THE GROWTH
OF VENTURE
CAPITAL

THE GROWTH
OF VENTURE
CAPITAL

A Cross-Cultural
Comparison

Edited by Dilek Çetindamar

Westport, Connecticut
London

Library of Congress Cataloging-in-Publication Data

The growth of venture capital : a cross-cultural comparision / edited by Dilek
Çetindamar.
  p. cm.
  Includes bibliographical references and index.
  ISBN 1–56720–581–X (alk. paper)
    1. Venture capital—Cross-cultural studies.   I. Çetindamar, Dilek, 1967–
  HG4751.C43   2003
  332'.04154—dc21   2002026965

British Library Cataloguing in Publication Data is available.

Library of Congress Catalog Card Number: 2002026965
ISBN: 1–56720–581–X

First published 2003

JK
Praeger Publishers, 88 Post Road West, Westport, CT 06881
An imprint of Greenwood Publishing Group, Inc.
www.praeger.com

Printed in the United States of America

The paper used in this book complies with the
Permanent Paper Standard issued by the National
Information Standards Organization (Z39.48–1984).

10 9 8 7 6 5 4 3 2 1

Copyright Acknowledgments

The editor and publisher gratefully acknowledge permission to quote from the
following sources:

Jeng, L. A., and Wells, P. C. "The Determinants of Venture Capital Funding: Evidence
across Countries," *Journal of Corporate Finance*. Vol. 6, No. 3, September 2000, pp.
241–89. Reprinted with permission from Elsevier Science.

"The Swedish Venture Capital Industry—an Infant, Adolescent, or Grown-up?" by
Dilek Çetindamar Karaömerlioglu and Staffan Jacobsson, *Venture Capital*, 2:2 (2000),
pp. 61–88. http://www.tandf.co.uk

To my mother,
with gratitude for her love and support.

Contents

Illustrations

FIGURES

TABLES

Preface

In the early part of my academic career in the United States and Sweden, one (research) question that often came to mind was related to how technologies and innovations came into existence in different countries. While contemplating this question, my focus slowly turned toward the financial problems of firms involved in innovation.

Since 1998, I have met with a number of colleagues at different conferences and have had the chance to work with some of them on a variety of projects. These projects were mainly in the field of venture capital and entrepreneurship. My greatest opportunity was to work with Staffan Jacobsson, with whom I studied the Swedish venture capital industry both theoretically and empirically. Together we were able to develop a comprehensive framework for the analysis of the evolution of a venture capital industry. When Hilary Claggett, my editor at Praeger Publishers, initiated this book project, I already had a number of colleagues from many different countries who were ready to share their experiences. They were enthusiastic about the book from the beginning, believed in it, and were very cooperative in turning it into reality.

This book aims to be accessible and of use to the general reader interested in learning about the venture capital industry as a distinct financial institution of the new century. It addresses members of academia, venture capital associations, policy-making institutions, and government agencies. The theoretical contribution of the book may be of more interest to academics, while the practical applications and country examples combined with theoretical issues may be more attractive to venture capital associations, policy makers, and government agencies. The analysis section of the book, with its explanations of what lessons can be drawn, may be most useful to countries planning to establish their own venture capital industry.

I have a lot of people I would like to thank for helping to make this book a reality. It is inevitable (as every author knows) that there is not enough space to thank all those people here, and in addition, if I forget anyone I apologize now. I would especially like to thank the following people in no particular order.

I give a big thanks to Hilary Claggett, who made my first book-writing experience comfortable, the publishing process seem easy, the book better, and all
my questions reasonable. Sinan Kesler and Steven Head Seggie made my text
much more compact and readable by putting in many hours of tedious work.
Bo Carlsson, Arnold Reisman, Annika Rickne, and Maximillian Von Zedwitz
made valuable suggestions on content and structure.

I am also grateful to Bo Carlsson and Staffan Jacobsson, who were incredibly
helpful in shaping my academic perspective through sharing their experiences
and insights in many areas, including the systemic view that constitutes the
basis of this book.

1

Introduction

Dilek Çetindamar

In the twenty-first century, with the continued globalization of the world economy, the competition among countries will continue at a frenetic pace. This competition in products, services, processes, and technologies is such that it entails the existence of a sound infrastructure. The venture capital industry (VCI) is an integral part of this infrastructure, and evidence from the 1990s has shown us that the existence of a strong VCI in a country leads to economic power and growth. We can logically extrapolate from this evidence that countries are at present (and will continue to be) engaged in a race to establish their VCIs as a means to create economic success.

Understanding the emergence and development of the VCI is of great importance not only for academia but also for venture capital (VC) associations, policy-making institutions, and government agencies. Thus, this book aims to increase the knowledge about the evolution of the VCI by searching answers for the following questions. How can VC ensure a competitive edge for countries? What is the role of the VCI in the new economy? How has the VCI developed in industrialized and developing countries? What are the infrastructure elements of the VCI? Are there any specific infrastructure characteristics of a successful VCI that can be taken as applicable across countries? How does VC evolve over time? What are the dimensions that measure the maturity of a VCI? What could be some policy suggestions for countries aiming to establish a VCI?

These questions need to be answered, and this book sets out to do just that. By using both theoretical and empirical analysis the book aims to identify the significant factors affecting the development and performance of a VCI in all the stages of its development. The majority of existing academic studies analyze the U.S. VCI, thereby ignoring the experiences in other countries. Because it is our intention here to look at the full spectrum of VCIs, the book presents a wide variety of examples from different countries. Thus, having collected a fuller sample of data from different countries, we will find ourselves in a better position to answer our aforementioned questions, in particular the question referring to policy suggestions for countries aiming to establish a VCI.

In addition, we also intend to shed light on the evolution of existing VCIs as a means of aiding in the understanding of and comparing the performance of VCIs in different countries. Our examination of the evolution and also of the issue of maturity will lead to insights into the realm of policy discussion for setting up VCIs. Logic dictates that there can be no "one size fits all" policy for establishing a VCI and instead that it is essential to have "tailor-made" policies for each different country. However, it is our intention here to show that while each country will have different requirements, it is possible to learn from the empirical evidence available and it is not necessary to completely reinvent the wheel.

In our analysis of the VCI we are operating under the assumption that financial organizations are just one of the actors shaping the functioning of this industry. In addition to these financial organizations it should also be noted that large companies, governments, research organizations, and entrepreneurs are also influential in this shaping. As a result, my analysis of the industry will be systematic so as not to ignore any of the influential actors and so as to ensure that there is no lessening of the impact of any conclusions we may reach.

The introductory chapter consists of four sections. The first section contains a short definition of VC. The development of the VC industry, both in industrialized and developing countries, is presented in the second section. Then, the third section introduces the role of VC in entrepreneurship and innovation. Finally, the last section presents the outline of the book.

VENTURE CAPITAL

The VCI supplies private equity funds to start-up firms, private firms in financial distress, and public firms seeking finance for a buyout. In reality, therefore, firms in the VCI act as financial intermediaries between investors and entrepreneurs (Smith and Smith 2000; Fenn, Liang, and Prowse 1995). These firms draw their funds from a wide variety of sources including pension funds, banks, and insurance companies. These funds are then invested in firms that are seen to have the potential for high growth and profit. In return for this investment the VC firm receives equity shares in the firm that they invest in. The period of the investment is usually between five and ten years, and in this time the venture capitalists provide a range of different services to the investee firm. Included in these services (on top of the obvious financial support) are planning, marketing, and strategic and managerial support. When the investment period comes to an end, the VC firm exits from its investment through either an initial public offering (IPO) or trade sales. The revenue raised from the IPO or trade sale is mainly transferred to the fund owners (i.e., banks, insurance companies, pension companies), with venture capitalists receiving a certain percentage of the profit in addition to salaries for the management services provided. Regarding return, all parties (if the venture is successful) enjoy a high rate of profit commensurate to the high risk undertaken. This rate has been calculated to be in the range of 20 percent to 56 percent per year (NVCA 2002).

There are five main differences in the VC firms active in the industry. First, firms specialize in different organizational types; for example, some firms prefer limited partnerships while others may prefer government-run firms. Second, the involvement in the management of the investee firms may be either active or passive. Third, firms may receive their funds from either banks or pension funds. Fourth, different firms specialize in firms at different stages of development (seed, start-up, expansion, late stage for management buyouts). Finally, firms often specialize in one particular technology field, such as biotechnology (Smith and Smith 2000; Gompers and Lerner 1999; Mason and Harrison 1999).

Another difference of note regards the definition of VC firms across countries. In particular there is a difference between the U.S. definition of VC and the European definition. This difference stems from the field of specialization of the VC firm and its preference regarding the development stage of the firm invested in. In the United States, private equity firms supplying buyout and restructuring funds to large and established firms are not accepted as being "proper" venture capitalists and as such are subsequently not accepted as members of the North America Venture Capital Association (NVCA). In Europe, on the other hand, these types of VC firms are accepted as "proper" venture capitalists and thus are accepted as members of the corresponding association. This differentiation is propagated not only by these associations but also by some researchers as well. They also loathe to accept firms investing in late stages as "classic VC" firms (Bygrave and Timmons 1992). In this book, however, such a differentiation is not adhered to, and as a result, one chapter is devoted to understanding how these buyout specialists function and why they can be considered a full-fledged part of the VCI.

Another issue regarding the definition is the distinction between the formal and informal sectors of the VCI. The formal sector refers to firms and as such is self-explanatory, while the informal sector refers to wealthy individuals, not supported by any corporate structure, who invest in portfolio firms. These wealthy individuals are commonly referred to as business angels. Even though no precise value can be given to the funds at the disposal of these business angels, it is believed that their funds greatly exceed those at the disposal of formal VC firms (Mason and Harrison 1999). This explains why business angels, as significant players in the VC industry, are included within the study of VC in this book.

THE DIFFUSION OF THE VENTURE CAPITAL INDUSTRY

The seeds of the modern VCI are considered to have been sown in 1946, the year in which the first VC firm was established in the United States (Bygrave

and Timmons 1992). The VCI in the United States is the largest and most
mature in the world (as would probably be expected given the time of its
formation) and in the period from 1998 to 2000 was able to raise a total of
U.S.$249 billion of cumulative funds (Fenn, Liang, and Prowse 1995; NVCA
2002). Table 1.1 shows quite clearly the incredible growth of the industry in
this period, and if we also include management buyouts, the funds increase to
a staggering U.S.$453 billion (Karaomerlioglu and Jacobsson 2000; NVCA
2002). The year 2001 created quite a setback for the industry, though, with the
terrorist attack in New York coming on the back of the crisis in the stock
market. As a result, there has been a marked slowdown in the industry, and
the level of funds in 2001 was fairly low in comparison to previous years: a
relatively miserly U.S.$30 billion (NVCA 2002).

If we compare the European VCI to the one in the United States, then we
can see that the VCI in Europe was a very late starter; its establishment dates
only back as far as the 1980s. This late start probably partly explains why VC
firms only raised some U.S.$71 billion of long-term capital during the period
from 1985 to 1997 (EVCA 1998). In the late 1990s, though, rapid growth began
to take hold in many European countries, with Sweden being one particularly
good example (Mason and Harrison 1999), which then led to a growth in the
European VCI. This rapid growth shows a similarity to the rapid growth of the
U.S. VCI in the second half of the 1990s. For example, in 1997 alone, VC firms
in European Union (EU) countries raised nearly U.S.$16 billion of U.S.$71
billion accumulated in twelve years. Then, in 1999, funds raised in one year
increased to U.S.$22.5 billion, and in 2000, the figure was U.S.$43 billion,
almost double the 1999 figure (EVCA 2001). This almost exponential increase
in funds has been met by a virtually parallel increase in the prominence of
non-EU funds in the European VCI. In 2000 half the funds raised were foreign,
with 20 percent of them originating from the United States. The share of the
non-EU funds shows a radical increase in Europe. In just one year, from 1999
to 2000, these funds increased 135 percent (EVCA 2001). We can extrapolate

Table 1.1
VC Investments in the U.S., Excluding MBOs and LBOs, 1990–2000

Year	The number of investee firms	Total Investment (Million dollars)
1990	1,317	3,376
1995	1,327	5,608
1996	2,004	11,278
1997	2,696	17,207
1998	3,155	22,576
1999	3,956	59,164
2000	5,458	103,849

Source: NVCA, 2002.

from this increase that, in the future, the weight of non-EU funds will increase to a significant level.

The boom in the VCI that we have observed in the 1990s has not been limited to industrialized countries, though. There have been some positive signs emanating from the developing countries, in the Far East in particular, that show the strengthening of their VCIs. The total funds available in the Far Eastern VC pool rose from a fairly modest U.S.$21.9 billion in 1991 to a more impressive U.S.$38.4 billion in late 1997 (Mason and Harrison 1999). If we then look at 1998, we can see that private equity funds based solely in Hong Kong and China were able to raise a total of U.S.$7.2 billion in capital, of which two-thirds came from outside Asia. The single largest source of this capital was, perhaps as is to be expected, U.S. institutions (Folta 1999). However, 65 percent of the cumulative funds came from Asian sources. If we concentrate specifically on Hong Kong, then astoundingly the 1998 sum, U.S.$4.1 billion, was more than the total raised by professional private equity organizations in the previous sixteen years since the first fund came into being. Another Asian country with a successful VCI is Taiwan. The total VC funds raised in this small country have been calculated at approximately U.S.$20 billion, half of which was raised by business angels (Chen and Lee 2001). Despite the positive developments in a number of countries in Asia, Japan experienced problems in its VCI. Due to the financial crisis in the country, its VC funds dropped from U.S.$2.5 billion in 1991 to U.S.$1.2 billion in 1998 (Finlayson 1999).

The Pacific Rim, eastern Europe, and south Africa are just a few of the other areas where multiple private equity funds have seen recent improvements or currently are being raised (Mason and Harrison 1999). For example, the Australian VCI set a record in 2000 by raising more than U.S.$1.2 billion , of which 24 percent came from abroad, with Asia being the main source (Venture Economics 2001). The majority of total Asian funds (63 percent), including Japan, Australia, New Zealand, and other smaller Asian countries, came from Asian sources in 1998 (Folta 1999). In recent years, Asian funds have been going international and diffusing to other markets, such as Europe. For example, in 2000, 3 percent of non-European funds entering into European VC funds came from Asia (EVCA 2001). Because some of the Asian countries are the fastest growing economies of the world, the rise of Asian funds and their globalization may not be surprising. However, the size of international Asian funds is low compared to the U.S. funds.

Two successful countries that can be considered to have bridged the gap between being a developing country and an industrial country are Israel and Ireland (although strictly speaking, Israel is still seen as a developing country). As Israel has crossed this great divide between the "haves and have-nots," we have been able to observe a transformation not only in their industry but also with respect to their VCIs. Their industries have been transformed into ones based on high technologies, and at the same time, there has been rapid growth in their VCIs. The first Israeli VC fund was established in 1985, with available resources of U.S.$25 million. It was not until the 1990s, though, that the first real growth could be observed (Abbey 1999; Leibowitz 2000; Mlavsky 2000). In 1992 the government introduced special VC funds called Yozma that continued to be available until 1996. Yozma funds contributed a significant amount of VC funds as well as attracted foreign funds due to special incentives offered along with Yozma funds. In 2000 the Israeli VCI managed to raise a record U.S.$3 billion, an amount equivalent to all funds raised during the period from 1991 to 1999. Considering Israel's population of only 5.7 million, the total fund size can be interpreted as a great success. Almost half of these funds (45 percent) go to high-technology fields such as information technology and pharmaceuticals. Israel receives a great deal of funds from the United States; it receives the highest share (7.7 percent of total) of the U.S. VC funds that are invested in foreign countries. We have witnessed a similar rapid growth in the case of Ireland (Murphy 2000). The Irish VCI took off in 1994 after changes were made to pertinent regulations and certain aspects of the tax system. The Irish government introduced incentives to encourage the establishment of VC firms, with professional fund managers to run capital coming from pension funds and insurance companies. Both Israel and Ireland had many common regulation changes, including research grant aid, reductions in capital gain taxes, and tax treatment of share options. Another similarity that is perhaps relevant to the growth of their VCIs is that in these countries a high percentage of the population are engineers or technology graduates.

A number of international VC funds have been set up with the intention of helping developing countries. For example, the World Bank has been involved in the promotion of VC funds in developing economies through its International Finance Corporation. This corporation invested U.S.$196 million in forty-nine VC funds during the period from 1979 to 1995. The majority of these funds were targeted toward low-income countries (Aylward 1998). The European Investment Bank and European Venture Capital Association (EVCA) have also organized an international program to foster the establishment of VC in central and eastern European countries (EVCA 2001). Special training programs were conducted during the period from 1993 to 1997, and VC firms were given financial incentives to invest in these countries. An example of the end result of this initiative is the Romanian VCI, which achieved a volume of U.S.$500 million, the majority coming from the United States, the United Kingdom, and Germany (Cautis 2000). Because of the success of these programs, they have been extended to Russia, the Ukraine, and Kazakhstan (EVCA 2001).

The analysis of the developments in industrialized countries indicates that the establishment of a VCI in a country requires the existence of a number of organizations and institutions (Aylward 1998; Jeng and Wells 2000; Gompers, Lerner, Blair, and Hellmann 1998; Mason and Harrison 1999; Sagari and Guidotti 1992). It is important to highlight here that, depending on the stage of the VCI, the actors in the industry and their tasks change over time (Murray

1996; Gompers and Lerner 1999). For example, the government can be significant in the start-up phase but its dominant role may diminish once the regulations and institutions are in place. Hence, policy makers need to observe the evolution of the VCI and develop policies accordingly. The evolution of the VCI will be measured by using its three characteristics as a base (Karaomerlioglu and Jacobsson 2000):

- Size refers to the absolute magnitude of the VCI. This can be measured either by taking the number of VC firms or calculating the total funds available as VC funds. The larger the size, the greater are the opportunities available for entrepreneurs and inventors.

- Diversity shows the presence of diverse actors that differ from each other with respect to their level of concentration in a specific industry, technology, geography, or development stage of portfolio firms. The more diverse the actors are, the more opportunities there are for a wide spectrum of companies and hence more opportunities for a flourishing, successful industry .

- Competence indicates the degree of skill and the capabilities that venture capitalists have at their disposal. Venture capitalists who have experience in their field and who have reached a certain level of professionalism are then in a position to make a real difference regarding the amount of added value that they can bring to their portfolio firms.

THE ROLE OF VENTURE CAPITAL IN ENTREPRENEURSHIP AND INNOVATION

In recent years there has a been a transformation in the economies of the industrialized countries to what has come to be referred to as the new economy. The main pillars of this economy are no longer labor and raw materials, as was the case with the "old" economy, but now consist of production based on high technology and business processes carried out over the Internet (1999; OECD 1999, 2001). If we look at the U.S. economy in the late 1990s, we see a great period of economic growth. It is widely accepted that this economic growth was the result of technological investments that took place in the 1980s, particularly investments in information technologies (OECD 2001).

If we turn to the example of the EU, then we see here that industry is coming to be dominated by high technology. During the period from 1995 to 1999, employment in high-technology industries in the EU grew by an annual average of 0.9 percent, compared to a total manufacturing growth rate of 0.3 percent. During the same period, jobs in knowledge-intensive services grew by an annual average of 2.9 percent, compared to a growth of 1.8 percent for the service sector as a whole. In 1999, the share of manufacturing output based on high technologies was, on average, 38 percent of all manufacturing output in the EU, whereas this share was almost half (48 percent) in service industries

(Eurostat 2001). It is safe for us to conclude from these statistics that this new economy is the driving force behind modern-day economic growth, and we can extrapolate from this conclusion that countries with entrepreneurs able to create and commercialize technological innovations will benefit from a spur in economic growth (OECD 1998).

There are many functions of the new economy, but bearing in mind the focus of our book, we are mainly interested in its function as a generator of new technologies and entrepreneurs (Hisrich and Peters 1998). As previously noted, the new economy is driven by technological development, and the basis of technological development is new technologies, which come from inventions. However, having inventions is by itself not enough; there also needs to be the successful commercialization of these inventions. The question now is, what can countries do to ensure that this step takes place? It is here that the role of the entrepreneur comes to the fore, because this person is the one who will develop projects, take risks, and tirelessly work to succeed in the commercialization of new products, services, and processes. The government's role in this process is to foster this entrepreneurship, because it is an important means of capturing technological opportunities and transforming them into value added to the economy (Carlsson 2002; OECD 1998). If we accept the premise that invention and entrepreneurship are at the heart of national advantage, the twenty-first century will be one in which the difference between economic success and failure will be the existence and utilization of technology, innovation, and entrepreneurship (OECD 2001; Jalava and Pohjola 2002; Porter 1990). Successful utilization will be the spur toward economic growth for countries.

Policy makers often make use of the national innovation systems approach since it analyzes not only innovations but also the actors creating innovations and institutions systematically affecting the interactions among actors (Carlsson and Stankiewicz 1991; Lundvall 1992; Nelson 1993; Patel and Pavitt 1994). In this book we also make use of this system, albeit in a watered-down version. Our aim in using this system is to help us understand the financial problems or barriers that prevent entrepreneurs and inventors from innovating or commercializing their inventions (Carlsson 2002). Financial constraints can often prevent small and medium-sized companies, particularly firms based on new technologies, from expanding their operations (Moore 1994; OECD 2001; Westhead and Storey 1997). Thus, a substantial number of studies have been done and literature produced on the subject of innovation financing (Bygrave and Timmons 1992; Sapienza, Manigart, and Vermeir 1996; Kortum and Lerner 1998; Christensen 1997). These studies highlight the unique role of the VCI as an innovation-financing mechanism (Bygrave and Timmons 1992). However, they are focused on the United States and other industrialized countries and, by and large, ignore developing countries (Mason and Harrison 1999; Çetindamar 1999). To ensure some sort of balance, this book focuses on the

VCI and its development in many different countries across the full development spectrum.

Inspired by the national innovation systems approach, we have created an innovation-financing system as shown in figure 1.1. This system will allow us to analyze the VCI from both the demand and supply sides. By *demand side*, we are referring to organizations like universities and research organizations, which provide entrepreneurs and innovators. When we refer to *supply side,* we are considering the sources of finance for VC firms and the exit mechanisms available to them. The range of interactions among these diverse organizations depends on the institutional infrastructure and the entrepreneurial climate. The institutional infrastructure affects both the demand and the supply side. The infrastructure consists of institutions that are either formal (laws, patent laws, government regulations of bank conduct, regulations regarding the installation of electrical equipment, etc.) or informal (common law, customs, traditions, work norms, practices, etc.) (Edquist 1997). These institutions reduce uncertainty by providing information, making it easy to manage conflicts and cooperation among organizations, and providing incentives (Edquist 1997).

As mentioned earlier, the focus of this book is organizations involved in the VCI. We chose the VCI is because it is considered a crucial element in the financing of entrepreneurs and inventors. Many of the new technology-based firms have great difficulty in finding the finance required to stimulate their growth (OECD 1998). There is a multiplicity of factors behind this difficulty. The first one is that these firms have no tangible assets, and investors are less keen to directly finance the operations when no guarantee can be given in

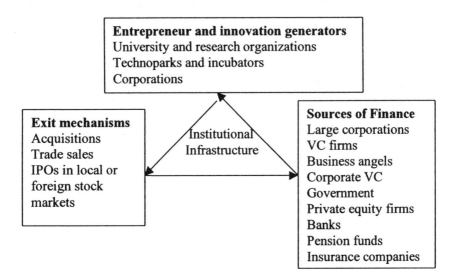

Figure 1.1 Innovation-financing system

return. Second, these firms are put into the category of high risk because there is a general difficulty in putting a figure to the economic value of intellectual property rights. The final factor is the wariness on the part of investors to finance risky investments such as these, because it is very difficult to evaluate new technical developments and potential breakthrough innovations (Moore 1994; Rickne 2000).

In addition to their obvious financing role, VC firms, particularly in the early stages, also concentrate on strategic, interpersonal, and networking roles as a means of adding value to the portfolio firms (Sapienza, Manigart, and Vermeir 1996; Eliasson 1997). Because innovation requires the creation of new knowledge, it is essential for the innovating firms to learn from all possible sources. These sources include universities, the firm's own activities, and other firms they are in contact with (Lundvall 1996). The value-adding role of the VC firm in this learning process is as a bridge that allows the investee firm to form networks with all the potential knowledge sources that might be useful for the company (Carlsson 2002).

There are situations, though, in which the role of the VC firm is purely on the financial level. This is the case when the role of the VC firm is played by a bank or investment house, as is often the case in later stage investments (and perhaps one of the reasons why the U.S. definition of VC does not include these later stage investments). The shift observed in the late 1980s in the United States toward later stage investments has been followed by a corresponding loss in the value-added and learning roles, often referred to as a loss in the competence of the VCI (Bygrave and Timmons 1992; Camp and Sexton 1992). Loss of competence has been the main complaint about the European VCI. The European VCI is predominantly focused on later stage investments and low technology industries, with little or no risk capital being directed toward new high technology. The predictable result of this focus is that the VCI only functions as a provider of finance and not as a tool for adding value or stimulating learning. In an attempt to counter this loss of competence, the EU has established funds to be used for new high technology, and they hope to supplement these funds with funds from individual governments' own special programs (Murray 1998).

To back up our previous assertion that a strong VCI leads to economic growth, we can also point to several empirical studies. For example, an analysis of 530 venture-backed and non-venture-backed firms has shown that the presence of venture activity in an industry significantly increases the rate of patenting, in other words, the output of innovative activities (Kortum and Lerner 1998). Similarly, studies show that VC-backed firms have faster rates of growth in employment, investment, and exports than do FT-Excel 500/Fortune 500 companies (Mason and Harrison 1999). The existence of well-developed VC networks in technology-based regions significantly accelerates the pace of technological innovation and economic development in those regions (Florida and Kenney 1986; Saxenian, 1994). A recent study by the National Venture Capital

Association (NVCA 2002) revealed that companies originally backed by VC generated U.S.$736 billion in revenue in the year 2000. According to the study, VC-backed companies represented 3.3 percent of the United States's total jobs and 7.4 percent of gross domestic product in 2000.

This proven impact of VC in innovation financing and entrepreneurship has been the main thrust behind the establishment of VC industries in several countries. For example, the EU launched a number of new initiatives to increase the supply of early stage VC in order to increase the entrepreneurship in EU states (Murray 1998; Bygrave and Timmons 1992; Christensen 1997; OECD 1998; Swedberg 2000).

THE OUTLINE OF THE BOOK

There are three parts to this book. The focus of the first part is the three different performers in the VCI: innovation financiers, business angels, and buyout specialists. The variety of roles performed by these three performers are individually discussed in three subsequent chapters. Chapter 2 delves into theoretical issues regarding innovation and how VC firms fill an important function of innovation financing in modern economies. By showing how traditional finance theories fail in understanding important aspects of VC financing of innovation, this chapter introduces a systemic view based on the national systems of innovation approach. Chapter 3 focuses on business angel networks. The chapter provides a short introduction of business angels and then analyzes angel networks based on empirical data collected on about forty angel networks in the United States and Europe. Chapter 4 contains a discussion of how VC firms performing leveraged buyouts can result in increased performance of the investee firms in their radical restructuring process. Considering that buyouts account for slightly less than half the total amount of European VC investments, these buyout specialists need to be taken into consideration in any VC study.

The second part of the book relates the historical development of the VCI in an assortment of different countries. Chapter 5 has a study of twenty-one countries, including most of the countries in the European Union and the United States. In addition to a statistical analysis of these twenty-one countries, this chapter introduces case studies of three countries (Portugal, Israel, and Germany). The statistical analysis in this chapter shows that IPOs are the strongest driver of VC investing across countries. Pension funds, labor market rigidities, and government policies are other important factors that influence the development of the VCI. The chapter also points out that factors affecting early-stage and late-stage VC financing show differences. Chapters 6 and 7 examine Sweden and Denmark, two small countries in Europe that established successful VCIs. These chapters present detailed accounts of the development of the VCI in these countries and show that both countries have reached substantial size, although they suffer from a lack of competent and experienced venture capitalists. Chapter 8 is a detailed analysis of Canada, an intriguing example of a mature VCI that shows a wide variety of VC funds. The chapter gives particular emphasis to the role of VC financing for knowledge-based or potential fast-growth firms in Canada. Chapter 9 presents the Israeli VCI, and chapter 10 focuses on developing countries with the example of Turkey. Although Israel and Turkey are both considered developing countries, the former has a VCI that had a very successful launch, whereas the latter is still at the very early stage of setting up an industry. The success of the Israeli example shows clearly the importance of the demand side in the development of the VCI, in other words, the existence of entrepreneurs and innovations demanding VC. However, the Turkish study exemplifies the difficulties that developing countries face, such as weaknesses in institutional infrastructure. Chapter 10 ends with suggestions for developing countries that aim to establish and develop the VCI in their countries.

As is inevitable, each chapter in part II of the book differs according to the conditions peculiar to each country. However, as a means of preserving some sort of consistency and ensuring that we have a basis for comparison, each chapter attempts to refer to all the following features: stock markets, economic conditions, pension funds, the technological opportunity set available, entrepreneurial culture, availability of funds, and regulations.

The final part of the book shows the impact of VC firms on innovative high-technology firms that are operating in the fields of biomaterials. Chapter 11 is an empirical study of biomaterials firms from three different locations: Sweden, Ohio, and Massachusetts. Therefore, this chapter indicates not only how VC firms can influence the development of firms based on new technology but also how entrepreneurs and the availability of technological opportunities can improve the performance of VC firms. This chapter shows that VC firms play a vital role for both firm formation and firm development and growth, particularly for young science-based firms. Then the chapter offers some suggestions for enhancing the functionality of the capital market for entrepreneurial firms.

Overall, this book is an early attempt to compare the VCIs of different countries through the full range of pertinent variables, from business angels at one extreme to investee firms at the other. A wide and realistic picture of the industry's functions is presented. It is the intention of this book to trigger studies on understanding the cross-cultural issues in the establishment and development of the VCI in different countries.

REFERENCES

Abbey, A. D. 1999. *Venturing Toward Growth.* Jerusalem: Israel Seed Partners Publication.

Aylward, A. 1998. *Trends in Venture Capital Finance in Developing Countries.* World Bank, Washington, D.C.: IFC (International Finance Corporation) Discussion Paper No. 36.

Bygrave, W. D., and J. A. Timmons. 1992. *Venture Capital at the Crossroads.* Boston, Mass.: Harvard Business School.

Camp, S. M., and D. L. Sexton. 1992. "Trends in Venture Capital Investment: Implications for High-Technology Firms." *Journal of Small Business Management* 30 (3): 11–20.

Carlsson, B. 2002. *New Technological Systems in the Bio Industries: An International Study.* Eindhoven: Kluwer.

Carlsson, B., and R. Stankiewicz. 1991. "On the Nature, Function, and Composition of Technological Systems." *Journal of Evolutionary Economics* 1 (2): 93–118.

Cautis, M. 2000. "Romanian Venture Capital Activity on the Rise." *Venture Capital Journal,* 1 July, pp. 47–48.

Çetindamar-K., D. 1999. "The Role of Venture Capital for Innovation in Developing Countries." Paper presented at 16th International Association of Science Parks Conference, 31 August–4 September, Istanbul, Turkey.

Chen, N. V., and M. D. Lee. 2001. "Taiwan: Asia's Venture Capital." *International Financial Law Review.* Supplement: Private Equity and Venture Capital, pp. 98–102.

Christensen, J. L. 1997. *Financing Innovation.* TSER Project Report: Innovation Systems and Europe 3.2.3. Denmark: Aalborg University.

Edquist, C. 1997. *Systems of Innovation.* London: Pinter.

Eliasson, G. 1997. "The Venture Capitalist as a Competent Outsider." KTH/IEO/R-97/6-SE. Stockholm: The Royal Institute of Technology.

European Venture Capital Association (EVCA). 1998. *1998 Yearbook: A Survey of Venture Capital and Private Equity in Europe.* Zaventem, Belgium: European Venture Capital Association.

European Venture Capital Association (EVCA). 2001. *Annual Survey of Pan-European Private Equity and Venture Capital: EVCA Network News.* Zaventem, Belgium: European Venture Capital Association.

Eurostat. 2001. *Science and Technology in Europe: A Statistical Panorama of the EU Knowledge-based Economy,* No. 33/2001.

Fenn, W., N. Liang, and S. Prowse. 1995. *The Economics of the Private Equity Market.* Washington, D.C.: Federal Reserve Bank.

Finlayson, G. E. 1999. "Japan: The Changing Venture Capital Market." *International Financial Law Review.* Supplement: Private Equity and Venture Capital, pp. 14–19.

Florida, R., and J. D. F. Smith. 1990. "Venture Capital, Innovation, and Economic Development." *Economic Development Quarterly* 4 (4): 345–61.

Florida, R. L., and M. Kenney. 1986. "Venture Capital, High Technology, and Regional Development." *Regional Studies* 22 (1): 33–48.

Folta, P. H. 1999. "The Rise of Venture Capital in China." *The China Business Review* 26 (6): 6–15.

Gompers, P. A., and J. Lerner. 1998. *The Determinants of Corporate Venture Capital Success: Organizational Structure, Incentives, and Complementaries.* National Bureau of Economic Research Working Paper No. 6725, Massachusetts.

Gompers, P. A., and J. Lerner. 1999. *The Venture Capital Cycle.* Cambridge, Mass.: MIT Press.

Gompers, P. A., J. Lerner, M. M. Blair, and T. Hellmann. 1998. "What Drives Venture Capital Fundraising?" *Brookings Papers on Economic Activity,* pp. 149–204.

Hisrich, R. D., and M. P. Peters. 1998. *Enterpreneurship*. New York: McGraw Hill.

"The Internet Age." 1999. *Business Week*, 4 October, pp. 44–60.

Jalava, J., and M. Pohjola. 2002. "Economic Growth in the New Economy: Evidence from Advanced Economies." *Information Economics and Policy* 14 (2).

Jeng, L. A., and P. C. Wells. 2000. "The Determinants of Venture Capital Funding: Evidence across Countries." *Journal of Corporate Finance* 6 (3): 241–89.

Karaomerlioglu, D. C., and S. Jacobsson. 2000. "The Swedish Venture Capital Industry—an Infant, Adolescent, or Grown-up?" *Venture Capital* 2 (1): 61–88.

Kortum, S., and J. Lerner. 1998. *Does Venture Capital Spur Innovation?* Working Paper, Harvard Business School, Boston, Mass.

Leibowitz, A. 2000. "Strong Technology Gives Punch to Israeli Venture Capital Market." *Venture Capital Journal*, 1 July, pp. 1–3.

Lundvall, B. 1992. *National Systems of Innovation: Towards a Theory of Innovation and Interactive Learning*. London: Pinter.

Lundvall, B. 1996. *The Social Dimension of the Learning Economy*. Aalborg: DRUID Working Paper No. 96-1.

Mason, C. M., and R. T. Harrison. 1999. Editorial. "Venture Capital: Rationale, Aims, and Scope." *Venture Capital* 1 (1): 1–46.

Mlavsky, E. 2000. "Gemini and Israelian Venture Capital." *TUBISAD-Sabanci University Venture Capital Conference*, 7 September, Istanbul.

Moore, B. 1994. "Financial Constraints to the Growth and Development of Small High-Technology Firms." In *Finance and the Small Firm*, ed. A. Hughes and D. Storey. London: Routledge.

Murphy, M. 2000. "Ireland: Venturing Far and Near." *European Venture Capital Journal* (September): 46–50.

Murray, G. A. 1998. "Policy Response to Regional Disparities in the Supply of Risk Capital to New Technology-Based Firms in the European Union." *Regional Studies* 32 (5): 405–19.

Murray, G. C. 1996. "Evolution and Change: An Analysis of the First Decade of the UK Venture Capital Industry." *Journal of Business Finance and Accounting* 22 (8): 1077–107.

Nelson, R. R. 1993. *National Innovation Systems*. Oxford: Oxford University Press.

North America Venture Capital Association (NVCA). 2002. http://www.nvca.com.

Organization for Economic Cooperation and Development (OECD). 1998. *Fostering Entrepreneurship: The OECD Jobs Strategy*. Paris: Organization for Economic Cooperation and Development.

Organization for Economic Cooperation and Development (OECD). 1999. *OECD Science, Technology, and Industry Scoreboard 1999: Benchmarking Knowledge-Based Economies*. Paris: Organization for Economic Cooperation and Development.

Organization for Economic Cooperation and Development (OECD). 2001. *Science, Technology, and Industry Outlook: Drivers of Growth—Information Technology, Innovation, and Entrepreneurship*. Paris: Organization for Economic Cooperation and Development.

Patel, P., and K. Pavitt. 1994. "National Innovation Systems: Why They Are Important, and How They Might Be Measured and Compared." *Economics of Innovation of New Technologies* 3: 77–95.

Porter, M. 1990. *The Competitive Advantage of Nations*. New York: Free Press.

Rickne, A. 2000. "New Technology-Based Firms and Industrial Dynamics." Ph.D. diss., Industrial Dynamics Department, Chalmers University of Technology, Gothenborg, Sweden.

Sagari, S. B., and G. Guidotti. 1992. *Financial Markets, Institutions and Instruments: Venture Capital—The Lessons from the Developed World for the Developing Markets*. Oxford: Blackwell Publishers.

Sapienza, H. J., S. Manigart, and W. Vermeir. 1996. "Venture Capitalist Governance and Value Added in Four Countries." *Journal of Business Venturing* 11: 439–69.

Saxenian, A. 1994. *Regional Advantage*. Cambridge MA: Harvard University Press.

Smith R. L., and J. K. Smith. 2000. *Entrepreneurial Finance*. New York: John Wiley.

Swedberg, R. 2000. *Entrepreneurship*. Oxford: Oxford University Press.

Venture Economics. 2001. www.ventureeconomics.com.

Weiss, C. 1990. "Scientific and Technological Constraints to Economic Growth and Equity." In *Science and Technology: Lessons for Development Policy,* ed. R. E. Evenson and G. Rains. Boulder, Colo.: Westview.

Westhead, P., and D. J. Storey. 1997. "Financial Constraints on the Growth of High Technology Small Firms in the United Kingdom." *Applied Financial Economics* 7: 197–201.

Part I
New Directions in Venture Capital

2

Venture Capital and the Innovation Process

Jesper Lindgaard Christensen

INTRODUCTION: RESEARCH IN VENTURE CAPITAL AND INNOVATION

In general, economic theory has tended to make a sharp distinction between monetary and real phenomena. Likewise, innovation theory has tended to be preoccupied with the real aspects of the process.[1] Innovation theory has truly explained to us thoroughly the special characteristics of an innovation process as opposed to ordinary investment in known products or processes, but it seems obvious that this difference should be explained with regard to implications for the financing of the process.

Doing something new usually implies some degree of uncertainty. Innovation is by definition characterized by novelty and uncertainty. It thus should not be surprising that financiers are reluctant to join innovation projects. On the other hand, people do not always dislike taking risks, as illustrated by the following excerpt, in which the Organization for Economic Cooperation and Development (OECD) compares innovation financing with expenses on gambling.

In many countries about 5% of the GNP is spent on traditional gambling—casinos, lotteries, football pools, horse-racing—and one must ask why is so little spent on innovation financing? (OECD 1982, p. 119)

In innovation financing, as in gambling, the chances of financing a successful, radical innovation are relatively small, but the potential gains are large. A consequence of uncertainty is that innovators, be they firms or financiers, must carefully consider the technical practicability and market prospects before putting the innovation process into effect.

This approach was echoed in the writings of Joseph Schumpeter, who may be considered the grandfather of theorizing on the special problems associated with financing innovations. Schumpeter emphasizes the importance of a close

contact between borrower and lender in the screening and monitoring function
of the banker. Thus, the financier

should know, and be able to judge, what his credit is used for and . . . the banker must
not only know what the transaction is which he is asked to finance and how it is likely
to turn out, but he must also know the customer, his business, and even his private
habits, and get, by frequently "talking things over with him," a clear picture of his
situation. But if banks finance innovation, all this becomes immeasurably more important. (1939, p. 90)

Although Schumpeter's comment mentions banks, the argument is clearly also
applicable to venture capital firms.

We can only speculate about why so little research has been devoted to
innovation financing after Schumpeter. One of the reasons for our ignorance
on this subject is the difficulties in giving normative prescriptions linked to the
intrinsic impossibility of estimating the optimal level of innovation financing.
Financial institutions function as selection mechanisms by not financing projects assessed as commercially fragile. However, this assessment is an ex ante
selection based on guesses about the future, whereas the actual outcome is only
possible to measure ex post. In other words, there should be financial barriers
to innovation but it is not possible to estimate to what degree there should be
barriers.

Another reason why studies on this issue are few is that it is rarely possible
to separate the financing of innovation and the financing of the firm as a whole.
When financiers assess a project proposal, they take into consideration the
viability not just of the innovation project but of all the activities of the firm
(in some cases including possible other potential businesses of this potential
customer, such as insurance).

A third factor is the lack of statistics. Not only do we have limited data about
some of the areas relevant for innovation financing, but we also have limited
statistics overall. There is no doubt, for instance, that the informal venture
capital and the corporate venture capital are of great importance. However,
although several rough estimates have been made, we are not in a position to
accurately quantify the importance of these sources, and the general knowledge
on these sources is sparse.[2] Likewise, even the statistics on the formal venture
capital market are not very well developed, although they have improved lately.

Finally, to study the interplay between people—particularly when money is
involved—requires interdisciplinary approaches. We are still not very good at
using such an interdisciplinary approach.

Lately, increased interest, from both policy makers and academia, has been
directed toward the relationship between finance and innovation, but the research in the area is still sparse. The increased interest has, in the mid-1990s,
mainly been in the impact of the financial system on innovation.[3] Now we are
also witnessing an increase in the research on venture capital. For example, we
now see more journals that either focus particularly on venture capital or have

a still larger share of papers on venture capital. This increase may be partly triggered by the general upswing of the industry.

In the many new papers on venture capital, we now see a growing recognition of the importance of an understanding at the micro level—that is, the relationship between the firm and the venture capital firm. One of the main arguments for this understanding is that often problems with financing new ventures are not only a question of price and/or quantity of capital. Rather, barriers to financing are rooted in the lack of information, trust, and competencies between the parties. I shall explain in further detail the nature of these barriers, which are often denoted agency problems. It is often claimed in the literature that such barriers may be mitigated by the hands-on character of venture capital financing, involving close interaction between the firm and the venture capital firm, which facilitates the buildup of trust and mutual understanding between the parties (de Clercq and Sapienza 2001; Shepherd and Zacharakis 2001). Rarely, however, is consideration given to possible counterarguments or inexpedient effects resulting from such close relationships. My purpose in this chapter is to discuss suitable theories on this important issue in venture capital research and to discuss what the established theories have to offer. In doing so, I take into account the possible drawbacks to close interaction, and I discuss any trends in the way innovation is done today that may require a rethinking of current sound theoretical bases for an understanding of venture capital financing.[4]

This chapter sets out to specify the just-mentioned possible changes in innovation. In the third section I discuss established theories, and I point out needs for further theoretical development and how this research avenue should be pursued. The fourth section pinpoints critical issues in the relationship between the firm and the venture capitalist. The fifth section discusses the pros and cons of such relationships using theoretical considerations derived from the third section. This chapter is not meant to be a literature review. Rather, it points to issues that, in spite of their potential to bring this part of venture capital research forward, are rarely discussed in the venture capital literature.

A NEW ROLE OF VENTURE CAPITAL IN INNOVATION?

Venture capital has been said by many observers to be attracted to innovative firms. This attraction might be linked to the great opportunities of investments in such firms. Paradoxically, innovative firms have often been said to be particularly suffering from a financial constraint (e.g., Murray and Lott 1995; Lockett, Murray, and Wright 2002; Bank of England 1996). On this point, however, different hypotheses have been made during the past decade. One hypothesis is that high-tech firms are met with severe financial constraints due to the more explorative character of the innovation process and subsequent high failure rates. An alternative hypothesis is that medium-tech innovations are likely to suffer from underfinancing because they are too risky for banks, the potential return is too small for venture capital firms, and they are not eligible to receive government aid (OECD 1993, p. 59).[5] On the other hand, commercial banks think they are too risky. Finally, it could be argued that traditional, low-tech firms are likely to suffer from underfinancing with risk capital due to the general assertion that it is innovations and new technologies that are associated with high returns.

It is possible to argue for the validity of all these three hypotheses. Each of them may have different explanatory power in different sectors and in different periods of time. The recent boom in IT-related venture capital investments may be said to support the latter hypothesis. However, when the bobble—as some observers have denoted the development—exploded, Internet-related firms experienced severe financial constraints.

Nevertheless, the distribution of venture capital investments by sector strongly indicate that venture capital firms are important in innovation. As one paper states:

Given that a significant proportion of venture capital-backed companies are in technology sectors, venture capital plays a direct and significant role in the process of innovation and technology-based development in modern industrial economies. (Mason and Harrison 1999, p. 1)

This excerpt illustrates the importance of venture capital in the innovation process.[6] Even quite some years ago, Timmons and Bygrave (1986) pointed to the qualitative role played by venture capitalists in the innovation process. Florida and Kenney (1988) contended that venture capital has a key role to play in a *new* model of innovation. In their perception, the new model of innovation is based on integrating components of how Schumpeterian theory sees the change in the way innovation takes place.[7] Thus, Florida and Kenney see venture capital–backed innovation as a new form of innovation in between the (individual) entrepreneurial-driven and the (large) corporate and R&D-driven innovation process.

One of the key changes in the innovation process is the increased use of networks between an increasing number of different types of actors such as large corporations, investors, universities, consultants and other organizations. This development has spurred the upcoming of an understanding of innovation as being *systemic*. Thus, theories within the "innovation systems approach" have emphasized aspects like the diffusion of knowledge and the interaction between organizations. Some even argue that what has been denoted the "new economy" is a steep increase in what may be termed knowledge externalities. Such externalities are nonpecuniary in the sense that knowledge produced by one agent—or a set of agents—may benefit other agents without financial compensation (Foray 2000, p. 2). The externalities contribute to the buildup of the general knowledge base of the society, which is, in turn, beneficial for future

innovators. The interaction between different types of agents is much emphasized in the innovation systems approach and in evolutionary theories on technological change. This interaction is likely to expand the knowledge frontiers
of society as a whole and to enhance the knowledge base of the firms involved
in such interaction.

In this setting the venture capital firm may have an important intermediary
role. Venture capitalists are important parts in networks and are furthermore
in between, and central to, several different types of networks. In Florida and
Kenney (1988, p. 127) these networks are grouped in four, although they do
overlap. The first of these is the financial network, which includes the venture
capital fund and its back funding to syndication partners like other venture
capital funds and business angels as well as complementary financing sources.[8]
The second network is used in the location of investment opportunities and
their screening. This group spans from other venture capitalist and business
angels to accountants and universities. A third network surrounding venture
capital firms consists of accounting firms, lawyers, consultants, and other professional service firms. Finally, a personal network is used to ensure the human
resources in the innovation process, on both the management and the technical
side.

An important prerequisite for this venture-backed innovation process to succeed is a well-developed technological infrastructure—or in Florida and Kenney's own words, "social structures of innovation" (1988, p. 120). Perhaps even
more important, as reflected in this chapter's focus, is the microeconomic, personal interaction between the parties.

Although Florida and Kenney do not address it in their work (1988), the
social structures of innovation would often constitute completely different
things in different national and even regional contexts. Stimulation of such
social structures ought to be subject to policy development, but until recently
it has largely been overlooked by policy makers in the European countries.
This oversight may perhaps be explained by the unwillingness of national
authorities to differentiate policies, whereas on a regional policy level, wide
discussions have taken place about the extent to which such social structures
of innovation could be stimulated.

Although this model certainly is developed with the U.S. institutional environment in mind, and should perhaps be used primarily for this environment,
it does illustrate some generic, new features of the innovation process and the
implications for venture capital. Cooke (2001) extends the discussion on the
implications of changes in production to argue that the manner in which venture capital firms operate in the new economy is more important than venture
capital per se. In a study of biotech in the United Kingdom, United States, and
Germany Cooke points to three factors that explain differences in the development of the biotech industry: exploitation of basic science, venture capital,
and cluster formation. In discussing venture capital Cooke points out that the
superior biotech innovation system in the United States should be explained

not by the *quantitatively* larger venture capital market in the United States but rather in the ability of the venture capital system to organize the management of the commercialization of science.

What, precisely, is the content of the change in the mode of innovation? For example, is the Florida and Kenney model an adequate description of the changes? Most observers, at least, would probably agree that a significant change has indeed taken place within the past few years.

A different view of the change in modes of innovation is that the change is primarily related to the changes in work organization, with more emphasis on knowledge, interaction, and learning (Lam 2000). This view has implications both for the mere relative importance of the human resources factor compared to other production factors, and for the skill requirements from both industrial firms and venture capital firms. Thus, Lam sees the knowledge production to have shifted from a mode 1 to mode 2, where knowledge production in mode 2 is characterized by

- creation in the context of application involving multiple actors as opposed to governance by the academic community
- transdisciplinary as opposed to disciplinary
- heterogeneity of producers as opposed to homogeneity
- practical and tacit knowledge still more important than academic knowledge
- institutionalization in flexible, socially distributed systems rather than at universities
- creativity induced in groups rather than individually

Clearly, such changes imply immense challenges to those financiers who are used to applying traditional methods of credit assessment.

A third way to describe changes in the mode of innovation has been denoted the "new economy." This concept has been used primarily in the business press, but has in the business press rarely been properly defined.[9] The new economy might impose a challenge for venture capital firms if it is defined broadly as, among other things, an increase in networking; extensive use of knowledge; decreased transaction costs; heavy investments in the information, communication, telecom, and biotech industries; and extensive use of information and telecom technologies in most firms. Not only have changes taken place in the behavior of firms rendering new requirements to how venture firms should assist the management in the portfolio firms, but even the due diligence and screening of potential investments has become a different ball game. Traditional models for assessing the value of a firm are often inadequate; for example, cash flow is often absent and so is collateral (Commission of the European Communities 2001, p. 17; see also footnote 6). To a much larger extent, the role of the venture capital firm in the future can be expected to be that of a network mediator, and the initial screening is likely to be increasingly based on the assessment of "knowledge assets"—the quality, uniqueness, and volatility of the knowledge and whether it is subject to fluctuations, for example, by heavy reliance on the knowledge of one person who may move from the organization.

Regardless of the exact character of the changes, the role of venture capital firms in innovation has changed significantly. This change is enhancing the importance of the hands-on relationship between the firm and the venture capital firm. We need to consider more carefully these micro aspects of the relationships. Moreover, the new modes of innovation have implications for an agenda on the development of an adequate theory of venture capital. Before discussing new theories, let's briefly look into established theory.

LESSONS FROM ESTABLISHED THEORY

As mentioned above, the research in innovation financing is somewhat sparse and scattered. The bulk of studies within financial theory are rarely focused upon the special features of financing innovation, and they rarely consider the institutional characteristics of the financial system, for example, the role of venture capital firms and complementary institutions.

On the one hand, innovation theories are preoccupied with the real side of the process and, with few exceptions, barely mention the financial aspects. Conversely, financial theory focuses upon monetary phenomenon and suffers from fundamental deficiencies with respect to analyzing innovations. Financial theory has mainly been preoccupied with price relations and arbitrage. As Neave (1991) puts it:

Neoclassical financial theory is similarly limited in its ability to explain financial system change. Indeed, it may fairly be said that the theory is better at explaining well established practices rather than it is at illuminating the creative or exploratory aspects of finance, the dynamics of technological change, or the evolution of sophisticated financial systems from primitive ones. (p. 5)

Traditional corporate finance theories are concerned with either the undertaking of investments or the financing of investments. The former is analysis of the decisions as to whether funds should be allocated to investments in securities, acquisitions, valuation models, and so on. The latter is more concerned with implicit and explicit ways of organizing the payback to the shareholders, including the incentives for management to act in accordance with the interests of shareholders.[10]

Compared to these traditional corporate finance theories, venture capital financing involves important differences. Venture capital is characterized by illiquid equity investments involving high degrees of information asymmetries. This requires relative intense monitoring, which is one explanation why venture capital firms exist: due to the specialized abilities to screen potential deals and to cope with asymmetric information, venture capital firms use this competence to invest in firms with a high risk/high return profile and where returns are highly uncertain. In contrast, traditional corporate finance theories often presume information on just those aspects that are usually not known in venture investments: price/earning ratios may be impossible to calculate because the shares are not quoted and consequently not priced at a market; cash flows are often very fluctuating if they have begun at all; historic information may not be available and dividend payments are often absent.[11]

Because traditional finance theories most often operate with dispersed and passive ownership, the governance mechanisms are quite different. Immediate exit may be an option in liquid markets but not in most venture investments. In general, corporate governance mechanisms in traditional finance theories may be characterized as indirect rather than direct; there may be voting rights in the election of the board of directors and various remuneration mechanisms for bringing management incentives into alignment with those of the shareholders. In contrast, venture capital firms depend more on "voice" (Hirschman 1970) for influencing the development in the investee firm.

Within financial theory with a microeconomic perspective, a large branch of literature has developed with the basic assumption that asymmetric information between a lender and a borrower may have deterrent effects on loan markets because of moral hazards and adverse selection effects.[12] Another, related, theory is the principal-agent theory, in which it is discussed how a principal (for example, a provider of funds for a venture capital firm) can set up a compensation system to motivate an agent (for example, the management of a venture capital firm) to act in the principals' interests. It is presupposed that there are potential conflicts of interests and that the principal cannot directly observe the actions of the agent.

Venture capital firms are special in the sense that the principal-agent relationship is double-sided. In relation to the portfolio firm, the venture capital firm is the principal; however, the venture capital firm is the agent in relation to the providers of the funds. There are several agency problems involved in this double interplay. Even after the investments, the venture capital firm may have an incentive to report to fund providers an overoptimistic valuation of the value of the portfolio firms. In some venture capital firms, this value is reported in the annual report with the size of the investment, whereas other venture capital firms use the market value principle. Because there is no market valuation of unquoted shares, there is bound to be a high degree of subjectivity in the valuation by the venture capital firms' management, which can create agency problems.

These theories seem at first sight a natural starting point for a microeconomic analysis of the relationship between the firm and the financier, in this case a venture capital firm (Reid 1999; Shepherd and Zacharakis 2001). Indeed there is some appealing research within this area, and the literature is to some extent valuable for an analysis of the role of venture capital firms in innovation financing. In particular, the literature directs our attention to the impact of information incompleteness. The notions of asymmetric information, credit rationing, adverse selection, and moral hazards highlight important features of the nature of loan markets, which are also relevant to innovation financing broadly, but less so for venture capital firms because venture financing is usually with equity. This strand of theory also points to the importance of relationships between the financier and the firm. The specific character of these relationships is, in this theory and in principal-agent theory, described with a relatively narrow focus because it is primarily focused upon incentive structures to avoid opportunistic behavior.

On the other hand, there are some deficiencies of the information and economics literature in relation to using this theory as a basis for explaining the micro aspects of venture capital financing. Specifically, it is unable to analyze the *process* of innovation financing. The approach is static and lacks an incorporation of a time perspective. Furthermore, the institutional setup is almost disregarded. Most often agents are assumed to take decisions under conditions of risk rather than uncertainty and their computational abilities are assumed to be unlimited. Innovations are, however, by definition characterized by novelty and uncertainty. In addition, the lack of a differentiated institutional environment for innovations, and of different types of financing institutions, further limits the use of these theories. The selection problem is solely described as a selection between projects seen from the chair of the financier. The recent upswing of the venture capital industry, increased number of venture capital firms, and increased competition among venture capital firms indicates that the selection problem is rather a question of the right match of the parties; innovating firms looking for capital need to screen the venture capital firms as well. The information asymmetries are presumably not any less than in the reverse situation. Entrepreneurs are highly uncertain about which competencies and networks they are getting access to by making an agreement with one venture capital firm rather than another.

Therefore, even this branch of standard financial theory is inadequate in relation to venture capital financing of innovations. There is a gap in the literature in this area. A first step toward an alternative theory is to discuss more specifically what is important in the interaction between the parties.

CRITICAL POINTS IN THE INTERFACE BETWEEN INDUSTRIAL INNOVATORS AND VENTURE CAPITAL FIRMS

What possible barriers for financing innovations may exist in the interface between industrial innovators and venture capital firms?

From established theory, we can identify problems with information, because this is often either limited or asymmetrically distributed. The concept of "moral hazards" from the information and economics literature suggests that trust is also an important aspect of the interplay between the parties. In addition, it was mentioned above that venture capital firms exist because of their comparative advantages in distinguishing good deals from bad ones and their postinvestment nursing of the investee firm. In other words, the assessment and assistance competencies are crucial in the interplay.

I have grouped innovation financing problems under three headings: problems stemming from lack of (1) information, (2) trust, and (3) competencies. Let us now consider these in turn.

Information and Knowledge

Lack of information, be it amount or quality of information, is naturally a hindrance for innovation financing by venture capital firms if the basis for decision making becomes inadequate. What kind of information do innovators and venture capital firms need? This question is probably difficult to answer in a general manner because the information required may differ. For example, the upswing of the IT industry, and specifically the Internet firms, caused many venture capital firms to finance new Internet-based firms on the basis of rather limited information. Moreover, and related, there is likely to be an element of herding behavior in the venture capital industry. Thus, the financing of Internet-based firms made venture capital firms focus even more on this segment, and funds were allocated and created specifically for investments in these firms. Conversely, in the recession of the IT industry, the venture capital available for Internet-based firms has been constrained.

Information and knowledge are, however, two different things. Among several taxonomies in the literature, Lundvall and Johnson (1994) mention four kinds of knowledge: know-what, know-why, know-how, and know-who. Know-what is knowledge about facts, or concrete information that may be checked since this information is usually codified. Know-why is knowledge on the driving forces behind, for example, the development in nature. It therefore includes physical laws. Know-how is skills, the capability of an individual, organization, or team to apply useful knowledge and information to solve a problem. Know-who is the knowledge about who knows what and who knows what to do. With increasing complexity of society and increasing use of different knowledge bases in development activities, know-who knowledge becomes still more important. If the new economy is denoting—among other things—the increased tendency to create networks among firms and a highly developed division of labor, then it becomes immensely important to have know-who knowledge. Know-who knowledge links closely to the ability of venture capital firms to act as intermediaries, as discussed in the previous section.

Likewise, it may be argued that know-what, understood as knowledge of accounts, budgets, and so on, is still important, but the relative importance has shifted toward know-who. It is often said that one of the main contributions of venture capital firms is to bring their network to the use of the innovator (NUTEK 1999). It may therefore be concluded that theories on the innovator–

venture capital firm interaction must take into account not only the information and knowledge of the two parties in question, but also the contribution of the network of the two parties in this respect.

Trust

Because of the particular risk of moral hazard associated with innovation financing, it is essential that the parties trust each other. It is a precondition not only for initial financing but also for an established relationship to develop qualitatively. It is, however, not possible for a venture capital firm to screen potential deals optimally. The venture capital firm may wish to have more information on the moral rectitude of the innovator, that is, whether the innovator is willing to act in accordance with the terms of contract and not take undue risks. The venture capital firm may also wish to have information on the ability of the innovator to undertake the project. However, this kind of information is difficult to obtain regardless of the search costs spent on it.

Some firms in the portfolio may behave opportunistically, and moral dimensions of the relationship are difficult to eliminate by contracting. In principle both the financier and the innovator may act opportunistically. However, because of asymmetrically distributed information—that is, innovators are likely to know more about the project than do venture capital firms—it is usually lack of trust of the innovator that is the financial barrier to innovation financing. A related aspect that should also be mentioned is that chemistry between the parties is essential.

Competencies

The third group of financial barriers to innovation financing has to do with competencies on the part of both the venture capital firm and the innovator. Venture capital firms need competencies, either internal or acquired externally. High-level knowledge on both technical and market matters is unlikely to be held by one person or sometimes not even by one organization. Venture capital firms use competencies to assess the technical aspects of projects, the market uncertainty of projects, the knowledge base of the firm, and the ability of the management of the firm to successfully execute the business plan. Venture capital firms also need to be competent sparring partners for the firm during the project and in the fine-tuning of the business plan.

The innovator may need competencies in economic management and in preparing and presenting a business plan. It has been pointed out in the literature that often the competencies of the venture capital firm and the innovator are directed differently. On the one hand, it has been argued that venture capital firms focus on assessing economic features such as accounts, budgets, and collateral, whereas innovators are very preoccupied with the technical features of their projects.[13] This disparity is not necessarily a disadvantage; in fact, complementarity of competencies is important. Nevertheless, the parties should be able to talk together using the same codes and should not be too distant. In theoretical discussions on knowledge transfer, it has been argued that an absorptive capacity is necessary to keep the parties in alignment. I shall discuss this in further detail later.

In summation, the main problems of financing may stem from three groups of barriers. A contract or relationship between a financier and an innovator may be hampered by information/knowledge problems, lack of trust/chemistry, or either lack of or mismatch of competencies.

For venture capital firms in general, it is an important strategic consideration if/how relationships to portfolio firms are managed. Some venture capital firms have chosen a very hands-on approach, whereas others are more passive in relation to the investee company. Under the presumption that the venture capital firm has adequate competencies, it would generally affect the barriers positively (that is, reduce them) if the venture capital firm is massively involved in the running of the portfolio firms. However, there are disadvantages associated with this involvement.[14] Therefore, the next section discusses some of the considerations in this strategic choice.

ARGUMENTS FOR AND AGAINST CLOSE RELATIONSHIPS BETWEEN INNOVATORS AND VENTURE CAPITAL FIRMS

If we consider the range of different financing sources with respect to their involvement in the firms they finance, it is clear that financing sources can be very different. Some financiers are even anonymous to the investee company. Even though venture capital firms are usually said to be particularly hands-on, within the venture capital firms family are found huge differences in this respect. These differences may reflect a division of labor on the capital market, because some venture capital firms specialize in early-stage, small, monitoring-intensive investments and others have specialized in more passive, larger investments. The disparity may, however, also reflect a difference in perception of the benefits and costs associated with different types of investments.

One of the implications following the theories on credit rationing due to asymmetric information is that the barriers of lack of information, trust, and competencies can be alleviated through closer relationships between innovators and financiers (de Clercq and Sapienza 2001; Sharpe 1990). It is, however, important to understand the limitations of this argument, because there are both costs and benefits related to well-established relationships between financial institution and innovator. An acceptable level of knowledge can reduce the problems of uncertainty about a project and the persons undertaking it, and often this knowledge will ease access to finance. One way to provide information and confidence is by repeated contracts between a firm and a financier, so that both parties can accumulate knowledge through learning processes.[15]

The benefits of close relationships between the venture capital firms and investee firms may be related to several features. First, the information level increases, and the effect is that search costs with respect to both screening and monitoring are reduced, which may increase profitability of the venture capital firms. Second, uncertainty on the moral rectitude of the innovator decreases. In other words, a close relationship facilitates development of mutual trust. Another aspect of this close relationship is that the venture capital firms will have better possibilities to influence if something goes wrong with the project. This increased possibility of monitoring may prevent moral hazards with the innovator. Third, the competencies of both parties are built up in the interaction. The venture capital firms will accumulate specific knowledge about the technical aspects of the projects and the industry in general. On the other side, the innovator will learn about strategic issues from the regular sparring.[16] In addition, the fund-raising ingenuity will improve. Fourth, channels and ways of communicating will improve, which in turn can save costs for both venture capital firms and innovator, and will facilitate further smooth information exchange. Fifth, cultural proximity may improve, and the parties are likely to increase their understanding of each other.

The advantages for the innovator are—as already mentioned—an increased competence and knowledge on the logic, culture, and organization in the capital market. Efficiency in the firm may also increase as a result of close interaction with a venture capital firm. This will come about through an increased stock of expertise and advice available through the network of the venture capital firm. Time horizons with financiers in an established relationship are likely to be longer. In other words, the firm has access to "patient capital," which may be particularly important for innovations. Finally, it is likely that the above-mentioned network effects will be higher. Thus, the venture capital firms may be an entrance to important industrial collaborators, allowing for synergies among the portfolio firms.

As mentioned, the very transmission of information is easier when relationships have been established and ways of communication that are understandable by both parties have been worked out. Once a code of communication has been established, innovators may be unwilling to pay the cost of building up new relationships that require a new series of learning processes. Arrow (1974) emphasizes this point:

A communication system has some cost of initial investment which is irreversible. In particular, a communication channel is used to greatest capacity when it has an optimal code for transmitting messages. This "code" need not be interpreted literally; the term refers to all patterns of communication and interaction within an organization, patterns which make use of conventional signals and forms which have to be learned. Once learned, however, it is cheaper to reuse the same system than to learn a new one; there is a payoff on the initial learning investment but no way of liquidating it by sale to others. (p. 19)

Such close relationships tend to be stable, which may be both beneficial and a disadvantage. This dichotomy has to do with several features of the relationships. One is the mutual irreversible dependence that develops between the firm and the venture capital firm once the deal has been accepted. Even if the project does not show the expected performance, the venture capital firm has an interest in keeping the firm solvent as long as there are still opportunities related to the product of the firm. It is thus likely that venture capital firms are reluctant to withdraw from the deal. Innovators may also incur considerable costs in breaking up the relationship. First, as mentioned in the citation in the previous paragraph, the innovator will have to pay the costs of searching for a new financier and building up new codes and channels of communication. Second, other venture capital firms may perceive a broken relationship as an indication that the previous venture capital firm had discovered information on the innovator that may harm the situation. In other words, the mere shift of financial connection may harm the reputation of the innovator, and consequently, other financial institutions may charge a cautiousness premium to cover for this potential, hidden information.

Essentially, the argument put forward by Arrow (1974) implies that venture capital firms, when looking at situations of unprofitable terminations of a deal, will consider not only the capital involved but also the time and effort that were spent setting up the information exchange, developing trust, and so on. In many cases these costs are sunk and should therefore be considered real expenditures. The sunk costs in the relationships are difficult to stipulate ex ante, because they depend not only on the asset specificity of the project, which to some degree may be assessed in advance, but also on the specificity of the relationship and how it evolves. But once these costs are "paid," they will tend to preserve already established relationships because they cannot be reallocated to another relationship. Thus, the higher the exit costs from a relationship, the more the sunk costs are the glue in the relationship. To assess these exit costs, we need to use more than just an absolute calculation. The exit costs should also be assessed against the estimated costs of building up alternative relationships. Information on this is not readily available and involves immense uncertainty. This deficiency in the assessment of alternative relationships may in itself be a hindrance to establishing new relationships.

A prerequisite for efficient information exchange is common channels and codes of information, effectively distributed and understood. The specific channels and codes will reflect the cultural, geographical, and organizational differences between the firm and the venture capital firm. Thus, there may be difficulties in the ability to process information. Information gathering on the innovator would in theory proceed until the marginal costs of more information exceed the expected benefit from additional information. The trouble with this way of reasoning is, of course, that it is impossible to stipulate with accuracy when this point is reached—one does not know the value of the information before it is known, and innovation projects are characterized by uncertainty on the future benefits. Consequently, venture capital firms know that they will always be bounded rational in their decision making. They do not have costless, unlimited computational efforts; they prefer instead to gather information to a satisfactory level, even if that level does not include all relevant information. Therefore, the interaction must lead to ways of pooling the information in a manner suited to the receiver's organizational structure and ability to process informational signals. The more specialized the organizational design, the more effective the receiving and processing of information. Less flexibility is, however, the negative side of this trade-off.

This method indicates that there is bound to be a mutual adaptation of the other party's ways and habits of interacting. A venture capital firm may, for example, talk differently to a thirty-year-old firm with 100 employees than it would to a single entrepreneur. In this way the venture capital firm takes the absorptive capacity of the other party into account. The idea of absorptive capacity was, at least in the Cohen and Levinthal work (1989), meant as an argument for why firms prefer to do R&D for other reasons besides making new products or processes. It may be, according to this theory, that firms increase their ability to assimilate external information. A firm that engages in intramural R&D will be in a much better position to assess what is relevant external information and what is not relevant. Moreover, it becomes easier to interact with other researchers due to the proximity in culture, logic, and language. For the venture capital firm, the concept of absorptive capacity is highly relevant because the capacity is related not only to the size and age of the innovating firm but also to the degree of specialization of the venture capital firm and whether the competencies of the two parties match.

This argument that absorptive capacity is related to the degree of specialization may at first seem counterintuitive. The reverse hypothesis, that broad scope will increase one's ability to interact with many types of people, may be plausible. However, as venture capital firms experience an increasing degree of specialization at a number of markets, they increase not only their knowledge of the market and the technologies involved but also their ability to interact with certain types of firms. The second point is that it is important that the absorptive capacity of the two parties match. This proper matching is even more important than a high level of absorptive capacity on both sides. For example, a biotech entrepreneur may be well equipped for understanding what is discussed in the negotiations with a technology-focused venture capital firm. However, if the same entrepreneur approaches a venture capital firm that specializes in Internet-based firms, the two parties may have quite different understandings of time horizons and other aspects of the relationship. It may therefore be argued that absorptive capacity is a relevant aspect of understanding the interaction between venture capital firm and innovator, but perhaps this aspect ought to be seen as a relative concept and not something that reflects an absolute level of, for example, specialized knowledge.

CONCLUSIONS

This chapter drew attention to some general trends in the innovation mode because these trends may affect the role of venture capital firms in innovation. Specifically, I argued that innovative firms are increasingly dependent on networking. A venture capital firm may, in an innovation setting, be increasingly important as a mediator and as a bridge to other networks.

Discussions of innovation inevitably lead to discussions of knowledge and interaction. Innovation is closely linked to the generation, transfer, and use of knowledge, and is becoming increasingly so. In addition, and again increasingly, firms are collaborating on innovation not only with a single partner but also with many different types of partners, including venture capital firms.

I argued that traditional financial theories may bring us only a little step toward understanding the role of venture capital firms in innovation. The traditional finance theories fail to address important aspects of venture capital financing of innovation, such as the genuine uncertainty in innovation and the buildup of trust in close relationships between the parties. Such close relationships may mitigate problems with lack of information, competencies, and trust (de Clercq and Sapienza 2001); however, there are also costs associated with establishing and maintaining such relationships. I argued that it is important to take into account the absorptive capacity of the parties, but this should be done using a relative perception of this concept, thus allowing for differences in the parties' ways and habits of interacting. In fact, researchers dealing with venture capital, rather than starting with traditional finance theories, may generally benefit more by starting with theories on interfirm relationships and exchange of knowledge and then adapting and applying these theories to venture capital situations.

NOTES

1. One remarkable exception is the work by Schumpeter ([1912] 1934), who made the first thorough treatment of the financing aspects of innovations. Among other classical, early contributions are the selected writings of Thorstein Veblen. However, in most other early writings, direct references to innovation financing are scattered.

2. Included in estimates of the importance of informal venture capital is an estimate for the United Kingdom (Mason and Harrison 1996) that suggests that the informal venture capital industry is twice as large as the institutional venture funds in terms of amount invested in the small and medium-sized enterprises sector. Bannock (1995) supports this estimate, whereas others (Stevenson and Coveney 1994) suggest that these estimates are too low. Estimates for Finland also suggest that the informal venture market is at least twice as large as the professional market (Suomi and Lumme 1995), and according to SITRA, a government agency for business promotion, there are likely to be around 4,500 potential business angels in Finland in the year 2000. Moreover, potential business angels considerably outnumber active angels. Wetzel and Freear (1996) suggest that there may be up to ten times as many potential angels as active

angels, and Riding et al. (1993) estimate that there are approximately one hundred thousand potential informal investors in Canada. Although there is indeed considerable uncertainty on these estimates, they do show beyond doubt that informal investors are a major source of financing for small firms.

3. The exact socioeconomic impact of financing innovation in general—and venture capital in particular—is difficult to estimate. Levine (1997) discusses the importance of economic development of financial systems in general, whereas only a few other studies have focused directly upon venture capital (BVCA 1999; NUTEK 1999; Manigart, Bayens, and van Hyfte 2002; Christensen and Christensen 2002).

4. By taking this micro-perspective it is not my intention to discuss theories specifically on the evolution of the venture capital industry; rather I intend to focus upon the micro-aspect of venture financing. The macro trends in innovation that I mention are thus closely related to a possible change in the role of venture capitalists in the financing process.

5. This hypothesis is supported by results from an analysis in the United States (The Advanced Manufacturing Programme; Jacobs 1991, p. 161) in which it was found that small, basic businesses feel that their needs are not glamorous enough to attract venture capital.

6. This importance is also supported by recent statements from the European Commission. Among numerous such statements it is mentioned in one paper that "Intangible assets offer no or only very limited collateral for bank loans, and venture capital is often the best solution for innovation financing" (Commission of the European Communities 2001, p. 17).

7. Changes in the mode of innovation has, however, long been discussed by many authors; see, for example, the well-known discussion of a Schumpeter Mark I and II mode of innovation. In short, Mark I is the entrepreneurial mode that has the creative individual as the driving force, whereas innovation in Mark II is driven by R&D departments of large firms. More recently, innovation theory has discussed extensively the existence of and changes in technological regimes.

8. Venture capitalists are important intermediaries in relation to their portfolio firms as well. It is a deliberate strategy in some venture capital firms to place a limited number of managers on the boards of several portfolio firms, thus stimulating networking across these firms.

9. See Petit (2000), Foray (2000), Freeman (2000), and OECD (2000) for more thorough discussions on the new economy. Also, Cooke (2001) devotes a section to defining what is meant by "new."

10. Classical corporate finance textbooks include those by Copeland and Weston (Addison Wesley) and by Brealey and Myers (McGraw-Hill).

11. These problems are reinforced in the case of innovations.

12. Stiglitz and Weiss (1981) is a classical article in this line of research; others include Leland and Pyle (1977) and Myers and Majluf (1984).

13. This idea of a competence mismatch is not new either. Veblen spelled it out very convincingly in his 1919 article titled the "Captains of Finance and the Engineers," and more recently, Prakke (1988) states that "Financiers will place over-reliance on accounting procedure and mentality. The candidate entrepreneur will overestimate the importance of the technical qualities of his new product to the detriment of market assessment. There is a mismatch of priorities due to the differences between the two cultures" (p. 85).

14. This is not confined to the venture capital firms. In the financial sector, banks apply techniques on customer relationship management.

15. However, the models within the information and economics tradition are rarely two-period models that allow for such learning effects. An additional criticism against these theories is that they are not really dealing with genuine uncertainty but rather calculable risk. Often, however, innovation is characterized by true uncertainty, and the ventures supported by the venture capital firms are particularly uncertain.

16. In a survey on venture-backed firms in the United Kingdom, respondents listed "sounding board for new ideas" as the most important contribution by venture capital firms, with 60 percent of the venture-backed firms listing this contribution as either crucial or of large importance (BVCA 1999).

REFERENCES

Arrow, K. 1974. *The Limits of Organisation*. New York: Norton.

Bank of England. 1996. "The Financing of Technology-Based Small Firms." October. Report.

Bannock, G. 1995. "Corporate Venture Capital." Background paper for the European Innovation Monitoring System Innovation Policy Workshop "Innovation Financing." Luxembourg.

British Venture Capital Association. 1999. "The Economic Impact of Venture Capital in the UK." London: Bannock Consulting.

Chan, Yuk-Shee. 1983. "On the Positive Role of Financial Intermediation in Allocation of Venture Capital in a Market with Imperfect Information." *The Journal of Finance* 38 (5): 1543–68.

Christensen, C. E., and J. L. Christensen. 2002. "The Impact of Venture Capital in Denmark." In *Management of Technology: Growth through Business, Innovation, and Entrepreneurship*, ed. M. Zedtwitz et al. Oxford: Pergamon Press.

Christensen, Jesper L. 1992. "The Role of Finance in National Systems of Innovation." In *National Systems of Innovation*, ed. B. A. Lundvall, pp. 146–68. London: Pinter.

Cohen, W., and D. Levinthal. 1989. "Innovation and Learning: The Two Faces of R&D." *The Economic Journal* 99: 569–96.

Commission of the European Communities. 2001. "Enterprises' Access to Finance." Commission Staffs Working Paper, SEC 1667.

Cooke, Philip. 2001. "New Economic Innovation Systems: Biotechnology in Europe and the USA." *Industry & Innovation* 8 (3): 267–89.

Coveney, P., K. Moore, and J. Nahapiet. 1996. "Business Angels: Tapping the Potential of Individual Investors in Britain." The Oxford Executive Research Briefings, Templeton, Oxford.

de Clercq, D., and H. J. Sapienza. 2001. "The Creation of Relational Rents in Venture Capitalist-Entrepreneur Dyads." *Venture Capital* 3 (2): 107–27.

Florida, R. L., and M. Kenney. 1988. "Venture Capital-financed innovation and technological changes in the U.S.A.", Research Policy 17, 119–137.

Foray, D. 1997. "Generation and Distribution of Technological Knowledge." In *Systems of Innovation: Technologies, Institutions, and Organisations*, ed. C. Edquist. London: Pinter.

Foray, D. 2000. "Rachid and Joe: On the Essence of the Knowledge Economy." Paper presented at DRUID (Danish Research Unit Industrial Dynamics) Conference, June, Rebild, Denmark.

Freear, J., J. E. Sohl, and W. E. Wetzel. 1997. "The Informal Venture Capital Market: Milestones Passed and the Road Ahead." In *Entrepreneurship 2000*, ed. D. L. Sexton and R. W. Smilor, pp. 47–69. Chicago: Upstart Publishing.

Freeman, Chris. 2000. "A Hard Landing for the 'New Economy'? Information Technology and the United States National System of Innovation." Institute of Economics, Federal University of Rio de Janeiro, Nota Técnica 1.

Gompers, P. A., and J. Lerner. 1997. "What Drives Venture Capital Fundraising?" Working Paper, Harvard Business School.

Greenwald, B. C., and J. E. Stiglitz. 1990. "Asymmetric Information and the New Theory of the Firm: Financial Constraints and Risk Behavior." National Bureau of Economic Research Working Paper 3359.

Harrison, R. T. 1995. "Development in the Promotion of Informal Venture Capital." Paper presented at the European Innovation Monitoring System Innovation Policy Workshop "Innovation Financing." Luxembourg.

Hirschman, A. 1970. *Exit, Voice, and Loyalty*. Cambridge, Mass.: Harvard University Press.

Jacobs, M. 1991. *Short-Term America*. Cambridge, Mass.: Harvard Business School Press.

Lam, Alice. 2000. "Skills Formation in the Knowledge-Based Economy: Mode 2 Knowledge and the Extended Internal Labour Market." Paper presented at the Conference on the Learning Economy—Firms, Regions, and Nation Specific Institutions, DRUID, 15–17 June, Rebild, Denmark.

Landström, H. 1993. "Informal Risk Capital in Sweden and Some International Comparisons." *Journal of Business Venturing* 8: 525–40.

Leland, H. E., and D. H. Pyle. 1977. "Informational Asymmetries, Financial Structure, and Financial Intermediation." *The Journal of Finance* 32 (2): 371–87.

Levine, R. 1997. "Financial Development and Economic Growth: Views and Agenda." *Journal of Economic Literature* 35: 688–726.

Lockett, A., G. Murray, and M. Wright. 2002. "Do UK Venture Capitalists *Still* Have a Bias against Investments in New Technology Firms?" *Research Policy* 31: 1009–30.

Lundvall, B.-A., and B. Johnson. 1994. "The Learning Economy." *Journal of Industrial Studies* 1 (2): 23–42.

Manigart, S., K. Bayens, and W. van Hyfte. 2002. "The Survival of Venture Capital–Backed Companies." *Venture Capital* 4 (2): 103–24.

Mason, C. M., and R. T. Harrison. 1996. "Informal Venture Capital and the Financing of Small and Medium Sized Enterprises." *Small Enterprise Journal—The Journal of SEAAN* 2 (3): 33–56.

Mason, C. M., and R. T. Harrison. 1999. "Editorial, Venture Capital: Rationale, Aims and Scope." *Venture Capital* 1 (1): 1–46.

Murray, G. 1999. "Seed Capital and the Tyranny of (Small) Scale." Presented at the Conference on Financing Entrepreneurship and Innovation in Science-Based Industries, 22–23 January, Mannheim, Germany.

Murray, G. C., and J. Lott. 1995. "Have UK Venture Capitalists a Bias against Investment in New Technology-Based Firms?" *Research Policy* 24: 283–99.

Myers, Stewart C., and Nicholas S. Majluf. 1984. "Corporate Financing and Investment

Decisions When Firms Have Information That Investors Do Not Have." *Journal of Financial Economics* 13 (2): 187–221.

Neave, E. H. 1991. *The Economic Organisation of a Financial System.* London and New York: Guildford/Routledge.

NUTEK. 1999. *Effekter av venture kapital.* Stockholm: NUTEK.

Organization for Economic Cooperation and Development (OECD). 1982. "Innovation in Small and Medium-Sized Firms." Background report. Paris: Organization for Economic Cooperation and Development.

Organization for Economic Cooperation and Development (OECD). 1993. *National Systems for Financing Innovation.* Paris: Organization for Economic Cooperation and Development.

Organization for Economic Cooperation and Development (OECD). 2000. *A New Economy? The Changing Role of Innovation and Information Technology in Growth.* Paris: Organization for Economic Cooperation and Development.

Petit, P. 2000. "Some F.A.Q.s about the New Economy and Its Future." Paper presented at Conference on the Learning Economy—Firms, Regions, and Nation-Specific Institutions, DRUID, 15–17 June, Rebild, Denmark.

Prakke, F. 1988. "The Financing of Technological Innovation." In *Innovation, Technology, and Finance,* ed. A. Heertje. Oxford: Blackwell.

Reid, G. C. 1999. "The Application of Principal-Agent Methods to Investor-Investee Relations in the UK Venture Capital Industry." *Venture Capital* 1 (4): 285–302.

Riding, A., et al. 1993. "Informal Investors in Canada: The Identification of Salient Characteristics." Ottawa: Carleton University.

Schumpeter, J. A. [1912] 1934. *Theory of Economic Development.* Cambridge, Mass.: Harvard University Press.

Schumpeter, J. A. 1939. *Business Cycles: A Theoretical, Historical, and Statistical Analysis of the Capitalist Process.* New York: McGraw-Hill.

Sharpe, Steven A. 1990. "Asymmetric Information, Bank Lending, and Implicit Contracts: A Stylized Model of Customer Relationships." *The Journal of Finance* 45 (4): 1087.

Shepherd, D. A., and A. Zacharakis. 2001. "The Venture Capitalist-Entrepreneur Relationship: Control, Trust, and Confidence in Co-Operative Behaviour." *Venture Capital* 3 (2): 129–50.

Stevenson, H., and P. Coveney. 1994. "Survey of Business Angels." Venture Capital Report Ltd., www.vcr1978.com.

Stiglitz, J., and A. Weiss. 1981. "Credit Rationing in Markets with Imperfect Information." *American Economic Review* 71: 393–410.

Suomi, M., and A. Lumme. 1995. "Informal Private Investors in Finland." Helsinki: SITRA.

Timmons, J. A., and W. D. Bygrave. 1986. "Venture Capital's Role in Financing Innovation for Economic Growth." *Journal of Business Venturing* 1 (2): 161–76.

Veblen, T. 1919. "Captains of Finance and the Engineers." *Dial,* June, pp. 599–606.

Wetzel, W., and J. Freear. 1996. "Promoting Informal Venture Capital in the U.S.: Reflections on the History of the Venture Capital Network." In *Informal Venture Capital: Evaluating the Impact of Business Introduction Services,* ed. R. Harrison and C. Mason. Hemel Hempstead: Woodhead-Faulkner.

Wright, M., and K. Robbie. 1998. "Venture Capital and Private Equity: A Review and Synthesis." *Journal of Business Finance Accounting* 25: 521–570.

3

Angel Networks for the Twenty-first Century
An Examination of Practices of Leading Networks in Europe and the United States

Julian Lange, Benoît Leleux, and Bernard Surlemont

Developments in web technology are creating new opportunities for entrepreneurs and venture investors alike and are facilitating the emergence of new breeds of introduction services that connect these parties more efficiently. This chapter relies on clinical analyses of over forty identified "best practice" angel networks in the United States and Europe to provide a systematic study of the newest and most innovative practices in angel networks, focusing in particular on the use of information technology to facilitate the flow of ideas and capital to start-ups and early-stage companies and its implications for tomorrow's private equity markets and the financing of high-potential ventures. It highlights two simultaneous polar developments, one toward the mass distribution of information regarding start-up opportunities (entrepreneur-centric networks) and the other, in reaction to the first, toward extreme screening of the information for a select audience (investor-centric networks).

INTRODUCTION

Informal venture capital represents a pool of high-risk growth equity estimated conservatively at ten times the size of formal venture capital, a significant force in the financing of start-up firms and hence of critical importance to economic development. Angel networks are taking full advantage of the new information technologies to become more efficient in generating deals and distributing information about private equity activities, significantly reducing the

This paper was first presented at the 2000 Babson College/Kauffman Foundation Entrepreneurship Research Conference and published in Summary form in *Frontiers of Entrepreneurship Research 2000*.

informational and search costs associated with the old "atomistic" format of angel investing. Yet little is understood about the key success factors of angel networks for the twenty-first century.

ANGEL INVESTORS AND NEW VENTURE FUNDING

Informal venture capital, also referred to as angel capital, represents a pool of risk equity fundamental to the start-up and initial growth phases of high-potential ventures. The term *angel* originated in the early 1900s and referred to investors on Broadway who made risky investments to support theatrical productions (Utterbach et al. 1999). Today, the term refers mainly to high net worth individuals who invest in and support start-up companies in their early stages of growth.[1] In addition to providing financing, angels typically support the company by providing guidance and assistance with recruiting, management, networks, distribution connections, and so on. Also referred to as informal or independent investors, they are said to represent the largest pool of equity capital in the United States, many times larger than formal venture capital (Wetzel 1986a, 1986b).

Collectively, they are the oldest, largest, and most often used source of external equity for entrepreneurial firms (Van Osnabrugge and Robinson 2000). The value they add has been clear for many years. In 1874, Alexander Bell used angel money to start Bell Telephone; in 1903, Henry Ford launched his automobile empire using the funds provided by five angel investors. Apple, Amazon.com, and The Body Shop are other examples of businesses developed primarily with the use of angel funds.

Business angels come from various backgrounds. Typically, they are well-educated individuals with a high net worth and significant income. A UK study titled "Barriers to Investment in the Informal VC Sector" revealed that around two-thirds of business angels' principal source of wealth was their own past business ventures, not inheritance. Since most angels are themselves former entrepreneurs, they have a successful history in business development and a wealth of knowledge and connections to provide in addition to funds.

Most angels invest in companies that are not ripe for venture capitalists (VCs)—angel funds account for over 60 percent of early financing compared with less than 30 percent provided by VCs. Angels typically invest during the seed or start-up stages of companies operating in the markets and technologies they are familiar with. Their role is often to fill an equity gap between the money an entrepreneur is able to secure from the bank and the funds he or she is able to obtain from a venture capital firm.

According to the most recent figures from the U.S. Small Business Administration (SBA, http://www.sba.gov/), out of 350,000 small companies searching for angel funds about 10 percent were able to secure angels' support by way of equity or debt. The SBA conservatively estimated that roughly 250,000 angels invested $20 billion annually—twice as much as VCs. Van Osnabrugge and Robinson (2000) argue that the United States has nearly 3 million angels investing more than $50 billion in entrepreneurial firms each year. They estimate that business angels invest up to five times more money than any other investor type. According to the SBA, angels also invest in approximately fifteen times as many companies as institutional venture capitalists. Van Osnabrugge and Robinson's findings show that angels fund thirty to forty times more ventures each year than venture capitalists do, but they tend to focus on the smaller, earlier stage deals.

The angel investor literature (Van Osnabrugge and Robinson 2000; Harrison and Mason 1996) gives many examples of characteristics that distinguish angels from other types of investors. In particular, angel investors have been shown to

- invest in smaller deals than VCs do: investments generally range between $100,000 and $500,000, but can be as low as $25,000 or as high as $1 million. Angels usually resist investing more than $1 million, whereas VCs seek initial investments of at least $3 million to $10 million.

- syndicate aggressively: most angel investors tend to invest as part of a larger group because they can make more of an impact when their funds are pooled and there is a feeling of safety in numbers.

- source deals mainly through personal networks and referrals: groups of friends, informal contacts, business associates, and personal searches are prominent sources of potential deals.

- prefer seed and very early stage start-ups: those stages leverage better their limited financial resources; correspond to the bigger "financing gap," in other words, periods during which it is most difficult for the new ventures to obtain funding; and provide the best environment to contribute actively to the development of the company and hence provide the highest potential for personal satisfaction.

- invest in virtually all industry sectors, but are inclined to concentrate on the industries they are most familiar with.

- have a wide range of functional expertise in terms of length of senior management, professional, and industry experience: in addition to the money they invest, they are eager to share their expertise, experience, and contacts. Even so, they normally do not insist on the level of control that venture capitalists usually demand. They can either be "active" investors, serving on boards of directors, or be providers of guidance, serving in less formal counseling or mentoring roles.

- have a tendency to devote very significant amounts of time post-investment supporting the ventures: as a consequence, their average investment portfolio size is often constrained by the amount of time they are prepared to commit to their investment activities. Most will indicate they can manage five or six companies effectively.

- have a distinct geographical preference for deals within a few hours' drive of home (Wetzel 1983), so that meetings with entrepreneurs can be easily arranged without spending much time and money on long-distance travel and accommodation.

- be more flexible in their financial decision making than VCs are. They can afford the risk inherent in private investment, and at the same time, they are inclined to act—contributing time and money—based in part on their feel for a business or the confidence they have in the entrepreneur.

- be willing to assume bigger risks and accept lower rewards when they are attracted by the nonfinancial characteristics of an entrepreneur's proposal.

- have investment time horizons very much in line with other early-stage private equity investors, normally in the three-year to five-year horizon.

- have relatively efficient investment decision processes that do not involve high upfront fees: most angels like to be involved in the venture and enjoy helping grow their businesses. They share their enthusiasm, build value, and feel social responsibility. Significant secondary investment considerations for angels include making use of tax breaks (significant in some countries) and the desire to support the next generation of entrepreneurs.

- be more geographically dispersed than the formal VC market: angels can be found everywhere and are not confined just to metropolitan centers.

- have a tendency to be opportunistic in their deals, investing on average once every two years, with over 98 percent of the deals involving a syndicate of other investors.

As far as motivations are concerned, angel investors tend to combine the traditional venture capitalist's concern for financial profitability with other nonfinancial motives such as personal satisfaction, opportunities to influence the outcome of a new venture, and so on. Their expected returns are very much in line with the venture investment industry: start-up companies are expected to earn about ten times the investment within five years.

The willingness of many angels to invest (1) in first-time entrepreneurs, (2) at the search or seed levels of development, and (3) reasonably small amounts of capital (less than $100,000) makes invaluable contributions to the pre-formal venture capital development of many technology ventures. An early study by Freear and Wetzel in 1990 on the financing of 284 New England high-tech firms founded between 1975 and 1986 found that out of the 62 percent that had to rely on external equity for their growth, individual angel investors were the most common source of funds, providing 177 rounds of equity financing for 124 firms. Ninety firms raised equity from venture capital funds in 173 rounds. Table 3.1 summarizes the distribution of individual angel investors and venture capitalists in the various rounds of financing. A more recent study by Benjamin and Margulis (1996) similarly finds that more than 61 percent of the 480 start-up firms in their sample were financed through business angels, while friends and family accounted for 18 percent on average, and venture capital firms, corporate investors, and IPOs accounted for less than 2 percent overall.

In recent years, angel investing has seen rapid growth and increased professionalization. Evidence of such increased activity can be found in the increase in angel group enrollment. From 1995 to 1998, the number of members in the Band of Angels organization, a Silicon Valley angel group, grew from 12 to

Table 3.1
Angels and Venture Capitalists Contributions to New Venture Fundings

Financing Round ($k)	Number of Individual Angels Investing	Distribution of Angels Investing (%)	Number of Venture Capitalists Investing	Distribution of VCs Investing (%)
<250	102	58	8	5
250–500	43	24	14	8
500–1,000	15	8	31	18
>1,000	17	10	120	69
Total	177	100	173	100

Source: Freear and Wetzel (1987)

110 (McLaughlin 1999). The Band of Angels invested in nineteen deals in 1995 and twenty-three deals in 1997. The average investment per company increased from $290,000 to $535,000. The growth occurred not only in Silicon Valley but also across the United States, in Europe, and in other countries. For example, in the last five years, the Boston/Route 128 area has seen the emergence and growth of at least a dozen new angel groups (Utterbach et al. 1999). In Europe, starting from a few confidential entrepreneurs' clubs in 1995, angel networks and other new venture support groups now number in the hundreds.

ANGEL INVESTORS AND VENTURE SUPPORT SERVICES

The market for informal venture capital is said to suffer from two related crippling inefficiencies: the extreme discretion of most business angels, and the high search costs of angels for businesses and businesses for angels (Riding, Duxbury, and Haines 1997; Wetzel 1986a). These inefficiencies are often invoked to support the existence of a "funding gap," preventing valuable opportunities from materializing.

As a response to these perceived shortcomings, a number of organizations have been created, referred to alternatively as matchmaking services, angel networks, venture support bureaus, or business referral services (Harrison and Mason 1996). A forerunner in the effort was the Venture Capital Network (VCN), established in 1984 in New Hampshire, now called the Technology Capital Network operated by the MIT Enterprise Forum. From these pioneering days, angel networks have mushroomed and taken on more and more different shapes and modus operandi to cover more varied business realities.

The development in the 1990s of the "network economy," capitalizing on the new opportunities created by the Internet, has also affected the angel network community. From mostly limited access subscription services, venture support networks have developed new means of serving the needs of both investors and entrepreneurs: from matchmaking events to Internet cocktail parties à la First Tuesday, from incubators to specialized publicly listed early-stage funds, new means of closing the perceived funding gap have been hatched. This chapter investigates innovative practices in the angel networking field across a number of countries in an attempt to understand the key drivers of "performance" in this vital field of endeavor.

RESEARCH METHODOLOGY

Any major effort to understand best practices in the global networked economy needs to take a global perspective. This research effort surveys forty leading angel networks across eight European countries (United Kingdom, France, Belgium, Spain, Switzerland, Finland, the Netherlands, and Germany) and the United States. Open-ended interviews of business angel network managers were conducted by phone or through face-to-face meetings. The interviews, taped or recorded, covered a number of different aspects of the networks' operational histories as well as underlying motivations and rationales. The aspects covered included the history of the network from inception to its current form; its sponsors, financing, and mode of operation; rules for admission and continued participation; services provided to members; screening rules; and so on. Table 3.2 lists the names of the angel networks in the sample as well as their country of origination. Some of these networks operate across boundaries, such as UniversityAngels.com, taking advantage of the networking capabilities and scalability of the Web. Table 3.3 presents the major survey questions.

A TYPOLOGY OF ANGEL NETWORKS

This study does not focus on characteristics of business angels but rather investigates the innovative operating models of business angel *networks*. The Bank and Finance Commission in Belgium (CBF) defines a business angel network (BAN) as a "structured network which offers business angels the possibility to access projects in need of financing." As such, the typical roles undertaken by BAN include part or all of the following: (1) identify investors and entrepreneurs; (2) organize some channels through which the two parties can meet; (3) coach and mentor entrepreneurs and their projects; (4) provide feedback mechanisms for entrepreneurs to build on investor comments and suggestions; (5) facilitate later rounds of financing by providing connections to banks and venture capitalists; and (6) guarantee the confidentiality of all parties involved. The BAN literature typically distinguishes four fundamental types of networks (Coveney and Moore 1998; Mason and Harrison 1997) but the survey conducted here supports the need for a finer typology, presented in Table 3.4. The typology relies on seven criteria, which are detailed next.

Table 3.2
Sample of Angel Networks in the Study

Angel Network Name (founding year)	Country
First Tuesday - London (1998)	UK
British Venture Capital Association (1983)	UK
Natwest Angels Service (1995)	UK
National Business Angels Network (1997 as NBAN; LINC before)	UK
European Technology Forum (1998)	UK
Great Eastern Investment Forum (1994)	UK
Venture Capital Report Ltd (1978)	UK
Xenos (1997)	UK
Cambridge Network (1998)	UK
E-Start (1999)	UK
OION - Oxfordshire Investment Opportunity Network - Oxford	UK
Group Professional Networks (1994)	France
IPEN - International Private Equity Network (1996)	France
BusinessAngels.com (1998)	France
International Venture Capital Forum (1997)	France
Planet Start-Up (1999)	France
Capital-IT (1999)	France
Defi Start-Up (1998)	France
Leonardo Finance (1995)	France
Invest'Essor	France
ICEVED - Intl Center for Venture Development (1999)	Spain
Sitra (1996)	Finland
Smart Capital (1999)	Switzerland
Vlerick Business Angel Network - Gent	Belgium
WABAN – Mons	Belgium
SOCRAN – Liege	Belgium
BAMS - Business Angels Matching Services - Louvain La Neuve	Belgium
BeBAN – Brussels	Belgium
NEBIB	Netherlands
BAND	Germany
Business Angels Club Berlin	Germany
Wellspring Angel Fund (1998)	USA
Walnut Venture Associates	USA
128 Venture Capital Group (1983)	USA
Angeltips.com, Inc. (1999)	USA
UniversityAngels.com (1999)	USA
CommonAngels.com (1998)	USA
The Enterprise Corporation	USA
Technology Capital Network (1984)	USA
Colorado Capital Alliance – Boulder (1996)	USA
PEAK – Boulder	USA

Financing Mode

Whereas most of the early players on the European scene were publicly funded and supported, a number of new actors are now set up and operate on purely private grounds. Examples include BAMS, BusinessAngels.com, and First Tuesday. Irrespective of their public or private nature, most networks rely

Table 3.3
Angel Networks Survey Questions

Network Descriptive Characteristics
- History of the network: when founded, by whom, with what goals in mind, etc.
- Organization: sponsors, physical facilities, annual budget, funding, etc.
- Number of full-time employees, if any, status, etc.
- Revenue-generating sources (Inscription fees, sponsors, other)
- Number of members (investors) and other statistics on affiliation
- Registration process: how to become a member angel, fees, commitments made
- Type of services offered by the network
- Type and source of deals offered to members
- Type and source of member angels: age distribution, wealth, how active, track records
- Databases managed: deals done through the network, contacts established, etc.
- What is the definition of "satisfactory" performance for the network?
- Marketing channels used
- Relationships with other angel networks
- Biggest challenges the network will likely face in the future and contingency plans

Investment Activities
- Number of deals looked at / considered / done over the last 3 years
- Amount invested globally and by deal

Reference Networks
- Source of information on investment opportunities (informal sources, formal sources, etc.)
- Source of information for the deals that were actually done (informal sources, formal sources, etc.)

Investment Characteristics
- Investment preferences by industry, geographical location, deal size, development stage
- Decision-making process
- Preference for single deals or syndications with other investors
- Preference for minority or majority equity stakes
- Level of participation in invested company: none, board of directors, advisory board, part-time involvement, etc.

Investment Motivations
- Project evaluation criteria
- Lead factors in the decision to invest
- Lead factors in the decision NOT to invest
- Risk evaluation: informal, formal, syndicated, reference investor, etc.
- Return expectation guidelines
- Exit expectations: means, time to exit, alternatives considered, etc.
- Performance of actual investments already done
- Satisfaction with respect to the above

Table 3.4
Typological Dimensions of Angel Networks

Typological Criteria	⇐	⇒
Financing Mode	Private	Public
Profit Orientation	For Profit	Not For Profit
Preferred Financing Stage	Early Stage Preferred	All Stages
Investment Sectors	Specialist	Generalist
Screening and Support	Active	Passive
Geographical Reach	Regional or Local	National or Pan-National
Type of Services Offered	Introduction Services Only	Broad Offering (coaching, mentoring, incubating, team building, funding, etc.)

heavily on sponsoring and subscription revenues to operate. An EU commission report estimates that, on average; a BAN can only break even after five years of existence (EBAN and EURADA 1998). In the United States, most angel groups have been suppliers of private capital funded by high net worth individuals.

Profit Orientation

Profit orientation can often be related to the financing mode, with public BANs often operating relatively simple forums for introduction on a nonprofit basis, whereas private BANs tend to offer enlarged service offerings and are clearly intent on generating revenues from the activities. In the United States, most angel groups are driven by an underlying profit motive on the part of their participants but are nonprofits themselves. They generate revenues to cover costs but leave the profit orientation to the investors who fund particular deals (e.g., Walnut Venture Associates, CommonAngels.com, Technology Capital Network). Recently, some BANs have emerged with a distinct profit-making approach, taking compensation in the form of fees for introductions and equity or warrants in companies that are funded through their network (e.g., Angeltips.com). Hybrids do exist, such as NBAN in the United Kingdom, which is financed both by the Department of Trade and Industry and by private sponsors such as Barclays and Lloyds.

Preferred Financing Stage

By definition, BANs were mostly created to bridge the early-stage funding gap. This is particularly true in the United States, where there is a well-developed and funded venture capital community. However, some BANs do not hesitate to invest in all stages of a company development. For example, PEAK (Colorado), OION, and NBAN have few restrictions in terms of stage of financing.

Investment Sectors

Many angel groups concentrate on particular sectors, with many emphasizing high-tech investments in telecomm, information technology, and the Internet. For example, in the United States, Walnut focuses on information technology companies in rapidly growing markets. OION defines itself as high-tech oriented. An extreme case of specialization in the United Kingdom is First Tuesday's Internet "cocktail party" and matchmaking events. Other BANs seem to have followed the latest fashion into "new media" projects: the International Venture Capital Forum of Sophia Antipolis struggled in 1999 to maintain a decent representation of biotechnology projects in its annual lineup simply because of a lack of projects presented.

Screening and Coaching

Some intermediation services take very active roles in screening projects to be presented to investors and coaching them to ensure consistent quality and satisfactory presentation. CommonAngels.com selects potential investments through an initial screening questionnaire and submission of an accompanying executive summary submitted by entrepreneurs. Firms that pass through that initial screen must then make a presentation to a small group of network members and, if successful, are then permitted to present to a breakfast meeting of the entire membership (approximately fifty investors). Another example is the International Venture Capital Forum in Sophia Antipolis, which actively screens projects submitted for presentation at the annual matchmaking event (keeping less than 25 percent of all the projects submitted) and requires attendance and participation at presentation coaching sessions organized by a major sponsor, Deloitte and Touche. Still other angel groups provide a more classic caveat emptor approach.

Geographical Reach

In the United Kingdom, networks such as OION (Oxford) or LINC (Scotland) act primarily on a local basis, whereas NBAN offers a nationwide coverage. Similarly in Germany, the Business Angel Club Berlin has a regional focus, whereas BAND claims a national reach. In France, Invest'Essor focuses on the Paris area, whereas BusinessAngels.com has a national audience, as does NEBIB in the Netherlands. Most groups in the United States have had a regional focus (e.g., Walnut, 128 Venture Capital Group); recently, however, groups with a national focus are beginning to emerge (e.g., Angeltips.com, garage.com).

Three interesting outliers with a pan-national dimension are worth mentioning. First, BAMS operates across Belgium, Luxembourg, and Northern France. Second, and most notably, First Tuesday operates a network of local chapters now represented in some sixty-five cities across Europe. The First Tuesday model is described in more detail below. Finally, UniversityAngels.com uses alumni affiliation as a channel to link up entrepreneurs and start-up financiers across boundaries.

Types of Services Offered

From the traditional matchmaking role, BANs have developed a broad range of service offerings for entrepreneurs and investors alike. Even in matchmaking, a number of models have evolved. The simplest introduction format is the nonthreatening networking event organized by First Tuesday: screening is minimal and anyone with an interest in the Internet economy is welcome to join the fray. At the other end of the spectrum are pay-for-service matchmaking groups that actively match investors and projects for a fee (e.g., Angeltips.com). Beyond matchmaking, BANs are also offering business plan coaching, directly or indirectly (the International Venture Capital Forum, for example, partners with Deloitte and Touche for the active coaching of selected projects before presentation at the annual investment conference); active financing support; team building and management recruitment services; incubation support (logistics, shared offices, etc.); and even direct investment into the projects.

AN EXAMPLE OF VIRAL NETWORKING: FIRST TUESDAY'S FIREBALL

First Tuesday's debut was nothing short of astounding. Modeled along the lines of the *Churchill Club* or the *DrinksExchange* in San Francisco, in what is referred to as the Silicon Valley format, First Tuesday offered an informal cocktail-party-style forum for anyone interested in the new economy and new media, in other words, the Web. The gatherings appealed to both actual and would-be entrepreneurs, investors and professionals alike, anyone with an interest in keeping abreast of the latest developments in the field. No gimmicks, no beauty contest,[2] just a friendly, casual atmosphere, a chance to mingle with like-minded individuals who share a common interest in the cause of the Internet, and an opportunity to hear speeches from highly visible flag bearers of the new economy.

By late 1999, a short year after the first gathering in a crowded and noisy London pub, First Tuesday was launched across Europe and the rest of the world, in seventeen cities, creating venues where anybody with a bright idea could come to start building a new media business. By March 2000, First Tuesday had operating chapters in thirty-eight cities over four continents: cities such as London, Amsterdam, Budapest, Tel Aviv, Geneva, Hamburg, Sydney, Moscow, Frankfurt, and Paris, with more opening every month. Over forty thousand people had requested announcements and information from all over the world. More than ten thousand people were attending First Tuesday events worldwide every month, and more than sixty cities were on the waiting list to get onto the First Tuesday bandwagon.

The First Tuesday business model relies on at least five different revenue streams: (1) matchmaking, physical and online; (2) online job databases; (3) special conferences and events, mostly financed through sponsors and subscriptions; (4) website revenues for advertising services provided to a very targeted clientele; and (5) brand licensing through partnerships with international service providers. Beyond the traditional BAN support functions, First Tuesday is also adding to the mix the ability to actually invest directly or indirectly in projects, to leverage the resources of its extensive chapter base, and to tap the large intellectual bandwidth of its members and partners.

INTERNET AND BUSINESS ANGEL NETWORKS

A common theme encountered across all surveys is the tremendous impact the Internet economy is having on venture support services. Not only is the new economy putting a reinforced urgency on the need to network, but the new information technologies on which the economy is built are also changing the very channels through which these networks can be established.

Disintermediation is already taking place, according to many angel networks surveyed: it is becoming more and more difficult for many classic matchmaking services to charge for their basic introduction services since entrepreneurs find it relatively easier to access the financing sources without their help. More refined billing systems are taking shape, for example with introduction services taking direct equity stakes in their pupils or charging only on a success fee basis.

At the same time that some of the classic foundations of start-up intermediation are being attacked, opportunities are also being created all around. Active and continuing venture support services—in the form, for example, of incubators and hatcheries—are emerging everywhere. The strict financial focus is giving way to a broader definition of "resourcing" the firm, to include help in structuring the management team, recruiting key players for growth, or establishing solid boards of directors and advisors. The reduction in search costs also means entrepreneurs have a better ability to shop their deals around, increasing the likelihood of funding and a better match with investors. Increasingly, projects can be found on multiple network services at the same time.

Angel groups are generally taking advantage of the Internet to keep in touch with their dispersed membership, with some groups highlighting their "virtual" characteristics (e.g., CommonAngels.com describes itself as a virtual organization). Most of the information exchange takes place through e-mail and attachments of backup data or presentations, with face-to-face meetings being reserved for due diligence activities and presentations by entrepreneurs to the full membership of the angel group.

EMERGING PLAYERS IN THE BUSINESS OF ANGEL NETWORKS

Most BANs operate on the basis of matchmaking. Their major purpose remains the provision of services and opportunities for matching supply and demand for finance of start-ups and early stage businesses. From a financial point of view, many of these actors are playing the game of economies of scale and try to quickly gain a critical mass to finance their activities through membership fees and consulting services. Consequently, most BANs try to build volume and keep an equilibrium between business angels and entrepreneurs in an attempt to remain neutral. It is interesting, however, to notice that many business angels complain about the services provided by some BANs and in particular about the lack of selectivity and the poor quality of projects they provide. For instance, a common angel complaint is that only secondhand projects go through organized networks.[3]

Consequently, there are pressures on BANs, as on any intermediaries, to add value to their services. For angels, value means credibility and confidence in the projects that are proposed to them. BANs have to develop the ability to organize a very careful selection among the business investment opportunities and to ensure that the selection criteria agreed to by the angel network membership will be closely followed.[4] During our interviews, we observed emerging initiatives that are going in the direction of helping entrepreneurs to structure their businesses, hire professional management, develop strong business plans, manage intellectual property rights, and so on. These activities are often supported by business angels and mostly originate in the private sector. Some are developed by individuals acting as a network of "professional" business angels, like Innode in Belgium. Others group professional partners coming from complementary horizons, like the Vlerick Venture Coaching that is backed by a legal firm (one of the big five), a major bank, and the University of Gent. Still others are purely spin-offs of major players, like the recent Arthur Andersen initiative to develop business incubators, or are groups of ex-consultants backed by business angels, like Peak Business Development Co. in Denver, Colorado.

Our expectation is that BANs will evolve toward such a new profile: moving toward a role of investment recommendations and business coaching, exerting a very high selectivity on projects, financing their activities through participation in the projects (stock or options) and with a much smaller base of business angels that trust and rely on the network they back. Concurrently, high traffic / low selectivity marketplaces will continue to develop, such as UniversityAngels.com, NVST.com, or FindYourAngel.com, providing raw intermediation with little value-added services, relying on advertising-based revenue streams to sustain themselves. These "Internet turbo-charged" angel networks very much still follow the traditional model but they take advantage of the web scalability. These emerging models are described in Table 3.5.

CONCLUSIONS AND DISCUSSIONS

With the twenty-first century at our doorstep, it was interesting to hear from established and new players in the business angel network community about their fears and expectations, reviewing some new modes of operations and challenging older ways of doing things. The survey conducted here highlights the very dynamic nature of the industry, which has been riding on the coattails of the Internet revolution and its networking focus. New angel networks are emerging every day, and new models are being created every other week. In particular, the new information technologies are helping bridge the decades-old problem of connecting early-stage projects and risk investors.

Where a clear trend toward disintermediation is already visible, challenging existing fee-for-service introduction services, the increasing resource needs of start-ups open up a new world of opportunities for venture support services. Equity-for-service models are being adopted rapidly, leading to more dynamic realignment of risk and returns between parties involved with launching new ventures. The attention is also shifting away from pure financial intermediation services to a more global resourcing approach, where finance is just one piece

Table 3.5
Evolving Models of Business Angel Networks

	Traditional Angel Networks	Investor-Centric Angel Networks	Entrepreneur-Centric Angel Networks
Core business	Matchmaking Education/Services	Investment Screening Project Structuring Business Incubation Coaching/Mentoring	Networking Project Exposure Link-ups
Projects selectivity	Low to Moderate	Very high	None to Low
Mode of financing	Membership Fees Consulting Fees Service Fees	Consulting Fees Equity Stakes	Web Banners Traffic Referrals
Size (# of angels)	Large	Small	Huge

of a very complex puzzle. Increased attention is being placed on team building, management recruitment, the assembling of world-class advisory boards, and the provision of highly visible and competent directors. The creation of macro-networks (networks of networks) is also seen as a natural extension of services to a global audience.

Defining what constitutes performance for venture support systems is an issue that deserves further discussion. In many instances, the creation of active venture networks is sufficient performance. Clearly, being able to provide evidence of actual start-up funding and resourcing, and consequent value creation in the economy, would be even better. Quantifying such value contributions would, of course, challenge many systems' abilities and would be open to bias charges of one sort or another.

NOTES

1. In the United States, the term *angel* is often associated with "accredited investors" defined under SEC Rule 501 as an individual with a net worth of at least $1 million or earnings in excess of $200,000 per year (Levin 1994).

2. *Beauty contest* is the colloquial name for the more classic angel network presentation model in which entrepreneurs are given the opportunity to present their projects to a select audience of potential investors in the hopes of arousing their interest and ultimately enticing them to part with their money.

3. It is actually interesting to note that very few BANs track or provide records of successful investments. From our fieldwork, we have reason to suspect that one reason for this might be their very poor performance.

4. Although in some countries (e.g., Belgium and the United Kingdom) legislation forbids BANs to formulate investment recommendations.

REFERENCES

Benjamin, G. A., and J. Margulis. 1996. *Finding Your Wings: How to Locate Private Investors to Fund Your Venture.* New York: John Wiley & Sons.

Coveney, P., and K. Moore. 1998. *Business Angels: Securing Start Up Finance.* New York: John Wiley & Sons.

EBAN and EURADA. 1998. "European Business Angels Network: Dissemination Report on the Potential for Business Angels Investment and Networks in Europe." Brussels: European Business Angels Network. February.

Freear, J. J., and W. Wetzel. 1990. "Who Bankrolls High-Tech Entrepreneurs?" *Journal of Business Venturing* 5: 77–89.

Harrison, R. T., and C. Mason. 1996. *Informal Venture Capital: Evaluating the Impact of Business Introduction Services.* Hemel Hempstead: Woodhead-Faulkner.

Levin, Jack. 1994. *Structuring Venture Capital, Private Equity, and Entrepreneurial Transactions.* Chicago: CCH.

Mason, C., and R. Harrison. 1997. "Business Angels Networks and the Development of the Informal Venture Capital Market in the UK: Is There Still a Role for the Public Sector?" *Small Business Economics* 9: 111–23.

McLaughlin, G. 1999. "Angel Investing: Silicon Valley." In *Venture Support Systems Project: Angel Investors*, ed. M. Utterbach, K. Morse, H. Stevenson, and M. Roberts. Cambridge: MIT Entrepreneurship Center.

Riding, A., L. Duxbury, and G. Haines Jr. 1997. "Financing Enterprise Development: Decision-Making by Canadian Angels." *Conference Proceedings for the Entrepreneurship Division of the Association of Management and International Association of Management*, pp. 17–22.

"UK Business Angels Invest Record Amount." 1999. *European Venture Capital Journal* 80: 10.

Utterbach, M., K. Morse, H. Stevenson, and M. Roberts. 1999. *Venture Support Systems Project: Angel Investors.* Cambridge: MIT Entrepreneurship Center.

Van Osnabrugge, M., and R. J. Robinson. 2000. *Angel Investing: Matching Startup Funds.* San Francisco: Jossey-Bass.

Wetzel, William E. 1983. "Angels and Informal Risk Capital." *Sloan Management Review* 24: 23–34.

Wetzel, William E., Jr. 1986a. "Entrepreneurs, Angels, and Economic Renaissance." In *Entrepreneurship, Intrapreneurship, and Venture Capital*, ed. R. D. Hisrich, pp. 119–39. Lexington, Mass.: Lexington Books.

Wetzel, William E., Jr. 1986b. "Informal Risk Capital: Knowns and Unknowns." In *The Art and Science of Entrepreneurship*, ed. D. L. Sexton and R. W. Smilor, pp. 85–108. Cambridge Mass.: Ballinger.

4

The Role of Venture Capitalists in Going-Private Transactions

Arman Kösedağ

INTRODUCTION

"Going private" through management buyout (MBO) and its consequences has been the subject of frequent debates among policy makers and financial economists during the last twenty years.[1] By no means does this era constitute the entire period of these highly levered transactions, however. In fact, leveraged buyouts (LBOs), known as "bootstrapping," trace back to the early 1960s. In its earlier versions, an LBO was a practice by which the owner/founder, seeking to cash out his investment, transferred the firm to managers or younger family members, who would put up a small amount of capital and borrow the rest.

Today, LBOs differ from their earlier appearance in that they have been applied to those companies that are not only large, but also publicly traded.[2] Such a dramatic change in the structure of LBO deals can mainly be attributed to the emergence of junk bond financing and venture capital firms *(or buyout specialists, as they are called within the context of LBO transactions)*. Buyout specialists appear as large-block equity investors in most cases and are usually appointed to the board of directors with an active role in monitoring management's activity and performance.

It is true that the venture capital firms originally were associated with the start-up and/or second-stage financing of high-tech companies. In early 1980s, there was a surge of LBOs, many of them generating enormous returns to equity investors. For example, following a LBO of $80 million (of which only $1 million was equity capital) from RCA Corporation in 1982, Gibson Greeting Cards was sold to the public for $280 million in sixteen months (Fuqua 1988). The buyout of Goodmark by its managers from the parent company General Mills presents a similar case. The management team invested only $200,000 in equity as a part of financing the $15 million bid in 1982. In November 1985, the company was taken to public with a market value of $45 million. The management team liquidated part of its investment for $6 million while keeping 62.5 percent ownership of the company (Clark, Gerlach, and Olson 1996).

Venture capital firms were quick both in recognizing and taking a part in these highly profitable deals. Venture Lending Associates, First Chicago Venture Capital, Citicorp Investing, Manufacturers Hanover VC Group, and First Venture Capital Corp. are among the list of venture capital players in LBOs provided by Michel and Shaked (1988). Following this initial spree, some of the VC firms, either individually or pooling funds together, emerged into a new type of financial intermediary known as buyout specialists, or LBO firms who would engage specifically in financing LBOs. Wesray, Kohlberg Kravis Roberts & Co and Gibbons, Green van Amerongen are examples of such firms (Michel and Shaked 1988).

Contrary to the previous chapters, where venture capital firms are viewed (in accord with their original purpose of establishment) as the fund providers in start-ups and/or in expansion financing, this chapter views them as buyout specialists and discusses their role in going-private transactions. As such, the emphasis is put on levered corporate transactions that differ in terms of presence/absence of a buyout specialist.

While some are cautious not to use the terms *buyout specialist* and *venture capital firms* interchangeably or not to recognize the LBO specialists as a subset of venture capital firms (see page 243 in Jeng and Wells, 2000, for example), others make it explicit that there is a high degree of similarity between the two.[3] According to Wright and Robbie (1998), "venture capitalists can essentially be viewed as seeking a return on their specific and distinctive skills in identifying, investing and monitoring new and/or radically changing firms (such as management buy-outs and buy-ins undergoing restructuring)." We follow the latter and, hence, view the LBO specialists as a form of venture capitalists.[4] This definition is also consistent with the statistics of *EVCA Quarterly Newsletter* (November 2001) where buyouts account for 43.6 percent of the total amount of European venture capital investments within the first half of 2001 (6 percentage points up from its 2000 level) as opposed to 1.6 percent seed, 13.2 percent start-up, and 32.8 percent expansion financing.

To understand the role of venture capitalists in buyout transactions, it is necessary to understand why they occur. To this end, I classify the principal motives of LBOs in six categories and discuss them in detail. Beforehand, however, I introduce various aspects of these highly levered transactions from their characteristics—as they relate to motives underlying LBOs—to their economic significance.

CHARACTERISTICS OF GOING-PRIVATE TRANSACTIONS

Going-private deals differ from other corporate control transactions primarily in that they do not combine two previously separate entities into a single public economic unit, but instead create a privately held company with a limited number of investors. Since incumbent management often appears as the bidder and since such transactions are usually financed largely with debt, these activities are called MBOs, LBOs, or (more descriptive, but used less frequently) leveraged management buyouts (LMBOs). There is a tendency for management's equity ownership to increase as a result of the MBO. To secure the loans, management pledges the assets and future cash flows of the subject-company as collateral.

As a natural result of going-private transactions, registration and other public ownership expenses cease. Such savings are not without costs, however, as the liquidity of a firm's claims (especially equity claims) is reduced because of lost or limited access to public equity markets after the buyout. One last, but not least, characteristic of MBOs is the participation of large-block equity investors, who in most cases are buyout specialists. These large-block investors are usually appointed to the board of directors and maintain an active role in monitoring management's activity and performance.

As clear as the organizational changes briefed above are the substantial wealth increases experienced by the shareholders of target companies. A 30 percent to 40 percent premium—paid to the shareholders over the pre-buyout market price—has been documented by a number of studies including De-Angelo, DeAngelo and Rice (1984); Marais, Schipper, and Smith (1989); Lehn and Poulsen (1989); and Kaplan (1989a, 1989b). This agreement among studies mitigated the public criticism of LBOs with respect to welfare of target shareholders. The source(s) of this wealth increase, however, became the core of the public controversy concerning LBO transactions. It was not surprising, then, that MBOs, particularly with regard to their effect on the efficiency/market value of firms and the source of wealth, have occupied the agenda of many academicians. In fact, the issue of excess gains accruing to pre-buyout stockholders has, in itself, been the subject of several studies. For example, Torabzadeh and Bertin (1987) do not test any specific hypothesis of LBOs, but show significant positive abnormal returns of 23.26 percent realized by target shareholders as a result of the buyout announcement. Torabzadeh and Bertin view this result as justification of the economic rationality of MBOs, when in fact it could simply be a means of wealth transfer (from other stakeholders of the firm, including bondholders and Internal Revenue Service),[5] as the critics would argue.

Why, given some obvious advantages to leveraging including the value gain accruing to target shareholders, did firms wait until the 1980s to engage in LBOs? An obvious driving force behind the LBO era was the entrepreneurial spirit of corporate managers with a desire to increase personal and shareholders' wealth, partly fueled with the broad publicity of earlier LBO success stories. This factor would have been insufficient, however, if a favorable economic climate did not exist. In this respect, positive growth in the economy, relatively low and stable interest rates, availability of surplus funds in financial institutions including commercial banks and pension funds, the development of junk bond financing,[6] and the involvement of venture capital firms appear to be the main impetus to LBOs in America.

As a result, the 1980s experienced a dramatic increase in the number and volume of LBOs. In 1982 total value of LBO transactions was $3.5 billion, accounting for 5.8 percent of the total merger activity. The upward trends in these two figures continued until the peak year of 1989, when the annual numbers reached $65.7 billion and 20.3 percent, respectively. In 1999 the value of LBO transactions was $62 billion, compared to the $1,393.9 billion value of total mergers (Weston, Siu, and Johnson 2001). While the relative value of LBOs among total merger activities has diminished, the substantial dollar amount poured into these transactions should be sufficient to reflect their continuing economic significance.

EXPLANATIONS FOR LEVERAGED BUYOUTS

This section presents six possible explanations or hypotheses for LBOs. These include cost savings, undervaluation of stock, management manipulation, tax savings, wealth transfer from bondholders, and agency-theory-based explanations—management incentives and performance improvements, and free cash flow. The last one is particularly important because it explicitly recognizes the role of buyout specialists in LBOs. As such, a large portion of this section is devoted to agency-theory-based explanations.

Cost Savings on Shareholder Relations

An immediate gain that going private can generate is the saving of registration, listing, and other public ownership expenses, such as disclosure requirements, which can be especially significant for smaller firms. DeAngelo, DeAngelo, and Rice (1984) are first in proposing and examining this potential source of value. In their hypothetical setting, an annual potential saving of $100,000 from such items translates into a present value of $1,000,000 at a 10 percent discount rate. The importance of this example is strengthened by the findings of Maupin (1987), who estimates the direct costs (excluding management time and indirect costs such as additional audit fees) of public ownership to range between $60,000 and $250,000 per year. By itself, however, this explanation is sufficient only for the smallest scale MBOs.

At least two drawbacks of this explanation are in order: (1) cost savings on shareholder relations cannot rationalize the reverse LBO[7] phenomena observed by Cummings (1989), Muscarella and Vetsuypens (1989, 1990), and Ainina and Mohan (1991); and (2) this rationale ignores the fact that LBOs with outstanding debt continue to incur some public relations costs since they must still file 10Q and 10K reports with the Securities and Exchange Commission. In fact, even in the absence of public debt, buyout firms may seek some costly means to disseminate the information about their financial performance to the market. They do this because greater uncertainty about the firm results in a lower price when they go public again. Muscarella and Vetsuypens (1989) argue, for example, that the public knows more about firms re-entering the capital markets (reverse LBOs) than firms entering the market for the first time. In support of their argument, they report statistically significant less underpricing for the reverse LBO firms at their "second" initial public offering than for those firms that go public for the first time. It seems necessary, therefore, to keep the market informed so that the LBO can command a higher price when it goes public again.

Undervaluation of the Firm's Stock

There is an apparent conflict of interest in a management buyout, since the purchasing managers have an information advantage over both current stockholders and other potential purchasers. It is plausible, therefore, to posit information asymmetry as an explanation for going-private transactions. The rationale behind this assertion is that going-private transactions are, in a sense, an extreme form of corporate stock repurchase by a management team that possesses private and valuable information about the future prospects of the firm's cash flows. This contention is in line with Myers and Majluf's (1984) suggestion that common stock issuance (purchase) will be chosen by management if it believes the stock price is too high (low).

Both Smith (1990) and Ofek (1994) cast doubt on the information asymmetry hypothesis. Their findings attribute performance improvements to completed buyout proposals only. Specifically, Smith reports no increase in cash flows following a failed buyout proposal, and he reports a similar performance for completed management-proposed buyouts and for buyouts initiated by a takeover threat or by outsiders. Ofek reinforces Smith's findings and reports that, at cancellation announcements (of MBO proposals), returns drop to 2 percent (from 27 percent measured over one month before the buyout announcement to the day after the MBO offer announcement), which is insignificantly different from zero, and persist there for the following two years. Ofek attributes poor performance of uncompleted MBO offers to the absence of organizational changes in the completed buyouts rather than to information asymmetry. That is, if a buyout is motivated by undervaluation, then abnormal returns should remain positive regardless of the outcome of the buyout offer. The very fact that Ofek's study finds no evidence of improvements in operating performance in unwillingly canceled offers rules out the possibility that the cancellation results from bad information and, hence, strengthens the doubts about the information advantage hypothesis.

Management Manipulation Hypothesis

It is also often indicated in the literature that managers may even distort the operating data through manipulations of accounting information to reduce the acquisition price.[8] Evidence supporting the manipulation hypothesis is limited. Kaplan (1989a) casts doubts, although indirectly, on management's manipulation. He reports that post-buyout operating performance in the first two years after the buyout is below the projections provided to prospective lenders by managers in the buyout proxy statements. This finding is contrary to the view that buyout company managers purposely mislead public shareholders by understating the projections.

DeAngelo (1986) explicitly considers the management manipulation issue and also fails to support it. She studies the accounting decisions made by managers of sixty-four firms that proposed to go private during the period from 1973 to 1982. Her findings give no indication that managers of sample firms systematically understate earnings in periods before an MBO proposal. As a possible explanation, DeAngelo suggests that outside scrutiny by public shareholders and their financial advisers deters management manipulation.

Tax Savings

The most frequently cited benefit of going private is the tax saving. In fact, both Lowenstein (1985) and Frankfurter and Gunay (1993) argue that the use of debt in buyout deals is attributable to tax subsidy only. In addition to the tax shield of higher interest costs, buyout reduces the tax liability through the increased depreciation deduction associated with the write-up of assets following the buyout.

The evidence presented by Lehn and Poulsen (1988); Marais, Schipper and Smith (1989); Kaplan (1989b); and Muscarella and Vetsuypens (1990) supports the tax advantages of LBOs. For example, using a sample of seventy-six management-led going-private transactions undertaken in the period from 1980 to 1986, Kaplan (1989b) estimates a median value of tax-driven benefits (both from interest and depreciation deductions) that is between 21 percent and 142.6 percent of the premium paid to shareholders. Kaplan reports a strong correlation between the excess return to pre-buyout shareholders and potential tax benefits generated by the buyout. He does not find any significant relation between the excess return to post-buyout shareholders and potential tax benefits of the buyout, however.

All the above studies agree, nevertheless, that the total value created in an LBO cannot be explained by tax advantages only. This point is confirmed by one of the advocates of debt (due to the interest tax shield it creates) in a firm's capital structure. Miller (1991) states, ". . . tax savings alone cannot plausibly account for the observed LBO premiums."

Wealth Transfer from Bondholders

Leverage is not without its cost. Large increments of additional debt can increase the potential for bankruptcy and hence raise the cost of debt financing. Moreover, in an option-pricing framework, any risk-increasing activity of the firm will enhance the position of the stockholders at the expense of bondholders. Lehn and Poulsen (1988); Marais, Schipper, and Smith (1989); Asquith and Wizman (1990); and Cook, Easterwood, and Martin (1992) consider the wealth transfers from the bondholders of the target firm to stockholders (due to the substantial increase in debt-equity ratio) as a possible portion of premiums paid to shareholders.[9]

Lehn and Poulsen (1988) report an average price decline of 1.42 percent based on thirteen bonds (of various LBO firms) traded on the exchange during the twenty-day period centered on the LBO announcement date. This decline is considerably smaller than the 7.21 percent average drop in the twenty-bond index (reported daily in *The Wall Street Journal*) for the same period. Marais, Schipper, and Smith (1989) also find minimal effects of going-private transactions on debt claims. In fact, the negative average abnormal return for a period from the buyout announcement to the completion of transaction is both statistically insignificant and limited to nonconvertible bondholders.

Asquith and Wizman (1990) report a loss of 6.8 percent of the gain accruing to the equity holders experienced by bondholders with no protective covenants accounts only. Consistent with this result, Cook, Easterwood, and Martin (1992) find (depending on restrictive covenants) the presence of significant bondholder losses that, on average, are 3 percent of the market value of bonds. Overall, the evidence provided by these studies is inconclusive, and the magnitude of the bondholders' losses is insufficient to explain shareholders' gains. This result, not surprisingly, necessitates (and generates) the consideration of other factors as the sources of gains.

Agency-Theory-Based Explanations: Management Incentive and Performance Improvements, and Free Cash Flow Hypotheses

Change in ownership structure brought about by an MBO provides a good fit to the agency theory. Specifically, within the agency theory, management no longer shares the costs of its shirking and its consuming perquisites that may provide incentives to improve the firm's operating and management performance. With a substantially increased stake by management, managerial and stockholder interests are presumably aligned more closely.[10] Moreover, a closer monitoring of managers' actions is conducted by other major investors, compared with that of a diffused ownership structure.

Jensen (1986, 1988) extends the agency-theory-based management incentive hypothesis of LBOs by assigning debt a special role in these transactions. His argument differs from the conventional view of debt as a tax advantage. According to Jensen, many of the benefits in going-private transactions stem from debt's "control function" on managers with respect to free cash flow, which is defined as cash flow in excess of that required to fund all positive net present value (NPV) projects of a firm. The payout of free cash flow to shareholders is consistent with the value maximization principle. In Jensen's framework, debt is the sole candidate to fit the role in distributing the free cash flow through periodic interest payments. A permanent increase in dividends does not achieve a similar result because such a promise is considered weak (i.e., there is no contractual obligation) since dividends can be cut in the future. Periodic coupon payments on debt puts significant pressure on managers and ensures a better management performance, which in turn is reflected in operating costs and value added to the firm.

These two agency-theory-based explanations gather considerable support from empirical researchers with respect to both predictions of the free cash flow hypothesis and efficiency gains stemming from organizational changes and asset control as suggested by the management incentive explanation.

An implication of the free cash flow argument for going-private transactions is that, in order to be a LBO candidate, a firm must have substantial free cash flow at the discretion of management. Accordingly, firms or divisions of large firms that have stable business histories and low growth prospects are more likely to be subject to LBOs. Empirical studies make observations consistent with these predictions. Most LBOs take place in mature industries (Lehn and Poulsen 1988; Kieschnick 1989), and the growth rates and capital expenditures of LBO firms are lower than those of comparable firms in the same industry (Kaplan 1989b; Lehn and Poulsen 1988, 1989).

Lehn and Poulsen (1988) show that their proxy for the free cash flow and the premium paid in LBOs are positively related. In a follow-up study, Lehn and Poulsen (1989) use a logistic regression equation and, in line with their previous finding, obtain a significantly positive relationship between undistributed cash flow and a firm's decision to go private. Similarly, Opler and Titman (1993) conclude that the main characteristics of firms initiating LBOs are unfavorable investment opportunities and high cash flows.

On the efficiency gains stemming from organizational changes and asset control, Kaplan (1989a), Smith (1990), Muscarella and Vetsuypens (1990), Lichtenberg and Siegel (1990), Opler (1992), and Ofek (1994) provide comparable results. In general, their findings show increases in industry-adjusted operating profit/sales, operating profits per employee, and operating cash flow/ operating assets for the post-LBO firms. Kaplan (1989a) analyzes the post-buyout operating performance of forty-eight MBOs completed between 1980 and 1986. His results indicate that 76 percent of the sample firms experienced an average increase in operating income of 40 percent within two years of going private. Over a three-year post-buyout period, average operating income was

42 percent higher than that for the year preceding the buyout. Moreover, operating income measured net of industry changes remained essentially unchanged in the first two post-buyout years and became 24 percent higher in the third year. Kaplan's conclusion that efficiency gains constitute a major source of pre-buyout shareholders gains is driven by the high correlation found between the premiums paid to pre-buyout shareholders and post-buyout performance improvements.

Smith's (1990) examination of fifty-eight MBOs, completed during the period from 1977 to 1986, provides results consistent with Kaplan's (1989a); that is, operating cash flow per employee and the operating cash flow per dollar book value of assets increase relative to the year preceding the buyout. Like Kaplan, Smith finds that cash flow improves under private ownership. Smith attributes this finding to better management of working capital, which is reflected as a reduction in the inventory holding period and in the accounts receivable collection period.

Unlike Kaplan (1989a) and Smith (1990), who analyze company-level data, Lichtenberg and Siegel (1990) examine total factor productivity (output per unit of total input) of approximately one thousand plants involved in LBOs during the period from 1981 to 1986. They find an improvement in plant productivity, which moves from 2.0 percent above the industry mean in the three pre-buyout years to 8.3 percent above the mean in the three post-buyout years.

At the case study level, Baker and Wruck (1989) examine O. M. Scott and Sons, a division bought by its managers and by Clayton and Dubilier (a LBO specialist) from the parent company, ITT, in December 1986. By the end of September 1988, earnings before interest and taxes were up by 56 percent and sales were up by 25 percent. Both research and development expenses and marketing and distribution expenses have also increased over the same period, suggesting that a reduction on these items is not responsible for increased sales and earnings figures. The authors credit organizational changes, characterized by heavy debt load and management equity ownership, for the improved operating performance of the company, O. M. Scott and Sons. They view a stronger incentive compensation plan, a reorganization and decentralization of decision making, and monitoring by sponsors as equally important.

Leveraged Buyouts Versus Leveraged Recapitalizations

It must be clear that some of the motives for LBOs are unambiguously beneficial to all parties involved, the last motive discussed—agency theory—being the most obvious and gaining the most empirical support in this respect. In this vein, the Baker and Wruck (1989) study discussed earlier is noteworthy because it explicitly recognizes the role of buyout specialists and credits them as one of the sources of value created in LBOs.

The role of buyout specialists, and hence their direct effect on the wealth creation in highly levered transactions, become more apparent when LBOs and

leveraged recapitalizations are compared. Leveraged recapitalization (or leveraged recap, or LR) is a relatively new form of corporate restructuring but carries
many features of a typical LBO transaction, as outlined by Gupta and Rosenthal
(1991):[11]

- Substantial increase in debt.
- Substantial increase in management ownership of equity.
- A more efficient management team and reduced agency costs of free cash flow (due
  to increased managerial ownership and the "control role" of debt).
- Similar tax implications for the subject firms.

There are, however, two important differences between these two seemingly
similar transactions that make the comparison of LBOs and LRs noteworthy
for the purpose of this chapter:

- LRs remain as public entities—and therefore enjoy the liquidity but carry the costs
  associated with public ownership.
- LRs lack the presence of a large-block equity investor (buyout specialists or institutional investors) and are owned by a large number of small shareholders.

As discussed earlier, the wealth increase of target shareholders in LBOs is a
well-documented fact. Gupta and Rosenthal (1991) investigate whether, like
LBOs, LRs increase the wealth of the firm's equityholders. While results indicate positive excess returns accruing to shareholders in LRs, the magnitude
of this wealth effect is smaller than that gained by shareholders of LBO transactions. Further analysis that focuses on the reduction in the agency cost of
free cash flow and wealth transfer from existing bondholders supports the former as a possible source for observed value gain in LRs.

Kracaw and Zenner (1996) examine the wealth effect of bank financing announcements on LBOs and LRs. They find, in addition to gains associated with
the initial announcements of these two highly levered transactions, that LBO
targets gain an additional 2 percent whereas LR targets lose about 2 percent at
the bank financing announcement. The authors also report positive gains (although marginal) accruing to the participating banks' shareholders with the
announcements of bank financing agreements. This finding suggests that gains
to target LBO shareholders are not due to wealth transfer from banks involved
in financing—contrary to the view that the involvement in highly levered
transactions deteriorate the financial stability of the banks.

One can deduce, although indirectly, that a higher value gain realized by
shareholders of LBO targets may be attributed, at least partly, to the presence
of buyout specialists in these transactions. Fortunately, there are some studies
that exclusively investigate this issue, such as Denis's (1994) comparison of
Kroger's recapitalization and Safeway's LBO, both operating grocery store
chains.[12] While both firms received buyout offers from Kohlberg, Kravis and

Roberts (KKR), only Safeway agreed to be acquired by KKR and a group of incumbent managers in a LBO. Kroger, on the other hand, rejected KKR's offer and implemented a leveraged recapitalization plan. Although both transactions resulted in debt levels of more than 90 percent, Kroger's managers were not as successful as Safeway's in improving profits and cash flows. Denis attributes this result to Kroger's lack of increased managerial shareholding, the close linking of managerial compensation to company performance, and sponsor's ownership and monitoring. With respect to the role of sponsor, he adds the following:

The evidence suggests that Safeway's increase in value comes at a personal cost to Safeway managers in the form of substantially closer monitoring of top executives. Therefore, it is possible that Kroger's managers were willing to give up some expected value in exchange for a corporate governance system that involved less monitoring. (p. 222)

In a more recent study, Bae and Simet (1998) use a large sample of LBO and LR firms in comparing two important aspects of these two highly levered transactions: (1) the returns accruing to stockholders and (2) the attributes of firms associated with these gains. The announcements of both transactions result in significant positive average excess returns, with the LBO group experiencing substantially larger returns than the LR group. Additional analyses show that the level of a firm's free cash flow is responsible for this difference. That is, while free cash flow and stockholders' return on both transactions are positively correlated, the association is more pronounced for LBO group. These findings suggest that firms with free cash flow benefit more via a LBO rather than a LR on the reduction of associated agency costs.

SUMMARY

The 1980s witnessed a rather unusual form of corporate restructuring: leveraged buyouts. In addition to positive economic growth and lower interest rates for debt financing, the development of junk bond and venture capital financing made these highly leveraged transactions possible. Opponents argued that LBOs were nothing but purely tools of transferring wealth among corporations' various stakeholders, including movement of wealth from the IRS through tax shields of debt expenses, and that little or no economic value was created as a result of LBOs. In addition to this explanation, many others are offered as motives of buyouts and thus sources of gains accruing both to pre-buyout shareholders and equity investors in the deal. Among those explanations, the most supported appear to be savings on shareholder relations, tax benefit of debt financing, and reduction in agency costs (due to the alignment of managerial interests with company objectives and monitoring of buyout specialists). High insider ownership, monitoring by LBO specialists, and the control function of debt on free cash flow are believed to be the main reasons behind the improved operating efficiency and increased cash flows.

The role of buyout specialists or venture capitalists become much more apparent in studies that compare LBOs with leveraged recapitalizations. While both transactions result in enormous debt levels in companies, the latter lacks the presence of buyout specialists. The empirical evidence favors LBOs as a form of corporate restructuring: both the value gain accruing to shareholders and the performance of the firms (in terms of improving profits and cash flows) is higher in LBOs than in leveraged recapitalizations.

NOTES

1. In this chapter, the terms *management buyout* (MBO) and *leveraged buyout* (LBO) are used interchangeably to define a buyout transaction implemented by the management team of the company.

2. The RJR-Nabisco buyout in 1988, with a purchase price of $24.6 billion, is known as the biggest going-private deal.

3. "Though the LBO industry in the US is typically seen to be distinct from the venture capital industry, venture capitalists are extensively involved in funding buyouts especially smaller ones (see e.g. Malone 1989). In the UK, there is probably much greater overlap between venture capitalists and what may be seen as LBO Associations" (Wright and Robbie 1998).

4. Schilit (1996) also defines LBOs as a special case of venture financing.

5. Wealth transfer from bondholders is covered later in this chapter. The wealth transfer from the IRS refers to the tax practice that allows the deductibility of debt financing cost from taxable income. Payments (dividends) on equity financing, on the other hand, are not tax deductible (and, in fact, are subject to double taxation—one at the corporate level and one at the personal level as the shareholders pay income taxes on them).

6. Junk bonds are high-yield and, thus, high-risk bonds issued by companies with a great deal of default risk. They are either rated below investment grade by debt rating agencies (below Baa, based on Moody's, and below BBB, based on Standard and Poor's, Duff and Phelp's, or Fitch) or not rated at all. Of course, high-yield high-risk bonds are not new to financial markets, but traditional ones originally would receive an investment rating with subsequent lower grades with their higher likelihood of default risk (and, hence, the term *fallen angels*) whereas junk bonds would receive lower grades at their issuance. Junk bonds were originally initiated by Michael Milken of Drexel Burnham and Lambert and later developed into a major financing tool of LBO deals.

7. The term *reverse LBO* defines a firm (or a division of a firm) that is taken private via a leveraged buyout transaction and brought back to market through a public offering.

8. "The CEO (of Regina), who held about 50% of the stock during the buyout, sold one-tenth of his stake for $2.1 million. Regina exhibited very strong stock price performance in the first two years following its IPO. In 1988, the CEO abruptly resigned and confessed to having manipulated the firm's reported results" (DeGeorge and Zeckhauser 1993).

9. Surrounding the first announcement of RJR Nabisco's LBO, RJR Nabisco's common stock price increased 50 to 60 percent, while the price of its outstanding bonds declined 15 to 20 percent, according to various studies.

10. Kaplan (1989a) estimates a median post-buyout equity ownership by management as 22.6 percent. According to Muscarella and Vetsuypens (1990), it is 63.4 percent—far higher than in public companies.

11. The characteristics of leveraged recaps draw heavily from the list provided by Gupta and Rosenthal (1991).

12. Firms in retail food business have been attractive LBO candidates primarily due to their steady cash flow patterns.

REFERENCES

Ainina, M. Fall, and Nancy K. Mohan. 1991. "When LBOs Go IPO." *Journal of Business Finance & Accounting* 9: 393–403.

Asquith, Paul, and Thierry A. Wizman. 1990. "Event Risk, Covenants, and Bondholder Returns in Leveraged Buyouts." *Journal of Financial Economics* 27: 195–213.

Bae, C. Sung, and Daniel P. Simet. 1998. "A Comparative Analysis of Leveraged Recapitalization versus Leveraged Buyout as a Takeover Defense." *Review of Financial Economics* 7: 157–72.

Baker, George P., and Karen H. Wruck. 1989. "Organizational Changes and Value Creation in Leveraged Buyouts: The Case of the O. M. Scott & Sons Company." *Journal of Financial Economics* 25: 163–90.

Clark, John C., John T. Gerlach, and Gerard Olson. 1996. *Restructuring Corporate America*. Orlando, Fla.: The Dryden Press–Harcourt Brace.

Cook, Douglas O., John C. Easterwood, and John D. Martin. 1992. "Bondholder Wealth Effects of Management Buyouts." *Financial Management* 21: 102–13.

Cummings, Stephen E. 1989. "The Recycled LBO: A Second Dose of Leverage." *Mergers and Acquisitions,* November/December, pp. 53–56.

DeAngelo, H., L. DeAngelo, and E. Rice. 1984. "Going Private: Minority Freezouts and Stockholder Wealth." *Journal of Law and Economics* 27: 367–402.

DeAngelo, L. 1986. "Accounting Numbers as Market Valuation Substitutes: A Study of Management Buyouts of Public Shareholders." *The Accounting Review* 61: 400–420.

DeGeorge, Francois, and Richard Zeckhauser. 1993. "The Reverse LBO Decision and Firm Performance: Theory and Evidence." *Journal of Finance* 48: 1323–48.

Denis, David J. 1994. "Organizational Form and the Consequences of Highly Leveraged Transactions: Kroger's Recapitalization and Safeway's LBO." *Journal of Financial Economics* 36: 193–224.

Frankfurter, George M., and Erdal Gunay. 1993. "Management Buyouts and Anticipated Gains to Shareholders—Theory and Testing." *International Review of Financial Analysis* 2: 33–50.

Fuqua, J. 1988. "Business Cycles and Shareholder Value in the LBO Era." *Management Review* 77: 26–29.

Gupta, Atul, and Leonard Rosenthal. 1991. "Ownership Structure, Leverage, and Firm Value: The Case of Leveraged Recapitalizations" *Financial Management* 20: 69–83.

Jeng, L. A., and P. C. Wells. 2000. "The Determinants of Venture Capital Funding: Evidence across Countries." *Journal of Corporate Finance* 6 (3): 241–89.

Jensen, Michael C. 1986. "Agency Costs of Free Cash Flow, Corporate Finance, and Takeovers." *American Economic Review* 76: 323–39.

Jensen, Michael C. 1988. "Takeovers: Their Causes and Consequences." *Journal of Economic Perspectives* 2: 21–48.

Kaplan, Steven N. 1989a. "The Effects of Management Buyouts on Operating Performance and Value." *Journal of Financial Economics* 24: 217–54.

Kaplan, Steven N. 1989b. "Management Buyouts: Evidence on Taxes as a Source of Value." *Journal of Finance* 44: 611–32.

Kieschnick, Robert L. 1989. "Management Buy-Outs of Public Corporations: An Analysis of Prior Characteristics." In *Leveraged Management Buyouts,* ed. Yakov Amihud. Homewood, Ill.: Dow Jones-Irwin.

Kracaw, W., and M. Zenner. 1996. "The Wealth Effects of Bank Financing Announcements on Highly Levered Transactions." *Journal of Finance* 51: 1931–46.

Lehn, Kenneth, and Annette Poulsen. 1988. "Leveraged Buyouts: Wealth Created or Wealth Redistributed." In *Public Policy Towards Corporate Takeovers,* ed. Murray Weidenbaum and Kenneth Chilton. New Brunswick, N.J.: Transaction Publishers.

Lehn, Kenneth, and Annette Poulsen. 1989. "Free Cash Flow and Stockholder Gains in Going Private Transactions." *Journal of Finance* 44: 771–87.

Lichtenberg, Frank R., and Donald Siegel. 1990. "The Effects of Leveraged Buyouts on Productivity and Related Aspects of Firm Behavior." *Journal of Financial Economics* 27: 165–94.

Lowenstein, L. 1985. "Management Buyouts." *Columbia Law Review* 85: 730–84.

Malone, S. 1989. "Characteristics of Smaller Company Leveraged Buy-outs." *Journal of Business Venturing* 4: 349–59.

Marais, L., K. Schipper, and A. Smith. 1989. "Wealth Effects of Going Private for Senior Securities." *Journal of Financial Economics* 23: 155–91.

Maupin, Rebekah J. 1987. "Financial and Stock Market Variables as Predictors of Management Buyouts." *Strategic Management Journal* 8: 319–27.

Michel, Allen, and Israel Shaked. 1988. *The Complete Guide to a Successful Leveraged Buyout.* Homewood, Ill.: Dow Jones–Irwin.

Miller, Merton H. 1991. "Leverage." *Journal of Finance* 46: 479–88.

Muscarella, Chris J., and Michael R. Vetsuypens. 1989. "The Underpricing of 'Second' Initial Public Offerings." *Journal of Financial Research* 12: 183–92.

Muscarella, Chris J., and Michael R. Vetsuypens. 1990. "Efficiency and Organizational Structure: A Study of Reverse LBOs." *Journal of Finance* 45: 1389–1413.

Myers, S. L., and N. Majluf. 1984. "Corporate Financing and Investment Decisions When Firms Have Information That Investors Do Not Have." *Journal of Financial Economics* 13: 187–221.

Ofek, Eli. 1994. "Efficiency Gains in Unsuccessful Management Buyouts." *Journal of Finance* 49: 637–54.

Opler, Tim C. 1992. "Operating Performance in Leveraged Buyouts: Evidence from 1985–1989." *Financial Management* 21: 27–34.

Opler, Tim, and Sheridan Titman. 1993. "The Determinants of Leveraged Buyout Activity: Free Cash Flows vs. Financial Distress Costs." *Journal of Finance* 48: 1985–99.

Schilit, W. Keith. 1996. "Venture Catalysts or Venture Capitalists?" *The Journal of Investing*, Fall, pp. 86–95.

Smith, Abbie J. 1990. "Corporate Ownership Structure and Performance: The Case of Management Buyouts." *Journal of Financial Economics* 27: 143–64.

Torabzadeh, Khalil M., and William J. Bertin. 1987. "Leveraged Buyouts and Shareholder Returns." *Journal of Financial Research* 10: 313–19.

Weston, J. Fred, Juan A. Siu, and Brian A. Johnson. 2001. *Takeovers, Restructuring, and Corporate Governance*, 3d ed. Upper Saddle River, N.J.: Prentice-Hall.

Wright, Mike, and Ken Robbie. 1998. "Venture Capital and Private Equity: A Review and Synthesis." *Journal of Business Finance & Accounting* 25: 521–70.

Part II
National Experiences

5

The Determinants of Venture Capital Funding
Evidence across Countries

Leslie Ann Jeng and Philippe C. Wells

This chapter analyzes the determinants of venture capital for a sample of 21 countries. In particular, we consider the importance of IPOs, GDP and market capitalization growth, labor market rigidities, accounting standards, private pension funds, and government programs. We find that IPOs are the strongest driver of venture capital investing. Private pension fund levels are a significant determinant over time but not across countries. Surprisingly, GDP and market capitalization growth are not significant. Government policies can have a strong impact, both by setting the regulatory stage, and by galvanizing investment during downturns. Finally, we also show that different types of venture capital financing are affected differently by these factors. In particular, early stage venture capital investing is negatively impacted by labor market rigidities, while later stage is not. IPOs have no effect on early stage venture capital investing across countries, but are a significant determinant of later stage venture capital investing across countries. Finally, government funded venture capital has different sensitivities to the determinants of venture capital than non-government funded venture capital. Our insights emphasize the need for a more differentiated approach to venture capital, both from a research as well as from a policy perspective. We feel that while later stage venture capital investing is well understood, early stage and government funded investments still require more extensive research.

We thank Paul Gompers, Josh Lerner, and Andrei Shleifer for helpful conversations. We also thank Carl Kester and the participants of the Harvard Industrial Organization seminar for comments. Furthermore, we gratefully acknowledge Chris Allen, the Bureau of Labor Statistics, the European Venture Capital Association, FIBV, The Giza Group, InterSec Research Corp., Macdonald & Associates Limited, Nomura Securities, OECD and the Toronto Stock Exchange for help in obtaining data. We appreciate the financial support of the Division of Research at Harvard Business School. All errors and opinions are our own.

INTRODUCTION

Venture capital has been the driving force behind some of the most vibrant sectors of the US economy over the past two decades. Venture capitalists were instrumental in fostering the tremendous growth of firms such as Microsoft, Compaq, Oracle, and Sun Microsystems, which were all founded less than 20 years ago, but have rapidly become dominant players in the high technology arena. While the contributions venture capital makes to the economy overall are underexplored, there exists a widespread belief that venture capital is instrumental in bringing innovations to market at a rapid pace, thereby creating economic growth, jobs, and opportunities for further technological innovation. The 1997 National Venture Capital Association annual study on the impact of venture capital sheds light on some of the job-creating abilities of the sector. The study reveals that between 1991 and 1995, venture-backed companies increased their staffs on average 34 percent per year. Over the same time period, Fortune 500 companies decreased staffing levels 4 percent per year.[1]

The growth rate of venture capital funding has been high in many countries, but funding levels still vary significantly (see Table 5.1). In this chapter, our goal is to understand the determinants of growth in the venture capital industry. Our work builds on that of Black and Gilson (1998), who examine the importance of well-developed stock markets and IPOs for venture capital financing. Black and Gilson's empirical work tests only the significance of IPOs over time in the US. We test a number of other factors in addition to IPOs, and use panel data for ten years and fifteen countries. The factors we test are the ones enumerated in the literature on venture capital: initial public offerings, GDP and market capitalization growth, labor market rigidities, financial reporting standards, private pension funds, and government programs.

Our results indicate that IPOs are the most important determinant of venture capital investing. Private pension fund levels impact venture capital over time, but not across countries. Our analysis demonstrates the necessity of separating venture capital into early (seed and startup) and later (expansion) stage investing, both for the purposes of analysis and for policy considerations. In particular, we show that different types of venture capital are differently affected by the determinants of venture capital. Thus, labor market rigidities negatively affect early stage venture capital investments, but have no impact on later stage venture capital investments. IPOs have no impact on early stage investments across countries, but are a significant determinant for later stage venture capital investments. Government funded venture capital is not as strongly determined by IPOs as non-government funded venture capital. Finally, our qualitative analysis of government programs gives further insight into the role government funds can play as a catalyst for private sector funding.

This chapter is organized as follows: The second section discusses the role of small firms in the economy and the link between these firms and venture capital from the perspectives of financial intermediation, corporate governance,

Table 5.1
Country Comparison

Countries	Venture Capital ($ US in millions)			Early Stage ($ US in millions)			Private Equity New Funds ($ US in millions)		
	1986[25]	1995[26]	CAGR %	1986[25]	1995[26]	CAGR %	1986[27]	1995[28]	CAGR %
Australia	$417	$888	45.9%	$17	$54	76.5%	$239	$249	0.8%
Austria	1.9	1.4	-3.8	2	0.4	-16.5	1	2	1.6
Belgium	195	139	-3.7	67	8.4	-20.7	344	210	-5.4
Canada	152	412	15.4	65	182	15.7	230	1,133	19.4
Denmark	22	19	-1.6	4.6	4.5	-0.2	32	37	1.7
Finland	9.7	38	21.7	1.5	1.0	32.4	54	69	3.4
France	195	444	9.6	32	35	1.2	168	1,055	22.6
Germany	43	694	36.4	9	116	32.8	50	274	20.9
Ireland	17	25	4.7	8	1	-18.9	34	16	-7.9
Israel	NA	NA	NA	NA	NA	NA	60	139	18.0
Italy	21	246	31.5	11	60	20.9	203	354	6.4
Japan	2,351	2,524	7.4	18	11	-38.3	258	604	23.7
Netherlands	128	471	15.6	31	100	14.0	260	337	2.9
New Zealand	0.7	3.8	461.9	NA	0.9	NM	14	33	135
Norway	14	154	40.9	1.2	7	28.6	14	60	22.8
Portugal	0.3	57	101.1	0.3	9	54.3	2	143	67.4
Spain	34	180	20.4	14	24	5.7	0	190	-2.35
Sweden	61	31	-7.1	7	9	3.0	114	614	20.5
Switzerland	13	28	9.0	10	1	-22.7	6	64	29.5
United Kingdom	65	883	3.5	158	36	-15.2	777	2,363	13.2
United States	3,181	3,651	1.5	333	1,093	14.1	8,800	28,369	13.9

Venture Capital includes seed, startup and expansion stage investments. Early stage includes only seed and startup investments. Private Equity New funds raised is defined as committed, but not yet paid, capital to private equity funds, i.e., includes money raised for all stages of investment.

Source: European Venture Capital Journal, The Guide to Venture Capital in Asia, Venture Economics for US figures, MacDonald & Associates Limited for Canada's figures and the Giza Group for Israel's figures.

and entrepreneurship. The third section explains how venture capital firms are organized and how they work. The fourth section surveys the theories that explain what factors affect venture capital investments. The fifth section discusses the data, while the sixth section covers the regression methodology. The seventh section presents our empirical results. The eighth section discusses the role of government programs and includes case studies of the venture capital experience of Israel and Germany. The final section concludes.

THE ROLE OF VENTURE CAPITAL IN THE ECONOMY

Before we discuss venture capital in more detail, we first need to clarify our use of the term, since it is defined differently in the US and Europe. Venture capital, as we use the term, refers to one type of private equity investing. Private equity investments are investments by institutions or wealthy individuals in both publicly quoted and privately held companies. Private equity investors are more actively involved in managing their portfolio companies than regular, passive retail investors. The main types of financing included in private equity investing are venture capital and management and leveraged buyouts. Outside of the US, the term venture capital is frequently used to describe what we have just referred to as private equity.

The definition of venture capital, as it is used in the US, and as we use it in our chapter, comprises three types of investing—seed, startup, and expansion investment—and excludes buyouts. These types represent three stages of investing which are defined with reference to the stage of development of the company receiving the investment.

Seed capital is the very first type of financing a newly founded company might want to secure. These funds are typically used to fund initial product research and development and to assess the commercial potential of ideas. Startup investments, on the other hand, are targeted at companies that have moved past the idea stage and are gearing up to produce, market, and sell their products. Companies at this stage still use more cash than they generate. Investments in either seed or startup stage are also referred to simply as early stage investments.

After a company has passed through the early stage, it becomes a potential candidate for expansion stage investing. In the expansion stage, a company that has already established its product in the marketplace often needs additional capital to fund the growth of its manufacturing and distribution capacity, as well as to fund further R&D.

The other category of investments included in private equity, in addition to venture capital, is buyouts. Buyouts are usually applied to more mature companies. In a leveraged buyout, debt is used to acquire a company and reduce its equity base. Management buyouts are leveraged buyouts where current management takes control of its company.

Our primary interest is specifically in venture capital, not private equity. We believe venture capital in particular merits interest for several reasons. The past performance of venture capital-backed companies shows that venture capital has been very successful at backing companies with innovative technologies and tremendous growth potential. Companies such as Apple, Compaq, Digital Equipment Corporation, Intel, Microsoft, and Sun Microsystems were all backed by venture capital. As a measure of the success of these companies, we can consider their total market capitalization, which in July 1997 was $369 billion.

The National Venture Capital Association 1997 report gives further evidence on the beneficial impact of venture capital. In addition to creating jobs at a much faster rate than Fortune 500 companies, venture capital-backed firms have done well even when compared to other high growth companies. 1995 revenue growth for venture capital-backed high growth companies was 36.8 percent compared to 23.8 percent for non-venture capital-backed high growth companies.

The Role of Venture Capital in Financial Intermediation

Venture capital firms serve as financial intermediaries in a market where lenders and borrowers find it costly to get together. The costs are due to adverse selection and moral hazard, and the cost of administration, information gathering, and search efforts. By and large, the literature focuses on the important role banks play as financial intermediaries (Mayer, 1988; Fama, 1985; Myers & Majluf, 1984). However, for startup ventures, bank financing may not be optimal. In the US, for example, banks are prohibited from holding equity. But startups have few other tangible assets, and the prohibition makes it difficult for banks to obtain reasonable collateral on loans to startups. This severely restricts banks' willingness to take the additional risk associated with these new companies. In addition, since startups require a lot of cash in the early stages to finance their growth, debt-based finance is usually inappropriate from a cash management perspective as it strictly ties the cash flows of companies.

Even in countries such as Japan and Germany, where banks can hold equity, startup ventures are not highly funded by banks. This is to a large extent due to corporate governance issues discussed in the next section.

Given the need for financial intermediaries for startups and the unsuitability of banks to this role, the venture capital organization arose to fill this void in startup financing. American Research and Development, founded in Massachusetts in 1946, was the first modern venture capital organization. Venture capital is especially attractive because its equity finance structure gives companies the necessary leeway in their repayment schedule. In addition, by focusing on startups, venture capital firms achieve expertise and economies of scale in locating and financing potentially successful startup ventures.

Gompers (1994) examines "Angels" as an alternative source of funding for startups. "Angels" are essentially wealthy individuals who finance startups out of their own funds. While "Angels" represent an important source of financing, their scope is limited by the wealth of these individuals. "Angels" are not a viable source for large amounts of capital. Another source of startup financing is large corporations. However, Sykes (1990) finds that these programs have had limited success.

Venture Capital vs. Other Forms of Corporate Governance

Startup firms present a unique set of issues for corporate governance which makes venture capital particularly suited to the sector. They operate in new markets, where information about the nature of the market is generally poor. Furthermore, they do not have an established track record which could be used as a baseline performance measure. Because so much of their value lies in their potential for future growth and so little in their current, tangible assets, start-ups place particular demands on monitors of financial performance. Jensen (1993) describes the type of investor needed in this environment as "active investor."

Active investors are investors who have a large financial interest in their investments, and can still provide an impartial view of the management of these firms. Some of the most common financial intermediaries, such as pension funds, insurance companies and money managers, are unable to perform the role of active investor due to legal structures and customs. Roe (1990) outlines the various restrictions on US banks, insurance companies, and mutuals, which prevent them from holding a large equity stake in any one company and from being actively involved on the boards of their investment companies.

Sahlman (1990) and Jensen (1993) find that venture capitalists solve the corporate governance and monitoring problem through extensive initial due diligence about startup companies' businesses. Furthermore, they maintain a close relationship by frequently visiting and talking to company management. The venture capitalists also sit on the boards of directors. In some instances, they even perform some key corporate functions for the firm, such as running the corporate finance department and working with suppliers and customers.

While countries such as Japan and Germany do not have restrictions on equity holding by banks, their banks are still not very adept at filling the necessary role as monitor for startups due to institutional design. A few banks dominate Japan's and Germany's banking industry and, often, only those companies with close relationships to these banks can obtain financing. Also, because they are large and provide a wide range of services, these banks do not have the specialization and focus required to handle small startups. Their involvement in management issues at the firms they lend to is often minimal. Edwards and Fischer (1994) document that German banks do not play an active role in management and that bank representation on boards is generally very small.

Large companies can also play an active role in the development of smaller enterprises with new ideas. However, this governance model possesses many attributes that reduce the chances of success for startups. Hardymon et al. (1983) find that legal difficulties often arise over whether the corporation has access to ventures' proprietary information. In addition, corporate venture capital groups within large organizations may not be able to operate autonomously

(Seigel et al. 1988). Furthermore, Sahlman (1991) points out that the approval process within large enterprises is neither fast nor effective enough. He also notes that the entrepreneur is not sufficiently motivated, due to the absence of any equity participation and any negative repercussions of failure.

Thus, venture capitalists are the only ones who can really successfully provide the type of corporate governance that startups need.

Venture Capital and Entrepreneurship

While the entrepreneurship literature does not emphasize the role of venture capital, its insights suggest that venture capital can be quite important in the context of entrepreneurial challenges. The recent literature, as summarized by Holmes and Schmitz (1990), focuses on the importance of technological innovation and of matching up entrepreneurs with appropriate projects.

Opportunities for creating new products arise over time as a consequence of technological innovation and demographic change, while the ability to exploit these opportunities varies across the population. Not everyone is capable of starting a new business, and those who have started one are not necessarily capable of managing it competently. Even good business projects must be matched with an appropriate entrepreneur if they are to succeed. If the success of a project hinges vitally on finding a suitable entrepreneur, venture capitalists can greatly aid the success of a project by providing a matching function. They can also assist the process by developing the manager's skills after she has been brought in, and by bringing in additional management talent as needed.

Furthermore, the literature on entrepreneurship finds that liquidity constraints are binding and, therefore, critical to entrepreneurs (Evans and Jovanovic 1989). This underscores the importance of venture capital as a way to circumvent liquidity constraints.

VENTURE CAPITAL STRUCTURE AND FUNCTIONING

Both the private equity and the venture capital sectors differ across countries. Their differences start with organizational form. In the US and UK, firms are organized as limited partnerships, while in France and Germany they have a different organizational structure with far more involvement of banks (Lerner 1995). Another difference in organizational form is the prevalence of so-called captive funds in Europe and their relative absence in the US. Funds are labeled captive if more than 80 percent of their financing derives from one source. In many instances, captive funds are subsidiaries of banks. In France, in 1995, captive funds accounted for 37.1 percent of new funds raised.

The management style of venture capitalists differs across countries as well. In Japan and Germany, venture capital firms are not as actively involved in managing their investments as in the US. Japanese and German venture capitalists have traditionally not held board representation, nor have they been involved in day-to-day management issues. Hurry et al. (1991) present evidence on the different degree of involvement of US and Japanese venture capital firms. They show that US firms tend to make fewer investments, but take larger equity stakes in each investment. This strategy confers an advantage over the Japanese one because it allows the venture capitalists to better focus on managing and understanding a few companies and gives them a greater incentive to monitor.

The composition of funding sources also differs dramatically by country. If we consider all private equity investing, the US private equity market received 38 percent[2] of its funds from pension funds in 1995. In Germany, by contrast, pension funds supplied only 8.6 percent of new funds raised and banks supplied 57.2 percent in that same year.[3]

Tables 5.2 through 5.4 indicate how levels of venture capital and private equity differ across time and across countries. In order to compare the order of magnitude of private equity and venture capital funding across countries, we normalize our figures by average GDP for each country. Table 5.4 shows how, in relative terms in 1995, the US had the greatest amount of new fund flows into private equity. Averaged over the whole time period, however, the UK had slightly higher flows into private equity than the US.

The compound annual growth rate of new funds raised was also similar for both countries. This, however, masks some strong differences between the two. US private equity suffered a downswing which bottomed out in 1990, and then steadily rebounded over the next five years. UK private equity hit its trough only one year later, but then stagnated until 1994.

An even more interesting difference, from the perspective of this chapter, concerns the difference in early stage investment patterns between countries. If we again look at the US and UK, we see that the UK suffered a steady, unabated decline in early stage investing that took place over the whole time period (see Table 5.3). As a per mil of GDP, early stage investing dropped from 0.19 to 0.04 in the UK from 1986 to 1995. In the US, by contrast, early stage investing followed closely the development of private equity, with a trough in the early 1990s and steady recovery since then.

The emphasis on early stage investing is strong and growing in some countries, such as Australia, Canada, the Netherlands, and the US. In other countries—Germany, Japan, and the UK, to name just a few—private equity is more involved in later stage financing. For example, in 1994, 36 percent of Germany's private equity[4] was invested in later stage investments. However, for the same time period, only 18 percent of US private equity[5] was similarly invested.

While we recognize that great differences exist in venture capital and private equity firms across countries, we limit our description of organizational structure to the case of the US limited partnership. Since our main interest lies with

Table 5.2
Venture Capital Investment as per mil of Average GDP

Country	1986	1987	1988	1989	1990	1991	1992	1993	1994	1995	Average Level (per mil)	Average Growth (%)	CAGR (%)
Australia	NA	NA	NA	NA	NA	NA	0.364	0.358	1.198	1.336	0.814	82 %	54 %
Austria	0.014	0.027	0.011	0.058	0.044	0.025	0.006	0.004	0.002	0.007	0.020	60	-7
Belgium	1.207	1.056	0.282	0.444	0.370	0.612	0.737	0.414	0.327	0.628	0.608	8	-7
Canada	0.206	0.252	0.275	0.229	0.197	0.270	0.267	0.413	0.569	0.855	0.353	20	17
Denmark	0.201	0.243	0.211	0.123	0.111	0.168	0.072	0.134	0.170	0.132	0.156	5	-5
Finland	NA	NA	0.087	0.064	0.182	0.203	0.174	0.262	0.282	0.358	0.202	34	22
France	0.194	0.302	0.558	0.516	0.551	0.620	0.464	0.433	0.539	0.336	0.451	12	6
Germany	0.031	0.036	0.045	0.108	0.334	0.386	0.362	0.342	0.376	0.375	0.240	45	32
Ireland	0.425	0.876	0.655	0.416	0.795	0.892	0.584	0.377	0.629	0.557	0.620	15	3
Israel	NA	NA	NA	NA	NA	NA	NA	NA	NA	NA	NA	NA	NA
Italy	0.021	0.060	0.081	0.208	0.168	0.403	0.418	0.234	0.210	0.295	0.210	54	34
Japan	NA	NA	NA	NA	NA	NA	0.052	0.038	NA	0.216	0.102	-28	61
Netherlands	0.532	0.482	0.546	0.503	0.783	0.795	0.684	0.608	1.063	1.433	0.743	15	12
New Zealand	NA	NA	NA	NA	NA	NA	NA	0.016	0.041	0.517	0.191	658	463
Norway	NA	NA	0.126	0.011	0.520	0.465	0.242	0.420	0.689	1.337	0.476	645	40
Portugal	0.004	0.127	0.072	0.217	0.588	0.727	0.709	1.073	1.185	0.990	0.569	378	84
Spain	0.087	0.221	0.171	0.154	0.125	0.376	0.302	0.322	0.307	0.425	0.249	36	19
Sweden	0.313	0.250	0.131	0.163	0.202	0.079	0.055	0.148	0.524	0.158	0.202	27	-7
Switzerland	0.068	0.010	0.175	0.166	0.205	0.122	0.245	0.159	0.222	0.105	0.157	17	5
UK	0.793	1.057	1.080	1.224	1.076	0.883	0.816	0.726	0.100	1.033	0.969	5	3
US	0.556	0.867	0.434	0.408	0.308	0.177	0.366	0.349	0.457	0.638	0.456	12	2

Venture capital investment levels for 21 countries. Venture capital investment is defined as startup + seed + expansion investments. Data on venture capital is taken from the EVCA yearbooks, AVCA yearbooks, MacDonald & Associates Limited, and Venture Economics. Average growth is the arithmetic annual growth rate over the time period considered. CAGR is the geometric annual growth rate over the time period considered.

venture capital and not private equity, we find it advantageous to use the US as an example given the specialization in venture capital that prevails there.

Venture capital firms in the US are typically organized as limited partnerships with the venture capitalists serving as general partners and the investors serving as limited partners. It was not until the early 1980s that the limited partnership became the predominant form of venture capital funds in the US. In 1980, only 40 percent of funds were limited partnerships, but by 1992, over 80 percent of venture capital funds were organized as such (Gompers and Lerner, 1996). The US venture capital industry exhibits a high degree of geographic concentration. Gompers and Lerner find that 25 percent of US venture capital firms were based in California over the 1972–1992 time period. A large portion of new capital committed comes from pension funds, endowments, and insurance companies and banks. In 1995, they provided 38 percent, 22 percent and 18 percent, respectively, of new capital committed.

Table 5.3
Early Stage Investment as per mil of Average GDP

Country	1986	1987	1988	1989	1990	1991	1992	1993	1994	1995	Average Level (per mil)	Average Growth (%)	CAGR (%)
Australia	NA	NA	NA	NA	NA	NA	0.069	0.044	0.191	0.526	0.207	159 %	97 %
Austria	0.014	0.027	0.001	0.053	0.012	0.006	0.000	0.001	0.0001	0.002	0.012	1300	-19
Belgium	0.417	0.311	0.085	0.146	0.061	0.170	0.089	0.071	0.091	0.038	0.148	-0.4	-23
Canada	0.082	0.100	0.118	0.088	0.067	0.112	0.138	0.176	0.178	0.376	0.144	25	18
Denmark	0.041	0.037	0.050	0.089	0.057	0.051	0.009	0.033	0.036	0.031	0.043	25	-3
Finland	NA	NA	0.013	0.028	0.082	0.102	0.078	0.090	0.074	0.096	0.071	48	33
France	0.032	0.039	0.119	0.088	0.105	0.033	0.042	0.016	0.026	0.027	0.053	20	-2
Germany	0.007	0.012	0.012	0.035	0.027	0.031	0.036	0.039	0.060	0.063	0.032	39	28
Ireland	0.194	0.299	0.315	0.017	0.028	0.127	0.037	0.099	0.071	0.026	0.121	43	-20
Israel	NA	NA	NA	NA	NA	NA	NA	NA	NA	NA	NA	NA	NA
Italy	0.011	0.014	0.002	0.019	0.014	0.066	0.067	0.007	0.053	0.071	0.033	184	23
Japan	NA	NA	NA	NA	NA	NA	0.005	0.003	NA	0.047	0.018	-45	105
Netherlands	0.127	0.059	0.107	0.058	0.094	0.103	0.082	0.085	0.173	0.304	0.119	24	10
New Zealand	NA	NA	NA	NA	NA	NA	NA	0.000	0.019	0.062	0.027	237	237
Norway	NA	NA	0.011	0.006	0.067	0.027	0.023	0.091	0.153	0.061	0.055	176	28
Portugal	0.004	0.047	0.029	0.037	0.178	0.133	0.110	0.090	0.143	0.087	0.086	153	41
Spain	0.037	0.155	0.098	0.076	0.033	0.094	0.077	0.046	0.033	0.056	0.070	41	5
Sweden	0.034	0.080	0.012	0.041	0.024	0.008	0.006	0.012	0.012	0.043	0.027	57	3
Switzerland	0.050	0.036	0.040	0.073	0.072	0.014	0.002	0.018	0.035	0.004	0.034	70	-26
UK	0.194	0.191	0.254	0.218	0.160	0.086	0.070	0.066	0.082	0.042	0.136	-12	-16
US	0.058	0.055	0.068	0.070	0.045	0.021	0.074	0.062	0.102	0.191	0.075	36	14

Early stage investment levels for 21 countries. Early stage investment is defined as startup + seed investments. Data on venture capital is taken from the EVCA yearbooks, AVCA yearbooks, MacDonald and Associates Limited, and Venture Economics. Average growth is the arithmetic annual growth rate over the time period considered. CAGR is the geometric annual growth rate over the time period considered.

In general, a venture capital firm will manage several pools of capital. Each of these pools of capital, also referred to as funds, is structured as a separate limited partnership. Venture capital firms invest in a broad range of industries, not just high technology startups. A fund will invest in projects over the first three to five years of its existence. Investments and appreciation are paid out to the partners over the remainder of the fund's life.

We have already spoken about the importance of the monitoring that takes place between venture capitalists and entrepreneurs. The relationship between venture capitalist and entrepreneur is marked by the following monitoring and control arrangements:

- Monitoring frequency. Gompers (1995) shows how decreases in industry ratios of tangible assets to total assets, higher market to book ratios and greater R&D intensities lead to more frequent monitoring.

Table 5.4
Private Equity New Funds raised as per mil of Average GDP

Country	1986	1987	1988	1989	1990	1991	1992	1993	1994	1995	Average Level (per mil)	Average Growth (%)	CAGR (%)
Australia	NA	NA	NA	0.829	0.157	0.964	0.314	0.713	0.881	1.672	0.790	101%	12%
Austria	0.011	0.032	0.115	0.016	0.007	0.000	0.000	0.000	0.000	0.009	0.019	43	-2
Belgium	2.133	2.409	0.218	0.414	0.221	0.592	0.522	0.635	0.549	0.946	0.864	22	-9
Canada	0.483	0.835	0.840	0.384	0.235	0.501	0.621	1.195	1.520	2.349	0.896	32	19
Denmark	0.288	0.331	0.215	0.079	0.358	0.246	0.099	0.128	1.028	0.253	0.302	93	-1
Finland	NA	NA	0.484	0.316	0.230	0.109	0.042	0.145	0.526	0.641	0.312	50	4
France	0.168	0.758	0.697	1.754	1.079	1.273	0.907	0.855	1.077	0.799	0.937	49	19
Germany	0.036	0.238	0.114	0.178	0.543	0.642	0.636	0.152	0.215	0.148	0.290	80	17
Ireland	0.864	1.091	1.263	0.628	0.515	1.087	1.243	0.848	5.254	0.360	1.315	55	-9
Israel	NA	NA	NA	NA	NA	0.896	1.478	3.313	1.642	0.716	1.610	21	-5
Italy	0.204	0.129	0.268	0.260	0.224	0.256	0.526	0.421	0.450	0.419	0.316	17	8
Japan	NA	NA	NA	0.088	0.288	0.245	0.258	0.161	NA	0.400	0.240	45	29
Netherlands	1.080	0.412	1.063	0.721	0.380	0.475	0.395	0.551	1.063	1.025	0.717	17	-1
New Zealand	NA	NA	NA	NA	NA	NA	NA	0.340	0.694	0.231	0.422	19	-18
Norway	NA	NA	0.129	0.002	0.630	0.368	0.136	0.730	0.440	0.520	0.369	3658	22
Portugal	0.036	0.184	0.163	1.926	0.426	0.227	0.329	1.779	2.388	NA	0.924	206	54
Spain	0.000	0.489	0.239	0.175	0.409	0.374	0.470	0.575	0.187	0.450	0.337	21	-1
Sweden	0.592	0.598	0.135	0.180	0.991	0.613	1.855	0.864	1.633	3.101	1.056	78	20
Switzerland	0.033	0.451	0.109	0.198	0.566	0.119	0.258	0.371	0.284	0.240	0.263	167	25
UK	0.955	2.363	2.403	4.053	2.758	1.665	1.669	1.752	5.433	2.761	2.581	35	13
US	1.539	3.095	2.221	2.518	1.110	1.226	1.751	2.243	3.384	4.960	2.405	23	14

Private equity new funds raised for 21 countries. Private equity new funds raised includes funds raised for
venture capital and buyouts. Data on venture capital is taken from the EVCA yearbooks, AVCA yearbooks,
the GIZA Group, MacDonald & Associates Limited, and Venture Economics. Average growth is the arithmetic annual growth rate over the time period considered. CAGR is the geometric annual growth rate
over the time period considered.

- Compensation schemes that are designed to provide the entrepreneur with the appropriate incentives. Equity-based compensation gives the entrepreneur the incentive
  to focus on growth.

- Active involvement of the venture capitalist with the company through board representation. Lerner (1995) shows that venture capitalists' involvement as directors is
  more intense when the need for oversight is greater.

- Use of convertible securities. These give the venture capitalists the option of selling
  their stake back to the entrepreneur.

The need for monitoring also extends to the relationship between the investor and the venture capitalist. Just as the entrepreneur has an incentive to
deviate from behavior that is optimal for the venture capitalist, the venture
capitalist has an incentive to deviate from behavior that is optimal for the
investor. Investors monitor venture capitalists in the following ways:

- The life of the venture capital fund is limited, which means that the venture capitalist cannot keep the money forever. The limited lifespan of venture capital funds also ensures that disagreements over when and how to distribute funds are minimized.

- Limited partners can withdraw from funding the partnership after the initial capital investment. In practice, limited partners rarely withdraw their funds from the partnership. They are more likely to withhold new funds from venture capitalists in future fundraising efforts.

- Venture capitalists are explicitly prohibited from self-dealing, i.e., receiving preferential investment terms different from those granted to the limited partner.

In the late 1980s the use of covenants became very popular. The average number of covenants used per contract grew from 4.4 to 7.9 between the two periods of 1978–82 and 1988–92, respectively (Gompers and Lerner, 1996). However, Gompers and Lerner (1996) find that restrictive covenants are only used in the most serious cases because they are very costly to negotiate. They also find that the use of covenants decreases during periods of high demand for venture funding, since the supply of venture capitalist services is rather limited. In this situation, the reduction of covenants is viewed as increased compensation for the venture capitalist.

FACTORS THAT AFFECT VENTURE CAPITAL

The previous section described how venture capitalists manage their investments. This section lays out the theoretical underpinnings of our empirical analysis, and explains what the driving forces are behind venture capital flows. We recognize that we have not included all factors that practitioners would deem important for venture capital. Specifically, we think that capital gains tax rates and the efficiency of bankruptcy procedures also impact venture capital. We encounter difficulties, however, in finding good measures for these variables to include in our empirical analysis. Thus, for instance, while we believe that capital gains taxes are important, using data on individual capital gains tax rates, we find no statistically significant impact on venture capital and, for this reason, we do not report the results in our regressions.

Initial Public Offerings

The main risk faced by investors and venture capitalists is the risk of not getting their money back. Thus, a viable exit mechanism is extremely important to the development of a venture capital industry. Furthermore, an exit mechanism is essential to the entrepreneur for two reasons. First, it provides a financial incentive for equity-compensated managers to expend effort. Second, it gives the managers a call option on control of the firm, since venture capitalists relinquish control at the time of the IPO (Black and Gilson, 1998).

Table 5.5
Percentage of Divestments That Are Public Offerings

Country	1991	1992	1993	1994	1995	Mean
Austria	0%	0%	0%	NA	0%	0%
Belgium	2%	NA	0%	20%	39%	15%
Denmark	24%	55%	0%	0%	0%	16%
Finland	0%	0%	0%	0%	1%	0.2%
France	10%	2%	12%	21%	8%	11%
Germany	NA	NA	NA	NA	NA	NA
Ireland	0%	0%	0%	0%	0%	0%
Italy	5%	0%	3%	0%	12%	4%
Netherlands	8%	5%	20%	12%	6%	10%
Norway	1%	17%	37%	6%	31%	18%
Portugal	0%	0%	0%	0%	NA	0%
Spain	2%	1%	0%	1%	0%	1%
Sweden	1%	0%	16%	0%	52%	14%
Switzerland	0%	2%	8%	15%	0%	5%
UK	13%	34%	36%	47%	45%	35%

Public offerings and divestments are measured in local currency terms. Divestments include all private equity. The number reported represents public offerings as a percentage of divestments. The data are taken from the EVCA yearbooks.

We focus on IPOs as an exit mechanism for the following reasons. While there are many mechanisms to liquidate a fund, the literature shows that the most attractive option is through an IPO. A study conducted by Venture Economics (1988) finds that $1.00 invested in a firm that eventually goes public yields a 195 percent average return (or an average cash return of $1.95 over the original investment) for a 4.2 year average holding period. The same investment in an acquired firm only provides an average return of 40 percent (or a cash return of only 40 cents) over a 3.7 year average holding period. Also, if regaining control is important to the entrepreneur, IPOs are clearly the best choice, given that the other option, trade sales, frequently entails loss of control. Trade sales are sales of a startup company to a larger company (also referred to as a strategic buyer). Table 5.5 shows the importance of trade sales in Europe. The percentage of divestments accounted for by trade sales ranges from 30 percent in the UK to 76 percent in Portugal over the whole time period considered (Table 5.6).

To account for the importance of exit mechanisms, we include both current and lagged IPOs in our statistical analysis. We do not have an explicit measure of trade sales. Increased volume of IPOs should have a positive effect on both

Table 5.6
Percentage of Divestments That Are Trade Sales

Country	1991	1992	1993	1994	1995	Mean
Austria	22%	50%	100%	NA	24%	49%
Belgium	52%	NA	57%	51%	32%	48%
Denmark	24%	7%	70%	62%	85%	50%
Finland	67%	37%	0%	10%	48%	32%
France	41%	56%	57%	33%	48%	47%
Germany	NA	NA	NA	NA	NA	NA
Ireland	82%	76%	19%	13%	64%	51%
Italy	86%	89%	57%	21%	52%	61%
Netherlands	48%	44%	22%	24%	44%	36%
Norway	15%	49%	18%	40%	15%	27%
Portugal	NA	100%	57%	90%	56%	76%
Spain	72%	62%	20%	31%	24%	42%
Sweden	13%	40%	78%	43%	25%	40%
Switzerland	40%	4%	24%	33%	47%	30%
UK	24%	22%	41%	30%	36%	30%

Trade sales and divestments are measured in local currency terms. Divestments include all private equity. The number reported represents trade sales as a percentage of divestments. The data are taken from the EVCA yearbooks.

the demand and supply of venture capital funds. On the demand side, the existence of an exit mechanism gives entrepreneurs an additional incentive to start a company. On the supply side, the effect is essentially the same; large investors are more willing to supply funds to venture capital firms if they feel that they can later recoup their investment.

Labor Market Rigidities

Labor market rigidities present an obstacle to venture capital growth. Sahlman (1990) discusses how labor market rigidities form a large barrier to the success of venture capital investing in countries such as Germany and Japan. In Japan, for instance, leaving a company is not only considered dishonorable, but departing individuals also lose valuable benefits of seniority. Also, should the individual fail in his new venture, it would be difficult for him to find new employment, which would lead to a further loss of social standing. Labor market rigidities are frequently cited as one important reason why venture capital is not more prevalent in Europe and Asia.[6]

Labor market rigidity should impact the demand for venture capital funds negatively (i.e., the higher labor market rigidity, the less demand for venture capital funds we would expect). Strict labor laws make hiring employees difficult for companies, because they deprive the company of the flexibility to let people go later on, should this become necessary. In addition, large benefits payments, which typically accompany more rigid labor markets, make it more expensive to hire in the first place.

We use two measures of labor market rigidity. One reflects rigidity in the market for skilled labor, the other reflects rigidity in the overall labor market.

Financial Reporting Standards

Small startup firms are risky prospects. If the market does not have good information on these companies, investors will demand a high risk premium, resulting in more expensive funding for these companies. This cost of asymmetric information can be reduced if the country in which the company operates has strict accounting standards. With good accounting regulation, venture capitalists need to spend less time gathering information to monitor their investments.

We include an independent variable that measures the level of accounting standards in the various countries for public firms. Since we are dealing with private firms in our sample, we use this variable as a proxy for reporting standards of private firms. On the supply side, this variable should have a positive effect on the supply of venture capital funds.

Private Pension Funds

Raising money from pension funds provides numerous advantages to the venture capitalist. Venture capitalists can quickly raise a large amount of investment capital solely by approaching a few large pension funds. Furthermore, with only a few investors, a venture capital firm can economize on the amount of time expended on keeping its investors apprised of its activities. In addition, with changes in legislation and perceived high rates of return, many pension funds became eager to lend to venture capitalists. For all these reasons, private pension funds are an important source of venture capital funds in the US. In 1994, pension funds provided 46 percent of venture capital money in the United States (Black and Gilson 1998).

On the other hand, raising money from pension funds may present a few disadvantages. For instance, in the US, there may be regulatory compliance issues with ERISA. In addition, managers of pension funds are sophisticated investors who may require additional disclosure. However, these issues do not present a huge barrier for venture capitalists to raise money, especially for venture capitalists with good reputations.

We have included private pension fund data as an independent variable in our regressions. Private pension funds should have a positive effect on the supply of new funds to venture capital firms. There is no reason to believe that private pension funds have any effect on demand for venture capital funds.

Macroeconomic Variables

The state of the country's economy will also have an effect on venture capital. Acs and Audretsch (1994) suggest that macroeconomic fluctuations influence startup activity in general. Macroeconomic expansions are found to lead to an increase in the number of startups. Since an increase in startup activity increases demand for venture capital funds, we expect a positive relationship between macroeconomic expansion and venture capital investing. We use GDP growth to measure macroeconomic fluctuations in our analysis and expect this variable to be positively correlated with venture capital investment.

We also include growth in market capitalization as an explanatory factor for venture capital investing. We believe that increases in market capitalization create a more favorable environment for investors in general. Therefore, increases in market capitalization should be met by greater supply of funds to venture capital investments.

Government Programs

Many governments have begun to recognize the benefits of venture capital and have made efforts to fund startup businesses. Lerner (1996) provides preliminary evidence that government funded programs can yield favorable benefits. However, O'Shea (1996) points out that there may also be disadvantages to these efforts. For instance, government spending on venture capital may hinder the development of a private venture capital sector. Furthermore, many are skeptical about the government's ability to appropriately target healthy ventures. In addition to looking at government funding in our statistical analysis, we also discuss on a more descriptive level the importance of various government programs on pages 105–107.

DATA

This chapter empirically examines 21 countries: Austria, Australia, Belgium, Canada, Denmark, Finland, France, Germany, Ireland, Israel, Italy, Japan, the Netherlands, New Zealand, Norway, Portugal, Spain, Sweden, Switzerland, the United Kingdom and the United States. These countries are selected based on availability of information.

We use panel data covering the years 1986–1995. Data on venture capital investments, early stage investments, and new funds raised are obtained from The European Venture Capital Journal, Asian Venture Capital Journal, The

GIZA Group for Israel figures, Macdonald's & Associates Limited for Canada figures and Venture Economics for US figures.

Venture capital investments refer to the total amount disbursed by venture capitalists for seed, startup and expansion stage investments. Early stage investments only include funds used for seed and startup investments. Our New Funds Raised number is dictated by data availability. Ideally, we would look at new funds raised for venture capital. However, the closest we can come to that figure is new funds raised for private equity. New Funds Raised is defined as total funds raised for all private equity investing and includes committed, but not yet paid, capital. Typically, the capital promised by investors to venture capitalists is not immediately paid to the venture capitalists. Most agreements call for a 25–33 percent cash commitment up-front and stipulate when addition cash is to be phased in at future dates (Sahlman, 1990). The total amount of investment promised to the venture capitalists is referred to as committed capital, even though only approximately one third is initially paid in.

Country Gross Domestic Product (GDP) data in local currency are provided by the IMF's International Financial Statistics Yearbook. Market capitalization data (annual end of period figures) in billions of US dollars are provided by the IMF's Emerging Markets Fact Book. Total Private Pension fund figures in US Dollars are provided by InterSec Research Corporation. Exchange rates (annual end of period rates) are obtained from the IMF's International Financial Statistics and are expressed as national currency unit per SDR.

Initial Public Offering data are available for 1986–1995 for Canada, Japan and the US, 1989–1995 for the UK, and 1991–1995 for Australia, other European Countries and New Zealand. They are provided by the Federation Internationale des Bourses de Valeurs, Securities Data Corporation, Nomura Securities and the Toronto Stock Exchange. These figures exclude privatizations, real estate trusts, utilities and closed-end funds.

Ratings on accounting standards are measured by an index provided by International Accounting & Auditing Trends, Center for International Financial Analysis & Research, Inc. This index is created by examining and rating companies' 1990 annual reports on their inclusion or omission of ninety accounting items. A minimum of three companies in each country were studied.

We include two measures of labor market rigidity. Our first measure gauges the amount of flexibility in a country's skilled labor market, by measuring the average job tenure of individuals who have completed some or all tertiary education. This statistic best represents the class of individuals who are likely to start new enterprises. For the US, this figure is 7.4 years while for Germany and Japan it is 10.5 and 9.5 years respectively. Our second measure refers more generally to the entire labor market. It measures the percent of the labor force that has job tenure greater than ten years. This statistic attempts to capture the flexibility of all individuals to leave their current position to join a startup. While there exist better measures of labor turnover,[7] none offers as broad a cross-section as these two statistics. Data for these two measures are provided by the OECD's 1997 Employment Outlook, Chapter 5 (Draft) and 1994 Employment Outlook, respectively.

We also use variables from the law and finance literature (La Porta et al.) to measure the efficiency of financial markets. The categorization of legal systems as reported by La Porta et al. (1996) divides countries into four legal traditions: English, French, German, and Scandinavian. The English legal tradition is also referred to as the common law tradition, while the other legal traditions can be grouped together as the civil law traditions. The different legal traditions differ by the extent to which shareholder and creditor rights are protected in the various countries. The common law tradition provides the best legal protections, while the French tradition is the worst in this respect.

The variables Rule of Law, Anti-director Rights, and One Share One Vote all describe the amount of protection that shareholders can expect in a given country. They are taken from La Porta et al. (1996). Rule of Law reflects the law and order tradition in a country, as measured by the International Country Risk Guide. The scale ranges from 0 to 10, with lower scores for a weaker law and order tradition. Anti-director Rights is an index aggregating shareholder rights. This index is formed by adding one for each of the following conditions: (1) when the country allows shareholders to mail their proxy vote; (2) when shareholders are not required to deposit their shares prior to the General Shareholders' meeting; (3) when cumulative voting is allowed; (4) when an oppressed minorities mechanism is in place; or (5) when the minimum percentage of share capital that entitles a shareholder to call for an Extraordinary Shareholders' Meeting is less than or equal to 10 percent. The index ranges from 0 to 5. One Share One Vote equals one if the company law or the commercial code of the country requires that ordinary shares carry one vote per share. Otherwise it is zero.

Table 5.7 provides a summary of the variables used in this chapter and their sources.

METHODOLOGY

We use a linear specification for the supply and demand schedules of venture capital funds. In our regression analysis, we estimate the coefficients of the equilibrium specification.

Supply and Demand Structural Equations

As explained previously, we believe the following factors (in addition to return percentage) influence the supply of venture capital: IPOs, accounting standards, GDP growth, and market capitalization growth. The following simple equation describes the supply of venture funds in the economy:

Table 5.7
Variable Descriptions

Variable	Description	Sources
Early Stage Investments	Early stage investments (Seed and Startup both government and private sector funded) divided by average GDP	European Venture Capital Journal, Asian Venture Capital Journal, Macdonald's & Associates for Canadian data and Venture Economics for US data
Early Stage Investments w/o government funds	Estimated Early Stage Investments, funded by private sector sources, divided by average GDP	European Venture Capital Journal, Asian Venture Capital Journal, Macdonald's & Associates for Canadian data and Venture Economics for US data
New Funds Raised	Annual New Funds raised (both government and private sector funded) domestically divided by average GDP. Includes committed but not yet paid capital	European Venture Capital Journal, Asian Venture Capital Journal, Macdonald's & Associates for Canadian data and Venture Economics for US data
New Funds Raised w/o government funds	Annual New Funds raised domestically divided by average GDP. Excludes Government funds. Includes committed but not yet paid capital	European Venture Capital Journal, Asian Venture Capital Journal, Macdonald's & Associates for Canadian data and Venture Economics for US data
Venture Capital Funds	Annual Expansion and Early Stage Investments (both government and private sector funded) divided by average GDP.	European Venture Capital Journal, Asian Venture Capital Journal, Macdonald's & Associates for Canadian data and Venture Economics for US data
Venture Capital Funds w/o government funds	Estimated Expansion and Early Stage Investments, funded by private sector sources, divided by GDP.	European Venture Capital Journal, Asian Venture Capital Journal, Macdonald's & Associates for Canadian data and Venture Economics for US data
IPOs	Total Market Value of IPOS divided by average GDP	FIBV, Nomura Securities Securities Data Corporation, Toronto Stock Exchange
Labor Market Rigidity (educated)	Average tenure of Employees with some or completed tertiary education	OECD's Draft 1996 Economic Outlook Chapter 5
Labor Market Rigidity (general)	Percent of labor force with a tenure greater than 10 years	OECD's 1993 Economic Outlook
Accounting Standards	Ratings on Accounting Standards	International Accounting & Auditing Trends, Center for International Financial Analysis & Research, Inc.
Private Pension Growth	Percentage change in Private Pension Fund Levels	InterSec Research Corporation
Private Pension Levels	Private Pension Fund Levels divided by GDP	InterSec Research Corporation
Market Capitalization Growth	Percentage change in Market Capitalization	*Emerging Market's Fact Book*, International Monetary Fund
GDP Growth	Percentage change in GDP	*International Financial Statistics*, International Monetary Fund 1995

$$\text{Venture capital funds supplied}_{it} = \alpha_o + \alpha_1 \text{ Return percentage}_{it} + \alpha_2 \text{ IPOs}_{it} +$$
$$\alpha_3 \text{ Accounting standards}_i +$$
$$\alpha_4 \text{ GDP percentage growth}_{it} +$$
$$\alpha_5 \text{ Market capitalization percentage growth}_{it}$$

The fourth section of this chapter also describes the variables that we believe are important for demand for venture capital: IPOs, accounting standards, labor market rigidities, GDP growth and market capitalization growth. A simple equation for the demand side of venture capital is as follows:

Venture capital funds demanded$_{it}$ = β_o + β_1 Return percentage$_{it}$ +
β_2 IPOs$_{it}$ + β_3 Accounting standards$_i$ +
β_4 Labor market rigidities$_i$ +
β_5 GDP percentage growth$_{it}$ +
β_6 Market capitalization percentage growth$_{it}$

To obtain the equilibrium, we solve the supply equation for return percentage, and substitute this expression into the demand equation. Then, taking into account the equality in equilibrium of supply and demand, we solve for the equilibrium quantity.

Equilibrium Condition:

Venture capital funds$_{it}$ = π_o + π_1 IPOs$_{it}$ + π_2 Accounting standards$_i$ +
π_3 Labor market rigidities$_i$ +
π_4 GDP percentage growth$_{it}$ +
π_5 Market capitalization percentage growth$_{it}$

where, in equilibrium

Venture capital funds supplied$_{it}$ = Venture capital funds demanded$_{it}$
= Venture capital funds$_{it}$

The equilibrium for new funds raised is analogous. The only difference is that the supply of new funds is also affected by private pension funds. Our regression analysis considers two different forms of the equilibrium equation: the cross sectional form and the within form.

Between Regression (Cross Section Regression)

The between regression captures the difference in venture capital investments between countries as a result of differences in characteristics across countries.

Venture capital funds$_i$ = π_o + π_1 IPOs$_i$ + π_2 Accounting standards$_i$ +
π_3 Labor market rigidities$_i$ +
π_4 GDP percentage growth rate$_i$ +
π_5 Market capitalization percentage growth rate$_i$

where

Venture capital funds$_i$ = Average of venture capital funds over time

and likewise for other variables.

The dependent variables used in the between regressions are: new funds committed, venture capital investment (seed, startup and expansion stage investments) and early stage investment (seed and startup investments). Each variable is normalized by average GDP. Early stage investments, venture capital investments, and new funds raised all include government funds. However, we believe that government funding is driven by considerations different from the ones driving private sector funding. Therefore, we also consider the three dependent variables without public source funds.

Within Regression (Fixed Effects Regression)

The within regression captures the difference in venture capital funds due to changes over time of the independent variables.

$$\text{Venture capital funds}_{it} - \text{Venture capital funds}_i$$
$$= \pi_o + \pi_1(\text{IPOs}_{it} - \text{IPOs}_i)$$
$$+ \pi_2 \text{ (GDP percentage growth rate}_{it} -$$
$$\text{GDP percentage grow)}_i +$$
$$+ \pi_3 \text{ (Market capitalization percentage growth rate}_{it} -$$
$$\text{Market capitalization percentage growth rate}_i)$$

where, Venture capital funds$_i$ = average of Venture capital funds over time and similarly for other variables.

The dependent variables examined are the same ones that we use in the between regressions. We also consider lags of GDP and market capitalization growth. However, these independent variables are not significant and the results do not change. For this reason, we do not report these regressions.

RESULTS

Tables 5.8 through 5.11 report the results from the between regressions. Tables 5.12 through 5.14 contain results from the within regressions.

Between Regression Results

Table 5.3 reports results from the between regression of venture capital investments on IPOs, accounting standards, labor market rigidities, market capitalization and GDP growth. The explanatory power of all the regressions is high, with R^2s ranging from .49 to .71. The coefficient on IPOs is positive and statistically significant for virtually all specifications. This lends support to the hypothesis advanced in Section 4 that high levels of IPOs in a country will lead to more venture capital.

In addition to the explanation we present above, one could offer another explanation for why the coefficient on IPOs is positive. This explanation involves reverse causality: Since venture capital investments frequently end up as IPOs, a higher level of such investments will lead to a higher level of IPOs down the road. Thus, our coefficient would be positive not because more IPOs

Table 5.8
Venture Capital Investments, Between Regressions

Independent Variables	Dependent Variables					
	1 Venture Capital w/o gov't funds	2 Venture Capital w/o gov't funds	3 Venture Capital w/o gov't funds	4 Venture Capital	5 Venture Capital	6 Venture Capital
IPOs	0.0953[a] (2.934)	0.0718[b] (2.067)	0.0976[a] (3.986)	0.0901[b] (2.180)	0.05814 (1.382)	0.0899[a] (2.851)
Accounting Standards	-0.00002[c] (-1.723)	-0.000005 (-0.341)	-0.00002[a] (-2.514)	-0.00002[d] (-1.482)	0.000006 (0.349)	-0.00002[b] (-2.039)
Labor Market Rigidity (educated)	-0.00003 (-0.612)		-0.00003 (-0.634)	-0.00002 (-0.270)		-0.00002 (-0.296)
Labor Market Rigidity (general)		-0.00001 (-0.969)			-0.00001 (-0.580)	
Market capitalization growth	-0.0002 (-0.294)	-0.0004 (-0.537)	-0.00018 (-0.320)	-0.00013 (-0.163)	-0.00007 (-0.081)	-0.0001 (-0.171)
GDP growth	0.0005 (0.117)	0.0007 (0.176)		-0.00005 (-0.010)	0.0019 (0.393)	
Constant	0.0014[c] (1.603)	0.0010 (0.769)	0.0015[b] (1.984)	0.0015 (1.297)	0.00015 (0.097)	0.0015[c] (1.545)
R-Squared	0.6502	0.7119	0.6497	0.4924	0.6004	0.4923

Between regression of 15 countries. The dependent variables are venture capital (i.e., early stage and expansion) investments with and without government funds, divided by average GDP. The independent variables are (1) IPOs divided by average GDP; (2) Accounting Standards; (3) Labor Market Rigidity (educated); (4) Labor Market Rigidity (general); (5) Percentage change in Market capitalization; (6) Percentage change in GDP. T-statistics for coefficients in parentheses.

a = Significant at 1% level, b = Significant at 10% level, c = Significant at 15% level, d = Significant at 20% level

lead to more venture capital, but because higher levels of venture capital eventually show up as greater amounts of IPOs.

To test for this reverse causality story, we examine several subpanels of our original panel, where the subpanels cover shorter time periods. The time periods are chosen such that investment projects started during the period will not have had enough time to progress to the IPO stage. The time periods are 1992–1995 and 1993–1995, and the results are contained in Table 5.9A. The results allow us to reject the reverse causality story, as the coefficient on IPOs remains positive and significant.

Table 5.9A
Venture Capital Investments, Between Regressions (1993–1995)

Independent Variables	Dependent Variables			
	1 Venture Capital w/o gov't funds 1993 - 1995	2 Venture Capital w/o gov't funds 1994 - 1995	3 Venture Capital 1993 - 1995	4 Venture Capital 1994 - 1995
IPOs	0.1043[a]	0.0814[a]	0.0929[a]	0.0701[a]
	(5.070)	(4.925)	(3.731)	(3.693)
Accounting Standards	-0.00003[a]	-0.00002[a]	-0.00003[a]	-0.00002[a]
	(-4.566)	(-3.215)	(-3.416)	(-2.263)
Labor Market Rigidity (educated)	-0.00005	-0.00004	-0.00005	-0.00002
	(-1.171)	(-0.846)	(-0.916)	(-0.320)
Market capitalization growth	0.00134[a]	0.0021[a]	0.0015[a]	0.0026[a]
	(2.857)	(2.723)	(2.692)	(2.875)
GDP Growth	-0.0071	-0.0096[b]	-0.0069	-0.0111[b]
	(-1.352)	(-1.851)	(-1.089)	(-1.858)
Constant	0.0025[a]	0.0024[a]	0.0024[a]	0.0020[a]
	(3.543)	(3.161)	(2.741)	(2.322)
R-Squared	0.8102	0.8447	0.7161	0.7885

Between regression of 15 countries for 1993 to 1995 time span. The dependent variables are venture capital (i.e., early stage and expansion) investments with and without government funds, divided by average GDP. The independent variables are (1) IPOs divided by average GDP; (2) Accounting Standards; (3) Labor Market Rigidity (educated); (4) Percentage change in Market capitalization; (5) Percentage change in GDP. T-statistics for coefficients in parentheses.

a = Significant at 1% level, b = Significant at 10% level, c = Significant at 15% level, d = Significant at 20% level

Another way to test the reverse causality explanation is to look at the factors underlying IPOs, which are not dependent on venture capital. La Porta et al. (1996) analyze the legal determinants of IPO finance as part of their study into the legal determinants of external finance. They find that Rule of Law has a large positive effect on the number of IPOs. Furthermore, a higher degree of Anti-director Rights also leads to more IPOs. Even when they correct for specific differences in shareholder rights, they find that civil law countries (the German and French origin ones in particular) still have a significant negative impact on the amount of IPOs in a country.

Table 5.9B
Venture Capital Investments, Between Regressions

Independent Variables	Dependent Variables					
	1 Venture Capital w/o gov't funds	2 Venture Capital w/o gov't funds	3 Venture Capital w/o gov't funds	4 Venture Capital	5 Venture Capital	6 Venture Capital
GDP Growth	0.0025 0.685	0.0033 0.634	0.0030 0.785	0.0028 0.700	0.0037 0.657	0.0030 0.707
Rule of Law	0.0000 -0.106	0.0000 0.020	0.0000 -0.002	0.0000 0.251	0.0000 0.324	0.0000 0.277
One Share One Vote		0.0001 0.221			0.0001 0.239	
Anti-director rights			0.0001 0.785			0.0000 0.316
French origin	-0.0001 -0.622	-0.0001 -0.558	0.0001 0.292	0.0000 0.018	0.0000 0.051	0.0001 0.269
German origin	-0.0004[b] -2.181	-0.0005[b] -1.908	-0.0003 -0.953	-0.0004[b] -1.895	-0.0004[c] -1.697	-0.0003 -1.044
Scandinavian origin	-0.0004[c] -1.762	-0.0004[c] -1.576	-0.0002 -0.845	-0.0003[d] -1.435	-0.0003 -1.258	-0.0003 -0.859
Constant	0.0006 0.505	0.0004 0.273	0.0001 0.107	0.0002 0.138	0.0000 -0.025	0.0000 -0.020
R-Squared	0.52	0.53	0.56	0.51	0.51	0.52

Between regression of 15 countries. The dependent variables are venture capital (i.e., early stage and expansion) investments with and without government funds, divided by average GDP. The independent variables are (1) GDP Growth; (2) Rule of Law; (3) One Share One Vote; (4) Anti-director Rights; (5) French legal origin; (6) German legal origin; (7) Scandinavian legal origin. T-statistics for coefficients in parentheses.
a = Significant at 1% level, b = Significant at 10% level, c = Significant at 15% level, d = Significant at 20% level

By regressing venture capital investments on shareholder rights and legal origin dummies in Table 5.9B, we can show to what extent these investments are dependent on the variables underlying IPOs. Rule of Law and Anti-director Rights are not significant in this regression. The civil law variables, however, are. The German and Scandinavian countries in particular have lower levels of venture capital investing. These results indicate that the same factors driving IPOs also drive venture capital investments. The connection between IPOs and

Table 5.10
Early Stage Investments, Between Regressions

Independent Variables	Dependent Variables					
	1	2	3	4	5	6
	Early Stage Investments w/o gov't funds	Early Stage Investments w/o gov't funds	Early Stage Investments w/o gov't funds	Early Stage Investments	Early Stage Investments	Early Stage Investments
IPOs	0.0044 (0.652)	-0.0007 (-0.117)	0.0073^d (1.395)	0.0024 (0.289)	-0.0040 (-0.579)	0.0049 (0.761)
Accounting Standards	-0.000001 (-0.582)	9.3 x 10^{-9} (-0.004)	-0.000002^d (-1.421)	-0.000001 (-0.409)	-0.000003 (0.985)	-0.000002 (-1.001)
Labor Market Rigidity (educated)	-0.00002^d (-1.469)		-0.00001 (-1.367)	-0.00001 (-0.981)		-0.00001 (-0.921)
Labor Market Rigidity (general)		-0.000006^a (-2.625)			-0.000006^b (-2.016)	
Market capitalization growth	-0.00003 (-0.233)	-0.0002 (-1.365)	-0.00004 (-0.297)	0.00002 (0.099)	-0.00007 (-0.493)	-0.00009 (0.060)
GDP growth	0.0006 (0.704)	0.00037 (0.509)		0.0005 (0.504)	0.0005 (0.681)	
Constant	0.00024 (1.269)	0.00029 (1.275)	0.0003^b (1.867)	0.0002 (0.939)	0.00008 (0.315)	0.0003^d (1.387)
R-Squared	0.3672	0.6760	0.3323	0.1740	0.6152	0.1507

Between regression of 15 countries. The dependent variables are early stage (i.e., seed and startup) investments with and without government funds, divided by average GDP. The independent variables are (1) IPOs divided by average GDP; (2) Accounting Standards; (3) Labor Market Rigidity (educated); (4) Labor Market Rigidity (general); (5) Percentage change in Market capitalization; (6) Percentage change in GDP. T-statistics for coefficients in parentheses.

a = Significant at 1% level, b = Significant at 10% level, c = Significant at 15% level, d = Significant at 20% level

venture capital investing appears more substantial than the reverse causality story would indicate. It appears that structural factors are driving the positive relationship between the two, and that we are not just observing the move, over time, of venture capital flows into IPO flows.

When we include government funded investments in total venture capital, the significance of IPOs drops, as measured by the t-statistic (Specifications 4–6). This implies that government investments are less sensitive to IPOs. From this, we infer that government funded venture capital supports investments in environments that are less favorable to venture capital (i.e., in environments where the IPO market is not strong).

The government funded projects might nevertheless be sensible from an economic perspective, and might offer adequate returns. In order to decide

Table 5.11A
Private Equity New Funds Raised, Between Regressions

Independent Variables	Dependent Variables					
	1 Private Equity New Funds Raised w/o gov't funds	2 Private Equity New Funds Raised w/o gov't funds	3 Private Equity New Funds Raised w/o gov't funds	4 Private Equity New Funds Raised	5 Private Equity New Funds Raised	6 Private Equity New Funds Raised
IPOs	0.2113[b] (2.125)	0.2429[b] (2.219)	0.2366[a] (2.856)	0.1928[b] (1.940)	0.2368[b] (2.237)	0.2143[a] (2.605)
Accounting Standards	0.00002 (0.558)	0.000002 (0.029)	0.00001 (0.368)	0.00003 (0.961)	0.000009 (0.121)	0.00003 (0.899)
Labor Market Rigidity (educated)	-0.00013 (-1.066)		-0.00011 (-1.024)	-0.0001 (-0.906)		-0.0001 (-0.875)
Labor Market Rigidity (general)		-0.00004 (-0.819)			-0.0004 (-0.779)	
Private Pension Fund growth	0.00075 (0.343)	-0.0003 (-0.191)	0.0003 (0.166)	0.0003 (0.131)	-0.0004 (-0.267)	-0.00008 (-0.043)
Market capitalization growth	-0.00041 (-0.346)	-0.0010 (-0.391)	-0.0005 (-0.467)	-0.0001 (-0.097)	-0.0008 (-0.336)	-0.0002 (-0.187)
GDP growth	0.0071 (0.533)	0.0056 (0.393)		0.0060 (0.455)	0.0068 (0.497)	
Constant	-0.00015 (-0.051)	0.0013 (0.196)	0.0006 (0.276)	-0.0011 (-0.376)	0.0007 (0.109)	-0.0004 (-0.175)
R-Squared	0.8332	0.8552	0.8253	0.8381	0.8639	0.8325

Between regression of 13 countries. The dependent variables are new funds raised for private equity (i.e., venture capital and buyouts) investments with and without government funds, divided by average GDP. The independent variables are (1) IPOs divided by average GDP; (2) Accounting Standard Regulation; (3) Labor Market Rigidity (educated); (4) Labor Market Rigidity (general); (5) Percentage change in Private Pension Funds; (6) Percentage change in Market capitalization; (7) Percentage change in GDP. T-statistics for coefficients in parentheses.

a = Significant at 1% level, b = Significant at 10% level, c = Significant at 15% level, d = Significant at 20% level

whether this is the case, it would be helpful to have data on rates of return. There is some US evidence that government supported venture capital can select good projects. Lerner (1996) shows that companies that receive SBIR awards experienced higher growth relative to a matched sample. However, without more comprehensive data on returns for the various funds in our sample, we are unable to say whether government funds support high-return projects in environments that otherwise would not have supported them, or

Table 5.11B
Private Equity New Funds Raised, Between Regressions

Independent Variables	Dependent Variables			
	1 Private Equity New Funds Raised w/o gov't funds	2 Private Equity New Funds Raised w/o gov't funds	4 Private Equity New Funds Raised	5 Private Equity New Funds Raised
IPOs	0.1409 (0.570)	0.2654^c (1.974)	0.1580 (0.636)	0.2619^c (2.033)
Accounting Standards	0.00002 (0.223)	0.000002 (0.023)	0.00002 (0.263)	0.000009 (0.106)
Labor Market Rigidity (educated)	-0.0001 (-0.586)		-0.0001 (-0.598)	
Labor Market Rigidity (general)		-0.00005 (-0.838)		-0.00005 (-0.849)
Private Pension Fund growth	0.0024 (0.468)	-0.0006 (-0.327)	0.0017 (0.327)	-0.0007 (-0.419)
Private Pension Fund levels	0.0010 (0.379)	-0.0007 (-0.414)	0.0006 (0.246)	-0.0008 (-0.482)
Market capitalization growth	-0.0008 (-0.333)	-0.0010 (-0.376)	-0.0006 (-0.262)	-0.0009 (-0.335)
GDP growth	0.0132 (0.581)	0.0009 (0.044)	0.0111 (0.487)	0.0016 (0.084)
Constant	-0.0007 (-0.108)	0.0022 (0.287)	-0.0007 (-0.103)	0.0017 (0.233)
R-Squared	0.8365	0.8630	0.8331	0.8737

Between regression of 13 countries. The dependent variables are new funds raised for private equity (i.e., venture capital and buyouts) with and without government funds, divided by average GDP. The independent variables are (1) IPOs divided by average GDP; (2) Accounting Standard Regulation; (3) Labor Market Rigidity (educated); (4) Labor Market Rigidity (general); (5) Percentage change in Private Pension Funds; (6) Private Pension Fund levels, (7) Percentage change in Market capitalization; (8) Percentage change in GDP. T-statistics for coefficients in parentheses.

a = Significant at 1% level, b = Significant at 10% level, c = Significant at 15% level, d = Significant at 20% level

whether government funds back low-return projects. Our result does, however, indicate that government involvement can generate venture capital investments where otherwise there would have been none.

The variable for accounting standards has a statistically significant negative coefficient. This result is surprising, as we expect a positive coefficient. This finding could be explained as follows: As we mentioned earlier, the accounting standards under consideration are those used by public firms. Therefore, they

Table 5.12
Venture Capital Investments, Within Regressions

Independent Variables	Dependent Variables			
	1 Venture Capital w/o gov't funds	2 Venture Capital w/o gov't funds	3 Venture Capital	4 Venture Capital
IPOs	0.0257[a] (3.094)	0.0148[a] (2.100)	0.0260[a] (2.882)	0.0164[a] (2.207)
Lagged IPOs	0.0076 (0.982)		0.0106 (1.269)	
Market capitalization growth	-0.00003 (-0.390)	-0.000007 (-0.097)	-0.00003 (-0.327)	0.000003 (0.037)
GDP growth	-0.0005 (-0.514)	-0.0000005 (-0.001)	0.0003 (0.243)	0.00073 (0.966)
Constant	0.0003[a] (5.289)	0.0003[a] (7.179)	0.0003[a] (5.084)	0.0004[a] (7.196)
R-Squared	0.1632	0.0586	0.1679	0.0733

Within regression of 17 countries. The dependent variables are venture capital (i.e., early stage and expansion) investments with and without government funds, divided by average GDP. The independent variables are (1) IPOs divided by average GDP; (2) Lagged IPOs; (3) Percentage change in Market capitalization; (4) Percentage change in GDP. T-statistics for coefficients in parentheses.
a = Significant at 1% level, b = Significant at 10% level, c = Significant at 15% level, d = Significant at 20% level

only provide a proxy for accounting standards at privately held firms. This proxy may not be correctly measuring the private firms' accounting standards. Furthermore, Wright and Robbie (1996) provide evidence that accounting information is only one part of the venture capitalist's assessment process. While accounting information is an important piece in the decision making process, other elements, such as discussions with personnel and access to unpublished and subjective assessments, are also widely used. This insight, however, could only explain why accounting standards do not have a positive significant coefficient. The statistically significant negative coefficient, however, can still not be entirely understood.

Table 5.10 contains the results from the between regression of early stage investments on IPOs, labor market rigidities, accounting standards, market capitalization and GDP growth. While labor market rigidity was not significant in the regressions on venture capital, the coefficients on labor market rigidities in

Table 5.13
Early Stage Investments, Within Regressions

Independent Variables	Dependent Variables			
	1 Early Stage Investments w/o gov't funds	2 Early Stage Investments w/o gov't funds	3 Early Stage Investments	4 Early Stage Investments
IPOs	0.0051[a] (2.271)	0.0018 (0.970)	0.0054[a] (2.309)	0.0020 (1.026)
Lagged IPOs	0.0008 (0.406)		0.0011 (0.512)	
Market capitalization growth	0.000002 (-0.099)	0.000002 (0.093)	0.0000007 (0.031)	0.000004 (0.209)
GDP growth	0.00002 (0.062)	0.0001 (0.629)	0.00005 (0.157)	0.0002 (0.815)
Constant	0.00004[a] (2.598)	0.00005[a] (3.858)	0.00005[a] (2.981)	0.00006[a] (4.293)
R-Squared	0.0919	0.0179	0.0970	0.0228

Within regression of 18 countries. The dependent variables are early stage (i.e., seed and startup) investments with and without government funds, divided by average GDP. The independent variables are (1) IPOs divided by average GDP; (2) Lagged IPOs; (3) Percentage change in Market capitalization; (4) Percentage change in GDP. T-statistics for coefficients in parentheses.

a = Significant at 1% level, b = Significant at 10% level, c = Significant at 15% level, d = Significant at 20% level

this specification, with early stage venture capital, are negative and significant. The significance for overall labor market rigidity is higher than that for rigidity of the more highly educated labor market. These results confirm the hypothesis advanced in Section 4 that labor market rigidities pose a hindrance to venture capital.

There are several reasons why labor market rigidities might affect early stage venture capital and not later stage venture capital. First, the probability of an early stage investment going bankrupt is higher, which increases the probability that the employees of the venture will have to find other jobs. All things being equal, this will be more difficult in a country with higher labor market rigidity. Also, given the liquidity constraints of an early stage venture which, in most cases, has no regular revenue stream, it is increasingly difficult to hire employees because the environment offers the employer less flexibility to let people go and imposes higher costs of benefits for unemployment insurance, etc.

Table 5.14A
Private Equity New Funds Raised, Within Regressions

Independent Variables	Dependent Variables			
	1 Private Equity New Funds Raised w/o gov't funds	2 Private Equity New Funds Raised w/o gov't funds	3 Private Equity New Funds Raised	4 Private Equity New Funds Raised
IPOs	0.0736[a]	0.0509[a]	0.0617[b]	0.0344
	(2.188)	(2.109)	(1.819)	(1.218)
Lagged IPOs	0.0721[a]		0.0632[a]	
	(2.355)		(2.043)	
Private Pension Fund growth	-0.0002	-0.00009	-0.0002	-0.00007
	(-0.388)	(-0.479)	(-0.481)	(-0.299)
Market capitalization growth	0.00007	-0.00002	0.000002	0.00007
	(0.234)	(-0.092)	(0.006)	(0.235)
GDP growth	0.0026	0.0023	0.0003	0.0039
	(0.585)	(1.048)	(0.064)	(1.181)
Constant	0.0004[c]	0.0006[a]	0.0006[a]	0.0007[a]
	(1.607)	(3.839)	(2.527)	(3.139)
R-Squared	0.2060	0.0504	0.1448	0.0450

Within regression of 14 countries. The dependent variables are new funds raised for private equity (i.e., venture capital and buyouts) with and without government funds, divided by average GDP. The independent variables are (1) IPOs divided by average GDP; (2) Lagged IPOs; (3) Percentage change in Private Pension funds; (4) Percentage change in Market capitalization; (5) Percent change in GDP. T-statistics for coefficients in parentheses.

a = Significant at 1% level, b = Significant at 10% level, c = Significant at 15% level, d = Significant at 20% level

It is surprising that the coefficient on IPOs in the early stage investment specification of Table 5.10 is not significantly different from zero. This implies that countries with higher levels of IPOs do not have significantly higher levels of early stage venture investments as well. This is particularly puzzling in light of our results later on, in Table 5.13, which show that early stage investments are sensitive to IPOs over time. Since IPOs are significant in the fixed effects, within regression specification of Table 5.13, it is likely that we have not identified all the variables which affect early stage venture capital in the between regression. Another signal that we do not have all relevant variables is that the

Table 5.14B
Private Equity New Funds Raised, Within Regressions

Independent Variables	Dependent Variables	
	1 Private Equity New Funds Raised w/o gov't funds	3 Private Equity New Funds Raised
IPOs	0.0731[b] (1.976)	0.0786[a] (2.110)
Lagged IPOs	-0.0078 (-0.206)	-0.0083 (-0.217)
Private Pension Fund growth	-0.0004 (-0.897)	-0.0004 (-0.898)
Private Pension Fund levels	0.0036[a] (2.552)	0.0036[a] (2.576)
Market capitalization growth	-0.0001 (-0.275)	-0.00006 (-0.179)
GDP growth	0.0036 (0.804)	0.0031 (0.684)
Constant	-0.0002 (-0.600)	-0.0002 (-0.545)
R-Squared	0.3426	0.3251

Within regression of 14 countries. The dependent variables are new funds raised for private equity (i.e., venture capital plus buyouts) with and without government funds, divided by average GDP. The independent variables are (1) IPOs divided by average GDP; (2) Lagged IPOs; (3) Percentage change in Private Pension funds; (4) Percentage change in Market capitalization; (5) Percentage change in GDP. T-statistics for coefficients in parentheses.

a = Significant at 1% level, b = Significant at 10% level, c = Significant at 15% level, d = Significant at 20% level

R-squareds for early stage investments, with a range of 0.15 to 0.68 (Table 5.10), are much lower than the R-squareds for venture capital investment, which range from 0.49 to 0.71. One variable that might account for some of the unexplained variation is the amount of trade sales that take place. Trade sales are another exit mechanism, in addition to IPOs. We do not, however, at present have a measure for the prevalence of trade sales.

When we consider new funds raised for all private equity endeavors in Table 5.11A and Table 5.11B, we find, as we found for venture capital investments, that IPOs have a positive and significant coefficient. As was the case for venture capital investments, the explanatory power of our regressions is quite high, with R-squareds ranging from 0.82 to 0.87. Since we are considering funds raised for projects that range in size and riskiness across a broad spectrum, a variable that affects smaller, riskier ventures such as labor market rigidity, does not have a significant coefficient.

The coefficients on pension fund levels and growth rates are not statistically significant. We think that this is due, in part, to the fact that pension funds are regulated differently in the sample countries. The regulations hypothesis is supported by the evidence in Tables 5.14A and 5.14B, which show that, once fixed effects are taken into account, pension fund levels do have a positive and significant impact on new funds raised.

In all regressions, contrary to our expectation, the coefficients on GDP and market capitalization growth are not statistically significant. The absence of significance on our macro-economic variable, GDP growth, underscores the importance of IPOs as the main explanatory factor for venture capital and private equity investments.

Within Regression Results

The within regressions allow us to understand how variation across time in the explanatory variables affects venture capital, early stage investments, and new fund flows. Table 5.12 reports the results of the within regression of venture capital investments on IPOs, lagged IPOs, market capitalization growth and GDP growth. The current level of IPOs has a positive, significant coefficient, emphasizing, once again, the importance of IPOs. The other variables are statistically insignificant.

Table 5.13 reports the results of the within regression for early stage investments. IPOs have a positive effect on the level of early stage investments from year to year. Thus, even though the average level of IPOs does not affect the amount of early stage investments (as we saw in Table 5.10), early stage investments are still affected by yearly fluctuations in the amount of IPOs.

Tables 5.14A and 5.14B report results on within regressions of new funds raised. IPOs are again strongly significant with a positive sign. Lagged IPOs are also positive and statistically significant in Specifications 1 and 3 of Table 5.14A. Table 5.14B shows that private pension fund levels have a positive and significant coefficient, as expected. Again, the implications of these results indicate the omission of an individual country effect in the between regressions which is being picked up in the fixed effect regression.

DESCRIPTIVE ANALYSIS

In addition to the statistically measurable factors of the previous section, specific details of institutions, regulation, and culture also affect venture capital. For this reason, we include a study of government programs for venture capital, as well as brief case studies on venture capital in Germany and Israel. In Germany, venture capital has grown a lot. However, it has still not reached the level of significance that it has in the US or the UK. Israel, by contrast, is an example of successful venture capital development outside of the US. In 1993, new funds raised (per mil of GDP) in Israel exceeded those of any other country within our sample.

The Role of Government Programs

Government schemes for assisting private equity vary widely, from providing legal infrastructure to establishing funds that invest directly in private equity projects. We examine some of the larger government programs, and show how they influence private equity flows.

Getting the basic legal and tax structures into place appears to be an important factor in aiding the development of private equity funds. For example, the US and the UK, which have good basic regulations, have high levels of private equity and venture capital investments as a percentage of GDP. Austria, on the other hand, lies on the opposite extreme of this spectrum. With no special legal structure for private equity firms and no tax or other incentives aimed at the industry, private equity investment languishes and shows no sign of growth in the near future.

Portugal furnishes another example of the importance of providing an appropriate legal environment for private equity. In 1986, when Portugal had even lower levels of private equity investment (again measured as a proportion of GDP) than Austria, the Portuguese government created a new type of corporate structure, the venture capital corporation. These venture capital corporations were granted a number of tax benefits as follows:[8]

- Exemption from the new company incorporation tax
- Exemption from income tax and other taxes during the year of incorporation and the three following years
- After this period, deduction from tax of the profits appropriated to reserves and reinvested in venture capital projects during the following three years

As a consequence, private equity investments in Portugal increased dramatically (by a factor of 38) between 1986 and 1987.

In addition, growth of private equity in Portugal benefited from direct government funding. Through a variety of government agencies (the most important being the two EC supported regional development agencies NORDEPIP and SULDEPIP), the Portuguese government contributed strongly to the growth in private equity funds in the early 1990s. In 1992, government agencies contributed Esc 460 million (US$ 3.1 million) to new funds raised, or 15 percent of the total. By 1994, this figure had grown to Esc 12.8 billion (US$ 80.5 million), which represented 57 percent of new funds raised. Thus, the large increase in government financing was met by a similarly large increase in private funds. The increase in private funding appears sustainable, independent of continued large government programs. Thus, when government funding decreased from Esc 12.8 billion (US$ 80.5 million) in 1994 to Esc 2 billion (US$ 13.4 million) in 1995, an increase in bank funding from Esc 8.9 billion (US$ 59.5 million) to Esc 13.7 billion (US$ 91.7 million) made up much of the shortfall.[9]

In Norway, government funded private equity investments appear to have been a strong factor involved in rebuilding private equity after the banking crisis of the late 1980s. In 1989, Norway's private equity market bottomed out with only NKr 8 million (US$ 1.2 million) in investments (less than 10 percent of the level of the previous year). The resurgence in the industry in 1990 (when NKr 392 million (US$ 66.4 million) was invested) is, according to the EVCA, in part a consequence of a NKr 800 million (US$ 120.9 million) program launched by the government in 1989 as a way of strengthening the Norwegian venture capital industry.[10]

In 1993, the Norwegian State Industrial and Regional Development Fund was started. This marked a transition point in the government's share of venture capital investing. From 1993 to 1995, government source investments increased from NKr 120 million (US$ 16 million) , which constituted approximately one third of total investments, to NKr 535 million (US$ 84.7 million), or 50 percent of private equity investments. Furthermore, the government's involvement appears to have spurred other types of investors, as total investment moved from NKr 350 million (US$ 46.6 million) to NKr 990 million (US$ 156.7 million) over the same period of time.[11]

Governments can also play a strong role in influencing the growth of other sources of funds. For example, Ireland experienced a large surge in new funds raised as a consequence of a government-recommended increase in private equity investments by pension funds. A commitment of IR £ 50 million (US$ 70.5 million) boosted new funds raised considerably, from IR £ 23 million (US$ 32.4 million) in 1993 to IR £ 150 million (US$ 232.1 million) in 1994.[12]

Similarly, in the US around 1980, a large flow of new funds in venture capital was unleashed with changes in the Employment Retirement Income Securities ACT (ERISA), that permitted venture capital investing for pension funds.[13] In Australia, a similar measure was undertaken in 1985, when the Reserve Bank changed its rules to allow banks to make equity investments in small and medium sized enterprises.[14] The Italian government has also recently given pension funds permission to invest in privately held small and medium sized enterprises.[15] In Finland, banks and pension funds were also encouraged to invest in venture capital and in 1995, the share of these institutions in total venture capital raised went to 79%, up from 20% in 1994.[16]

While government funding of private equity is minimal in the UK, government support of the industry occurs through the legislative structure of venture capital. The UK incentive schemes are:[17]

- Venture Capital Trust (VCT): VCTs provide income tax relief on investments and capital gains tax deferral in the case of capital reinvestment.

- Enterprise Investment Schemes (EIS): The EIS, successor program to the Business Expansion Scheme, provides up-front tax relief on investments, along with relief from capital taxation.

- Small Firms Loan Guarantee Scheme (SFLGS): SFLGS was introduced in 1981. Under this scheme, 41,000 loans were made between 1986 and 1996.

- Share option schemes, which allow innovative and precisely tailored incentive compensation plans to be implemented.

- Direct financing through grants and awards is also available. These programs, however, are fairly small. Thus, for example, two of the large technology-oriented programs distribute only £ 50 million (US$ 75 million) per year.

Another example of government involvement in a mature private equity market is the Netherlands. Government involvement in the Netherlands is still significant, but it is declining. The nominal figure for public investments has not changed substantially since the early 1990s, but its overall importance has declined, as the industry has grown. Thus in 1992, public sector investments were DFl 65 million (US$ 35.8 million) compared to DFl 55 million (US$ 34.3 million) in 1995. As a share of total investments, however, the public sector commitment dropped from 12 percent to 6 percent over the same time period.[18]

Furthermore, the Netherlands government has scaled back its venture capital commitments in other ways. The guarantee scheme for private venture capital companies launched in 1981[19] was a cornerstone of government support. Under this scheme, the government covered up to 50 percent of losses incurred by venture capital companies. This scheme was reduced in 1990, and discontinued at the end of 1995. However, the reduction of government support programs for venture capital has not reduced the size of the venture capital industry in the Netherlands. On the contrary, over the period from 1990 to 1995, private equity investments as a percentage of GDP grew from .11 percent to .15 percent. Given its level of maturity, the Dutch private equity industry was capable of maintaining its growth, despite the gradual withdrawal of government support.

Thus, whether we consider the legal and tax environment, loss guarantees, direct expenditures, or government encouragement of investment, it is clear that the government can play an important role in the development of private equity. Mature venture capital industries are quite capable of maintaining healthy levels even after this support is withdrawn.

Israel Venture Capital Case Study

Between 1988 and 1992, Israel's venture capital industry was still in its infancy with only one active venture capital fund of US$ 30 million. At this time, the major suppliers of capital to emerging companies were large established investment companies belonging to holding groups such Hapolain, IDB, Leumi, Israel Corp., Koor, Clal and Elron Groups.

In 1992, the Likud government began to promote the venture capital industry. It set up the Yozma venture capital program to provide financing for venture capital funds and to invest directly in companies. Yozma also encouraged foreign and local corporations to coinvest in high technology startups. In 1993, Yozma provided US$ 100 million to establish nine venture capital funds. By 1996, Israel's venture capital industry, which had raised more than US$ 1 billion, had experienced such phenomenal growth that the government decided to exit the market. However, to continue to foster its venture capital industry, the Israeli government enacted a temporary legislation allowing tax-free investing in Israeli venture capital funds by foreign venture funds which had tax-free status in their home countries. Currently, there are thirty-two venture capital funds with a total of US$ 500 million invested which represents 50 percent of raised capital.

Another attribute which fostered the growth of Israeli's venture capital industry is Israel's favorable taxation laws for individual investors. For persons not in the business of trading securities, capital gains on sales of securities on the Tel Aviv Stock Exchange (TASE) or securities of Israeli companies listed on recognized foreign exchanges are exempt from capital gains taxes in Israel. For individual residents, dividends are taxed at a maximum of 25 percent and interest is taxed at a maximum of 45 percent. Furthermore, some resident corporations receive a tax break on dividends. Finally, foreign investors face a maximum tax rate of 25 percent on dividends and interest. These laws made investing in equity securities extremely attractive which, in turn, produced a vibrant equity securities market. For reasons mentioned earlier, this provides a conducive environment for venture capital.

A record number of Israeli firms have successfully gone public. Some recent examples are M-Systems, Gilat Satellite, Mercury Interactive and DSP Group. The TASE is by far the strongest Middle East capital market with 654 listed companies in 1995. Total equity market capitalization as of December 1995 was US $37 billion, approximately 42 percent of Israel's GDP. Between 1991 and 1995, Israel's growth in market value was 589 percent in local currency. At the same time, Israel's economy had been very strong with GDP growth averaging 5.5 percent per year since 1991.

Initial public offerings for Israeli companies are not limited to TASE. In 1996, approximately fifty Israeli companies raised US$ 1.5 billion on US exchanges. In addition, trade sales are a very popular exit mechanism for venture capital startups. In 1995, foreign companies acquired a significant number of Israeli startups. Some recent examples are America-on-Line's acquisition of Ubique, Boston Scientific's acquisition of Medinol and Intel's acquisition of Shamy.

Most portfolio companies in Israel's venture capital funds are in the early stage with an average company age of approximately 1.5–2 years. Currently, Israeli venture capital funds are primarily invested in technology companies such as telecommunications, data communications, industrial electronic equipment, software, multimedia and medical technology.

The bulk of these startup companies were founded by scientists and engineers who left their previous jobs to start their own companies. Also, the immigration of many skilled scientists and researchers from the former Soviet Union fueled Israel's boom in technology research. Venture capitalists are especially attracted to these R&D startups because many of these new enterprises received grants from the Office of the Chief Scientist (OCS) of the Ministry of Industry and Trade. The OCS administers the Law for Encouragement of Industrial Research and Development which targets developing science intensive industry and expands the technology infrastructure of the state. The OCS's 1995 annual budget was US$ 370 million, up from US$ 110 million in 1990. Currently, it supports close to one thousand companies.

Finally, the BIRD Foundation (Binational Industrial Research and Development) promotes US/Israeli corporate partnership investments in Israeli high technology startups. The average budget is US$ 1 million over a 12–15 month period. BIRD typically provides half of all R&D expenses, but does not take an equity position in the enterprise. Instead, BIRD receives 150 percent repayment from successful projects. Currently, BIRD invests $114 mm in 391 different projects.

The venture capital industry in Israel is becoming a significant part of the country's economy. Several factors have contributed to its success. While the government has played an important role in nurturing the industry, Israel's strong equity markets, and cultural and institutional factors, have allowed venture capital to prosper.

Germany Venture Capital Case Study

Germany's tradition of government support for the business sector dates back to the post-WWII programs dedicated to rebuilding industry. While these programs bolstered the growth of small to medium sized companies in general, they did not focus on venture capital specifically.[20]

One of Germany's most important small and medium enterprise programs is the European Recovery Program (ERP) which was started in 1947. It focuses on growing small businesses, primarily by providing low interest loans. ERP funds are disbursed by the Deutsche Ausgleichsbank (German Bank for Compensation) and the Deutsche Bank fuer Wiederaufbau (German bank for Reconstruction).

The ERP also supports research and development programs, as do state and regionally administered funds. In addition to the federally funded and administered programs, the states also have programs intended to support small and medium-sized businesses. Most of these programs emphasize interest rate or loan subsidies to existing businesses, and do not therefore contribute much to the development of startups. Many of the programs weigh non-profit-maximizing objectives, such as labor market or environmental considerations, quite heavily.

Kapitalbeteiligungsgesellschaften (Equity Stock Companies) were initiated in the 1950s and 1960s as yet another government institution intended to foster growth in small and medium-sized companies. Kapitalbeteiligungsgesellschaften (KBGs) are owned and funded by banks and state governments. Depending on whether they are public or private, the KBGs are more or less profit oriented. They provide equity or near-equity to established small firms that require financing for expansion purposes. KBGs are regulated with respect to their portfolio holdings, and for this reason tend to shy away from risky startup ventures. KBG investments are very hands-off. The KBGs provide little management supervision or support even though they might be involved with a company for up to eight years.

Until the early 1970s, there was no institutional structure available in Germany for the support of more risky startup ventures. When, in the 1970s, Germany's economic growth started to slow, consideration was given to how more growth could be generated in the small business sector. This led to the founding of Germany's first venture capital company, the Deutsche Gesellschaft fur Wagniskapital (German Society for Venture Capital, WFG).

The founding of the WFG marked the beginning of modern venture capital in Germany. Its members were a group of 29 German financial institutions. Government involvement in the project was significant. The government agreed to cover 75 percent of capital losses, and also offered the prospect of generous assistance to cover operating expenses, should the need arise.

While it initially focused on startup enterprises, the WFG shifted emphasis somewhat in the early 1980s, when its funds were divided equally among startups—companies earning DM 1 to 10 million (US$ 0.6 to 6 million) per year—and companies earning between DM 20 and 50 million (US$ 11.4 to 28.6 million).

In 1984, the WFG was restructured. The emphasis shifted toward later stage investments, and the number of partners was reduced to five. The specific industry focus (on high technology) from earlier years was abandoned, and non-technology investments came to represent a larger portion of the portfolio. Involvement in management decisions was still fairly limited.

In 1988, the WFG underwent another organizational change. Deutsche Bank, one of the partners in the WFG venture, bought out the other partners and integrated the WFG into its own subsidiary.

Other players gradually entered the scene. The initial entrants all had government backing. The second venture capital firm to enter the scene was the Hannover Finanz GmbH, in 1979. The third venture capital firm appeared in 1982: the Landesfonds des Landes Berlin. In 1983, eight new companies entered the growing field of competitors. By 1995, the German Venture Capital Association had over 100 members.

From 1989 to 1995, Germany had a program called Beteiligungskapital fur Junge Technologieunternehmen (Equity Participation for Young Technology Companies, BJTU),[21] administered by a subsidiary of the government owned Deutsche Ausgleichsbank. This was a co-investment scheme which gave the owner of the business the option of buying out the government share at a premium over the initial investment. If the company did not fare well, the founder was given the option of selling his share to the government at a discount to book value.

A successor was created to the popular BJTU program. The Beteiligungs-kapital fur Kleine Technologieunternehmen (Equity Participation for Small Technology Companies, BTU) was created in 1995, and slated to last through 2000.[22] The BTU focuses on new firms. BTU funds will only be brought in at a level that matches the investment of a private investor. The program also contains a guarantee scheme which covers up to 50 percent of losses to the private investor.

The institutional structures in place in Germany over the 1980s and, to a lesser extent, the 1990s have hindered the development of a venture capital industry on the scale of the UK or the US. The tax system in Germany does not favor venture capital investments by corporations. They cannot obtain a capital gains tax rates reduction. Corporate investments are taxed at the 56 percent corporate tax rate. Trade taxes and capital transaction taxes provide an additional burden.

In 1987, the Geregelter Markt was established as a means to provide an exit mechanism for startup firms. The other two markets already available in Germany at this time, the Amtlicher Handel (main stock market) and the Tele-fonverkehr (an unregulated market similar to the US OTC market), did not provide a sufficiently liquid exit mechanism. However, listing companies on the Geregelter Markt is still not easy, and is subject to stringent requirements. The companies that satisfy these criteria tend to do well, but only a small number of companies can qualify. In 1995 plans were introduced to provide a new exchange, called the Neuer Markt, which would offer young and fast-growing companies a way to raise capital.

Germany has also experimented with regulatory incentives for venture capital. In 1987, Unternehmensbeteiligungsgesellschaften (Societies for Enterprise Participation, UBGs) were introduced, which benefit from a somewhat more favorable tax status than other types of investment vehicles. The pace of regulatory change increased in the 1990s, but still failed to introduce sweeping changes to the system. Regulations for public promoted venture capital companies were loosened in 1991. In 1994, the operating environment for UBGs was improved.

Despite government programs intended to encourage venture capital, venture capital in Germany is still relatively insignificant. New and early stage investments as a percentage of GDP were only 0.0063 in 1995. Part of the problem in Germany appears to be both a cultural and institutional[23] aversion to risk taking. While some recent success stories[24] on the German venture capital market indicate that this might be changing, Germany has still not evolved into a hotbed of venture capital activity.

CONCLUSION

Private equity and venture capital markets have been subject to strong cyclical fluctuations over the years. Bygrave and Timmons (1992) describe several cycles that have marked the US venture capital experience. A very slow start in the 1940s eventually led to a boom in the 1960s. A downturn through most of the 1970s gave way to another successful period in the 1980s. A brief but sharp downturn at the start of the 1990s has been followed by another boom. The experience outside the US has been marked by similar ups and downs, albeit over a shorter period of time, stretching back to the 1970s. We have compiled a statistical track record that allows us to not only understand these swings over time, but that also gives us insight into the differences in private equity and venture capital across countries.

We show that, over time, IPOs are the main force behind the cyclical swings in venture capital. This result confirms the conventional wisdom on venture capital. We also discover a surprising result, which is that early and later stage venture capital investments are affected quite differently by the determinants of venture capital. Over time, IPOs explain less of the year to year fluctuations in early stage than in later stage investments. Our finding across countries is even more surprising: While later stage venture capital investments respond strongly to different levels of IPOs across countries, early stage investments are unaffected.

These results point to the need for further research focusing on early stage venture capital investments, and reinforce the notion that the distinct stages of venture capital are fundamentally different. We believe that there are several factors that are determinants of early, but not later, stage venture capital. One of these factors which we have been able to identify is labor market rigidities. Labor market rigidities affect variation in early stage venture capital across countries, but do not explain variation in later stage venture capital.

Given the importance of IPOs it is surprising that venture capitalists in countries with underdeveloped IPO markets do not avail themselves of the more developed IPO markets in countries like the US. This strategy of bringing companies to the US for the purpose of an IPO has been pursued successfully by the Israeli venture capital industry. A number of Israeli firms have had IPOs on the NASDAQ. It is not clear why venture capitalists in other countries have not pursued a similar strategy.

There still appears to be a very strong home bias in the venture capital industry in general. This is expressed in two ways. First, venture capitalists tend to invest in their home country. The costs of monitoring distant companies (Lerner 1995) can at least partially explain why the home bias might affect investments. Second, venture capitalists also seek to exit their investments in the home country. This can again be partially explained by the time and effort it takes to sell a business. An IPO in a foreign country involves more cost and effort than an IPO in the home country.

The additional costs incurred do not appear very high, and are unlikely to be as high as the monitoring costs incurred by investing in a foreign country. There may also be certain fixed costs associated with exiting through a non-domestic IPO. Once the barrier is breached, as it clearly is the case with Israel's many successful IPOs in the US market, additional IPOs might become easy to arrange. For venture capital industries that have not yet had many foreign IPOs, as is the case with Germany's, it might still be very costly to arrange these transactions. Given the importance of IPOs and the apparent solution for low IPO countries of listing on markets like the NASDAQ, the question of why there is such a strong home bias needs to be further addressed.

Our results on private pension fund levels and growth rates point to a need for a greater understanding of cross-country determinants. In our analysis of new private equity funds raised, we find that pension fund levels are significant over time, but insignificant across countries. We believe that some of these additional determinants, which would help explain differences across countries, can be found in regulatory and policy structures.

Our qualitative analysis shows that government policies can act as catalysts to galvanize private fund flows and investments. On a more quantitative, statistical level, our study of government involvement has produced some interesting results. We show that, compared to private venture capital, government-funded venture capital is less sensitive to IPOs across countries. Once again, the story for early stage investing is different: The difference in sensitivity of government-backed and non-government-backed early stage investments to IPOs drops by half in some specifications. These differences are only present when we compare across countries. Over time, the differences between the sensitivity of private and public venture capital to IPOs are negligible.

Our observation that government-backed venture capital is less sensitive to IPOs across countries than non-government-backed venture capital indicates a direction for future research. Governments appear to be willing to finance early stage projects that would not be funded privately. To evaluate the usefulness of the government role, it is important to understand the economic value of these projects. If more data on returns were available, they could be used to better understand the role of government in venture capital.

By providing an empirical analysis of private equity and venture capital across countries, we have been able to confirm the value of having a well-functioning exit mechanism in the form of a strong IPO market. We have also shown that some segments of the venture capital market behave quite differently from others. Our findings regarding the need for a more differentiated approach to venture capital are especially important, in that they concern two areas—early stage investing and government involvement—that are of particular interest to policy makers today.

NOTES

1. *Seventh Annual Economic Impact of Venture Capital Study* (1997), National Venture Capital Association, Venture One Corporation, Coopers & Lybrand L.L.P.

2. Represents percent of capital committed to independent private funds. Does not include SBIC, family groups or corporate affiliates. Venture Capital Yearbook, 1996.

3. EVCA Yearbook

4. EVCA Yearbook.

5. Includes LBOs, Acquisitions, Bridge Loans and Public Purchases. Source: Venture Capital Journal, July 1996

6. *The Economist (1/15/97)*, "Venture Capitalists: A Really Big Adventure."

7. The Employment Outlook, OECD publishes labor turnover rates which measure the movements of individuals into jobs (hirings) and out of jobs (separations) over a particular period. In addition, it mentions that labor tenure is correlated with labor turnover.

8. EVCA Yearbook

9. ibid.

10. ibid.

11. ibid.

12. ibid.

13. O'Shea (1996)

14. ibid.

15. ibid.

16. ibid.

17. Bank of England: The Financing of Technology-Based Small Firms

18. EVCA Yearbook

19. ibid.

20. The following summary of German venture capital relies heavily on Harrison (1990) The West German Venture Capital Market

21. O'Shea 1996

22. ibid.

23. An example of an institutional barrier is the ban on a person becoming a director again, if a company goes bankrupt.

24. *The Economist,* June 28, 1997

25. 1988 figures for Canada, Finland and Norway. 1992 Estimated figures for Australia and Japan. 1993 estimated figures for New Zealand.

26. 1994 estimated figures for Australia and New Zealand. 1993 estimated figures for Japan. 1994 figures for Portugal.

27. 1989 figures for Australia and Japan. 1988 figures for Finland and Norway. 1993 figures for New Zealand 1990 figures for Israel.

28. 1994 figures for Australia, New Zealand and US and 1993 figures for Japan.

REFERENCES

Acs, Zoltan J. and David B. Audretsch. "New-Firm Startups, Technology, and Macro-economic Fluctuations." *Small Business Economics*, Vol. 6, 1994.

Black, Bernard and Ronald Gilson. "Venture Capital and the Structure of Capital Markets: Banks versus Stock Markets." *Journal of Financial Economics*, Vol. 47, 1998.

Bygrave, William D. and Jeffrey A. Timmons. *Venture Capital at the Crossroads*. Boston, MA: Harvard Business School Press, 1992.

The Economist. Venture Capitalists: A Really Big Adventure. 1/15, 1997.

Edwards, Jeremy and Klaus Fischer. *Banks, Finance and Investment in Germany*. Cambridge University Press, 1994.

Evan, D.S., Jovanovich, B. "An estimated model of entrepreneurial choice under liquidity constraints." *Journal of Political Economy*, Vol. 97, No. 4, 1989.

Fama, Eugene. "What's Different about Banks?" *Journal of Monetary Economics*, 1985: 15.

Gompers, Paul. "Optimal Investment, Monitoring, and the Staging of Venture Capital." *Journal of Finance* L (5), 1995.

Gompers, Paul. "The Rise and Fall of Venture Capital." *Business and Economic History*, Vol. 23. No. 2, 1994.

Gompers, Paul and Josh Lerner. "The Use of Covenants: An Empirical Analysis of Venture Partnership Agreements." *The Journal of Law and Economics* 1996.

Hardymon, G. Felda, Mark J. DeNino and Malcolm S. Salter. "When Corporate Venture Capital Doesn't Work." *Harvard Business Review*, Vol. 114, 1983.

Harrison, Elizabeth M. *The West German Venture Capital Market: An Analysis of Its Market Structure and Economic Performance*. Peter Lang, 1990.

Holmes, Thomas J., and James A. Schmitz Jr. "A Theory of Entrepreneurship and Its Application to the Study of Business Transfers." *Journal of Political Economy*, Vol. 98, 1990, pp. 265–94.

Hurry, Dileep, Adam T. Miller and E. H. Bowman. "Calls on High-Technology: Japanese Exploration of Venture Capital Investments in the United States." *Strategic Management Journal*, Vol. 13, 1991.

Jensen, Michael C. "Presidential Address: The Modern Industrial Revolution, Exit and the Failure of Internal Control Systems." *Journal of Finance*, Vol. 48, No. 3, 1993.

La Porta, Rafael, Florencio Lopez-de-Silanes, Andrei Shleifer and Robert W. Vishny. "Law and Finance." *Journal of Finance*, forthcoming, 1996.

Lerner, Josh. "The Government as Venture Capitalist: The Long-Run Impact of the SBIR Program." NBER Working Paper, 1996.

Lerner, Josh. *The European Association of Security Dealers: November 1994*, Harvard Business School Case Study, 1995a.

Lerner, Josh. "Venture Capitalists and the Oversight of Private Firms." *The Journal of Finance* L, Vol. 1, March, 1995b.

Mayer, C. "New Issues in Corporate Finance." *European Economic Review*, Vol. 32, 1988.

Myers, S. and N. Majluf. "Corporate Financing and Investment Decisions When Firms Have Information That Investors Do Not Have." *Journal of Financial Economics*, Vol. 13, 1984.

National Venture Capital Association. *Seventh Annual Economic Impact of Venture Capital Study.* Venture One Corporation, Coopers & Lybrand L.L.P, 1997.

OECD. *Employment Outlook.* Chap 5, Draft, 1997.

O'Shea, Margaret. "Government Programs for Venture Capital." OECD Working Group on Innovation and Technology Policy, 1996.

Roe, Mark J. "Political and Legal Restraints on Ownership and Control of Public Companies." *Journal of Financial Economics,* Vol. 27, 1990.

Sahlman, William A. "Insights from the American Venture Capital Organization." Working Paper, 1991.

Sahlman, William A. "The Structure and Governance of Venture-Capital Organizations." *Journal of Financial Economics,* Vol. 27, 1990.

Siegel, Robin, Eric Siegel and Ian C. MacMillan. "Corporate Venture Capitalists: Autonomy, Obstacles, and Performance." *Journal of Business Venturing,* Vol. 3, 1988.

Sykes, Hollister B. "Corporate Venture Capital: Strategies for Success." *Journal of Business Venturing,* Vol. 5, 1990.

Venture Economics. "Exiting Venture Capital Investments." 1988.

Wright, Mike and Robbie, Ken. "Venture Capitalists, Unquoted Equity Investment Appraisal and the Role of Accounting Information." *Accounting and Business Research,* Vol. 26, no. 2, 1996.

FURTHER READING

Asian Venture Capital Journal. *The Guide to Venture Capital in Asia,* 1991.

Acs, Zoltan J. and David B. Audretsch. *Innovation and Technological Change: An International Comparison.* Harvester Wheatsheaf, England, 1991.

Acs, Zoltan J. and David B. Audretsch. "Innovation in Large and Small Firms: An Empirical Analysis." *American Economic Review,* Vol. 78, No. 4, 1988.

Bank of England. *The Financing of Technology-Based Small Firms.* October 1996.

Brav, Alon and Paul Gompers. " 'Myth or Reality?' The Long-run Underperformance of Initial Public Offerings: Evidence from Venture- and Nonventure-capital-backed Companies." *Journal of Finance,* Vol. 52, No. 2, December 1997.

Cohen, Wesley M. and Richard C. Levin. "Empirical Studies of Innovation and Market Structure." *Handbook of Industrial Organization* 2, Chapter 18, 1989.

EVCA. *European Venture Capital Journal.* 1986–1996.

Freear, John E. Sohl and William E. Wetzel, Jr. "Angels: Personal Investors in the Venture Capital Market." *Entrepreneurship and Regional Development,* 1995: 7.

Gompers, Paul. "Grandstanding in the Venture Capital Industry." *Journal of Financial Economics* 42, 1996:1.

Gompers, Paul. "Venture Capital Distributions: Short-run and Long-run Reactions." *Journal of Finance,* forthcoming, 1998.

Grisebach, Rolf. *Innovations-Finanzierung durch Venture Capital.* Verlag V. Florentz GmbH, 1989.

GT Management, *The GT Guide to World Equity Market.* Euromoney Publications Ltd., 1995.

Hellwig, Martin, "Banking, Financial Intermediation and Corporate Finance." Chapter 3, *European Financial Integration.* Cambridge University Press.

Holmes, Thomas J., and James A. Schmitz Jr. "On the Turnover of Business Firms and Business Managers." *Journal of Political Economy,* Vol. 103, 1995: 5.

Holtz-Eakin, Douglas, David Joulfaian, and Harvey Rosen, "Entrepreneurial Decisions and Liquidity Constraints." *Rand Journal of Economics,* Vol. 25, No. 2, Summer 1994.

International Finance Corporation. *Emerging Stock Markets Factbook,* 1995.

International Monetary Fund. *International Financial Statistics Yearbook,* 1996.

"Israel Suspends Capital Gains Tax." *Venture Capital Journal.* Securities Data Publishing, Inc, 1996.

Jensen, Michael C. "Active Investors, LBOs, and the Privatization of Bankruptcy." *Journal of Applied Corporate Finance,* 1989.

Jensen, Michael C. and W. H. Meckling. "Theory of the Firm: Managerial Behavior, Agency Costs and Ownership Structure." *Journal of Financial Economics,* Vol. 3, 1976.

Kester, W. Carl and Timothy A. Luehrman. "The LBO Association as a Relational Investment Regime: Clinical Evidence from Clayton, Dubilier & Rice, Inc." Working Paper, 1993.

Kroszner, Randall S. "The Evolution of Universal Banking and Its Regulation in Twentieth Century America." Forthcoming in *Financial System Design: Universal Banking Considered,* 1995.

Lerner, Josh. "The Syndication of Venture Capital Investments." *Financial Management,* Vol. 23, No. 3, 1994a.

Lerner, Josh. "Venture Capitalists and the Decision to Go Public." *Journal of Financial Economics,* Vol. 35, 1994b.

Marcus, Amy Dockser. "Global Promise of Israeli Technology Spurs Growth of Venture Capital Funds." *The Wall Street Journal,* 04/08/1993.

OECD. *Employment Outlook,* 1994.

Ooghe, Hubert, Manigart, Sophie and Fassin, Yves. "Growth Patterns of the European Venture Capital Industry." *Journal of Business Venturing,* Vol. 6, 1991, pp. 381–404.

Pavitt, K., M. Robson and J. Townsend. "The Size Distribution of Innovating Firms in the UK: 1945–1983." *The Journal of Industrial Economics,* Vol. 35, No. 3, March 1987.

Pound, John. "Proxy Voting and the SEC: Investor Protection versus Market Efficiency." *Journal of Financial Economics,* Vol. 29, 1991.

Reinganum, Jennifer R. "The Timing of Innovation: Research, Development, and Diffusion." *Handbook of Industrial Organization* 1, 1989.

Robbie, Ken, and Wright, Mike. *Venture Capital.* Dartmouth Publishing, 1997.

Rosen, Sherwin. "Hedonic Prices and Implicit Markets: Product Differentiation in Pure Competition." *Journal of Political Economy,* Vol. 82, 1974: 1.

Securities Data Publishing. "Land of Milk and Money as Tech Ideas Flow Out of Israel, Venture Capital Pours In." *Venture Capital Journal,* 1996a.

Securities Data Publishing. *Venture Capital Journal.* Vol. 36, No. 7, 1996b.

Venture Economics. *Investment Benchmark: Venture Capital,* 1995.

Venture Economics. *Venture Capital Yearbook,* 1996.

6

The Swedish Venture Capital Industry
An Infant, Adolescent, or Grown-Up?

Dilek Çetindamar and Staffan Jacobsson

This chapter analyzes the evolution of the Swedish venture capital (VC) industry. The institutional infrastructure in the form of legal access to available savings, the incentive structure and the exit possibilities for the VC firm initially blocked the evolution of the VC industry but institutional changes initiated a catch-up process in Sweden in the 1990s. The size of the Swedish VC industry is now substantial, among the four largest in the OECD set in relation to population. A distinct structural change in the Swedish VC industry in favor of diversity is also taking place but the industry is not yet mature with respect to its competence. The key policy issues are related not only to expanding the size of the industry, but also to increasing its competence. Further institutional change is, therefore, warranted, not only in terms of tax reforms and improving the access to pension funds and other savings, but also in terms of distinct policies aiming at increasing the flow of competence to the VC industry.

INTRODUCTION

For many decades, Swedish industry has been dominated by a handful of multinational corporations, such as Volvo, ABB, Alfa Laval, SKF and Ericsson. With the growing internationalization of these firms, much attention has recently been given to the role of new technology based firms (henceforth NTBFs) as a source of industrial growth and employment. Such firms, more than other young and smaller firms, are dependent on a well functioning capital

Originally published as "The Swedish Venture Capital Industry—an Infant, Adolescent or Grown-up?" by Dilek Çetindamar Karaömerlioglu and Staffan Jacobsson, *Venture Capital*, Vol. 2, No. 2, 2000, pp. 61–88. The first author's surname changed in February 2000 and it became Dilek Çetindamar.

market for their survival and growth. Capital can be sought from a range of sources such as large customers, suppliers, banks etc. Venture capital is an additional, and a particularly interesting, source of funding as a functioning venture capital industry provides in addition to such funds, a competence which may be scarce in the NTBF. Up until recently, such a service industry hardly existed in Sweden. This presumably meant that NTBFs faced a growth constraint, which could only partly be overcome by securing capital and competence from other actors.

In the 1990s, we have witnessed a boom in the venture capital industry. This boom does not, necessarily, indicate that the growth constraint of an underdeveloped venture capital industry has disappeared. Clearly, as is well known from the literature on "infant industries" an industry can well exist without being fully mature and well functioning. The purpose of this chapter is to analyze the evolution of the Swedish venture capital industry, critically assess it with respect to its maturity and identify the key policy issues, which have a bearing on its further evolution. The chapter is organized as follows. In the next section, we provide some analytical points of departure. Later the chapter maps the evolution of the Swedish venture capital industry, analyzes the present structure of the industry and summarizes our main conclusions and draws some implications for policy.

SOME ANALYTICAL POINTS OF DEPARTURE

This section provides some analytical points of departure for our empirical study. These circle around four issues; first, what are the determinants, or driving forces, of the evolution of an industry; second; how can we analyze and measure the progress an industry makes towards maturity, third, what is the time horizon involved from the formation of an industry to the point where it has reached maturity and, fourth, what is the role of policy in the evolution of a venture capital industry?

Before we proceed with the discussion, we need to define the venture capital (henceforth VC) industry. VC is a private equity market, which has formal and informal segments. While the formal market consists of financial intermediary firms, the informal market is made up of wealthy individuals called "business angels." We focus on the formal VC industry.[1] The VC industry supplies funds for start-up firms, private medium-sized firms, firms in financial distress, and public firms seeking buy-out financing. Some researchers avoid, however, using VC for private equity firms focused on any other than start-up firms. Accordingly, in some literature, firms investing in portfolio firms which are in an earlier phase than initial public offering (IPO) are "classic VC" firms (Bygrave and Timmons 1992). In this study, we will use the term VC to refer to the private equity market as a whole, since this is the concept used both in statistics and in the bulk of the literature. Some emphasis will, however be given to the "classic" VC industry.

The Determinants of the Evolution of a VC Industry

The VC industry is a service industry, which should supply not only capital but also competence; "competent capital" is what distinguishes this part of the capital market from other parts, such as banks. A VC industry is a vehicle for channeling savings in the economy into investments in, amongst others, risky start-up firms. These savings can be of different sorts, for instance accumulated within private pension funds or within publicly run pension schemes. The VC firms typically have a quite limited time horizon for their involvement in a firm and they therefore need a mechanism for realizing any growth in value of their investments, an exit opportunity. The growth in the value of the investments is influenced by the competence of the VC firm, not only in selecting firms to invest in but also in helping the firm to develop. The skills involved are not only general management skills, but also industry and technology specific competence including the ability to connect the firm to a larger network of actors. Without access to competence, technical and industrial, competent capital can not be formed.

The institutional set-up in an economy is central to the formation of a VC industry. The institutional set-up determines the access to savings, the incentive structure and the exit possibilities. The mere existence of large savings is not enough if they are tied up in pension funds which, for legal reasons, can not be invested by VC firms, nor is money accumulated in private pension funds available to start-ups if the pension funds refrain from making the funds accessible to VC firms. In the US case, a landmark in the evolution of the VC industry was the 1979 Employee Retirement Income Security Act, which allowed pension funds to make substantial investments into venture capital firms. Hence, whereas in 1978, pension funds had supplied only 15 percent of the cumulated funds of US $424 million, by 1986, this share had increased to more than half of the cumulated funds of US $4 billion (Bygrave and Timmons 1992).

Access to savings is not sufficient for an industry to evolve. There must be incentives to invest in the VC industry. These incentives refer to the number of times profits are taxed and the rate of that tax. As shown in several studies in the US, one of the main reasons for the growth of the VC industry has been the reduction of the maximum capital gains tax rate from 49.5 percent to 28 percent in 1978, and to 20 percent in 1981 (Bygrave and Timmons 1992; Fenn et al. 1995).[2] There must also be appropriate governance forms—for example, limited partnership—which provide incentives to staff in the VC industry.

The accumulation of large savings and an appropriate incentive structure matter little, however, if there are inadequate exit mechanisms. Stock markets, in general, have a crucial role in the development of the VC industry, since they supply exits for VC investments through their portfolio firms' sale in initial public offerings. Many studies show a strong relation between stock markets and the VC industry (HBS 1994; Bygrave and Timmons 1992; Abbott and Hay 1995). The development of a VC industry in the US paralleled the developments in the stock markets, namely they first flourished in the early 1980s, then slowed down during the late 1980s and the first few years of the 1990s since when they have been growing. This was also the picture for the UK VC industry (Murray 1996). It is thought important to have particular exit opportunities for NTBFs, which require that special, segmented, markets develop. In the US, NASDAQ was established in 1971, providing such an early exit opportunity for venture capitalists.

Analyzing the Maturity of a VC Industry

Measuring the progress an industry makes towards maturity requires an appropriate conceptualization of that process. Within industrial economics, very little work has been done on the evolution of industries, with notable exceptions such as Saxenian (1994). In development economics, however, the whole debate of infant industries treats precisely this issue. In that context, a commonly held view was that the maturation of an infant industry could be conceptualized as a gradual reduction from the initially high costs of production to a point where the production costs are equal to, or below, the import price of the product. This highly simplistic view of industrial development was later modified by adding that price is not the only competitive dimension, performance also matters as does the technological change capability required to modify price/performance (i.e., develop new technology) (Jacobsson 1993).

In the context of the VC industry,[3] we would argue that there are three dimensions which are suitable for not only measuring the evolution of the VC industry but also its present maturity. These dimensions are the size of the industry and the diversity of the industry and the competence in the industry.

The *size* of the industry is a dimension which is quite self-evident. The main measure of size is the total cumulative funds raised for the private equity investments. Although it is impossible to say how much VC is optimal, it is clear that the industry must have some volume in order to fulfill its role as a supporting industry to NTBFs. The number of actors may also be important for some areas where the lead-time is very long from the initial project to market expansion. This is particularly so in the biomedical field where a project may need to be "passed on" between several VC firms.

The *diversity* of the industry is perhaps not as self-evident. The VC industry should provide adequate services to firms in a very broad range of industries and technologies. These services should also be available for all stages in the evolution of firms, from seed financing all the way to management buy-outs.[4] This presumably requires a great deal of diversity among the VC firms. These firms have to handle risks by either having a diversified portfolio or by developing deep industry/technology specific competencies in a narrow field. The latter strategy is particularly important for firms involved in a significant way in financing at an early stage where much of the uncertainty is related to the potential of the technology. Indeed, unless the VC firm is very large, it is likely that firms involved in early stage financing are more specialized than other VC firms. As Norton and Tenenbaum explain:

The knowledge base of venture capitalists include technological, market, and product expertise, as well as networks comprising experts and investors with similar interests. Venture capitalists seek to manage operating and technical risks by gaining access, by means of their reputation in their specialisation, to information flows and deal flows in networks. . . . We posit that venture capitalists that invest in firms involving the greatest amounts of technical and products risks (presumably early stage financing) should be more specialized, should have a more narrow industry focus, and may be less diversified than those who finance later stage deals. (1993: 435)

A key dimension in analyzing the maturity of the VC industry is therefore the existence of a diverse set of specialized firms covering early stage financing, although not necessarily exclusively so. Hence, the structure of a mature VC industry would include specialized as well as diversified firms where a number of the former in particular are involved in early stage financing.

As the literature on infant industries tell us, the mere existence of a diversified VC industry does not necessarily mean that it has adequate *competence.* The VC industry appears not to be subjected to international competition to the same extent as the manufacturing industry and is, therefore, largely national in nature. This means that, in principle, there may exist a large and diversified VC industry which is inefficient due to an inadequate competence.[5] There are at least three issues involved with respect to the growth of competence.

First, as mentioned previously, competence in specific industries/technologies is required to reduce risks and to mobilize networks of investors. The conventional analysis using information asymmetry or genuine lack of information as a justification of the existence of a VC industry is, therefore, inadequate. Whereas there may, of course, be a shortage of information, much of the evaluation problem rests on a lack of knowledge both how to search for information but also, and most importantly, how to assess information.

This brings us to the second issue, which is the access to competence in the wider economy. An industry/technology specific competence is, of course, not equally available in all fields as nations and regions specialize. The profile of competence is strongly path dependent and the learning of new competence is constrained by the earlier specialization profiles, implying that specialization tends to be "sticky" (Dalum *et al.* 1997). It is therefore not at all self-evident that even if incentives and financial resources are available in abundance that the necessary competence is in place in industrial/technological fields that are distant to those dominating the prevailing specialization pattern.

Shortages in competence refer also to experience of the particular context of the VC industry. Even in the US VC industry, the fast expansion of the industry in the 1980s led to the inflow of inexperienced people, with consequent failures; as the Harvard Business School (1994: 13) notes: "Many venture capitalists that received money in the 'boom' of the 1980's had little or no previous industry experience . . . experienced venture capitalists are and will be in short supply for some time." A shortage of competence constrains, of course, the rate of expansion possible, given that the VC should be competent.

Third, competence development of this type involves a process of increasing returns which favors nations which initiate experiments earlier than others. Through initial trial and error, an industrial/technological competence is built up. Some of that competence can, together with capital gained in earlier phases, be invested in new ventures via the formation of a competent capital market. This was allegedly the case of Silicon Valley in the US where some of the early and successful entrepreneurs sold off their firms and became venture capitalists (Saxenian 1994).

The Time Horizon Involved in the Formation of a VC Industry and Government Policy

The discussion above suggests that the length of the period involved in the formation of a VC industry—the learning period—can be substantial. Not only does an appropriate institutional set-up need to be in place. In addition, competence has to be formed and a diversified structure of the VC industry needs to evolve. This is expected to be a highly complex process involving firms, academia as well as government.

A prerequisite for the formation of a VC industry is that an appropriate institutional set-up should be in place. Indeed, without such an institutional set-up the learning period may well be infinite. Hence, an essential objective of policy is to shape an appropriate institutional framework. This requires insight among policy makers and patience with respect to maintaining a stable set-up. The stability may have to be maintained for a period which, perhaps, goes far beyond the expectations of policy makers. If we are to judge from the process of forming new industries, such as the Japanese automobile industry or the Korean machine tool, electronics or excavator industries, the time horizon must be decades rather than years (Jacobsson 1993).

Until the industry is mature, NTBFs will face a growth restriction. Unless society is prepared to wait for the maturation of the VC industry, compensation mechanisms have to be set in place. These may be of various types and some may already be in place. For instance, acquisitions of NTBFs by large firms are argued, in the Swedish case, to be an important, although imperfect, substitute to a functioning capital market (Karaomerlioglu and Lindholm-Dahlstrand 1999). Other mechanisms can be government participation in the capital market. This has always been substantial, even in the US. In particular, we observe a comeback of government after a regulation change in 1992 regarding the Small Business Investment Corporations (SBICs).[6] In 1997 alone, government invested about US $2.2 billion through SBICs, more than half (60 percent) being the equity investment. This is a significant amount when compared with the entire VC industry that invested around US $14 billion in the same year (SBIC, 1999).[7]

This come-back indicates that direct government participation in the capital market may not only be limited to the learning period but that a functioning venture capital market may be very difficult to develop on the basis of market forces alone (Lerner 1996). In particular, in the seed phase, the uncertainties are so great that VC firms may not invest enough to sustain a sufficiently high degree of experimentation in the economy. These were the main reasons behind both the programs launched by the European Union such as the European Seed Capital Fund Pilot Scheme (Murray 1998) and many advanced countries' specific government initiatives (Jeng and Wells 1998).

In the remaining parts of this chapter, these analytical points of departure will be used in the following manner. In the next section, the evolution of the Swedish VC industry will be analyzed. Later, the focus is on analyzing the maturity of the Swedish VC industry by analyzing its size, diversity and competence whereas the length of the learning period is discussed in the final section.

THE EVOLUTION OF THE SWEDISH VENTURE CAPITAL INDUSTRY

This section begins with a brief description of the evolution of the Swedish VC industry as shown in figure 6.1. The determinants of this evolution are then discussed restrictions to the further growth of the industry are pointed out.

A Brief Description of the Evolution of the Swedish VC Industry

In the 1970s, the Swedish economy entered a period of stagnation and industrial production fell 25 percent in the period 1973–82 (Fredriksen 1997). The Swedish government considered VC as one out of many tools to take the country out of the crisis. Hence, whereas the first semi-private VC firm had been established already in 1973,[8] the initial development of a venture capital industry was essentially done through direct government participation in the market. In particular, in the period of 1975–81, central and regional government bodies established a number of regional development corporations in areas with special unemployment problems.[9]

The first big *private* VC wave in Swedish history came when 20 private VC funds (and an additional 30 new regional and government run investment companies)[10] were established in the period of 1982 and 1984 (Olofsson and Wahlbin 1985). From 1985, however, a shakeout period followed.[11] Whereas most of the private VC firms exited the industry, a few private VC firms such

as Euroventures and Skandia Investment and government funds kept the industry alive and expanded its size. For example, in 1983, there were 13 VC
funds with a total of SEK 478 million in cumulative funds, where government
funds were 20 percent of the total. In 1987 cumulative funds reached to SEK
4 billion, where government contributed SEK 1.7 billion (Statens Industriverk
1990). A second boom period in private VC came in the mid-1990s, particularly
after 1994. The industry received a whole range of new entrants, see (figure
6.2), a process which seems to continue also after 1998.

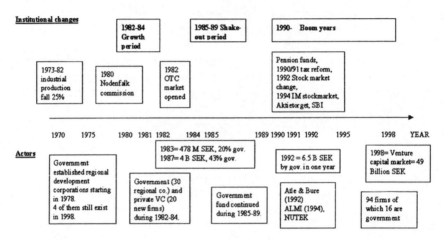

Figure 6.1 The evolution of the Swedish venture capital market

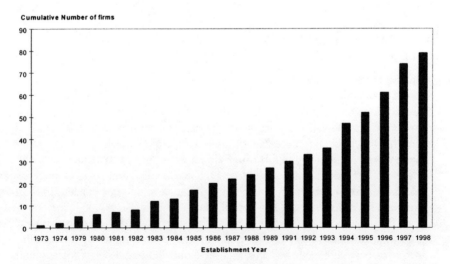

Figure 6.2 Cumulative number of firms in the Swedish venture capital industry
Source: Author's own database.

Government funds also flowed into the VC market in the 1990s.[12] In 1992, government created two investment corporations, Atle and Bure, and transferred SEK 6.5 billion to them. Government's holdings in Atle and Bure were later sold out (in 1995), only keeping about 10 percent indirectly, via its pension funds involvement in these firms (Isaksson and Cornelius 1998). Both Atle and Bure are now traded on the Stockholm stock exchange and they have become later stage investors.

Government also set up new institutions or transformed existing ones into new forms so that it could give soft money to potential entrepreneurs or NTBFs (OECD, 1998; NUTEK, 1997; Kilsved et al., 1997).[13] NUTEK (The Swedish Board for Technical and Industrial Development) expanded its programs in the 1990s to finance technical innovation at an early stage with seed capital. Support is provided in various forms such as loans, capital against royalty, or project guarantees to a maximum of 50 percent of the cost of the project. The Innovation Centre was established in 1995 and provides loans and seed capital to small firms. It also pays expenses taking place in the early stages of the innovation process, such as payments for technical and commercial licenses. Finally, Swedish Industrial Development Fund (Industrifonden) gives loans for specific projects (maximum 50 percent of total costs); capital against royalty (maximum 50 percent); credit guarantees (maximum 80 percent of the loan); and, in particular after 1996, VC in exchange for shares or convertible loans.[14]

The Determinants of the Evolution of the Swedish VC Industry

Beginning in the 1980s, and especially in the 1990s, a series of institutional changes took place, which shaped the evolution of the Swedish VC industry. We will analyze these determinants of the industry under the three categories as mentioned in previously; access to savings, incentive structure and exit possibilities.

Access to Savings: From the early 1980s, institutional investors, such as insurance companies, have been allowed to invest in start-up firms. However, pension funds were not allowed to do so until 1996 when the 6th AP fund, a government pension fund, was formed basically to supply money to the equity market in Sweden. This fund manages SEK 12 billion of which 10 percent is directly used to support the VC market. Even though the fund management does not directly invest in high tech small firms, it puts money into various VC firms' funds that are invested in start-up firms. This was a significant change in the institutional set-up as it began to open up the vast pension funds, which have been accumulated as a part of government run pension schemes in Sweden.[15] The time lag of 17 years compared to when the US released pension funds for the VC industry is especially important to note as much of the savings in Sweden are done within the framework of public pension schemes. Moreover, the money in the sixth AP fund is but a small fraction of the funds available in the pension schemes. This means that the bulk of the savings for the purpose of pensions were not and still is not, available to the VC market.

Incentive Structure: The incentive structure for the VC industry experienced important changes in the 1990s. The main change was related to the governance form of the VC, namely the establishment of limited partnerships. Interviews with venture capitalists suggest that the management of the VC firms were inexperienced investment managers in the 1980s. Large companies, which owned VC firms, assigned one or two employers from their own financial departments. In the 1990s, when limited partnerships became dominant, the industry was able to attract talented investment managers and experienced managers to become venture capitalists.

Another change in the incentive structure concerned the taxes of the revenues of both investors and management of the VC firms. A first tax reform was introduced in 1982 and was based on the suggestions of "Growth Capital" report prepared by the Nodenfalk commission which was an inquiry into the financial situation of small and medium sized companies (Timmons 1982).[16] The second and more extensive tax reform dates 1990/91. The maximum personal income tax was reduced to 55–58 percent from as high as 85 percent while the corporate tax rate was lowered to 28 percent in 1994 (OECD 1998).

Whereas there have been some changes in the Swedish tax system, they have not been adjusted to the needs of a VC industry. In particular, profits are taxed at three levels. The company pays taxes for its business income; the VC fund pays taxes for the dividends it receives and the investor pays taxes for the dividends it gets from the fund. This reduces, of course, the incentives to invest in the VC business. In contrast, in the US, limited partnerships are exempt from taxes, which means that taxes are paid only at two levels. As Bergman *et al.* (1999) show, total capital gains tax add up to 49.1 percent for investments in unlisted VC firms while it is 31 percent for investment in listed investment firms and 30 percent for direct investment in listed corporations. Hence, the tax system biases the flow of investment away from the VC industry.

Exit Possibilities: A special exit opportunity, the over-the-counter (OTC) market, was created in 1982, 11 years after the equivalent in the US. In the 1990s, three new markets for small companies were formed; AktieTorget, Stockholm Bourse Information (SBI), and Innovationsmarknaden.[17] The value of these, and the conventional stock market, as exit opportunity was enhanced in the early to mid 1980s and in the 1990s by an unprecedented boom in the stock markets. The booming and more diversified stock market in Sweden created an attractive place for firms to be listed in order to raise money and a good exit mechanism for VC firms with high-expected returns through IPO sales of their portfolio firms. This in turn developed the image of VC firms as a profitable investment tool.[18]

Concluding Remarks

The evolution (and the considerable lag behind the US, see later in this chapter) of the VC market is easily explained by the institutional set-up in Sweden which constrained the access to financial resources accumulated in the pension system; delayed the formation of adequate incentive structure and was late in developing exit mechanisms. In part, government programs compensated for the weakness in the private industry. The very considerable expansion in the VC market post 1994 can, in turn, be explained by a relaxation of some of these constraints; the improved access to savings, the diffusion of limited partnerships and a substantial improvement in exit opportunities coupled to a boom in the stock market. Yet, as the boom in the stock market fades, the remaining constraints in terms of triple taxation and access to funds in the pension system may lead to a declining activity in the VC industry in the years to come.

THE PRESENT STRUCTURE OF THE SWEDISH RISK CAPITAL INDUSTRY

In this section, we will discuss the maturity of the Swedish VC industry using the three dimensions developed in a previous section. These dimensions were size, the diversity and the competence of the industry. Two different data sources are used and introduced in the following section.

The Data

The first data source is the European Venture Capital Association (henceforth EVCA) Yearbook. As the EVCA compiles its data from its members we would expect that the procedure is standardized, and that the data is reasonably reliable. Upon closer scrutiny of the Swedish VC industry, however, it has been found that the data is questionable in two ways. First, it includes a set of actors that are not venture capital firms proper. Second, the association does not have some important firms in the industry as members. We have therefore collected our own database of 94 firms in Sweden, in contrast to the much smaller number of firms listed by EVCA. We will use this database for our analysis of the diversity of the Swedish VC industry whereas the EVCA data is used in international comparisons in the following section.

The list of VC firms in Sweden is collected from a range of sources. We started with the list of the Swedish Venture Capital Association (SVCA 1998) and expanded it by including VC firms found in a number of studies: Industrifonden study (Industrifonden, 1998), Affärsdata database (1999),[19] newspaper articles (Dagens Industri, 1997a and 1997b), and surveys (NUTEK, 1997; Isaksson, 1999; E-Chron, 1998). We also conducted an Internet search and through various links[20] reached a number of VC firms. Finally, we added a few

VC firms into our list based on case studies conducted by Ph.D. students in our department. By bringing all these data together, we assembled a gross list of 99 firms.

Having identified these firms, we collected information about their funds, investment strategies and portfolio firms through annual reports, web pages, directories, and studies mentioned above. Further, we conducted interviews with 11 of these VC firms. We interviewed general partners of the firms for about two hours. On the basis of these sources, we "cleaned," the data, see appendix 2, and ended with a list of 94 firms in our database and a solid figure for the cumulated funds in these firms.[21]

After we had gathered the list of firms and determined their size in terms of funds, we categorized them on the basis of their diversity in two dimensions: their investment phase and whether or not they are specialized. We distinguished between firms investing in early stages only, in late stages only or across stages and between specialized or non-specialized firms. The former group of firms consists of focused firms with a maximum of four investment areas (either as technology or industry, for example, medical technology or telecommunications), while the latter group of firms invests more than four areas.

This process was tedious. We gave great attention to finding the correct information about the firm's specialization area and investment phase preferences. We relied on firms' own statements if they existed, otherwise we tried to put together information gathered from the SVCA's directory classifications, NUTEK and Industriförbundet's (1999) study, and Affärsdata database.[22]

In order to pursue an analysis of the competence of the Swedish VC industry (section 4.3), we relied on three additional unique databases:

- Isaksson's study (1998, 1999) is based on a survey of 249 portfolio firms. These firms received financial support from five foreign VC firms and 39 Swedish VC firms, all members of SVCA.
- E-Chron group (E-Chron 1998) in Stockholm conducted a survey entitled "the Swedish IT/Internet VC Survey 1998" that covers 20 Swedish VC firms and 17 IT/Internet entrepreneurs.
- A survey of NTBFs conducted by the Department of Industrial Dynamics at Chalmers University of Technology. It includes data on various issues from 365 NTBFs, including their financial sources (for details of the database, see Rickne and Jacobsson 1999).

The Size of the Swedish VC Industry

Previously in this chapter it was revealed that in the 1990s the Swedish the VC industry has grown rapidly. Although there was a general growth in the VC industry in Europe in the 1990s (Mason and Harrison 1999), Sweden still had the third largest stock of cumulative VC funds in Europe, relative to the size of the GDP already in 1995 (EVCA 1996). Since that year, the growth of the Swedish VC industry was phenomenal rising from SEK 16 billion in cumulative funds to about three times that figure in 1998. Our database suggests that the cumulative funds reached to 49.2 billion SEK (US $5.9 billion), which is close to the statistics of the Swedish Venture Capital Association that calculates the cumulated funds as SEK 41 billion (US $5 billion) (SVCA 1998). This probably means that Sweden further strengthened its position *vis-à-vis* other European countries.[23]

The figure for 1998 is more than ten times the figure in 1987 and 100 times the figure in 1983, indicating the phenomenal development of the VC in the 1990s (see table 6.1). The expansion was so rapid that Sweden greatly reduced the gap with the US in terms of cumulated funds in the VC industry. By 1998, cumulated VC funds in Sweden were about US $5.9 billion whereas the equivalent figure for the US was US $315.4 billion (Fenn *et al.* 1995; NVCA 1998; SVCA 1998). When adjusted with respect to population (Sweden with 9 and US with 260 million inhabitants), the US has about 1.9 times more cumulated funds by 1998. This is a significant improvement compared to 1994 figures where the US cumulative funds were 3.1 times larger.

In the 1990s, we can also see strong evidence for a growth in the number of VC firms, as was seen in figure 6.1. Indeed, the firms established from 1994 constitute 57 percent of all VC firms. As mentioned previously, the number of firms is important *per se*,[24] since there may be a need to pass the project between a number of VC firms. Hence, not only the volume of funds[25] but also the growth in the number of VC firms is a positive sign of the maturation process.

The Diversity of the Swedish VC Industry

The difference between our database and the EVCA statistics is revealed more forcefully in the stage orientation of VC firms. According to EVCA,

Table 6.1
Cumulative Venture Capital Funds Raised in Sweden and the U.S.

Year	Sweden (billion SEK)	Sweden (billion $)	Sweden * (billion $)	US (billion $)	Ratio (US/Sweden*)
1983	0,4	0,06	1,7	6,7	3,9
1987	4	0,5	14,4	39,3	2,7
1994	10,9	1,4	40,3	127	3,1
1998	49,2	5,9	169,9	315,4**	1,9

*Adjusted according to population, Sweden has 9 million, US has 260 million population.
**For estimation, see Appendix A.
Source: See Appendix A.

Swedish VC industry is strongly oriented towards later stages, in particular buy-outs, like in many European countries (Christensen, 1997; Jeng and Wells 1998). In Sweden, in average, only 2.5 percent of the large capital funds are suggested to have been oriented towards seed and start-up stages in the period 1986–95. If we take only one year, say 1995, the early stage investments represented only 1.4 percent of the total VC funds invested (EVCA 1996).

The database, given in table 6.2, however, suggests that over 37 percent of the private VC firms invest in *early stages* (seed, start-up and early growth) only and these account for slightly less than 12 percent of the funds. If we consider firms investing both in the early and across stages, then they represent 61 percent of firms with a 23 percent of the funds. That 61 percent of the firms have only 23 percent of the investments is not surprising considering that early stage investments require much lower capital compared to late stage investments (i.e., MBOs). Whereas this means that most of the VC industry's activities are in late stages and not "classic" VC activities, the share of early stage financing is much higher than what is reported by the EVCA and all other studies based on EVCA's data.[26] Yet, it is clearly lower than the US where early stages received between 24 and 38 percent of the funds during the period of 1987–96 (Rausch 1998).[27]

In table 6.3, we can see that there has been a significant growth in the number of specialized VC firms in the 1990s; i.e., firms investing in selected industry categories rather than being diversified across many industries. Indeed, 25 out of the currently existing 36 privately owned and specialized VC firms were established after 1990 and about half of all new entrants in the 1990s are specialized firms. The accumulated funds of the specialized firms established in the 1990s amounted to SEK 2.8 billion in 1998 whereas the funds accumulated by the specialized firms established in the 1980s is only SEK 750 million. Yet in terms of volume of cumulated funds, they are quite small as compared to the non-specialized firms' funds of SEK 41.7 billion. In spite of the relatively small funds, it is clear that we have seen a structural change in the VC industry with the emergence of a significant number of specialized firms.

Table 6.2
The Phase Distribution of the Swedish VC Industry—1998

	Number of firms	% of firms	Total VC funds (M SEK)	% of funds
Early-phase VC firms	35	37,2 %	5,225	11,6 %
Across-phase VC firms	22	23,5 %	5,735	10,6 %
Late-phase VC firms	29	30,8 %	36,401	73,8 %
Unknown-phase VC firms	8	8,5 %	1,933	4 %
Total	94	100%	49,294	100%
Of which government firms	16*	17,0 %	9,332	19 %

*13 of these firms in early stage with funds of SEK 2,829 million.

Table 6.3

The Distribution of Venture Capital Firms According to the Establishment Period, Investment Phase* and Industrial Specialization—1998

Establishment Period	Industrial Specialisation	Total (M SEK)		Early Phase (M SEK)		Across Phases (M SEK)		Late Phase (M SEK)	
<1980	Specialised	250	3	115	1	0	0	135	2
	Non-specialised	1650	5	400	2	1250	2	0	0
	Total	1900	8	515	3	1250	3	135	2
1980-1990	Specialised	750	8	700	5	50	1	0	0
	Non-specialised	18305	14	655	3	3115	4	14535	6
	Total	19055	22	1355	8	3165	5	14535	6
>1990	Specialised	2841	25	2350	14	435	6	56	4
	Non-specialised	21700	26	920	8	885	6	19895	12
	Total	24541	52**	3270	22	1320	12	19951	16
Total ***	Specialised	3841	36	3165	20	485	10	191	6
	Non-specialised	41655	45**	1975	13	5250	10	34430	18
	Total	45496	82**	5140	33	5735	20	34621	24
				(11.3%)	(40.2%)	(12.6%)	(24.4%)	(76.1%)	(29.3%)

The numbers in parenthesis indicate the share of firms in different phases by their number of firms and amount of funds raised.

*Some firms had no investment phase information.

**12 firms whose establishment year is unknown are excluded.

***Seed, establishment and early growth phases.

Table 6.3 also shows the combination of the stages of investment with a specialized or non-specialized strategy of the VC firms. A first observation from table 6.3 is that the number of specialized firms with a presence in early stage financing has increased a great deal in the 1990s when 14 such firms were established. A second observation is that there is a strong relationship between specialization strategy and presence in early or late stages. As was argued previously, a firm can reduce risks in early stage investments by developing deep industry/technology specific competence. A firm can still further reduce the risk by having a portfolio of investment objects, which vary across the stages, but largely being within the same industry/technology field. For example, Slottsbacken invests only in telecommunication and information technology firms by supplying seed, start-up or expansion finance. Adding the specialized firms who are active in early phases only, to those which are active also across phases, we find that these amount to 30 out of the 36 specialized firms. In contrast, only 23 out of 41 non-specialized firms are active in these phases. Hence, we can clearly see the expected pattern where a specialization supports early phase investments.

The substantial number of firms that invest in early stages is mainly focused on two high technology areas: IT and biomedicine, as is shown in table 6.4.

Table 6.4
The Characteristics of the Specialized VC Firms

Specialisation areas	No. of firms	Total firms (%)	No. of firms in early phase	Total early phase firms (%)
IT related business	34	35	17	52
BM related business	22	23	15	45
Both IT & BM related	13	14	10	30

IT-Information Technology; BM: Biomedicine.

Among these early-stage firms, 17 (out of 33 early stage firms in total) are working with IT and related technologies while 15 of them are investing in biotechnology and medical technology. Among these specialized firms, 10 of them overlap as they invest both in IT and biomedicine. Hence, IT and biomedicine dominate as investment foci for the early stage firms. In addition to these firms, there are a number of firms focusing on these sectors but on later stages. A significant part, (81 of 323)[28] of the NTBFs operating in Sweden in these two fields have received venture capital (see table 6.5). Half of those were in the IT field and about 20 percent each were in biomedicine and mechanical engineering respectively. The relatively large number of firms receiving VC in the IT field can be explained by the correspondingly high share of IT firms in the sample. In contrast, the biomedical firms were clearly over represented as recipients of VC. Indeed, close to 45 percent of the medicine-based firms received VC finance.[29] Thus, in the 1990s, a structure of the Swedish VC industry has evolved where a large number of firms are now both specialized and active in early phases. A VC industry characterized by diversity is evolving which, again, is a positive sign of maturation. Much of the activities among the firms in early stages are focused on IT and biomedicine where a substantial share of the NTBFs also receives finance from the VC industry.

The Competence of the Swedish VC Industry

As seen in the previous section, there were a large number of new entrants into the Swedish VC industry in the 1990s, connected to this, a structural change took place in favor of diversity. In itself, this is a positive sign also in terms of competence development as specialized firms are likely to be able to develop industry and technology specific competence in a way that diversified firms are not. It is also encouraging with the diffusion of limited partnerships which would be expected to have increased employment of experienced and skilled investment managers. Moreover, while in the 1980s, many firms preferred to work by themselves, in the 1990s, VC firms tend to syndicate with each other. As co-operation helps firms to exchange knowledge and broaden their networks, it increases the competence of VC firms.[30] Finally, we saw in the above section that, if anything, there is a bias of the VC industry in favor

Table 6.5
The Main Financial Sources of NTBF*

Technology Class of firms	Total	Percen-tage	Own capital	Bank loan	Govern-ment	VC	Customer
IT-Based							
Number of firms	174	54%	149	85	55	41	38
(% within tech. Class)	(311%)		(85,6%)	(48,9%)	(31,6)	(23,6%)	(21,8%)
% within the financial source**			55,6%	50,3%	50,9%	50,6%	56,7%
Medicine-Based							
Number of firms	36	11%	27	19	19	16	6
(% within tech. Class)	(397%)		(75%)	(52,8%)	(52,8%)	(44,4%)	(16,7%)
% within the financial source**			10,1%	11,2%	17,6%	19,8%	9,0%
Machinery-Based							
Number of firms	88	27%	71	51	27	19	22
(% within tech. Class)	(256%)		(80,7%)	(58,0%)	(30,7%)	(21,6%)	(25,0%)
% within the financial source**			26,5%	30,2%	25,0%	23,5%	32,8%
All Firms – Total							
Number of firms	323	100%	268	169	108	81	67
% within total	318%		83,0%	52,3%	33,4%	25,1%	20,7%

Figures in parenthesis show the percentage of firms within the technology class. It is calculated by dividing the number of firms receiving a certain financial source by the total number of firms in the specific technology class. This figure is higher than 100%, since firms use in general more than one source. For example, in the whole sample, firms have in general received capital from 3 different sources (318%).

*We only included the financial resources that at least 20% of NTBFs used.

**It is calculated by dividing the number of firms in each technology class that are receiving a certain financial source by the total number of firms in this category of financial source.

of IT and biomedicine which suggests that the orientation of the VC industry, at least the part dealing with early stage investments, is towards new technological fields. Hence, there are no obvious imbalances between the technological orientation of the VC industry and that of the NTBFs.

This does not, however, mean that the VC industry has matured in the sense of developing an adequate competence to supply besides finance. As the VC business is a service industry, portfolio firms perception and evaluation are important in assessing the competence level of the VC firms. Three different studies shed light on this issue. The most extensive study (Isaksson 1999) indicates that VC firms are significantly engaged in the development of the portfolio firms. However, the main input from VC firms has been advice in financial matters. At most one fifth of the firms perceive that the VC firms gave significant inputs of other type such as strategy forming and helping with networks. Firms receiving help from venture capitalists regarding market and product, such as commercialization issues and linkages with a wide range of networks of customers and suppliers, are only 3 and 6 percent of all portfolio firms, respectively (Isaksson 1999).[31]

An in-depth study of the IT industry has clearly shown that the majority of VC firms specialized in this sector are not competent according to entrepreneurs receiving finance from them (E-chron 1998). Indeed, as many as nine out of twenty VC firms admitted that they did not have IT/Internet and technical competence. Thus, they agreed that sometimes they cannot supply strategic and technical advice, help with the recruitment of key people, and provide customer contacts.

A study of biomaterial firms (that constitutes one segment of the biomedical industry) show that out of 18 interviewed firms in Sweden, five of them (27 percent) received VC finance in their development phase (Rickne 1999). These firms received no input in technology and market related issues from the VC firms, while one fourth of their counterparts in Ohio and Massachusetts had benefited from their VC firms' competence in these issues.[32] A similar study which compares biotechnology firms in Ohio and Sweden has also shown the limited managerial input of VC firms into biotechnology firms receiving VC capital (three out of eight Swedish firms) (Karaömerlioglu and Laage-Hellman 1999). Even though these two studies' numbers of firms are too small to generalize, the results are in line with the other studies described previously.

In sum, even though VC firms are becoming specialized, are increasingly investing in earlier phases and emphasize the importance of networks and competence, our analysis shows that the Swedish VC industry is not competent yet, but may be in a process of becoming one. This result is not a surprise, since it is important to keep in mind that the Swedish early-stage VC firms lack a substantial experience in terms of the actual involvement with portfolio firms through a complete cycle. As many as two thirds of the current Swedish VC firms were established in the 1990s, particularly during the period of 1994–98. Considering that investment duration for most of them is five to seven years, the majority of them are in their early investment phases yet. Until they exit from their investments and enter new range of investments, they may be expected to still be in the learning period in terms of competence building.

CONCLUSIONS AND SOME IMPLICATIONS FOR POLICY

The purpose of the chapter was to analyze the evolution of the Swedish venture capital industry, critically assess it with respect to its maturity and to identify policy issues, which have a bearing on its further evolution. We argued that a VC industry evolves as a function of the institutional set-up in the economy. This has a bearing on three specific drivers; access to available savings, the incentive structure and the exit possibilities for the VC firm. By mapping the evolution of the Swedish VC industry, we could identify how these three drivers blocked the evolution of the VC industry for some years but also how changes in the institutional set-up initiated a catch-up process in Sweden in the 1990s.

The mere existence of a VC industry does not mean that it is mature. We argued that the maturity of a VC industry could be analyzed with respect to the size, diversity and competence of the industry. The size of the Swedish VC industry is substantial, among the four largest in the OECD set in relation to population. It is also growing very rapidly. In the 1990s, and using our own database, we found a very significant structural change in the Swedish VC industry in favor of diversity. There were many new entrants, which are specialized VC firms and active in early stage investments, mainly in IT and biomedicine. In itself, this is to be expected to lead to an accumulation of industry and technology specific competence but available evidence strongly suggest that the Swedish VC industry is yet not mature with respect to its competence. Indeed, we expect that competence must be accumulated over a couple of investment phases before a significant learning can take place. As the bulk of the VC firms were established in the mid-1990s, we would therefore have to expect to wait until the end of the first decade of the next millennium for a mature industry to materialize. The length of the learning period is, therefore at best about three decades, assuming the start to be in 1982 when OTC was created as an exit mechanism and private venture capital firms entered on a large scale.[33]

Of course, as mentioned in the introduction to this chapter, VC is only one source of capital and there are other and complementary mechanism, such as competent acquirers. In a policy discussion, VC should only form one part and the whole risk capital market need to be analyzed. It should also be acknowledged that a VC industry is not a sufficient condition for stimulating the development of a high tech industry. It can not perform its role without having access to a strong science and technology base (Florida and Kenney 1990).

Limiting ourselves to the VC industry, our understanding of the present size and structure of the Swedish VC industry differs substantially from two recent Swedish studies (Bergman *et al.* 1999, NUTEK and Industriförbundet 1999). First, Bergman *et al.* suggest that Sweden has a substantially smaller VC industry than the EU average whereas our data suggest that Sweden is among the leading countries. Second, both studies suggest that the share of IT and biomedicine in VC investments was less than 4 percent in 1997 whereas our data on the specialization of the VC firms as well as the industrial distribution of firms receiving VC clearly shows a strong focus on these two sectors.[34] Third, we differ with respect to the importance of early stage investment in the Swedish VC industry. Both sources suggest that this is negligible in Sweden whereas our data suggest differently. Indeed, our analysis suggests a rapidly growing VC industry which is in the process of changing structurally in favor of specialized firms focusing on early stages and positioning itself *vis-à-vis* IT and biomedicine whereas the above mentioned studies portray a small[35] industry focusing on late stage investments, much in mature industries such as consumer goods.

However, whereas our perceptions differ greatly, we still agree that the Swedish VC industry is not yet mature; although it has grown phenomenally in the 1990s, Swedish still lags the US with respect to the size of the VC industry; much of the funds are still allocated to late stage investments and, perhaps most importantly, our analysis of the competence of the Swedish VC industry suggests that it still is far from mature.

Of course, the perception of the nature of the VC industry has a bearing on the specification of the policy problem. Bergman *et al.* (1999) focus on the tax issue which, as mentioned above, involves a triple taxation and discriminates against channeling funds to VC firms. Implicitly, the policy problem is seen as the (perceived) small size of the Swedish VC industry and tax reforms are required to induce capital to move into this sector. Of course, if a further growth of the VC industry is seen as important for growth, a triple taxation does not make any sense at all.

NUTEK and Industriförbundet (1999) put forward the idea of 'entrepreneurial funds' where the idea is to increase the flow of private savings which are channeled to small firms with a growth potential via the VC industry. Whereas this is a good idea in a country with a flat income distribution, it still assumes that the key issue is the size of the VC industry. This is a valid perception but the alleged small size of the Swedish VC industry has been exaggerated and, moreover, it is probably not the key issue in the further evolution of the industry. We would argue that the key issue is rather the underdeveloped competence in the VC industry which not only influences what the VC firms can supply beyond capital but also the propensity for the VC firms to undertake early stage financing.[36]

Competence must be drawn from current firms, be they large and established firms or NTBFs. The evolution of a competent VC industry builds on an earlier industrial activity, which generate the required technological and industrial competence. It is, thus, a cumulative process and a key policy issue, we argue, is to understand this process of cumulative causation. In particular, under what conditions do early entrepreneurs, or others, shift from industrial activities to becoming involved in the VC industry? We would expect that with a greater movement, not only would the competence of the VC industry increase but also the inclination to invest in early stages.

Abandoning triple taxation and introducing "entrepreneurial funds" would presumably attract new actors to the VC industry (NUTEK and Industriförbundet 1999). The tax system may also be designed to stimulate such a mobility by providing special, but temporary, incentives, to investors in the VC industry, a suggested by NUTEK and Industriförbundet (1999). The motive for such an "infant industry" policy is the difficulties to develop the competence required to obtain a reasonable profit level in the industry. It is, however, not self-evident that special incentives are required given the very considerable dynamics of the Swedish VC industry. Moreover, potential special incentives should accrue not to investors in general, as suggested by NUTEK and Industriförbundet

(1999),[37] but to investors in early stages where industry and technology specific competence is particularly needed.

In addition to such subsidies, there is a scope for policy measures, which aim at expanding networks and increasing the movement of competent people into the VC industry. Three such measures are worthwhile to mention. First, SVCA should increase its activities to gain legitimacy for VC business. By increasing the recognition of VC business, it can attract managers and entrepreneurs to become venture capitalists, a respected profession. To do so, it should increase its membership activities, strengthen the network among VC firms, educate venture capitalists, and create an identity of the VC industry. Second, the networking activities in VC business should be developed.[38] In particular, a network among entrepreneurs needs to be initiated similar to the VC establishment of the association in the US in which now (1999) has 8,000 entrepreneur members.[39] Such a network serves two main purposes: creation of potential venture capitalists and building a pool of managers that could be employed for portfolio firms. Third, not only SVCA but also individual VC firms, government organizations, researchers should aim to increase the awareness about the VC industry. Increased information flow about VC firms, deals, investment opportunities, revenues, and performances of VC firms needs to be institutionalized in order to create a transparent and reliable environment[40] not only for investors but also for venture capitalists. This environment together with new educational programs on entrepreneurship and VC could motivate people to become venture capitalists, since their concerns regarding the uncertainties in conducting VC business could be lessened.

Yet, even if these measures are implemented and a healthy and mature private VC industry is generated, there may still be a role for a direct government involvement in the VC industry—shown in the case of the US—as a complement to private actors focusing on early stages. The scope of this involvement needs though to be further studied. Here, and speculatively, the main issue may not be a potential "crowding out" effect but a too fast decline in government involvement.

APPENDIX 1: SOURCES OF DATA AND ESTIMATION PROCEDURE FOR TABLE 6.1

The Swedish data is collected from the following sources: data for 1983 comes from Olofsson and Wahlbin 1985; data for year 1987 from Isaksson and Cornelius, 1998; data for year 1994 from EVCA statistics; and data for 1998 from our database. For the US data, we had three sources: Fenn *et al.*'s (1995) study, Prowse's (1998) study and NVCA (National Venture Capital Association)'s annual figures for the 1996–98 period.

Fenn *et al.*'s (1995) study gave data for the cumulative commitments to private equity partnerships over 1980–94 that totaled US $127 billion. Of this total, US $33 billion was committed to VC firms dedicated to venture capital financing while a much greater amount, US $94 billion, was committed to VC firms supplying non-venture capital finance (Fenn *et al.* 1995). In their definition, non-venture referred to MBOs/LBOs that are not included in the Venture Economics statistics used by NVCA. Prowse's (1998) study supplied the 1995 and 1996 figures.

As NVCA figures (used for 1997 and 1998) did not include MBOs, we derived an approximate ratio between venture and non-venture capital finance by using Fenn *et al.*'s (1995) study. From their data for the period of 1984–94, the ratio between venture capital and non-venture capital was 2.6. So, we calculated the total venture capital funds given by NVCA during the period of 1997–98 and multiplied it with 2.6 to find the corresponding growth in the non-venture capital funds and added these two figures. NVCA data shows that the venture capital funds where MBOs are not included were US $4.2 billion in 1995 which increased to US $10 billion, US $14.4 billion and US $24.1 billion during the 1996–98 period (NVCA, 1998; NSF, 1999).[41]

APPENDIX 2

The "cleaning" of the gross list of VC firms involves the following steps:

1. Firms that are not private equity suppliers are deleted. Even though ALMI is listed as one of the VC firms in the SVCA, it only supplies loan. It is, further, a very old establishment, even though year of establishment is given as 1994 in the SVCA list. This is because it is restructured as a limited company in 1994 and gathered all regional investment companies under its umbrella organization. Similarly, three firms, namely, Scandinavian Securities, Söderlind, Dintler, Karlsson & Partners and Swedbank Markets Corporate Finance firms are not VC firms. The former two are stock market companies and the latter is a financial service firm. We excluded them from our list.

2. Some firms have partial VC activities, but they are not completely VC firms, particularly Sjätte AP-fund and Industrifonden. The former holds SEK 12 billion of which only SEK 1 billion is invested in VC activities,[42] while the latter has SEK 3.8 billion of which the majority is loan. Including these firms as VC firms in the Swedish market would certainly inflate the size of the industry. Moreover, it is important to note that these firms in general invest in an indirect way into the VC market investing their capital in funds of other VC firms. For example, Sjätte AP-fund puts its money into Healthcap while Industrifonden puts money into Emano. Including them to the total size of the VC industry would lead to double counting. We included these firms in our list but did not add their funds to the total cumulative. These funds show up and are counted in the firms into which they are invested.

3. In the case of Atle and Bure, we decided, for two reasons, to include them into our list even though they were transformed into investment companies. First, they were set up by government in 1992 to boost the VC industry. They

were privatized in 1995 and since then their focus shifted to later stage investments. But still their existence in 1992 helped to create a good climate for VC firms. Second, their contribution to the market was substantial, in one year SEK 6.5 billion, which may have had a snowball impact for the industry. Thus, we included them in our list but we avoided including their branch firms' funds (such as ATLE Enviretech firm) to the total funds in order to avoid double counting.

APPENDIX 3

Table 6.A1
Venture Capital* New Funds Raised

Country (1)	VC new funds in the period 1986-95 per million of average GDP (2)	Rank (3)	VC new funds growth rate** from 1986-95 Per million of average GDP (4)	Rank (5)
Norway	0,369	9	3658	1
Portugal	0,924	6	206	2
Switzerland	0,263	15	167	3
Denmark	0,302	13	93	4
Germany	0,29	14	80	5
Sweden	1,056	4	78	6
Ireland	1,315	3	55	7
Finland	0,312	12	50	8
France	0,937	5	49	9
Austria	0,019	16	43	10
UK	2,581	1	35	11
US	2,405**	2	23	12
Belgium	0,864	7	22	13
Spain	0,337	10	21	14
Netherlands	0,717	8	17	15
Italy	0,316	11	17	16

Note: The numbers in parenthesis show the number of column.

*Venture capital includes start-up, seed, expansion, and MBO investments.

** average of the growth rate per annum

*** 1994 figure.

Source: Jeng and Wells, 1998.

NOTES

1. Nineteen of the firms in the data base described in section 4 are probably "business angels" who have formed a company for tax reasons.

2. A recent study also shows that decreases in capital gains tax rates directly increase capital flow into VC industry (Gompers and Lerner 1997).

3. The only study we could identify with a similar objective is the extensive study of Murray (1996) who used the Porter model to analyze the maturity of the UK's VC industry.

4. Moreover, there should be an adequate amount of funding and competence supplied in each combination of industry/technology and stage.

5. An inadequate competence, moreover, acts as an obstacle to investment in early stage financing, thereby influencing the degree of diversity of the VC industry.

6. Small Business Investment Corporations (SBIC) was established in 1982 as a financial support mechanism for small business.

7. Moreover, government's role as soft loan supplier also increased in the 1990s. For example, the Small Business Innovation Research (SBIR) program invested $916 million in 1996. Another such award program, Small Business Technology Transfer, invested $64.5 million in high tech firms in 1996 (SBA 1999).

8. The oldest Swedish VC firm called Företagskapital was established in 1973. It was owned half by the state and half by merchant banks and initially its aim was to provide financial help for generation changes in family companies. However, it was later developed into a VC firm (Olofsson and Wahlbin 1985).

9. Regioninvest, Dala invest, Oxelöinvest, AC-Invest, Z-Invest, Malmöhus Invest, Start Invest were the most important of these corporations (Fredrikson 1997). Out of these, four of them still exist as independent bodies in 1998, namely AC-Invest, Z-Invest, Malmöhus Invest, Start Invest. These firms were eventually transformed into VC firms, while many of the remaining regional development corporations were transformed into branches of ALMI (established in 1994) which supplies loans to SMEs.

10. These were modeled after the US SBICs but had a regional focus.

11. According to one study (Olofsson and Wahlbin 1985) out of 35 VC firms in 1985, only four of them still existed as VC firms in 1998. These were Skandia Investment, Four Seasons, Euroventures, and Företagskapital.

12. In addition, universities started to get involved in commercialization activities through incubators and science parks. This has, so far, included the establishment of three VC firms for the purpose of commercializing university-developed technologies.

13. The most important one is ALMI. Even though this organization has existed in various forms, it became a loan supplier company in 1994. It provides new firms with soft loans, which are interest-free and not amortized during the first two years.

14. The involvement of the government into VC industry is not unique to Sweden as many advanced countries have special government programs oriented to the support of their VC industry (Gompers and Lerner 1997; Financial Times 1998b).

15. In contrast to some other countries, private savings are low in part due to government run pension schemes.

16. In addition to taxes, this report managed to initiate both the opening of an over the counter market (OTC) and the creation of private investment companies for small businesses according to the American small business investment company's (SBIC) model with regional-focus.

17. The opening up of these alternative stock markets is not limited to Sweden. In Europe, the largest national alternative investment market is the German Neuer Markt (established in 1997) whose market capitalization in 1998 is almost 350 million ECU with 63 listings. In addition to national markets, there are two competing cross-border markets, EASDAQ and Euro NM. While the former is located in Brussels and is a pan-European exchange market modeled on NASDAQ, the latter is formed by three national markets, namely the Nouveau Marche in France, the Neuer Markt in Germany, NMAX in the Netherlands and Euro NM in Belgium. In 1998, the market capitalization in EASDAQ (established in 1996) was around 270 million ECU (around 39 listings), while it is around 160 million ECU in Euro NM (over 100 listings) (Financial Times, 1998a; Economist, 1998; Economist, 1999). However, none of these markets are large when

compared to the US one, NASDAQ, the largest alternative stock market in the world, which holds 3,898 firms in its listing with US $1 trillion market capitalization in 1999.

18. In addition, the Stockholm Stock Exchange's monopoly on listing of equity was abolished in 1992 (OECD 1998). Individual stockbrokers started listing equity issues by small and unlisted clients on their electronic trading systems. This increased the involvement of individual investors and firms, building up trust on stock markets and making it an attractive investment tool.

19. This database gives detailed information on business activity of firms registered by the Swedish Ministry of Industry.

20. A few important Internet sites are http://www.tillvaxt.se/tillvaxtkapital.html and http://www.pi.se/vencap.

21. Nineteen of VC firms in the database are more of a business angel type of firm, since they are established with wealthy individuals using their own capital for investment rather than raising funds from outside investors. These individuals aim to avoid high taxes imposed on active business angels by establishing investment firms. However, they can be still considered in the pool of the VC industry for two reasons. First, they represent a portion of the informal VC industry that is a part of the VC industry. Interestingly, this "informal" VC industry segment is to some extent institutionalized in Sweden in the form of "formal" VC due to tax regulation. Second, as observed in our interviews many of these firms are established as business angels but then they are transformed into professional VC firms by becoming limited partnerships and raising venture funds.

22. In some cases there were contradictory statements. SVCA, for example, had in a table classified a firm as investing in early phase and then, on a subsequent page which described the firm in detail, SVCA indicated the firm as late stage investor. In these contradictory cases, we used our own judgment based on firms' general characteristics such as their investment size and so on.

23. If we analyze the whole period between 1986–1995, and thus, avoid the problem of large yearly fluctuations we can see, in table 6.A1, Appendix 3, (column 3), that Sweden had the fourth largest accumulated VC funds per million of GDP, after the UK, the US and Ireland. Moreover, the growth rate in the funds accumulated outpaced most other countries, (column 4).

24. For the VC industry in total, Sweden had more firms per capita than the US even if we use the more limited number of 55 firms in SVCA (1998). The US had about 700 firms (NVCA 1998).

25. Considering that many firms established since 1995 are in the process of raising new funds, we can expect that in the near future, the cumulative funds in the VC market will increase further.

26. Another characteristic of the VC industry in Sweden (which it shares with Europe) is that it is said to be not primarily oriented towards "high-tech" industries. In 1995, high tech investments by number of firms represented 51.2 percent and by amount of investment only 20.8 percent. However, this data should be handled with caution. A study of 249 portfolio firms that received capital from 44 VC firms shows that 68 percent of VC investments by number of firms were in high technology industries and that some of the remaining ones (8 percent), classified as service firms could well be heavily into such areas as IT services and software (Isaksson 1999). Another study has shown that there is a conflicting picture about the European VC industry's high tech orientation (Murray 1999). When the statistics of the national VC

associations are used, for example, 77 percent of the US VC investments were in technology-based companies in 1992, while it was only 19 percent in Germany and 18
percent in the UK (Abbott and Hay 1995: 200). However, by using the value of technology investments as a percentage of adjusted total value (i.e. total annual VC investment excluding the MBOs/MBIs in the UK and Europe and LBOs/Acquisitions in the
US), Murray (1999) shows a different picture. Accordingly, the value of technology
investments in the US is over 80 percent during the 1984–97 period, while the European
figure ranges between 30–50 percent. In the case of the UK, this figure stays in the
same range with the other European countries until 1992 then it increases significantly
reaching to a peak (80 percent) in 1995 but then drops to 60 percent in 1997. These
examples call further for a careful evaluation of the statistics supplied by national VC
associations.

27. As is plain from the table 6.3, the role of the government as a player in the VC
market is now limited. The focus of the state owned firms is, however, largely in early
phases where its share constitutes slightly less than one fourth of the volume of capital
in both early and across stages. As the volume of funds directed towards early stage
investments is lower than in the US, it is presumably so that the state initiatives sup-
plements private initiatives, i.e., the risk of a "crowding out" effect is probably low.

28. These 323 firms are part of a stock of about 1,100 NTBFs, which were identified
in an earlier study (Rickne and Jacobsson 1999) and were approached by questionnaire.

29. Interestingly, VC firms may have a bias against mechanical engineering-based
firms. In other words they represent 27 percent of NTBFs but only less than 22 percent
received venture capital in spite of the greater need for investments in machinery and
equipment in that industry than, say, in the IT field where many firms are consultancy
firms. This may be a reason for concern as Sweden has a very considerable competence
in mechanical engineering and in control systems related to that field, for example, in
robotics.

30. The communication between the VCs increased significantly through the development of the industry association (SVCA). SVCA was established in 1985 while its
European counterpart was established in 1983 and its US counterpart in 1973. Although
SVCA has today 14 years of existence, its growth in terms of members and activities
took place mainly in the 1990s. For example, its first published directory dates 1998.
Similarly, it organized the first Swedish seminar about VC at the same year. Through
this professional organization, VC firms have started to act together as interest group
and influence government decisions regarding the industry. As one venture capitalist
stated, the Swedish VC industry is in a phase where it tries to find its identity among
other industries.

31. Another study performed in 1990 concludes the same, showing that out of 59
portfolio firms only 12 percent of them received important input for their production
and 8 percent for their technology (Fredriksen et al. 1990).

32. The Ohio and Massachusetts samples have 15 and 24 firms respectively, where
six firms in the Ohio sample and 18 firms in the Massachusetts sample received venture
capital financing.

33. Given the large number of entrants in the mid 1990s, a shake-out may take place.
It is important that such shake-out does not lead to chaos in the industry and its falling
in disrepute.

34. Isaksson's (1998) study on the distribution of portfolio firms across industries
supports our position.

35. Nutek and Industriförbundet (1999) recognize the growth of the Swedish VC industry but does not make an international comparison of the size of the Swedish VC industry.

36. Oddly enough, this issue was not touched upon in the otherwise excellent review of the VC literature, including vital research issues, by Mason and Harrison (1999).

37. This refers to investors in "entrepreneurial funds."

38. This could be done in the manner of ALMI's initiative in 1998, which managed to bring together around 50 business angels.

39. The association is called the American Entrepreneurs for Economic Growth, a nation-wide network of close to 10,000 emerging growth companies employing well over one million Americans.

40. Murray (1996) considers the increased information about the VC industry as a measurement of the maturity of this industry.

41. Personal contact with Håkan Bohlin.

42. Industrifonden (established in 1979) started to have equity investments only after 1996.

REFERENCES

Abbott, S. and Hay, M. *Investing for the Future*. London: Pitman Publishing, 1995.

Bergman, L., Braunerhjelm, P., Fölster, S., Genberg, H. and Jakobsson, U. *Vägen till välstånd*. Konjukturrådets rapport 1999. Stockholm: SNS Förlag, 1999.

Bygrave, W. D. and Timmons, J. A. *Venture Capital at the Crossroads*. Boston, MA: Harvard Business School, 1992.

Cheung, M., Tat, A. K., Grandinson, C. J. *A Comparative Study of Venture Capital Companies in Silicon Valley, Singapore and Sweden*. A Masters Course project in the Department of Industrial Engineering and Engineering Management at Stanford University, California, USA, 1998.

Christensen, J. L. *Financing Innovation*. TSER Project Report: Innovation Systems and Europe 3.2.3. Denmark: Aalborg University, 1997.

Dagens Industri. *"Riskkapitalbolag"* 28 July 1997a.

Dagens Industri. *"Pensionskapital till Uppfinnare"* 12 June 1997b.

Dalum, B., Laursen, K., and Villumsen, G. *"Is There Such a Thing as a 'Good' Export Specialisation Pattern? A European Perspective"* paper presented at the EU-TSER/TEIS project seminar, Naples, 1997.

E-chron. *The Swedish IT/Internet Venture Capital Survey 1998*. Stockholm: E-chron, 1998.

The Economist. "IPO Venture Capitalism." January 25, 1997.

The Economist. "Europe's Great Experiment." June 13, 1998.

The Economist. "A German Coup." January 9, 1999.

EVCA (European Venture Capital Association). *1992 Yearbook: A Survey of Venture Capital and Private Equity in Europe*. Zaventem EVCA, 1992.

EVCA (European Venture Capital Association). *1996 Yearbook: A Survey of Venture Capital and Private Equity in Europe*. Zaventem EVCA, 1996.

Fenn, W., Liang, N., and Prowse, S. *The Economics of the Private Equity Market*. Washington, DC: Federal Reserve Bank, 1995.

Financial Times. "Newcomers Escape Upheaval Unscathed." November 27, 1998a.

Financial Times. "No Negative Noises Yet." November 27, 1998b.

Florida, R., Kenney, M. *The Breakthrough Illusion: Corporate America's Failure to Move From Innovation to Mass Production.* New York: Basic Books, 1990.

Fredriksen, O. *Venture Capital Firms Relationships and Cooperation with Entrepreneurial Companies.* Linköping Studies in Science and Technology Thesis no 625, Department of Management and Economics, Linköping University, 1997.

Fredriksen, Ö., Olofsson, C. and Wahlbin, C. *The Role of Venture Capital in the Development of Portfolio Companies.* Paper presented at the SMS Conference Strategic Bridging, Stockholm, September, 1990.

Gompers, P. A. and Lerner, J. "What Derives Venture Capital Fundraising?" Working Paper, Harvard Business School, 1997.

Harvard Business School (HBS). *A Note on the Venture Capital Industry.* Case Number: 9–295–065, November 1994.

House of Representatives. *Equity Investments, Venture Capital, and the Federal Role in the Availability of Financing for High Technology Companies.* Subcommittee on Economic Growth and Credit Formation of the Committee on Banking, Finance, and Urban Affairs, Washington, DC, Serial no 103–99, 1993.

Industrifonden. *Förteckning över Riskkapitalaktörer Versamma på den Svenska Marknaden.* Stockholm: Industrifonden, 1998.

Isaksson, A. *Effecter av Venture Capital I Sverige.* mimeo, Umeå: Umeå University, 1999.

Isaksson, A., and Cornelius, B. *Venture Capital Incentives: A Two Country Comparison.* Paper Presented at the 10th Nordic Conference on Small Business Research, Växjö University, Sweden, June 14–16, 1998.

Jacobsson, S. "The Length of the Infant Industry Period: Evidence from the Engineering Industry in South Korea," *World Development.* Vol. 21 (3), 1993, pp. 407–419.

Jeng, L. A. and Wells, P. C. The Determinants of Venture Capital Funding: Evidence Across Countries. Working Paper, Harvard Business School, 1998.

Karaömerlioglu, D. and Laage-Hellman, J. The Microlevel Analysis of Firms in the Biomedical System in Ohio and Sweden, mimeo, Department of Industrial Dynamics and the Department of Industrial Marketing, Chalmers University of Technology, Göteborg, Sweden, 1999.

Karaömerlioglu, D. C. and Lindholm Dahlstrand, Å. "Innovation Dynamics in Sweden" 44th ICSB Conference, Naples, Italy, 20–23 June 1999.

Karaömerlioglu, D. C. and Jacobsson, S. "The Swedish Venture Capital Industry—an Infant, Adolescent or Grown-up?", *Conference on Financing Entrepreneurship and Innovation in Science Based Industries.* Mannheim, Germany, 22–23 January 1999.

Kilsved, H., Hammarström, O., and Mogård, P. *Småföretagens Riskkapitalsituation.* Stockholm: IMIT, 1997.

Landström, H. "A Pilot Study on the Investment Decision-making Behavior of Informal Investors in Sweden." *Journal of Small Business Management.* 33, July 1995, pp. 67–76.

Lerner, J. The Government as Venture Capitalist: The Long-run Impact of the SBIR Program. Working Paper 96–038, Harvard Business School, 1996.

Mason, C. M., and Harrison, R. T. Editorial, Venture Capital: rationale, aims and scope; in *Venture Capital.* Vol. 1 No. 1, January-March, 1999, pp. 1–46.

Murray, G. "Evolution Change: An Analysis of the First Decade of the UK Venture

Capital Industry," *Journal of Business Finance & Accounting.* 22 (8), 1996, pp. 1077–1107.

Murray, G. "A Policy Response to Regional Disparities in the Supply of Risk Capital to New Technology-based Firms in the European Union: The European Seed Capital Fund Scheme," *Regional Studies.* 32 (5), 1998, pp. 405–419.

Murray, G. "Seed Capital and the Tyranny of (Small) Scale," *Conference on Financing Entrepreneurship and Innovation in Science Based Industries.* Mannheim, Germany, 22–23 January 1999.

Norton, E. and Tenenbaum, B. "Specialisation Versus Diversification As a Venture Capital Investment Strategy," *Journal of Business Venturing.* 8, 1993, pp. 431–442.

NVCA (National Venture Capital Association). *Annual Report.* NVCA: Washington DC, 1998.

NUTEK. *Finansierings-möjligheter I Sverige.* Stockholm: NUTEK, 1997.

NUTEK and Industriförbundet. *Entreprenörsfonder.* Stockholm: NUTEK, 1999.

NSF. Science and Engineering Indicators 1998. Washington DC: IUS Government Printing Office, 1999.

OECD. *Fostering Entrepreneurship: The OECD Jobs Strategy.* Paris: OECD, 1998.

Olofsson, C., and Wahlbin, C. *The Swedish Venture Capital Market—an Early Appraisal,* Frontiers of Entrepreneurship Research 1985, Proceedings of the Fifth Annual Babson College Entrepreneurship Research Conference, 1985, pp. 191–209.

Oxelheim, L. *Nordic Equity Markets in Transition.* Reprint No. 461, the Research Institute of Industrial Economics, Stockholm, Sweden, 1998.

Prowse, S. D. "The Economics of the Private Equity Market." *Economic Review Third Quarter,* 1998, pp. 21–34.

Rausch, L. M. Venture Capital Investment Trends in the United States and Europe, National Science Foundation, Directorate for Social, Behavioural, and Economic Sciences, Division of Resource Studies, Issue Brief, October 16, 1998.

Rickne, A. New Technology-based firms in the Evolution of a Technological Field—the Case of Biomaterials, paper presented at the 19th Annual Entrepreneurship Research Conference, South Carolina, US, May 12–15, 1999.

Rickne, A. and Jacobsson, S. "New Technology-Based Firms in Sweden—A study of their direct impact of industrial renewal," *Economics of Innovation and New Technology.* vol. 8, 1999, pp. 197–223.

Sapienza, H. J., Manigart, S., Vermeir, W. "Venture Capitalist Governance and Value Added in Four Countries" *Journal of Business Venturing.* 11, 1996, pp. 439–469.

Saxenian, A. *Regional Advantage.* Cambridge MA: Harvard University Press, 1994.

SBA, 1999, http://www.sba.gov/SBIR/otacc.html.

SBIC, 1999, http://www.nasbic.org/SBICs.html.

Schilit, W. K. and Willig, J. T. *Fitzroy Dearborn International Directory of Venture Capital Funds.* Fitzroy Dearborn: Chicago, USA, 1996.

SVCA. *Svenska Riskkapitalföreningen 1998–99.* Stockholm: SVCA, 1998.

Timmons, J. A. *Venture Capital in Sweden: A Comparative Study.* Frontiers of Entrepreneurship Research 1985, Proceedings of the Fifth Annual Babson College Entrepreneurship Research Conference, 1982, pp. 294–312.

Zider, B. "How Venture Capital Works," *Harvard Business Review.* November-December 1998, pp. 121–139.

7

The Rise, Fall, and Possible Sustainable Revitalization of the Danish Venture Capital Market

Jesper Lindgaard Christensen[1]

INTRODUCTION: GAPS IN SME FINANCING

It is widely believed that the problems associated with financing SMEs (small and medium-sized enterprises) have been alleviated in the second half of the 1990s. It is now the opinion of many observers that the supply of capital is sufficient and also that risk capital is generally available. An important explanation for this change is the improvement in the business climate. Another explanation is that the amount of capital has increased, as has competition on the supply side. Nevertheless, there is still a debate on a potential gap in the financing of new innovative firms, which also need additional competencies together with capital. This gap is enhanced if the firm is based on intangibles or high technology. In the debate, venture capital has been pointed to as an answer to these problems (EU 2001).

A number of surveys in Denmark in the 1990s have focused upon identifying the most typical, financial constraint to SME development while also examining the extent of such a constraint. Although a sensitive issue, the debates and surveys have led to a certain level of consensus being reached, thus giving the following conclusions:

- The magnitude of the problem has decreased during the 1990s with the improved general business climate.

- There is an increased supply of capital and financing sources, which means increased competition in the market.

- The market for debt financing is generally well-functioning with an adequate supply.

- Mezzanine capital has until recently been virtually nonexistent, even though firms would like loans with interest rates linked to performance, as long as the firm does not have to part with influence.

- The company facing financial constraints has one or more of the following characteristics:

  - Small

  - New

  - Innovative

  - Growth oriented

  - Based on intangibles

  - Demand equity in combination with competencies

A particular type of firm experiencing financial constraints is the research/high-tech–based new firm, which demands relatively small amounts of capital. However, these risky, small investments are not really appealing to most venture capital firms because the fixed costs on the investment are too high compared to the business potential. Risk is one of the main characteristics of traditional venture capital. Accordingly, a considerable number of investments can be expected to fail, while other investments succeed with high rates of return and thus compensate for the losses. Venture capital, even when it is not centered around early-stage investments and high-tech sectors, does involve a considerable risk in most European countries. These are generic problems. Murray (1999) refers to the uncertainty and the relative size of the investments in early-stage, innovative firms as a "tyranny" of SME financing.

A number of *government initiatives* have aimed to fill in these gaps. Like many other European governments, Danish government stimulates an expansion of the venture capital market in order to alleviate financial constraints, in particular for small and medium-sized innovative firms. The intention behind the design of initiatives on the capital market is that they should each contribute to the improvement of access to capital in different stages of the development of a firm. In general, all initiatives are inspired from similar schemes in other countries. A similar approach is taken in other countries as well: inspiration to policy formulation comes to a large extent from abroad.[2]

In addition to government initiatives there is also a trend toward structural changes on the private market. A few years ago private equity funds entered the market for medium-sized firms.[3] The general strategy is to invest heavily in these firms and prepare them for an IPO. Although this strategy has no direct influence on the small firms segment, it is likely to influence the prices on shares in this segment also. Another structural development following a number of mergers and buyouts in the corporate sector is a substantial increase in corporate venture capital activity. A number of large firms either establish captive organizations meant to be venture capital funds, extend their venture activities within the firm, or invest in venture firms already on the market. In fact, some of these firms establish internal business incubators meant to increase the synergies between the parent company and small, new enterprises with a profile interesting for the parent company. Such corporate venture capital is currently very active in other countries as well, and this is likely to further stimulate the development in Denmark. Even so, our knowledge on CVC (corporate venture capital) is remarkably limited. Except for a few studies in the United Kingdom (McNally 1994a, 1994b, 1995; Sykes 1990), the academic research into CVC is extremely sparse.[4] It is beyond the limits of this paper to deal with CVC, although it will be touched upon insofar as it is relevant for the development of the formal venture capital market in Denmark.

Both government initiatives and the private market–driven development have undoubtedly contributed to a narrowing of the financing gap mentioned earlier.

It is very important to bear in mind that problems of financing SMEs are not only a supply-side problem. Surveys have revealed that many SMEs, especially small firms, are not aware of available financing possibilities, and even if they are, they do not know how to approach them.[5] The results from such surveys point to a need for initiatives that raise the awareness of financing possibilities among firms.

This chapter takes a historical perspective on the development of venture capital in Denmark. The story of venture capital in Denmark is, however, not specific to this country only. Like in many other countries, the venture market flourished in the mid-1980s but rapidly declined in quantitative importance in the latter part of the decade and the beginning of the 1990s. Moreover, the industry turned its focus away from small firms as well as away from investments in innovations. The historical development in this chapter is supplemented with an analysis of the more recent state of affairs in the Danish venture capital market. The activity of the venture capital firms and the size of the market are discussed, and an estimate is made based on a much more thorough investigation than is usually done when EVCA (European Venture Capital Association) figures are used. The chapter also discusses whether policy makers can learn any lessons from the evolution of the venture capital industry.

THE ORIGIN, DEFINITION, AND MEASUREMENT OF VENTURE CAPITAL ACTIVITY

The venture capital concept originated in the United States in the 1940s after WWII. In 1946 J. H. Whitney and Company was established with the purpose of financing new, fast-growing industrial firms. Shortly after, Payson and Trask was established, followed by Rockefeller venture funds in the late 1940s. The first publicly listed venture fund (American Research and Development Corporation, or ARDC) was established in 1946. ARDC was the only listed venture fund until 1960 (Dominguez 1974, p. 1). At that time the U.S. venture capital firms were an important (often described as heroic) inducement in the creation of successful firms like Digital Equipment and Apple Computers. In many cases venture firms were spin-offs from universities or industrial firms.[6] An essential feature of venture financing was a gradual buildup of competence through a mutual beneficial learning process between industrial firms and the venture capitalist.[7] However, the original idea of venture capital firms seems to have vanished somewhat during the first half of the 1990s, not as much in the United States but especially throughout the rest of the world.[8] Rather than financing risky start-ups, which were often technology-based enterprises, the bulk of the venture capital industry financed mainly buyouts and buy-ins, restructuring of firms, and leveraged buyouts in established firms.[9] Thus, seed capital represented only 0.6 percent of the venture capital market in 1996 (Aernoudt 1999, p. 49).

One of the lessons from this short historical account of the origin of venture capital is that the very concept of venture capital is dynamic, not just the industry itself. As we shall see later, the definition of venture capital has a huge impact on the measurement of activity. Therefore, definitions of venture capital are important to make clear.

The main part of the statistics on venture capital comes from EVCA, which defines venture capital as

a means of financing the start-up, development, expansion, restructuring or acquisition of a company. Venture capital provides equity (share) capital to enterprises not quoted on a stock market and thus it is also referred to as private equity.

The venture capitalist provides medium or long-term financing in return for a proportion of the equity capital of the company it is funding. The venture capitalist may also provide "quasi" equity i.e. loans or bonds which may, under specific conditions, give the right to share capital. The source of venture capital can be either governmental, private organisations or individuals. (www.evca.com)

Bygrave and Timmons (1992) use a distinction between "classic venture capital" and "merchant venture capital." By doing so they illustrate that informal venture capital, to a much higher degree than the formal venture capital, has kept to the original definition of venture capital in their activities. They define "classic venture capital" as focused upon early-stage, hands-on, patient investments in which investors are typically adding value to the formation of the firm in terms of entrepreneurial skills. Conversely, "merchant venture capital" comes primarily from institutional investors and is focused upon larger, late-stage investments with a shorter time horizon. Know-how in financial engineering, transaction crafting, and fee generation are some of the important skills in this type of venture capital.

The definition employed in this chapter is closest to the definition by Bygrave and Timmons, although EVCA figures will be referred to also.

THE INFANT VENTURE CAPITAL INDUSTRY IN DENMARK

The venture capital industry in Denmark is relatively young. Most of its venture capital companies were established in 1983 (seven venture firms established, funds 545 mill.dkk), 1984 (708 mill.dkk) and 1985 (788 mill.dkk), and the industry developed rapidly shortly after the takeoff.[10] Not only did funds and investments increase, but also the number of venture capital firms increased.

Of the investments in the first two years (the seven largest funds made sixty-eight investments), machinery and electronics were apparently the most attractive sectors, with 17 percent and 20 percent of the investments respectively. The rest of the investments were spread over a wide number of different sectors. The investments were primarily in producer goods (sixty-four) rather than consumables (four) and primarily in real assets (fifty-nine) rather than intangibles (nine). Average investment size mid-1985 was 3.5 Mill. dkk, totaling 339.6 Mill.dkk.

There are several reasons for the boom in the number of venture capital firms shortly after the first were established. First, there was the effect of the rapid development of the industry abroad. Second, even though the level of interest rates decreased, making external financing attractive for the firms, the stock market was booming and so were investments in industry. This boom in investments created great optimism with regard to flotations on the stock exchange, and in the beginning most venture firms believed that an IPO was the most likely exit. Investments in bonds became less attractive for pension funds and other institutional investors and also as an effect of tax on real rates of interest; in addition, shares became more attractive due to legislative changes in the taxing of capital gains. Consequently, the need for capital in firms increased, and institutional investors wished to channel some of their investments through affiliated companies with a venture capital profile. However, legislation prevented them from putting too much capital directly into the corporate sector.

The venture capital industry has indeed been in flux in its first decade. Thus, in 1987 a magazine stated that

One thing is for certain: Venture capital is not a temporary phenomenon in Danish business. The industry is sustainable as an important partner and capital supply to especially young, fast-growing firms, who, within a reasonable time span, have possibilities for being introduced on the stock exchange III. (translated from Danish; *Børsens Nyhedsmagasin*, June 26, 1987, p. 32).

Only a few years later the industry declined rapidly to a negligible size. In 1990 a new deficit record for the Danish venture capital firms was set (dkk 78.5 million); the number of venture capital companies declined from a top level of twenty-six at the end of the 1980s to twelve, of which only four or five were investing; and both new corporate investments and capital supply to the venture capital industry became stagnant. An accumulated loss of dkk million 362 since the start of the industry added even more risk aversion to the cautious investment strategies operated by some of the firms. Out of the original twenty-six venture capital firms, only eleven or twelve were left in the period from 1990 to 1994, and four of these did not invest in either 1990 or 1991

(*Venture News,* May 1991, p. 12). Not all of the disappeared venture firms went bankrupt. Some were merged, bought out, or restructured. But the trend is clear: still fewer venture firms. The remaining eight venture firms can be grouped into two: one group with a relatively large amount of capital that is investing in well-known, established firms; and another group of venture firms with a smaller amount of resources that is either passively investing small amounts in larger firms or concentrating on a few small firms (ibid., p. 24). A possible exception to these groupings is Dansk Udviklingsfinansiering A/S (Danish Development Finance Corporation Ltd., or DUF), which continued to invest in innovative, small firms. This was, though, partly a result of the way this fund was set up, as it was initiated as a political response to the decline in such investments. In the original concept, DUF was meant to be fully back-funded by public money. However, in the final setup, the originally proposed dkk 1 billion was reduced to 500 million, and private investors became the funding sources, together with the Danish National Bank.

Moreover, in line with the development in European venture firms, the investment profile of the industry as such has changed in the first half of the 1990s toward risk-averse investment strategies, with the majority of investments occurring in the later stages of the firm's development (Christensen 1997). This development can even be traced back to the 1980s. See in table 7.1 that the share of investments in new firms decreases over time, especially when the activity of DUF is disregarded.

Because Venture News has stopped producing statistics on venture activity in Denmark, I have used EVCA statistical data on investments by stages to

Table 7.1
New Investments—Stages Distributed [% of firms]

	New firms	Expansion	Later stages	Number of firms
1983				3
1984	55	34	11	55
1985	39	42	19	52
1986	37	30	33	68
1987	29	35	36	52
1988	32	29	39	41
1989	47 (26)	29 (42)	24 (35)	38 (26)
1990	52 (29)	26 (35)	22 (36)	27 (17)
1991	43 (8)	35 (50)	22 (42)	23 (12)

()DUF excluded.
Source: Venture News, 5/92, p. 6.

show developments, although there is not a one-to-one correspondence between the ways that the two collect and compile the data. EVCA statistics may
be affected by large variances in single years, especially for small countries in
which the sample is relatively small; therefore, averages over a greater period
may be a useful validation of the results (see Figure 7.1).

Calculated in amounts invested, the picture is even more clear: for all countries, expansion and later business stages account for the majority of investments. In other words, the formal venture capital has gradually moved away
from early-stage businesses.[11] In addition, the average would be even higher
on buyouts if a weighted average were used, because the United Kingdom is
much above the average in the buyout phase and the amounts of British venture capital almost match the rest of the other European countries combined,
according to the EVCA statistics.

EVCA has taken different initiatives to counteract the trend illustrated
above, including an Early-Stage Programme, an Early-Stage Interest Group,
and several activities that were specifically targeted at early-stage investors:
portfolio partnering workshops in life sciences and IT; partnering trips to the
United States and Israel; newsletters; the first international conference on
Early-Stage and Technology Investment; and specialized training modules
within the EVCA Institute course.

RECENT DEVELOPMENTS OF THE DANISH
MARKET: A REVITALIZATION?

After the collapse in the beginning of the 1990s, the venture capital industry
in the mid-1990s followed the general upswing of the economy not only in

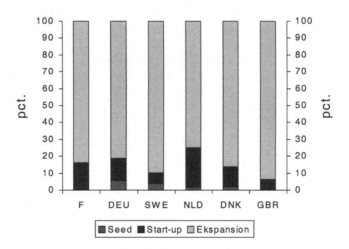

Figure 7.1 Venture investments by development stages, 1994–1996

Source: Kjærgård, Rolf (2000), European Venture Capital Association, selected yearbooks.

Denmark but throughout Europe. Not only did funds raised increase, but also the actual pace of investment began slowly to regain momentum and the number of venture capital firms increased, as will be shown with statistics later in this section. The business cycle does have an influence on the development of the venture industry. In particular, an upward trend in the stock market in combination with a few successful cases may spur an increase in venture capital activity. In addition, business cycles may have an impact on the behavior of market participants in that they may duplicate each other, thus reinforcing possible effects from business cycles. For example, a recession may cause venture capital firms to be reluctant to finance certain industries or types of firms in which losses have been experienced. Such patterns of behavior may become deeply rooted and widespread, which can cause inertia in the market: even when the capital market, which was previously constrained, recovers, it takes time to change the behavior of financiers.

The observed structural development suggests more general considerations about the possible cyclical character of the venture capital market. More specifically, the venture capital market is likely to be more volatile and business cycles are likely to have greater amplitude compared to ordinary product markets. At least three arguments support this claim. First, as is well known, the portfolio of firms is over-average risky and would probably be hit first and harder by a recession. Second, the development of venture capital indicates a herding behavior on the supply side. Third, the traditional adverse selection effects are likely to be reinforced by the heavy reliance on a "golden investment." Thus, many venture capital firms focus upon firms with high growth potentials, which are likely to be very risky investments. Even so, the importance of business cycles should not be exaggerated. In many countries, the government has had an impact on the development of the venture market, leveling out fluctuations caused by business cycles.

In the past few years, the venture capital industry has boomed. One of the reasons is a government guarantee to selected venture capital companies. The government has generally been active in stimulating the market with a combination of direct participation and arm's-length inducements to help market forces work. In addition, there has been great political awareness about the need for a more developed venture capital market, which in itself has created even more focus upon this financing source. A further spark to this development has been EVCA statistics that show that the size of the venture capital market in Denmark is relatively small compared to other European countries. For example, EVCA yearbooks for the late 1990s place Denmark near the bottom of the ranking of European countries if measured both as venture capital funds and as venture capital investments relative to GDP (gross domestic product; see table 7.2). This has contributed to a high political priority to stimulate the venture capital market. It should, though, be mentioned that the EVCA

Table 7.2
Total Private Equity/Venture Capital Investment

	% of GDP					
	1995	1996	1997	1998	1999	1995-99
United Kingdom	0.306	0.320	0.381	0.566	0.851	0.502
United States	0.074	0.143	0.210	0.248	0.643	0.278
Netherlands	0.147	0.183	0.229	0.303	0.463	0.263
Sweden	0.047	0.204	0.167	0.095	0.570	0.216
OECD-19	0.080	0.109	0.147	0.200	0.463	0.204
Canada	0.083	0.131	0.208	0.185	0.287	0.181
European Union	0.082	0.095	0.130	0.185	0.307	0.159
Europe	0.080	0.093	0.127	0.182	0.301	0.156
Iceland	0.014	0.014	0.075	0.293	0.285	0.147
Norway	0.107	0.067	0.124	0.126	0.185	0.121
Belgium	0.053	0.051	0.083	0.116	0.289	0.116
France	0.072	0.069	0.101	0.137	0.210	0.116
Finland	0.034	0.040	0.105	0.164	0.206	0.110
Germany	0.035	0.038	0.071	0.101	0.159	0.079
Italy	0.030	0.052	0.059	0.088	0.162	0.079
Ireland	0.038	0.066	0.052	0.084	0.123	0.076
Switzerland	0.021	0.054	0.024	0.092	0.181	0.072
Portugal	0.068	0.040	0.070	0.052	0.117	0.069
Spain	0.036	0.040	0.053	0.070	0.129	0.066
Denmark	*0.022*	*0.024*	*0.015*	*0.026*	*0.071*	*0.031*
Greece	0.009	0.033	0.015	0.018	0.061	0.028
Austria	0.001	0.000	0.010	0.027	0.046	0.016

Source: Parts of table in Baygan and Freudenberg (2000, p. 19) who use EVCA, various Yearbooks, NVCA, various Annual Reports, Canadian Venture Capital Association (CVCA)

statistics are highly uncertain and that better accounts are called for.[12] Later in this chapter I illustrate the deficiencies in the EVCA statistics.

The role of the government should not be underestimated, but precise effects are difficult to separate from the market-driven development. At the moment, the development of the market is very rapid, with market forces dominating. The market has now regained momentum not only in terms of the number of venture capital firms active on the market but also in the amount of capital for investments, the actual investments made, and the investment profiles of the market participants. Furthermore, complementary financing sources have developed hand in hand with the development of venture capital, notably corporate venture capital and, to some extent, business angel financing.

I attempt here to estimate the size of the market with considerably more accuracy than the estimations by EVCA (which have been used in a policy context). I also describe the structure of the venture capital market along several dimensions, both at the supply side and the demand side. The basis for these estimations and descriptions is a combination of several sources of information:[13]

- annual reports from venture capital firms
- websites of these firms (some venture funds are too new to have published annual reports)
- the business press
- a postal survey among all venture capital firms in Denmark

I have given careful consideration in this study as to whether relevant funds could be characterized as true venture or if they should be classified as complementary to the venture market. Funds normally investing in large firms, buyouts, and later stage firms are excluded from the analysis even if such funds are normally part of the EVCA definition of the venture capital market.[14]

Figure 7.2 shows the development during the 1990s, measured as the number of venture firms.[15] It is clear from figure 7.2 that 1995 is a turning point. The number of venture capital firms increases steadily from then onward, reaching an all time high of twenty-eight at the beginning of 2000. It should be added that twenty-eight is a very conservative figure. As already mentioned, the borderline between venture capital and other types of finance is blurred. Likewise, it is not at all clear what constitutes a venture capital firm. As explained

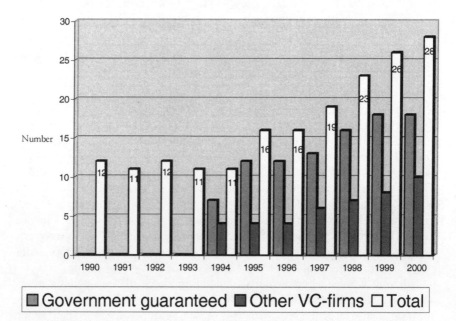

Figure 7.2 Number of Danish venture capital firms in the 1990s by types of fund
Source: Annual reports, homepages, business press.

earlier, some of the equity funds are not included in the present analyses. Also, funds have been established that are somewhere between a formal venture capital fund and a way of institutionalizing business angels' activity.[16] If such funds were included, the number of venture capital firms would total more than twenty-eight.

In addition to these structural developments, it is of particular interest to know the size of the market. Different measures are used to determine this size. One is the funds raised; another measure that is often used is the number of investments made. Both these measures are employed in the following discussion.

The information is derived from a survey done in the beginning of 2000 among all the Danish venture capital firms. In addition, in order to verify the information provided by the venture capital firms, annual reports and home pages from these venture capital firms have also been investigated, with a focus upon total equity capital and liquid funds (including securities) for each firm.

Table 7.3 shows funds available both as total equity capital (first column in each year) and as liquid funds and securities (second column in each year). For the last column, "Estimated capital available in 2000," the venture firms were asked to estimate what capital they would have available in the year 2000. The answers were checked and supplemented with similar information from two other surveys performed by two Danish business newspapers and with information from Internet home pages and annual reports. In some cases, information from these two surveys was not totally consistent. In these cases, we have relied on our own written information directly from the venture capital firms. In a few cases, phoning the venture capital firms was necessary. Even after these procedures, information was not available for all funds. In this case, the total equity from the latest year available was duplicated to 1999 and/or 2000. Table 7.3 shows selected results from this work.

The table shows a substantial amount of capital available as well as a rapid increase in this capital. The total size of the market can be estimated to almost

Table 7.3
Venture Funds in Denmark [capital available]

Name/group	Capital available in 1994	Capital available in 1998	Capital available in 1999	Estimated Capital available in 2000
All venture firms	2072	3152	3606	6345,7
Others*				1000
Total				7345,7

*NOVO 400 mio., two innovation funds 600
Source: Survey, annual reports, homepages, business press.

dkk 7 1/2 billion (1 billion EURO). This estimate may be conservative, because some of the important actors have made successful trade sales and are channeling substantial amounts of these revenues to venture activities.

Similar conclusions can be derived from investigations on investments made (see table 7.4). Again, even though a much more narrow definition of venture capital is used, the actual Danish figures are substantially higher than EVCA estimates. Thus, EVCA estimates investments in Denmark at euro 22 million in 1997 and euro 40 million in 1998. The present account shows an estimate of more than euro 100 million in 1998, in other words, more than double the EVCA estimates. Recent EVCA estimates have improved in quality and have also been much higher. In figure 7.3, two estimates are compared: one is the EVCA estimate, the other is the survey by Christensen and Borup. Estimates are substantially higher in the Christensen and Borup account. Although the two estimates appear to be similar in 1999, it should be noted that the two

Table 7.4
Venture Capital Investments in Denmark

Name/group	Capital invested in 1994	Capital invested in 1998	Capital invested in 1999	Estimated Capital inv. in 2000	Cumulative investments made pr.feb.2000
Foreign Venture Capital Firms	0	63,5	242	-	-
All venturefirms (incl. foreign)	212,6	708,9	1041	1373	3134

Source: Survey, annual reports, homepages, business press.

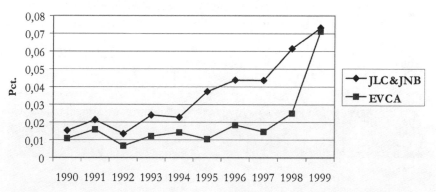

Figure 7.3 Two estimates of the Danish venture capital market, yearly investments, percentage of GDP.

Source: JLC & Borup estimate: survey among Danish venture capital firms. EVCA: EVCA Yearbooks, various years.

measures used different definitions of venture capital. Had the same definition been used, the Christensen and Borup figure for 1999 would have been much higher.

As mentioned, the EVCA figures include also later stage funds, whereas these funds are excluded from the estimate above. Even so, it is clear that the present, much more thorough, investigation of the size of the market renders considerably higher magnitudes compared to what has hitherto been thought.

Much of the rapid development has taken place within the past few years and, as is evident from table 7.4, this increase is expected to continue. Even if there is a substantial increase in venture capital activity, it is important to note that much of the increase in venture capital investments has been more investments in already established portfolio firms, whereas the number of new firms in the portfolio of the older venture capital firms is relatively stable, even in recent years.

The results in figure 7.4 explain why, even in countries with high growth in venture capital activity, entrepreneurs and small, new firms complain about finance constraints with respect to access to venture capital.

One possible explanation why venture capital firms may be reluctant to go into early-stage investments could be the routes of exit. It has often been claimed that the way out of the investment is important, both to the size of the rate of return on the investment but also—and related—to the mere decision of investing at all. Without the possibilities for harvesting the investments, it is likely that potential investors will be reluctant to consider investing in the first place. If the country does not offer appropriate exit routes, the development of a viable venture capital industry is likely to be hampered. Statistics on exit routes are somewhat uncertain due especially to the private

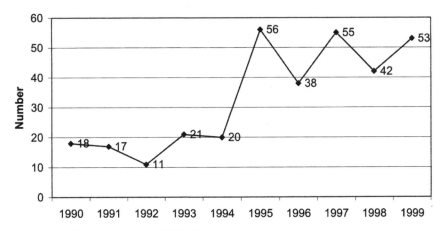

Figure 7.4 New investments, 1990–99.
Source: Survey among Danish venture capital firms.

nature of these transactions. This lack of statistics will undoubtedly cause an underestimation of the importance of, for example, trade sales compared to IPOs. Nevertheless, most accounts in most countries list trade sales as the most important exit. In the Anglo-Saxon countries, IPOs are also important, mainly due to the developed and highly liquid secondary markets in these countries.

But the importance of IPOs should not be overemphasized, as is the tendency in the business press and the academic literature alike.[17] For a venture capital market to flourish, the IPOs are more important as single success stories that may spur investors to increase funding rather than as a frequently used exit route. Instead, a lively M&A (mergers and acquisitions) market is more important, as trade sales is the single most important exit route used. This general statement should, however, be refined. Although the large-firm segment is not part of the venture capital definition used in this chapter (even if it is indeed included in the EVCA definition), the recent increase in activities of new Danish, large funds aimed at this segment would probably not have been at the same level had the stock exchange developed negatively. In other words, for venture activities at later stages, such as leveraged buyouts, the possibilities of an IPO may be important, whereas for the smaller deals most investors do not see an IPO as the most likely exit.[18] Even for smaller deals, a well-functioning stock exchange may in some cases facilitate a faster IPO for those firms that are determined to be listed. Thus, these firms are listed sooner compared to countries in which quotation is more difficult.

The changes have been not only quantitative but also structural and behavioral. One such structural change is the development in the medium and large firm markets in which a number of equity funds have become active. Although these funds are not necessarily targeting their investments toward the same firms as venture capital firms, nevertheless the markets are interrelated and an increase in the demand for shares in one part of the market may have spillover effects on the prices in other parts of the market.

In addition to the funds mentioned and, in this survey, defined as true venture capital, a number of other funds should be mentioned. These are either already on the market or under establishment. Capital is provided most notably by banks and also pension funds. A substantial part of the private equity capital raised is fund-of-funds, but independent funds meant for direct investments are set up as well. Some of these direct investments may also be characterized as true venture capital investments. This shows that a number of financial institutions are attracted to the venture capital market and that they are likely to provide the market with a substantial amount of capital.

Another trend is the increase in corporate venture capital, which not only is used for strategic acquisitions but is also in many cases true venture activity and indeed involves a substantial amount of money. A great number of industrial firms are now turning part of their activities to venture capital.[19] Also, it should be mentioned that it has become common for consultants to contribute with equity in some of their customer firms. This trend is seen especially in the Internet firm segment.

Finally, changes have taken place not just on the supply side. A number of success stories with IPOs and especially trade sales in Denmark and abroad have not only increased available capital and risk willingness on the supply side but have also improved the attitude toward taking a risk and the willingness to try to start up a new firm or to spin from an existing firm. This, in combination with improved support for making and testing a business plan, adds to the number of business opportunities and therefore increases the potential pool of investments. Increased numbers of business opportunities can be expected to change the investment profile of the aggregate venture capital industry. As the industry matures and as the debate on the so-called new economy has directed attention to small, innovative firms, it is likely that investments in the small firm segment will increase.

However, whereas analyses of the distribution of investments by firm size have until recently shown a fairly stable pattern, there is now a tendency toward a decrease in investments in the very small firms, as shown in figure 7.5.

EXPLAINING THE EVOLUTION OF THE VENTURE CAPITAL INDUSTRY

It may be concluded from the previous section that the development of the venture capital industry has followed a pattern in which a rapid takeoff was followed by a dramatic downswing and a subsequent shakeout of venture capital firms and a change of investment strategy in the remaining venture firms. I see six reasons for this change in the number of venture firms and in the investment strategies and frequencies of the remaining firms in the Danish market, which I explain below. However, the development of venture capital has been rather similar in the West European countries, and therefore these

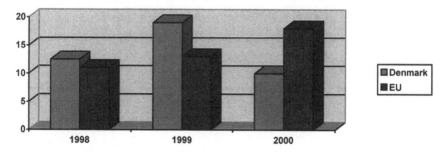

Figure 7.5 Seed investments as percentage of aggregate venture investments (amount)
Source: EVCA and Danish Business Development Fund.

explanations are to a large extent applicable to other countries as well, although with minor modifications.

First, the losses during the 1980s were to a large extent on start-ups. Data on losses in venture capital firms by size of portfolio firm are rarely available. One exception in Denmark is the venture capital firm Dansk Kapitalanlæg, which has been in the market long enough to break investments down into size classes. According to Dansk Kapitalanlæg (DKA), the results for 1997 clearly showed that the small firm group rendered the largest aggregate losses. A similar account of bank losses by size of amount lent shows clearly that there is a relationship between losses and the size of amount lent (which is a valid proxy for firm size; Finansrådet, May 1996, p. 24). There is no reason to believe that the pattern in DKA and the banks does not apply to Danish venture capital in general. Moreover, the portfolio of applicants is likely to have an aspect of adverse selection.[20] A relatively large share of applicants have presumably been rejected elsewhere due to bad reputation, inadequate documentation, disclosed information, and so on. This adds to the already risky profile of start-ups.

Second, venture capital firms have presumably underestimated the amount of resources (and possibly also the time horizon of the investments) they had to devote to time-consuming screening and monitoring of new, small firms. Especially when a new firm moved from the development stage to the marketing of the product, new problems arose, which took more resources and additional capital. Compared to the size of the investment, these resources were not in balance with the expected profits.

Third, there was a crowding-out effect from some of the funds traditionally labeled institutional investors, that is, mainly pension funds. Some of these funds were rather active in the venture market. Thus, the stock of unlisted shares between 1986 and 1994 increased (Venture News and Finanstilsynet).

Table 7.5
Stock of Unlisted Share in Pension Funds [book value]

	Mio.dkk
1986	929
1987	1069
1988	1557
1989	2313
1990	2546
1992*	2769
1993*	4374
1994*	5847

*ATP,LD, 1991 N.A.
Source: Venture News, 7/91, p.9, Finanstilsynet web-site.

In the beginning of the 1990s, most of these funds reversed their strategy and officially announced that they had underestimated the need and costs of monitoring and guiding small firms. Some of the institutional investors, who invested directly in the venture market, were at the same time owners in the "true" venture capital firms.

Fourth, it is questionable whether the venture capital firms actually had adequate amounts and types of resources. Some of them started with a capital portfolio that was too small. Thus, of sixteen venture funds in mid-1985, thirteen were established with a capital base less than or equal to euro 8 million (Rasmussen 1985, p. 31). The disadvantages of this are that they were unable to diversify their investments in order to minimize risk and that they were not always able to supply their portfolio firms with second and third round capital.

Fifth, the venture firms were not always competent to be active owners. Most venture firms were established "top-down," that is, established by one or more financial institutions rather than as a spin-off from the industrial sector, as in the early U.S. development of the venture capital industry. It is likely that some of the managers in the new venture firms came from the financial sector and brought with them investment policies and screening routines from that sector. In other words, the corporate sector did not always buy the "intelligent capital" that the venture capital concept is generally associated with. The institutional investors who were engaged in venture financing were especially not geared to venture investments with respect to organization and competencies.

Finally, it is beyond doubt that the worsening business climate in the late 1980s and early 1990s contributed to the crises. Firms in which venture capital typically invests (that is, over-average, technology-based, growth-oriented businesses often based on one or a few products) are often more sensitive to fluctuations than the average firm is. Therefore, a general recession is likely to hit the venture capital industry harder than it does the economy as a whole. This not only means worsened prospects for the firms in terms of declining demand, it also means that the equity provided by venture firms no longer replaces very expensive debt. A rapid shift from high inflation rates to low inflation caused even more trouble for many firms.

To illustrate that the development in other countries has followed a similar pattern, it is worth looking at Sweden (see chapter 6). Thus, SIND (1990, p. 55) quotes some of the main reasons for the decline of the industry in Sweden to be related to the venture firms who had (a) too small a capital base, (b) too short a time horizon on investments, (c) a lack of experienced, competent management who knew about developing small businesses. These reasons resemble those referred to in the Danish case.

Explanations on the upswing are likewise a multiple of different reasons, not just one single explanation. In summary, whereas the decline in venture capital activity may be explained above, the revitalization is most likely linked to five factors. First, the implementation of a Law on Guarantee on losses not only made the existing firms more risk willing, it also created a broader and more specialized supply side. Second, success stories of trade sales and more activity at both the stock market and the M&A market contributed to more venture capital activity. In other words, exit possibilities improved, just as was the case in other parts of Europe where new markets such as AIM, Neuer Markt, Le Nouveau Marché, and EASDAQ have emerged. Third, internationalization in venture capital has remained low in terms of quantity on a European level. Even so, there is increased collaboration and increased inflows of venture capital funds from abroad. It is therefore not just a question of Danish venture capital firms duplicating the behavior of foreign venture capital firms. In fact, the venture capital inflow into the Danish market has been substantial, according to Baygan and Freudenberg (2000). They highlight Ireland and Denmark as the two countries in which inflow has been substantial and has significantly increased the amount of venture capital in these countries (p. 12; see also note 14). Fourth, diversification and competition on financial markets, including the venture capital market, has increased. This is illustrated by the many new captive organizations, which have been spun off from, especially, banks and corporations. The increase in corporate venture capital has greatly expanded the pool of venture capital funds; however, another part of the informal venture capital market should be mentioned as well. The increased activity has made business angels more active. Fifth, the pure supply has increased from pension funds, fund-of-funds, and other institutional investors. Figure 7.6 illustrates the capital under management in 2000, by different types of funds.

These explanations both overlap with and add to those of Tyebjee and Vickery (1988). Their article points to the size of the technology sector, the culture of entrepreneurship, the financial markets for new companies, public policy initiatives, overall level of economic activity and cyclical economic factors in the country, and legislation on trade secrets and intellectual property.

LESSONS FOR POLICIES FROM THE DEVELOPMENT OF THE VENTURE CAPITAL INDUSTRY

This analysis shows a rapid increase both in aggregate size of the venture capital pool in Denmark and the investments made, and in the number of active organizations. I have shown that the EVCA figures underestimate the size of the Danish market substantially.

It has been discussed in many government bodies to what extent the government should be involved in the development of the venture capital market. Aernoudt (1999) claims that

Until recently, European policy makers were relatively absent from venture capital markets. . . . venture capitalists tended to agree with policy makers that no government involvement was needed in the field of venture capital. What was lacking, they said, was not capital, but good projects, and those could only come from creative individuals,

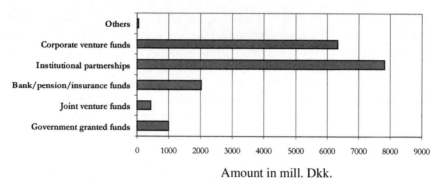

Amount in mill. Dkk.

Figure 7.6 Estimate of venture capital under management

not from public bodies. This, at first sight, attractive macro- or rather meso-economic rationale, can easily be deconstructed. (p. 47)

From the Swedish experience, it is obvious that direct government involvement has been vital in the creation of a viable venture market in Sweden. The active participation of the government contributed both to keeping the market "alive" and to the further development of the market. Since the mid-1990s, when the market revitalized, the government involvement changed character and became more indirect but still active. The state is now concerned with offering incentives for private individuals to provide back-funding for venture activities. In line with this argument, governments throughout the western world have developed schemes to stimulate investments in seed phases and start-ups. Even on a supernational level there are programs and institutions designed to support such investments. For example, the European Investment Bank has extended its activities from loan facilities and is now (after the Amsterdam summit) acting as a back-funding to technology-oriented funds in venture capital markets in a range of countries. The European Investment Fund likewise supports venture capital funds, as does the European Commission.[21]

It is evident from the evolution of the venture capital market in Denmark, and in other countries as well, that the inducement to grow, the sustainability of the market, and especially the ability of the market to recover after a downswing is highly dependent upon the government's playing a key role. This is reflected in the fact that in the majority of advanced countries the government has some form of special program aimed at supporting the venture capital industry (Gompers and Lerner 1997). Thus, the government clearly has a role to play in the very first stages of financing firm development. Government programs are primarily targeted toward this segment.

One of the lessons from the rise and fall of the venture capital market in Denmark, Sweden, and other countries is that adequate competencies have to be supplied, something which was generally not the case in the first years of expansion of the industry. Competencies also have to do with the possible cyclical character of the venture capital market, a wavelike development that I explained earlier in this chapter. In the past couple of years we saw in Denmark and the rest of Europe alike an immense amount of money flowing into the venture capital industry and new funds and venture capital firms popping up in a steady stream. The speed of new funds flowing into the industry exceeded the development of new business opportunities, and the consequences were that competition increased and prices on shares went up. Moreover, greater risks were taken and marginal deals were made to a greater extent, some of which were made by new entrants who may have been inexperienced to some degree. To counteract the increase in prices, some venture funds may look for opportunities in other markets.

Some contend that rapidly increased availability of funds for venture capitalists induce "venture capital myopia," in other words, a duplication of each others' investments (Sahlman and Stevenson 1985). This may subsequently lead to a much stronger shakeout than would otherwise have happened. Thus, according to Sahlman and Stevenson, herding behavior may lead to an excess demand relative to the investment opportunities. This overfunding of industries may in turn lead to overcapacity, declining income, failures, and falling returns in venture companies.[22] In a longer term, this myopia may have inexpedient economic consequences because certain industries may, even long after a recovery, experience financing constraints.[23]

Given the development described above, it is likely that there are still sound business proposals in Denmark seeking venture financing, and there is still room for developing the venture market even further. However, it is likely that the market could within a short time horizon be on the top of another cycle, which eventually may lead to another shakeout of actors on the market, a more cautious investment strategy of the remaining firms, and a reduction in funds to the venture industry. On the other hand, the amplitude of such a cycle may be reduced by active participation of government bodies. This is, however, likely to be successful only if there are competencies in the market. Furthermore, the skills of experienced venture capitalists may be important assets in counteracting a cyclical development because it is one characteristic of a competent venture capitalist to spot opportunities even in a declining market.

Even if a downswing and subsequent shakeout should occur, the development of the venture capital markets in many European countries, including Denmark, has meant an increased maturation. Thus, there is now much greater diversity and specialization among the venture capital companies. Moreover, the venture capital industry has reached a quantitative level at which we may talk about a critical mass. Therefore, even in a recession for the industry, it is likely that the two factors above—the diversity and the size of the market—will mean that the industry will not only stay alive and survive, but also keep up activities, again provided adequate competencies are present.[24]

NOTES

1. The author is grateful for comments on earlier drafts of this paper or parts of the paper. In particular, thanks to Peter Højme, former director of Dansk Erhvervsinvestering, Claus E. Christensen of Ministry of Industry, Morten K. Pedersen and Jacob N. Borup of Danish Business Development Fund, participants in DRUID-seminar in Aalborg November 1, 2000, and participants in a seminar on the development in Danish venture capital in Danish Business Development Fund December 10, 2001.

2. See OECD (1996b, 1996c) for a review of government initiatives to stimulate venture capital in OECD countries.

3. Some of the most important include Axcel, Polaris, and Nordic Private Equity Fund.

4. Recently the government-sponsored fund, The Growth Fund, made a mapping of the corporate venture capital activities in Denmark (Danish Growth Fund 2002). This is, however, largely the only information available on CVC in Denmark.

5. For example, in a survey from 1999 on business angels and innovative firms, ninety-six firms responded to the question "Assess the statement: It is difficult to get an overview of all possible financing sources in Denmark." Of these, 49 percent responded "Agree Fully" and 31 percent were "More in agreement than in disagreement."

6. The introduction of the Small Business Investment Act in 1958 further induced the investments by private funds although there have been periods with less successful SBA (small business administration). Thus the number of private investors with an SBA license decreased from 585 in 1966 to about three-quarters of that level in 1972.

7. Bullock (1983) describes this development.

8. See Christensen (1997) for an empirical account of this development.

9. There is probably not a single event explaining this development. However, one important inducement in the United States could be pointed to. December 12, 1980, Apple Computers was introduced on the stock exchange, and the tremendous success of this emission both attracted a lot of people and institutions to the venture capital industry and induced a boom in emissions of high-technology stocks. However, the newcomers to the industry were more directed toward fast, large profits than toward building up industrial firms (Finans/Invest, November 1984). The industry lost its original industrial base.

10. A somewhat similar development occurred in the other Nordic countries. By 1985 there were about twenty venture firms in Denmark, five to six in Norway (1984 figure), and twenty to thirty in Sweden.

11. In comparison, a similar picture cannot be found in the United States to the same extent. Traditionally, the U.S. venture funds have, to a larger degree than the European venture funds, been directed toward early-stage, technology-based investments. This is still the case when cross-country comparisons are made. Some accounts even suggest that the proportion of early-stage financing is declining in Europe but growing in the United States (OECD 1996b, p. 21). In the last few years, though, European venture capital has shown a growing interest in early-stage financing.

12. Baygan and Freudenberg (2000, p. 12) point to five major difficulties in international comparisons of venture capital activity, difficulties stemming from the lack of quality and comparability of statistics. One of these five points is that rarely are the data adjusted for international inflows and outflows. Usually data refer only to the location of the venture capital firm, whereas it is equally important, or perhaps even

more important, to know the capital available or investments made *in* a country rather than *by* a country. According to recent calculations, in an accounting of inflows and outflows of foreign investments, Denmark's position changes dramatically. If the usual "country of management approach" is used, Denmark is ranked seventeenth out of nineteen OECD countries in terms of total private equity investments as percentage of GDP in 1999, but it changes position to sixth if a "country of destination approach" is used (ibid., p. 22).

13. Thanks to student Jacob Borup for help in compiling the information on the Danish venture capital market.

14. Thus, funds like Polaris, Axcel, and Nordic Private Equity Partners are not considered part of the venture market.

15. This account is not totally consistent with what has been estimated by Venture News. In the present account are a number of venture firms that for some reason are not included in the Venture News statistics: Comlex (established 1990), Gaia Technologies (1992), novi (1988), DICO (1992), and Invest Miljø (1991). Therefore, Venture News mentions only ten venture capital firms in 1990, eight in 1991, and eight in 1992.

16. Two such examples are JT Invest and Growth.dk; in both cases, a successful businessman established his own venture-like fund.

17. It is even official policy in the Danish government to prefer IPOs to other types of exit. Thus, in an account of the goals for industrial policy (Regeringen 2000) it is stated as an objective that a certain number of technology-based IPOs should be reached by the year 2010.

18. In Britain, where relatively more venture activity takes place in later stages, the possibility of getting listed is seen as an important exit. Thus, in a survey for BVCA and PriceWaterhouseCoopers by Bannock Consulting published in 1999, 39 percent of venture-backed companies surveyed were expecting to obtain a stock exchange quotation.

19. In popular terms, we could denote this development as a stream of investments from "old" economics into "new" economics; thus, this transformation takes place through investments rather than through changes in demand and through competition that outperforms old industries.

20. There are, however, counterarguments to this. For example, Mason and Harrison list three arguments why the adverse selection argument is doubtful (1999a, pp. 32–33).

21. Aernoudt (1999, p. 47–57) provides an overview of current European policy toward venture capital.

22. In Denmark the hotel and restaurant industry is still suffering from credit constraints by some financial institutions, even though the investments in overcapacity were in the beginning of the 1990s.

23. On the other hand, some observers see mainly positive effects from such myopia (Bygrave and Timmons 1992).

24. Mason and Harrison are in line with this argument when they write "Efforts by governments to promote classic venture capital in countries that lack this form of finance may be constrained by the industry's human resource base" (1999a, p. 20).

REFERENCES

Aernoudt, R. 1999. "European Policy towards Venture Capital: Myth or Reality?" *Venture Capital* 1: 47–57.

Bank of England. 1996. *The Financing of Technology-Based Small Firms.* Report. October.

Bannock, G. 1995. "Corporate Venture Capital." Background paper for the EIMS Innovation Policy Workshop "Innovation Financing," Luxembourg.

Baygan, G., and N. Freudenberg. 2000. *The Internationalisation of Venture Capital Activity in OECD Countries: Implications for Measurement and Policy.* Paris: OECD, STI WP, 2000/7.

Bullock, M. 1983. *Funding of Technological Change: R&D for the 21st. Century. An Analysis of Trends Affecting Strategies for Industrial Innovation.* London: The Research and Development Society.

BVCA (British Venture Capital Association). 1999. *The Economic Impact of Venture Capital in the UK.* London: BVCA.

Bygrave, W. D., and J. A. Timmons. 1992. *Venture Capital at the Crossroads.* Boston, Mass.: Harvard Business School.

Christensen, J. L. 1997. *Financing Innovation.* Report, The European Commission, TSER-programme.

Christensen, J. L. 1998. *Den Danske Venturebranches Seed-finansiering* [Seed-financing in the Danish Venture Capital Market]. Aalborg: NOVI.

Christensen, J. L., L. Dyhrberg, P. Livoni, and J. Rygaard. 1998. "Finansiering af Innovationer—et Bidrag fra Private Investorer?" [Financing innovations—the role of business angels]. DISKO-rapport nr.5, Erhvervsudviklingsraadet.

Danish Business Development Fund. 2001a. "Det Danske Private Equity og Venture-marked år 2000" [The Danish Private Equity and Venture Market Year 2000]. Mimeo.

Danish Business Development Fund. 2001b. "Seed finansiering i Danmark: 2001" [Seed financing in Denmark, 2001]. Mimeo.

Danish Growth Fund. 2002. "Corporate Venture Capital i Danmark." Mimeo.

Davie, J. 1991. "Finding and Keeping Good Venture Capital Managers." *Venture Capital Journal,* July, pp. 21–26.

Dominguez, J. R. 1974. *Venture Capital.* Lexington, Mass.: Lexington Books.

EU, European Commission, Enterprise DG. 2001. Innovation, technology and risk capital. Enterprise Papers No. 5–2001.

European Venture Capital Association (EVCA). 1992. *EVCA Yearbook 1992: Venture Capital in Europe.* Antwerpen: KPMG and EVCA.

EVCA. 1994. *EVCA Yearbook 1994.* Antwerpen: KPMG and EVCA.

EVCA. 1996. *1996 Yearbook: A Survey of Venture Capital and Private Equity in Europe.* Zaventem, Belgium: EVCA.

EVCA. 1998. *Europe Private Equity Update.* No. 11. Antwerpen: EVCA.

Finansrådet. 1996. "Kreditvurdering og Finansieringsmuligheder" [Criteria for credit assessment and possibilities for financing]. Copenhagen: Finansrådet.

Gompers, P. A., and J. Lerner. 1997. *What Derives Venture Capital Fundraising?* Working Paper, Harvard Business School.

Isaksson, A. 1999. *Effecter av Venture Capital I Sverige* [Effects of venture capital in Sweden]. Stockholm: NUTEK.

Isaksson, A., and B. Cornelius. 1998. *Venture Capital Incentives: A Two Country Comparison.* Paper presented at the Tenth Nordic Conference on Small Business Research, Växjö University, Sweden, 14–16 June.

Karaomerlioglu, D.C., and S. Jacobsson. 2000. "The Swedish Venture Capital Industry— an Infant, Adolescent, or Grown-up?" *Venture Capital* 2 (1): 61–88.

Kjærgård, R. 2000. "Venturekapital Og Virksomhedsudvikling—Investeringsproces- sens Anatomi og Perspektiverne for en Offentlig Indsats" [Venture capital and development of enterprises—the genesis of investment process and perspectives for a government intervention). Copenhagen: Erhvervsministeriet.

Mason, C. M., and R. T. Harrison. 1999a. "Editorial, Venture Capital: Rationale, Aims, and Scope." *Venture Capital* 1 (1): 1–46.

Mason, C. M., and R. T. Harrison. 1999b. "Informal Venture Capital and the Financing of Emergent Growth Businesses." In *International State of the Art in Entre- preneurship*, ed. D. L. Sexton and H. Landström. Oxford: Blackwell.

Mason, C. M., and R. T. Harrison. 1999c. "Public Policy and the Development of the Informal Venture Capital Market: UK Experience and Lessons for Europe." In *Industrial Policy in Europe*, ed. K. Cowling. London: Routledge.

McNally, K. 1994a. "Bridging the Equity Gap? The Role of Corporate Venture Capital." Venture Finance Working Paper No. 10, October, University of Southampton.

McNally, K. 1994b. "Corporate Venture Capital Investment in the United Kingdom: Objectives, Strategies and Future Prospects." Venture Finance Working Paper No. 9, October, University of Southampton.

McNally, K. 1995. "External Equity Finance for Technology-Based Firms in the UK: The Role of Corporate Venture Capital." Venture Finance Working Paper No. 13, University of Southampton.

Murray, G. 1996. "Evolution Change: An Analysis of the First Decade of the UK Ven- ture Capital Industry." *Journal of Business Finance & Accounting* 22 (8): 1077– 1107.

Murray, G. 1999. "Seed Capital and the Tyranny of (Small) Scale." Conference on Financing Entrepreneurship and Innovation in Science Based Industries, Mann- heim, Germany, 22–23 January.

Organization for Economic Cooperation and Development (OECD). 1996a. *Government Programmes for Venture Capital.* Paris: OECD.

OECD. 1996b. *Venture Capital in OECD Countries.* Financial Markets Trends No. 63. Paris: OECD.

OECD. 1996c. *Workshop Proceedings: Ad Hoc Meeting on Experts on Venture Capital.* Paris: OECD.

Ooghe, H., S. Manigart, and Y. Fassin. 1991. "Growth Patterns of the European Venture Capital Industry." *Journal of Business Venturing* 6: 381–404.

Rasmussen, K. L. 1985. "Overvejelser ved Venturekapital Investeringer" [Considera- tions on venture capital investments]. Master's dissertation, Copenhagen Busi- ness School.

Regeringen [The Government]. 2000. "Pejlemærker for erhvervspolitikken." Copen- hagen: Regeringen.

Sahlman, W., and H. Stevenson. 1985. "Capital Market Myopia." *Journal of Business Venturing* 1 (1): 80–104.

Solomon, A. 1996. "Venture Capital in the U.S." In *Workshop Proceedings: Ad Hoc Meeting on Experts on Venture Capital.* Paris: OECD.

Statens Industriverk (SIND). 1990. *Riskkapitalet och de Mindre Företagen* [Risk capital and SMEs]. SIND, 1990, No. 3.

Stevens, W. 1996. "European Venture Capital Markets: Trends and Prospects." In *Workshop Proceedings: Ad Hoc Meeting of Experts on Venture Capital*. Paris: OECD.

Sykes, H. B. 1990. "Corporate Venture Capital: Strategies for Success." *Journal of Business Venturing* 5: 37–47.

Tyebjee, T., and L. Vickery. 1988. "Venture Capital in Western Europe." *Journal of Business Venturing* 3: 123–36.

Van Osnabrugge, A. 1999. "Comparison of Business Angels and Venture Capitalist Investment Procedures: An Agency Theory-Based Analysis." Paper presented at the Babson College–Kauffman Foundation Entrepreneurship Conference, University of South Carolina, May 12–15.

Venture News. 1998. T. Bak Jensen, consultants. Various issues.

Wright, M., and K. Robbie. 1998. "Venture Capital and Private Equity: A Review and Synthesis." *Journal of Business Finance Accounting* 25: 521–70.

8

Venture Capital in Canada
A Maturing Industry, with Distinctive Features and New Challenges

Charles H. Davis

INTRODUCTION

Venture capital (VC) is a form of private equity investment in early-stage businesses that are considered to have significantly high growth potential. It aims to generate income from appreciation of illiquid holdings and capital gains after disposal. VC shares agency and moral hazard problems with other forms of investment in private capital markets: unlike public markets where regulations ensure data disclosure, in private capital markets suppliers of capital must obtain their own information through due diligence and ongoing monitoring. VC investment is thus costlier and riskier than investment in public markets but also potentially much more lucrative. VC investments typically require patient investors who provide value-added advice and oversight to the recipient firm in the form of management, financial, and marketing know-how. Conventional financial institutions providing debt financing in the private capital market manage their risks with credit scoring applications and requirements for collateral. They are not able to make knowledgeable, hands-on investments to build technology-based businesses that create value primarily from intangible assets.

VC plays a disproportionately important role in driving industrial innovation through its selective and knowledgeable support of innovation in smaller companies, which enjoy comparative advantages in technology venturing due to their superior potential for coordinating marketing, design, and R&D (research and development) activities. In the United States between 1983 and 1992, venture capital accounted for 8 percent of industrial innovation (Kortum and Lerner 2000), although until the late 1990s venture capital represented less than 0.2 percent of U.S. GDP (gross domestic product). Private and public pension funds, endowment funds, foundations, corporations, wealthy individuals, foreign investors, governments, and professional venture investors are suppliers of venture capital.

The United States's venture capital industry is a key component in the U.S. innovation system, responsible for the development of tens of dozens of world-class technology companies. It is generally regarded as the most efficient and effective venture capital industry in the world, the model to emulate. This is especially so in Canada due to the close relationship between Canada and the United States. Canada is very sensitive to developments in the U.S. innovation system because of Canadian geographic, cultural, and economic proximity to the United States. The United States and Canada have the world's largest bilateral trade relationship. The two countries are also each other's largest trading partners. Canada has a large trade surplus in goods exported to the United States, and a large deficit in services imported from the United States. The United States is by far the largest source of foreign investment in Canada, accounting for 64 percent of direct investment in the country, and half of Canadian direct investment abroad is in the United States. Canadian firms are constantly exposed to U.S. firms as customers, suppliers, or competitors. However, the U.S. innovation system is so dynamic and resource-rich that for Canada to try to stay in the same league has been likened to the problem of "catching up with the Jetsons," that futuristic cartoon family with its endless supply of wondrous technologies.

It is a long and complex undertaking to develop an effective venture capital industry. In the case of Canada, the VC industry emerged slowly in the 1960s and 1970s, accelerated in the 1980s and expanded spectacularly in the late 1990s. The amount of venture capital under management in Canada has increased nearly fortyfold since 1981. Growth has been especially vigorous in this industry in the second half of the 1990s, driving an unprecedented technology venturing boom in Canada.

The Canadian venture capital industry has an unusual structural feature: funds are concentrated in vehicles dominated by "passive and semi-public investors." This is a major difference between Canada and the United States and Europe, where most venture funds are institutionally backed limited partnerships managed by professional VC managers. This structural feature is attributable to modifications in the Canadian tax regime introduced in the 1980s to encourage small retail investment in labor-sponsored venture funds. At the same time, the Canadian tax regime has imposed relatively high capital gains taxes on other kinds of venture capital investors. Historically, Canadian taxes and other factors appear to have reduced the incentives for active technology venturing in Canada, resulting in relatively greater conservatism on the part of Canadian venture investors compared to their U.S. counterparts. However, recent modifications of Canadian tax regulations have made the Canadian VC investment environment more like the American one.

The development of a venture capital industry can be conceptualized as a process of emergence and maturation. Maturity is measurable in terms of the industry's size, diversity, competence, and relative economic intensity (Karaomerlioglu and Jacobsson 2000). Relative economic intensity of venture capital activity is one indicator of the industry's maturity. In the case of Canada, the conventional reference point is the United States. The U.S. population is approximately nine times larger than Canada's, and the U.S. economy is approximately thirteen times the size of Canada's. The Canadian VC industry should therefore be between one-ninth and one-thirteenth the size of the U.S. venture capital industry. In recent years, taking into account the exchange rate of the Canadian dollar, Canadian venture capital activity ranged from 4 percent to 8 percent of its U.S. counterpart.[1] As for diversity, the venture capital industry should have enough breadth to encompass a range of industries, technologies, and sizes of deals. At the same time, the industry should be internally differentiated enough to possess firms with deep specializations in early-stage investments in particular industries or technologies. Industry competence refers to the industry's ability to obtain and assess information; the extension of the VC industry to industries, technologies, or regions that are not part of its original specialization pattern; and its depth of experience, including its ability to syndicate (Karaomerlioglu and Jacobsson 2000).

Many aspects of the Canadian VC industry are well documented, and quite detailed information about the industry is available through the Canadian Venture Capital Association and the firm Macdonald and Associates. However, a number of knowledge gaps exist concerning the behavior of this industry. This chapter examines the Canadian venture capital industry, describes its features, explains its distinguishing aspects, and discusses the issues facing it. The chapter is organized as follows. The next section describes the place of venture financing issues in the Canadian innovation agenda, provides an overview of issues regarding SMEs (small and medium enterprises) and their financial needs in Canada, and reviews the state of knowledge about availability of financing for "knowledge-based" or potential fast-growth firms. The following section analyzes the Canadian venture capital industry in terms of industry structure, characteristics, and tendencies. The third section explores three sets of issues currently affecting the development of venture capital in Canada: the fiscal and regulatory framework in which the industry operates, the investment gaps at the seed and start-up stages, and the availability of exits.

SMEs' CAPITAL NEEDS IN CANADA

Compared to its major trading partners, Canada's economic performance gives cause for concern. Canadian productivity has fallen in relative terms, and Canada's overall position on the influential World Competitiveness Scorecard has declined to ninth place in 2001 from sixth place in 1997. The many absolute improvements in Canadian competitiveness are overshadowed by loss of relative competitiveness across a range of indices (Porter and Martin 2000). In general, Canada's improvement in competitive performance in the 1990s is attributable primarily to improvement in macroeconomic factors, with bottlenecks and disconnects remaining in the microeconomic foundations of competitiveness (ibid.). This section reviews the known financial needs of Canadian SMEs, describes the investment needs that drive demand for venture capital, and examines available evidence about demand for venture capital among Canadian firms.

Against the background of declining relative competitiveness, national innovation policy-making in Canada has become more vigorous and more ambitious than it has been for decades. Many public and private actors are now actively promoting innovation-based competitiveness in Canada, advocating increased spending and adjustment of institutional arrangements to this end. Never before has an "innovation agenda" or the notion of an "innovation system" or "innovation clusters" enjoyed such a wide degree of interest and support within levels of government, the private sector, and the education sector as they currently do. Recent expressions are the House of Commons Standing Committee on Industry, Science, and Technology's report titled *Innovation Agenda for the Twenty-first Century* (Government of Canada 2001), and speeches by senior Canadian politicians. Financial issues are frequent items in the Canadian innovation agenda. In his response to the January, 2001, Speech from the Throne, Prime Minister of Canada Jean Chrétien announced a five-part plan to increase the country's innovation-based competitiveness: "at least double" federal investment in R&D by 2010; build excellence in Canadian universities; improve Canada's ability to commercialize research discoveries and technology; improve Canadian access to collaborative international research; and extend broadband Internet access everywhere in Canada by 2004 (Chrétien 2001). The Minister of Finance, Paul Martin, has called for Canada to adopt explicit innovation-related goals: that Canada have 5 percent of global e-commerce trade by 2003, and that Canada move from fifteenth to fifth in ranking of Organization for Economic Cooperation and Development countries' GERD (gross domestic expenditures on research and development)/GDP ratios, putting it in the same league as the United States and requiring expenditure of an additional 1 percent of GDP on R&D. Creating economic value from increased R&D spending requires innovation in the Canadian financial infrastructure—here the attention turns to venture capital. It is proposed that Canada strive to rank among the top three countries in the level of new venture capital investments per capita and to match the United States in dollar value per capita of initial public offerings (IPOs). In 1999, the dollar value per capita of IPOs by Canadian companies in Canada was half that raised by U.S. companies in the United States (Martin 2000).

Canada has about one million firms, of which only 0.2 percent have five hundred or more employees. About 75 percent of Canadian firms have fewer than five employees and about 22 percent have between five and fifty employees. In Canada as elsewhere, smaller firms account for the largest proportional increase in employment. Small firms created more than three-quarters of the net employment increase observed among all firms (Statistics Canada 2000). In 1997, businesses with fewer than five employees accounted for 26 percent of the gross increase in employment, but represented less than 9 percent of total employment. Businesses with less than fifty employees created 57 percent of the gross increase in employment but represented only 32 percent of total paid employment. Looking forward at 2001, the Canadian small business sector expected to create jobs at an average rate of 4.5 percent (Bruce 2000).

A recurrent theme in debates about Canadian economic performance is the adequacy of financial services for Canadian SMEs. The SME loan market is growing at greater than 7 percent annually and many nonbank actors have entered the market. The seven major Canadian banks authorized $70.9 billion in credit to small and medium businesses in 2000.[2] It is estimated that banks provide about half of all SME debt financing in Canada. The rest comes from nonbank sources such as credit unions, trust companies, specialized finance companies, credit card companies, life insurance firms, and public agencies.

Are financial services adequate? The general financial needs of SMEs are quite different from the financial needs of technology-based firms serviced by formal and informal venture investors. Mature firms with tangible assets appear to be adequately served by conventional debt financing institutions, while "knowledge-based" firms and other riskier groups such as infant firms, youth entrepreneurs, aboriginal entrepreneurs, or rural entrepreneurs often face difficulties in accessing start-up and working capital.

This generalization is supported by recent surveys of SMEs by national trade associations and banks. A survey of more than 22,000 Canadian Federation of Independent Business (CFIB) members in the second half of 2000 found that 29 percent of respondents considered that "availability of financing" was the most important issue facing them. However, more important to members than financing was a variety of regulatory, tax, and labor issues: the "total tax burden" (83 percent of respondents), employment insurance (64 percent), government regulation and the paper burden (62 percent), government debt (61 percent), workers' compensation (47 percent), shortage of qualified labor (46 percent), and cost of local government (42 percent; Canadian Federation of Independent Business 2001). A recent CFIB-sponsored study of members' experiences with financial institutions found that 84 percent of respondents declared themselves "very satisfied" or "somewhat satisfied" with services provided by financial institutions, major sources of dissatisfaction being service charges and branch closings (Bruce 2001). Respondents reported that about one in ten loan applications was rejected. However, about 21 percent of firms reported inability to secure adequate debt financing. Of these, the two largest groups were "less established" firms and "young high performing" firms (i.e., those less than ten years of age or with growth rates of 20 percent or more in the past three years). In Canada, new firms have a mortality rate of about 80 percent over a ten-year period (Baldwin et al. 1997). Only about 1 percent of the smallest firms (less than five employees) grow into the next size (Gorman and King 1998). Institutions providing conventional debt financing are aware of these risks and manage them by using increasingly sophisticated credit-scoring techniques and by requiring guarantees. A survey conducted in 2000 for the Business Development Bank of Canada found evidence of declining access to financial services by SMEs: 36 percent of respondents indicated that it is "somewhat or much more difficult" to obtain business financing today than five years ago.

Access to financing varies by the stage in the business life cycle, and Canadian start-ups are known to experience difficulty in obtaining bank loans (Riding 1998). Start-up firms have to provide personal guarantees, cosignatures, or fixed asset collateral to obtain loans. Once the firm has reached the growth stage and has a track record, access to debt financing is easier, although performance, fixed asset collateral, and personal guarantees are still required. Start-ups "do not expect much support when intangibles have to be financed, unless hard assets are pledged as guarantees" (Angus Reid Group 2000). Mature SMEs have an easier time; conventional financial institutions have targeted this group as preferred clients.

Entrepreneurial ventures can be divided into three types: "life-style" ventures with a five-year revenue projection of less than $10 million, middle-market ventures with a five-year projection of $10 million to $50 million, and high-potential ventures with a five-year revenue projection over $50 million (Wetzel 1997). The first category comprises more than 90 percent of all start-ups and is of no interest to venture investors. The second and especially the third categories of firms are the targets of venture investors.

Potential "gazelles," or fast-growth firms, make up a very small fraction of the total population of small firms, ranging from 16 percent to zero in about fifty counties in Québec studied by Julien and Lachance (2001). Fast-growth firms occur in every industry (Schreyer 2000). For example, small manufacturing firms that double their employment in five years may be considered high-growth firms (Julien and Lachance 2001). Canada's top ten fastest-growing technology firms in 2001 had truly astonishing five-year growth rates ranging from 73,068 percent (Stratos Global of Toronto) to 5,018 percent (Bridges.com of Kelowna, British Columbia). In 2001, forty-seven Canadian companies placed among Deloitte Touche's top 500 fastest-growing technology companies. They had average five-year growth rates of more than 6,000 percent (Deloitte Touche 2001).

Fast-growth firms may have distinguishing characteristics that can be detected ex ante by external service and resource providers (Fischer, Reuber, and Carter 1999). The two most important sources of capital for fast-growing SMEs in Canada are public equity and venture capital (Baldwin and Johnson 1996). Some types of "knowledge-based" firms, especially new technology-based firms, are potential fast-growth firms and are likely to require equity investment (Canadian Labour Market and Productivity Centre 1995a).

SIC codes (Standard Industrial Classifications) provide only an approximate indication of knowledge-intensity; reliable benchmarks for knowledge-intensity based on R&D ratios and indicators of human capital are not available. Venture capitalists define knowledge-based industries in terms of sectors that are known to use knowledge intensively: biotechnology, medicine and health, computers, communications, electronics and instrumentation, energy, environmental technology, and some areas of industrial equipment. Secor (1998) proposes a four-part typology of knowledge-based firms: science-based, high-tech craft, integrators, and technology users. Science-based firms are firms that commercialize products originating in scientific discoveries in research labs; examples are health biotechnology and new materials firms. High-tech craft firms produce state-of-the-art products requiring very highly skilled workers: examples are software and medical equipment. Integrators such as IT services or telecommunications companies assemble and deliver complex product and services. Technology users such as food processors or financial services use new technologies to improve the production and delivery of a mature product or service.

Knowledge-based firms do not have identical financial requirements. High-tech craft firms and science-based firms have more complex financial needs than do integrators and technology users, which "are often larger firms with financial needs and risks that can be addressed by financial institutions with more conventional products" (Secor 1998, p. 16). Science-based and high-tech craft are smaller, more innovative, have a longer product development cycle, and are therefore riskier than integrators and technology users (Secor 1998).

Few reliable estimates are available regarding the number of middle-market and high-potential start-ups in knowledge-based industries or their requirements for capital in Canada. Secor (1998) estimates that there are about 500 large knowledge-based firms (with loans above $5 million) in Canada, 8,000 small knowledge-based firms (with loans between $25,000 and $1 million), and 7,000 early-stage knowledge-based small firms with little business credit.

The new technology commercialization process is conventionally divided into five stages: research, seed, start-up, early growth, and expansion. Firms' financial needs vary according to stage of growth, and appropriate combinations of equity, debt, and (if the technology begins in a lab) public or private research support funding are necessary as the firm moves through its life cycle (see figure 8.1).

No objective assessment is available about the adequacy of the supply of research funding in Canada in domains that might yield economic benefit, or the appropriateness or effectiveness of the conditions under which this funding is made available with respect to the public policy goal of stimulating knowledge-based economic development. However, it is suspected that the supply of technology venturing opportunities in Canada could be increased by

Stage of growth	Research	Seed	Startup	Early growth	Expansion
Equity	Public or private grants	Founder capital/love money	Founder capital/Love money	mezzanine	mezzanine
		Zero-stage investment	First stage Venture capital	Venture capital	IPO
Debt	contracts	Working capital	Working capital	Working capital	
			Export financing	Export financing	Export financing
	Tax credit financing	Tax credit financing	Tax credit financing	Tax credit financing	
				Growth capital	Growth capital

Figure 8.1 Financing needs throughout the technology venturing process
Source: Adapted from Secor (1998).

increasing investment in university research in advanced areas of science and engineering.

Entrepreneurs have claimed for two decades that there exists a shortage of venture capital in Canada, and venture investors have claimed a shortage of interesting deals. The official view since the mid-1980s has generally been that the supply of venture capital in Canada is more or less sufficient, although supply may lag demand. Everyone agrees that the performance of the industry is determined by its structure and experience. In recent years the industry has maintained about one year's supply of investable capital. Today, however, the Canadian VC industry faces an unprecedented illiquidity challenge that will require increases in the supply of capital for later stage investments. The following section provides an overview of the Canadian VC industry, focusing on the formal venture capital market. The informal market is examined in a subsequent section.

AN OVERVIEW OF THE CANADIAN VENTURE CAPITAL INDUSTRY

Canadian venture investments have soared since the middle of the 1990s. Between 1994 and the end of 2000, venture capital under management in Canada more than tripled, rising from about CDN$5 billion in 1994 to nearly CDN$19 billion in 2000 (see figure 8.2). Annual VC investments increased by 350 percent between 1997 and 2000, rising from $1.8 billion in 1997 to $6.3

billion in 2000. That year about 1,400 rounds of financing (deals) involved nearly 2,600 separate investments (see figure 8.3). The $6 billion in venture capital invested in Canada in 2000 represents about 4 percent of the credit extended to the small firm sector by all financial service providers.

The precise number of players in the Canadian VC industry is unknown. An early study of venture investing in Canada (Crane and Poapst 1971) identified about 150 venture capital organizations, funds, venture managers, investment consultants, dealers, and holding companies claiming to be active in venture investing. The number of professionals in the industry increased from 89 to 160 between 1983 and 1986 (Macdonald 1987). The Macdonald and Associates database of the Canadian venture capital industry currently identifies about 600 professional investment firms and advisors, said to represent 90 percent of the players in the industry. The Canadian Venture Capital Association, established in 1974, has about 100 full members (i.e., with funds to invest).

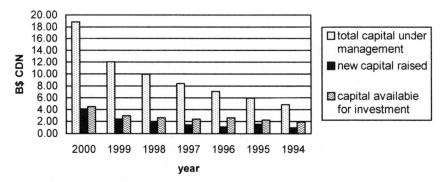

Figure 8.2 Venture capital in Canada, 1994–2000
Source: Compiled from publications of the Canadian Venture Capital Association and Macdonald and Associates.

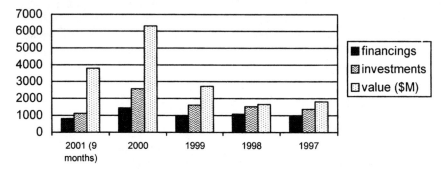

Figure 8.3 Canadian venture capital activity, 1997–2001
Source: Compiled from publications of the Canadian Venture Capital Association and Macdonald and Associates.

The structure of the Canadian venture capital industry is unusual: it is far more institutionally heterogeneous than its U.S. or European counterparts, "where all venture capital funds are institutionally-backed limited partnerships with professional venture capital managers" (Macdonald & Associates 1998, p. 5), and it contains an uncommon class of venture capital investment vehicles sponsored by organized labor. Excluding informal investors, six types of players are active in the Canadian venture capital market: private independent venture funds, labor-sponsored venture capital corporations (LSVCCs), corporate funds, institutional investors, government funds, and hybrid funds.

Private independent venture funds originated the Canadian venture capital industry in the 1950s and predominated until the late 1970s. By 1980 they shared the market with corporate venture groups. They are professionally managed funds that raise capital (typically from $20 million to $200 million) from pension funds, insurance companies, and other investors, and they are generally structured as limited partnerships with a ten-year lifespan (Macdonald and Associates 1998). Prominent Canadian examples are Hargan Ventures, McLean Watson Capital, MM Venture Partners, Fulcrum Partners, Telsoft, XDL Intervest, and Ventures West Management. Private independent funds were responsible for nearly $2 billion of the $10 billion of venture capital under management in 1998 (Macdonald and Associates).

Government funds accounted for as much as a third of the venture capital market in the 1980s but their saliency has since declined. The main government venture funds are operated by the Business Development Bank of Canada's Venture Capital Division; Innovatech (a fund established to invest in young technology in the Montreal area); the Export Development Corporation, which provides complementary debt financing but not venture financing; the venture investment arm of Hydro Québec (a crown corporation); and certain government-backed investment corporations such as the Community Futures Development Corporations (CFDC), a group of specialized public investment companies in Saskatchewan, and the three or four regional development agencies, such as the Atlantic Canada Opportunities Agency, that provide equity financing as a last resort as well as advising, training, and mentoring assistance. Several government venture funds such as the Innovation Ontario Corporation, Discovery Enterprise Inc. in British Columbia, and the Alberta Opportunity Company have suspended activities or exited from venture investing. Government funds represented about 9 percent of the $10 billion of venture capital under management in 1998 (Macdonald and Associates).

Corporate funds emanate from corporate groups. Those with venture capital activities in Canada include BCE Capital (Bell Canada—telephone services), Hollinger Capital (publishing), and the Dow Chemical Venture Capital Group. A prominent example of corporate venturing in Canada is Newbridge Networks's venture arm, Celtic House International. Corporate funds accounted for 17 percent of the $10 billion in venture funds under management in 1998 (Macdonald and Associates). Large technology-based firms may have corporate venturing programs or venture capital subsidiaries that are not widely visible in the venture capital industry. These firms operate as strategic investors that are not necessarily seeking rapid accumulation of capital but instead access to innovation, exposure to new markets, inside knowledge of a firm that might be regarded as a possible acquisition, protection of market share, development of a new product line, or other strategic objectives. Equity-based alliances and partnerships are a form of quasi-venture investing that is not well documented in Canada.

Institutional investors include subsidiaries or operating divisions of commercial banks, investment banks, life insurance companies, and pension funds. Since the late 1980s, this class of investors has been comprised primarily of financial institutions. In the late 1990s, some institutional investors began to make direct VC investments. Most of the major Canadian banks and financial institutions now have venture capital arms or divisions. Examples are Royal Bank Capital, TD Capital, Investissment Desjardins, RoyNat (Scotiabank), the CIBC Innovation Fund, and HSBC Capital. Financial institutional investors represented approximately 20 percent of commitments to the Canadian venture capital market in 2000.

The participation of Canadian trusteed pension funds in the private equities market may be a looming policy issue in Canada. Canadian pension funds control a huge pool of capital. However, this capital has not flowed into venture investments to an extent comparable to what has happened in the United States. In the United States, pension funds commit 5 percent to 8 percent of their assets to venture capital. The current rate is around 1 percent in Canada. The Pension Investment Association of Canada's 135 members control about a half-trillion dollars in assets, of which about 1.5 percent is in VC investments. The historical rate has been much lower: about 0.2 percent of total pension fund assets from 1985 until the mid-1990s, according to Canadian Labour and Business Centre (CLBC; 1999, p. 29). Canadian pension funds with VC investments include the Ontario Municipal Employees Retirement System (OMERS), the Ontario Teachers' Pension Fund, and the Caisse de dépôt. Investment in venture capital by Canadian pension funds at the same per-capita rate as U.S. pension funds would increase the pool of venture capital in Canada by $14 billion.

Ironically, Canadian pension funds helped to develop the VC market in Canada in the 1980s, after regulatory reforms broadened their investment powers. Canadian pension funds increased their investments in the institutional venture capital market, mainly through involvement in funds managed as limited partnerships. In 1985, pension funds contributed only $20 million to venture capital in Canada. In the following three years, they contributed $486 million. In 1989 the pension funds began an abrupt withdrawal from the VC market, and by 1990 they were back to $20 million. In following years their involvement in private capital markets remained at reduced levels. This period is sometimes recalled by VC old-timers as the "nuclear winter" of Canadian institutional investing in venture capital. What happened, and why did Canadian pension funds leave the VC market? CLBC interviews with pension fund managers found three sets of reasons: the recession of the late 1980s; the risk-adjusted substandard performance of pooled assets compared to rates obtained in the United States; and the difficulties in dealing with VC funds, some of which were attributable to fees and the complexities of monitoring, and others attributable to the lack of preparedness of pension funds to make illiquid investments (CLBC, 1999). The pattern of venture investments made by these funds during their market-making foray in 1986–1988 tended toward comparatively safe later stage deals with little involvement in technology (ibid.).

A survey of Canadian pension fund managers in 1997 and 1998 identified fourteen barriers to pension fund investing in the "new economy," including venture capital investing. Among these are: venture investing is too management-intensive and costly; there are too few experienced managers for specialized investing; failures are too glaring; risk-adjusted returns are unreliable; governing fiduciaries are unfamiliar with the complexities of private capital markets; critical market and performance information is lacking; small and medium-size pension funds (less than $1 billion) cannot afford such diversification; institutional memory of past negative experience with private capital markets; inconsistency of high-risk investing with fiduciary responsibilities toward pension plan members; valuation procedures are incompatible with those used for traditional asset valuation; lack of venture pool managers' familiarity with the needs of pension funds; and lack of investment opportunities of sufficient quality to warrant participation (CLBC, 1999).

Since 1997, Canadian pension funds have returned to the VC market, primarily through investments by large experienced public sector funds. Institutional investors (including pension funds) provided fully half the venture capital invested in the first nine months of 2001. It remains to be seen whether this is the beginning of consistent venture investment on the part of pension funds, latency in their investment dynamic, or discovery of a particular comfort zone within the set of venture investment opportunities.

Labor-sponsored venture capital corporations (LSVCCs), also called Labor-sponsored investment funds (LSIFs), are the most unusual feature of the Canadian VC industry. Similar in some respects to tax-subsidized employee share ownership plans in the United States and Europe, these funds have taken on an importance in Canada unequaled in other countries. LSVCCs are capitalized by small retail investors responding to the advantageous tax incentives offered by provincial and federal governments. Typically, the investor receives a tax credit of up to 30 percent on an investment limited to $5,000. The investment must be held for eight years or, in Québec, until age sixty-five. Depending on the province, investors may also receive tax credits related to retirement savings plans, so that a $5,000 investment can be purchased for less than half this amount. LSVCCs are also attractive because, through investments in these vehicles, investors can increase the amount of foreign content held in their retirement savings plans. LSVCCs are regulated as to the amount of equity they can hold in any individual company. They are also required to maintain relatively large cash reserves.

LSVCCs originated in Québec in the early 1980s and spread to other provinces through enabling federal legislation introduced in the late 1980s designed to restore the flow of capital to SMEs when pension funds reduced their commitments to venture investing. Canada now has around twenty-five labor-sponsored funds. Prominent examples of LSVCCs are the Fonds de Solidarité des Travailleurs du Québec (the Québec Workers' Solidarity Fund, the first LSVCC), the Canadian Medical Discoveries Fund, the Working Ventures Canadian Fund, the Working Opportunities Fund, and the Triax Growth Fund. Some funds are limited to investments in a specific province or region, and others are national in scope. LSVCCs have accumulated impressive amounts of capital—the Fonds des Travailleurs had a whopping $3.3 billion under management in 2000. Collectively, LSVCCs were responsible for fully half the $10 billion of venture capital under management in Canada in 1998 (Macdonald and Associates).

LSVCCs have investment mandates that are guided by economic and social goals that do not always converge. They are intended to help maintain or create employment and to help overcome barriers to capital flow to a variety of kinds of firms including SMEs, firms in nonmetropolitan regions, and technologically advanced firms. They are also intended to permit share ownership by working people, and they are in principle organized and controlled by a legitimate sponsoring labor union. The funds are required by statute to invest local capital in local firms, generally on a provincial basis, and gains realized on investments are the means by which other economic and social goals are expected to be attained (although LSVCCs do not have aggressive growth mandates like private independent venture firms). In principle, workers and unions are to be involved in enterprise-based decisions. LSVCC funds are also intended to serve as vehicles for cooperation between management and labor (Canadian Labour Market and Productivity Centre 1995b).

These principles have been deflected in a number of cases, leading to the accusation that LSVCCs are "rent-a-union" arrangements catering primarily to the interests of financiers. In response, five major LSVCCs have signed a declaration of principles: the First Ontario Fund, the Fonds de Solidarité, the Crocus Investment Fund, the Workers Investment Fund, and the Working Opportunity Fund. These "genuine" LSVCC funds have a higher index of social investment than do the other LSVCCs (Quarter et al. 2001). Between 1995 and 1998 the previously mentioned five funds delivered annual returns of 3 percent to 8 percent (Swift 1998).

Lost tax revenues attributable to investments in LSVCCs amounted to about $130 million in Ontario in 1995 (Riding 1998). As a matter of public policy it is not clear why fiscal advantages are accorded only to these investment vehicles among all venture capital funds (Vaillancourt 1997).

Hybrid funds are groups that have secured at least 50 percent of their capital from government or funds with government incentives or as a result of government policy, such as immigrant investor funds operating as venture capital funds. For example, ACF Equity Atlantic's $30 million fund is drawn from seven chartered banks, a credit union, the four Atlantic provinces and the federal government through the Atlantic Canada Opportunities Agency (ACOA), the regional development agency. A similar hybrid fund designed to provide capital to small firms, the British Columbia Focus Initiative, is privately managed with capital from two VC firms, three banks, and the provincial government acting as silent partner. Hybrid funds managed about 5 percent of the $10 billion in venture funds under management in 1998 (Macdonald and Associates).

The structure of the Canadian venture capital industry has evolved substantially and become much more complex during the past two decades. In 1981, independent venture funds were responsible for about half the capital under management in Canada. Corporate investors accounted for about 40 percent and government corporations, less than 10 percent. Crown-related corporations expanded their percentage of total capital under management into the decade but by 1991, LSVCCs and private independent funds each accounted for about 40 percent of capital under management. In 1995, LSVCCs captured 80 percent of the capital flowing into the industry. Each of the other investor types has subsequently expanded its amount of capital under management, with recent large increases in share by foreign firms and institutional investors from outside the VC industry such as mutual and pension funds. The approximate share of the $6.4 billion in venture capital investments in 2000 by each institutional type was corporate (14 percent), government (2 percent), LSVCCs (13 percent), private independent funds (16 percent), foreign funds (27 percent), and institutional investors (29 percent), of which about one-third came from newer institutional players, especially pension funds. However, in the first nine months of 2001, foreign firms and non-VC institutional investors accounted for almost half the venture capital investments in Canada.

The heterogeneity of the Canadian venture capital industry is reflected in the forms of finance that it uses and in the size of portfolios that firms manage. Cumming (2001b) finds that in the period from 1991 to 1998, Canadian venture capital firms did not consistently use convertible preferred equity as a form of financing, as is the case in the United States. Instead, they used a mixture of forms, with common equity and debt financing the two most frequent. However, they consistently used convertible preferred equity as a form of financing in high-technology firms. Cumming (2001a) suggests that the factors affecting the selected form of finance are the size of the deal, the degree of syndication, the kind of VC firm, and especially the stage of the investee firm. Private independent venture capital funds have much smaller portfolios than LSVCCs do, and this difference reflects the more active investment approaches of the private fund managers (Cumming, 2001b).

The bulk of Canadian capital under investment comes from individuals (high net worth individuals, via private independent funds, and individual retail investors, via LSVCCs), domestic corporate investors, and more recently, foreign corporate investors. In 1995, individual investors contributed more than $1.2 billion to the Canadian venture capital pool through contributions to LSVCCs. Pension funds left the Canadian venture capital market in the late 1980s and remained largely on the sidelines for a decade. The institutional investors "did (and still do) believe that there were simply not enough attractive opportunities in the Canadian market to justify their return to the venture capital arena" (Macdonald and Associates 1998, p. 10). The illiquidity issue in the Canadian venture capital industry is increasing efforts to attract greater numbers and variety of institutional investors into the market.

Some other salient characteristics of Canadian venture capital investing during the recent period may be briefly noted:

Increase in early-stage investments. Historically, Canadian VCs invested 30 percent or less of their funds in start-up or early development stage firms. However, the percentage of dollars disbursed in early-stage investments has increased from 36 percent in 1997 to 47 percent in 2000 to 58 percent in the first nine months of 2001 (see figure 8.4). The tendency is to make follow-on investments to companies already in a portfolio. In terms of size of investee firms, Canadian venture investments are distributed bimodally, with the largest shares of disbursed dollars going to small firms with revenues of less than $1 million and to larger firms with revenues greater than $9 million (see figure 8.5).

Increase in deal size and syndication. The average deal size in 2000 was $4.4 million, up from $2.7 million in 1999. Deals larger than $5 million captured 79 percent of all disbursements. Larger deals are related to an increase in syndication. In 2000, an average

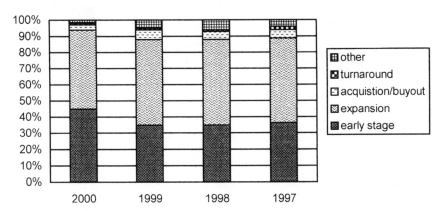

Figure 8.4 Venture capital investments (as percentage of dollars disbursed annually) by stage of investment

Source: Compiled from publications of the Canadian Venture Capital Association and Macdonald and Associates.

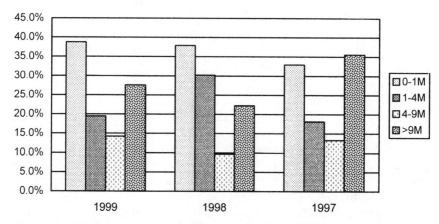

Figure 8.5 Venture investments (as percentage of dollars disbursed) in Canada by revenue of recipient firm in millions of dollars, average 1997–1999

Source: Compiled from publications of the Canadian Venture Capital Association and Macdonald and Associates.

of 3.4 investors were involved in financing deals for start-ups involving $5 million or more, and 4.2 were involved in other early-stage deals. The largest VC deal in Canada in 2000 was a seed investment of $115 million in Ottawa-based Innovance Networks, an optical networking company. This deal required a syndicate of six large American venture capital investors. All of the fifty largest VC deals in Canada in 2000 surpassed $20 million and required syndication ("Venture Capital Fifty" 2001).

High exposure to technology. Venture investors in Canada are showing a very strong preference for technology deals, in contrast to the situation in the late 1980s when technology accounted for around a quarter of investments and venture investors expressed disappointment over the supply of quality technology deals available (Macdonald 1991). Knight's 1994 study of Canadian venture capitalists' investment criteria reports that "several Canadian venture-capital firms suggested that being characterized as high technology was often a negative for deals" because "many high-technology firms are single-product firms" with limited marketing and financial skills. The Canadian VC industry's exposure to technology has steadily increased since about 1990, mainstreaming by the mid-1990s. In 1997, 66 percent of Canadian venture capital dollars were invested in technology firms, climbing to 89 percent in 2000. Figure 8.6 shows the sectoral composition of venture capital investments in Canada between 1997 and 2000. The share of investments captured by life science firms has remained steady, manufacturing's share and the miscellaneous share have shrunk, and the share taken by electronics, Internet-related, computer-related, and communications and networking firms has greatly expanded. Canada's recent technology venturing boom largely revolved around firms commercializing products and services based on information and communication technologies.

High geographic concentration. Canadian venture capital activity is very highly concentrated in a few city regions, particularly in Central Canada (see figure 8.7). Ontario

captured 43 percent of investment dollars disbursed between 1997 and 2000, and Québec, 26 percent. These disbursements are primarily located in the city-regions of Montreal, Ottawa, and Toronto-Kitchener-Waterloo. Calgary and Vancouver represent the
two other main pools of venture capital in Canada. These five city regions account for
over 90 percent of venture capital investments in Canada. Fourteen percent of Canadian
VC investment dollars were invested outside the country between 1997 and 2000, generally in the United States.

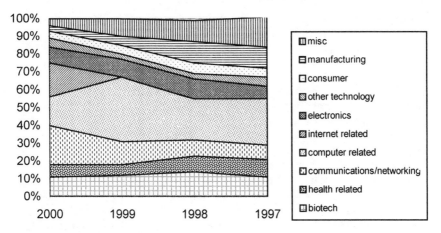

Figure 8.6 Sectoral composition of Canadian venture capital investments (in terms of
dollars disbursed annually), 1997–2000

Source: Compiled from publications of the Canadian Venture Capital Association and Macdonald
and Associates.

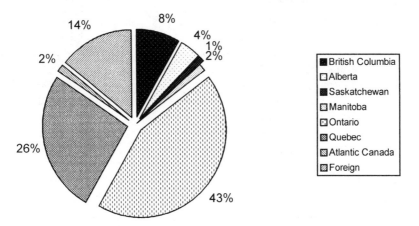

Figure 8.7 Regional distribution of venture investments (in terms of dollars disbursed)
in Canada, 1997–2000

Source: Compiled from publications of the Canadian Venture Capital Association and Macdonald
and Associates.

Investment criteria. Bachher's (2000) study of investment criteria used by VCs in the United States and Canada finds consistent use of criteria among VCs in the aggregate. In descending order of importance, VCs consider the management team, the target market, the offering, the venture's positioning within the competitive environment, capital payback projects, and the business plan. Although there exists a great deal of heterogeneity in use of decision criteria among VCs, the rank ordering of criteria is practically identical when VCs from California and Massachusetts are compared with VCs from Canada and elsewhere in the U.S (ibid.).

Positive economic impacts of venture capital. The Business Development Bank of Canada tracks the performance of VC-backed firms and provides an annual assessment of the economic impacts of venture capital.[3] VC-backed firms in Canada doubled their employment to an average of eighty-six persons per firm, of which 95 percent were located in Canada (Business Development Bank of Canada 2000). The average compounded annual growth rate of jobs was 39 percent for firms receiving VC backing between 1995 and 1999. IT companies' employment grew at 60 percent and labor-sponsored companies at 47 percent. These growth rates compare very favorably to those of the Canadian economy as a whole, which produced jobs at an annual rate of 1.9 percent, and the top 100 companies in Canada in terms of sales, which produced jobs at an annual rate of 4 percent (Business Development Bank of Canada 2000). Compounded growth rates for sales were 31 percent for all VC-backed firms in the sample, 53 percent for labor-sponsored firms, and 66 percent for IT firms. Similarly, VC backing enabled rapid export growth and significant annual increases in R&D activities (Business Development Bank of Canada 2000). Furthermore, VC-backed firms strongly outperformed non-VC-backed firms after IPOs (Business Development Bank of Canada 2000).

ISSUES IN THE DEVELOPMENT OF VENTURE CAPITAL IN CANADA

Generally speaking, the Canadian VC industry is now facing two broad sets of challenges. One concerns the illiquidity of the industry, its likely near-term needs for capital, and its options for profitably liquidating its investments. The other has to do with a funding gap at the seed or zero stage of technology venturing that is limiting the supply of bankable deals, exacerbating the highly skewed regional distribution of technology venturing opportunities, and hindering the development of new science-based industries, especially those originating in the life sciences. Both sets of issues are related to the fiscal and regulatory framework for venture investing in Canada.

The Fiscal and Regulatory Framework

In recent years, the e-business boom has drawn attention to deficiencies of the Canadian venture capital industry. The Canadian e-Business Opportunities Roundtable, a high-level advisory e-business body led by the business community, explained in a report why Canada was slower than the United States to take advantage of e-business opportunities:

The [investment] environment is less dynamic in Canada because the venture capital market here is dominated by passive and semi-public investors. Labour-sponsored funds, government funds and hybrid funds—none of which is permitted to take a large ownership stake in the companies in which it invests—make up over 60% of the Canadian venture capital pool. In contrast, only 1% of U.S. funds are under management by non-private investors. (Canadian e-Business Opportunities Roundtable 2000b)

The Canadian e-Business Opportunities Roundtable has continued its high-profile lobbying for modernization of the fiscal and regulatory framework for venture investing in Canada, identifying the following sticking points:

Capital gains. The Canadian capital gains tax is almost double the U.S. rate of 20 percent. Moreover, in the United States, capital gains taxes are reduced by half on shares of qualifying small business companies having undertaken IPOs if investors hold the shares for five years or more. The Canadian capital gains tax creates a disincentive for early-stage investors and an incentive for VC-backed companies to move to lower-tax environments. The Canadian e-Business Opportunities Roundtable advocates increasing the capital gains exemption to up to $1 million for "employees of qualified science and technology intensive companies" (1999). More generally, to compete with the United States in attracting risk investments for technology venturing, Canada cannot maintain a conspicuously higher capital gains tax. Capital gains taxes produce a very small revenue stream for Canadian governments: in 1992 capital gains revenues amounted to 0.3 percent of total revenues and 1.9 percent of personal income tax revenues (Grubel 2000).

Treatment of stock options. In Canada, firms with the status of "Canadian-Controlled Private Corporation" (CCPC; a Canadian private corporation that is controlled neither by nonresidents, nor by a public corporation or a combination of the two) receive tax advantages. One benefit is that employees of such companies with vested stock options do not pay capital gains tax when they exercise (purchase) their shares. They pay when the shares are sold. In other companies, capital gains taxes must be paid when employees exercise their shares. This tax provision clearly frustrates the practice of attracting and retaining valuable employees with stock options throughout the growth phase and the public offering. It also discriminates against foreign investor involvement in enterprise formation at the seed stage. The Canadian e-Business Opportunities Roundtable (1999) advocated that taxation of option benefits take place at the time of sale of redeemed shares and that registered retirement savings plans be expanded to include employee share option investments. The federal budget of 2000 introduced some changes that make employee stock options more attractive to non-CCPCs: employees may defer capital gains taxes on $100,000 of benefits annually.

Capital gains exemption for rollover investments. U.S. venture funds may defer taxation from capital gains that are realized on exiting an investment through a rollover provision for qualified reinvestments. The Canadian e-Business Opportunities Roundtable advocates that Canadian venture capital funds be allowed to defer capital gains taxes from investment exits if the gains are reinvested in a qualified firm. The February 2000 budget introduced a rollover provision for holders of shares in CCPCs and for firms with assets of between $2.5 million before the investment and $10 million after. This provision brought some relief to individual Canadian investors but it was far from matching the comparable U.S. regulation, which sets the upper limit on investable firms at thirty times the Canadian level, sets no limits on the size to which the firm can grow, and allows investments via partnerships (Canadian e-Business Roundtable 2000c). The Canadian government addressed these issues by introducing an improved rollover provision for capital gains in early 2001 (Sharwood 2001). However, eligibility still requires that the investee firm conduct most of its business in Canada during its first twenty-four months, mitigating the utility of this rollover provision for Canadian new technology-based firms that must quickly penetrate the U.S. market, as most such firms must do. Also, it was not clear whether investee firms would remain eligible after shares were disposed of through an IPO (ibid.).

Tax neutrality for foreign investors. Foreign investors who pool their fund as part of a limited liability company in the United States for purposes of investment in a Canadian fund are considered to be doing business in Canada and are subject to capital gains taxation as if they were residents of Canada. This limits Canadian venture capital fund managers' access to U.S. pension and endowment funds. Tax neutrality for nonresident investment in Canadian technology companies would encourage flows of foreign investment into Canadian companies and venture capital funds. The Canadian e-Business Opportunities Roundtable, citing the positive example of Israel, advocates the principle of tax neutrality for nonresident investments in Canadian businesses, regardless of the investors' investment vehicle (i.e., whether the investor is an individual investor, a pool of funds registered as a limited liability company in a country covered by a tax treaty, a direct investor in a Canadian company, or an investor in a Canadian-based venture capital fund that manages the investment on his or her behalf; Canadian e-Business Opportunities Roundtable 1999, 2000c).

Tax treatment of cross-border share-for-share mergers. Barriers exist to cross-border, share-for-share mergers with U.S. companies, an increasingly important exit route for Canadian VC-backed technology companies. Owners of equity in Canadian companies incur tax liability when shares are swapped in mergers or sales. This is not the case under U.S. rules. In order to avoid the tax liability, Canadian entrepreneurs find it useful to incorporate in the United States and establish an affiliate in Canada. To reduce this impediment to business formation in Canada, the Canadian e-Business Opportunities Roundtable recommends elimination of tax liability on rollovers of shares from a Canadian privately held company to a foreign company (1999, 2000c).

Restrictive IPO environment. The IPO environment in Canada is less expensive but also less attractive than in the United States because the Toronto Stock Exchange is comparably more restrictive in terms of listing requirements, resale restrictions, and escrow requirements for sale of shares in a company. Securities in Canada are regulated on a provincial basis, meaning that a company must list for trading in thirteen separate jurisdictions. Canada is the only G-7 country in which securities trading is regulated by subnational governments. The Canadian e-Business Opportunities Roundtable recommends that the Canadian IPO environment be made no less restrictive than the American one.

Clearly, most of the tax and regulatory issues have to do with removal of bottlenecks and impediments that make the risk/reward ratio of VC investing in Canada unfavorable compared to the United States. Others have to do with making the tax and regulatory aspects of VC investment linkages between the two countries less cumbersome. These issues have arisen in the context of significantly increased inflows of U.S. venture capital into Canada in the recent past. The investment flows were unleashed by aggressive marketing in the United States of Canadian investment opportunities by Canadian actors, by Canadian technology firms' deliberate selection of U.S. VC partners for later rounds of financing, and by the relative greater availability of U.S. funds for venture investment. Canadian preference for U.S. VC investors may be explainable by relatively higher dollar or opportunity costs of procuring capital in Canada, as suggested by Bergeron et al.'s study of Canadian biotechnology firms (2000). It certainly reflects the need of technology firms to grow quickly in the U.S. market. The scarcity of actively managed early-stage capital in Canada has allowed U.S.-based venture capitalists to induce Canadian firms with high growth potential to move their operations to the United States at an early stage. American venture capitalists then provide value by recruiting "a high profile and experienced board of directors, helping to find strong management, and making introductions to key suppliers and customers, thus facilitating the growth process and building a name for the company" (Canadian e-Business Opportunities Roundtable 2000a).

Ironically, the Canadian venture capital industry was better prepared to weather the recent major downward movement in stock prices because of its institutional shock absorbers. Labor-sponsored venture capital funds withstand stock market movements better than other kinds of riskier equity funds in technology-based industries because they are exposed to companies that have not yet gone public. Also, the LSVCCs' mandatory greater cash reserves have a stabilizing effect. However, the dampening of the Canadian venture capital system caused by its institutional arrangements only protects it from large market swings. Since most Canadian venture investments have yet not reached the exit stage, they are not highly exposed to the equities market.

Investment Gaps at the Seed and Start-up Stages

It is frequently observed that Canada suffers from a seed-stage investment gap. This gap extends to the start-up stage in many regions in Canada. The seed (or zero, or precommercialization stage) requires investment for purposes of R&D, proof of concept, product development, market research, preparation of business plans, or establishing a management team. The start-up investment brings the firm to a point at which it can do business by completing product development, marketing, and so forth.

Although venture capitalists' competitive advantage as investors lies in their efficiency in selecting and monitoring investments in the unique business environments of technology-based, fast-growth firms, within this context they rationally prefer projects in which monitoring and selection costs are relatively low or in which the costs and risks associated with informational asymmetry are relatively less severe, leading them to "favor firms with some track records over pure start-ups" (Amit, Brander, and Zott 1998). Investments at the seed stage are even riskier and so less favored by venture capitalists. Between 1991 and 1996, less than 2 percent of Canadian VC investments went to seed-stage deals (ibid.). The average size of seed investments ($621,000) was comparable to the much more frequent investments in start-ups ($721,000; ibid.), but the cost of managing these investments was necessarily greater.[4] "Very few venture capital companies do idea-stage investments," observes Denzil Doyle, chairman of the Ottawa-based venture fund Capital Alliance Ventures Inc. "It is just too labor-intensive. The lifting is just too darn heavy down in that end . . . Not enough of them finance R&D or the early stages of product development" (Doyle 1999). In response to seed and start-up funding gaps, Canadian policy actors have sought to mobilize the informal investment community and have established some specialized seed investment firms and agencies.

The angel capital market operates in "almost total obscurity" (Prowse 2000) in Canada as in other countries. Little is known about the size or scope of informal investing, the types of firms that raise angel capital, or the individuals that provide it. Informal investors in Canada represent a large pool of capital, believed to be several times larger than the pool of formal venture capital. Only about 5 percent of individuals with the financial profile of a potential angel are active business investors (Riding 1998). Most angel investments go to early-stage firms. Survey research conducted by the Canadian Labour Market and Productivity Centre (CLMPC, 1995a) documents that twice as many businesses have relied on investments from angels, at some point in their development, than on any other form of external equity investment, including institutional venture capitalists.

Furthermore, no systematic empirical evidence is available regarding the extent or nature of the seed-stage investment gap technology enterprises in Canada, although a recent review of reports and studies finds ample anecdotal evidence (Corkery and Brennand 1999). A proxy measure, university patent filings (ibid.), does not seem adequate since it is not known how many infant technology companies in the IT and telecommunication sectors spin directly out of universities. This trajectory appears to have been central in the establishment of Canada's newer high-technology clusters in Vancouver and Kitchener-Waterloo. However, the principal entrepreneurial trajectory in Ottawa seems to be graduation from a technology-intensive university, work in a firm in the industry, and then establishment of an infant technology company.

Practically nothing is known about Canadian angel investors who are active in technology industries. The activities of these informal investors produce a critical input for venture capitalists: a technology-based firm with a product. The problems of agency and moral hazard are just as acute at the earliest stages of firm formation as they are when venture capitalists enter the picture, while the degree of uncertainty is higher. Denzil Doyle, a father of technology venturing in Canada, believes that Canada faces a shortage of angel investors that is much more serious than any shortage in the United States. Angel activity should represent about five times VC investment, meaning that Canada should have a pool of angel capital of at least $5 billion to $10 billion. However, there is no evidence of technology-based angel investment activity on this scale in Canada.

Corkery and Brennand (1999) identify a series of gaps that, if overcome, would improve the match between seed capital supply and demand. To overcome an information gap, measures could be taken to help investors and entrepreneurs to find each other. In this vein, highly localized facilitation of face-to-face meetings has been more productive than distribution of codified information from a database of suppliers and seekers of seed capital. Institutions such as universities with potentially commercializable technology might overcome an identification gap by finding ways to interact with potential investors. A management expertise gap might be overcome by fostering the development or transfer of management skills for start-up companies. Finally, a research gap due to underinvestment in university research may result in a low supply of investment opportunities.

Others have identified a key incentive gap due to the high capital gains tax and the absence of rollover provisions in Canada, which make it unprofitable for potential technology investment angels to convert equity in one investment into equity in a new investment (Doyle 1999). Specialized "mentor capitalist" firms such as Eagle One Ventures, Reid Eddison, Venture Coaches, Skypoint Capital Corp., and StartingStartups are, however, emerging in the principal Canadian technology centers to bring direct management involvement as well as personal or partners' seed money into infant technology firms (Vardy 2001). Research is needed on the business models that support successful seed-stage venture investing in Canada.

Quite a few institutional mechanisms exist to foster seed-stage investments in Canada. Three main ones are in use. First, some mechanisms such as the federal Scientific Research and Experimental Development (SRED) tax credit or analogous provincial tax credits provide incentives for investment in R&D. Second, a certain number of seed-stage investment funds, designed to foster seed-stage ventures and spinouts from universities or research institutions, have been established in Canada. Examples are the University Medical Discoveries Fund; the Western and Eastern Technology Seed Investment Funds (consortia members are Ventures West, the Business Development Bank of Canada, and the Bank of Montréal); T2C2, a similar initiative in Québec; and biomedical investment funds established by a number of Canadian banks. Third, a variety of skills development and networking initiatives includes networks of experts, provision of specialized legal and support services, and support for seminars and investment-readiness exercises (see Corkery and Brennand 1999). Perhaps the most comprehensive initiative to mobilize local informal capital is the Canada Community Investment Plan (CCIP), a blueprint for a community investment facilitation service for potential fast-growth SMEs promoted by Industry

Canada through twenty-two pilot projects across the country. The CCIP provides a model for local leaders to determine if their community is right for an investment facilitation service (communities with economies dominated by agriculture, branch plants, or single employers are not), guidelines for organizing a group to create a facilitation service, and instructions on chartering, governing, and financing the service (CCIP 2001). CCIP-inspired investment facilitation initiatives are one kind among a broader range of local investment financing models (LIFMs) that exist across Canada (Canadian Labour Market and Productivity Centre 1998).

The key stumbling block in initiatives to mobilize informal capital in support of technology venturing outside the mainstream technology centers in Canada has to do with the skills and sectoral experiences of local business angels. Many communities possess high net worth entrepreneurial individuals with long business experience and the desire to invest in new ventures. However, if they made their fortunes in retailing or food processing, they cannot function as effective mentor capitalists in areas of advanced technology, even when viable opportunities exist. Johnstone (2000) describes this particular management skill bottleneck in the case of Cape Breton, a depleted local economy that generates infant firms in the software and new media sectors. These firms require capital and management mentorship in order to grow. To satisfy the capital requirements of these firms, local business angels would have to syndicate in groups of ten, which they are not eager to do. Of equal importance, entrepreneurs seek investor expertise in marketing, industry contacts, and management skills, which local investors are unable to provide (ibid.)

As a remedy to this management skill and experience deficit in the domain of technology venturing, some outlying communities in Canada are encouraging repatriation of native sons and daughters who are successful technology entrepreneurs in Central Canada or the United States. These repatriated individuals bring with them not just experience and investment capital but also social capital accumulated within the mainstream technology and investment communities.

Exits

The five principal exit strategies for venture capitalists are: (1) an initial public offering (IPO), involving the sale of a significant portion of the firm in the public market; (2) an acquisition, in which a third party purchases the entire firm; (3) a secondary sale, in which only the venture capitalist's shares are sold to a third party; (4) a company buyback, in which the investor's shares are repurchased by the entrepreneur; and (5) a write-off, in which the investor abandons the investment (MacIntosh 1997).

Cumming and MacIntosh (2002) find that VC investments in Canada have longer duration than in the United States for each development stage of the investee firm and form of each exit vehicle. This evidence supports the view that "there exists lower skill level among Canadian venture capitalists, and greater institutional barriers to efficient investment duration in Canada." Among the latter are "lower liquidity of secondary trading markets, Canadian legislation establishing LSVCCs, and onerous escrow and hold period requirements" (ibid.). These are factors that constrain the development of "smart" value-added venture capital investment activity in Canada.

In descending order of firm quality, as measured by the firm's market/book ratio, the normal pattern of exits would be IPOs, acquisitions, secondary sales, buybacks, and write-offs (Cumming and MacIntosh 2000). The most lucrative way to liquidate a venture capital investment is via an IPO. As figure 8.8 shows, the return on investment of equity in firms taken through an IPO is the highest of all forms of disposition of venture investments. IPOs provided a multiple of 4.29 times the cost of the original investment in the 687 venture capital dispositions in Canada in 1997 and 1998. Acquisitions and secondary sales provided the second most profitable group of exit routes, with multiples of 2.05 and 1.95. Company buybacks and mergers yielded relatively modest multiples of 1.27 and 1.14, respectively.[5]

IPOs are not the most frequently used means of disposing of venture investments in Canada. Of the 687 dispositions in 1997 and 1998, only about 10 percent were accomplished through IPOs and subsequent sale of shares. About 9 percent of dispositions were acquisitions of investee firms by third parties, 2 percent were mergers, 10 percent were write-offs, and 23 percent were secondary sales (Cumming and MacIntosh 2000).

In 1999, 92 IPOs were completed in Canada, of which 24 were in the technology and media sector and 7 in the life sciences sector. In 2000 Canada had

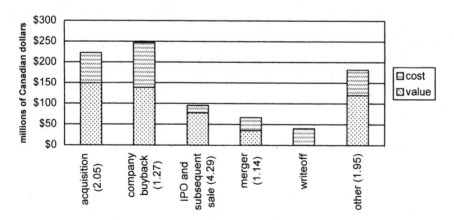

Figure 8.8 Venture investment dispositions, Canada, average of 1997 and 1998

Numbers in parentheses show the ratio between the cost of investment and the value when liquidated.

Source: Calculated from publications of the Canadian Venture Capital Association and Macdonald and Associates.

101 completed IPOs, of which 35 were in technology and media and 11 in the life sciences sector (PriceWaterhouseCoopers 2001, 2000). The number of advanced technology IPOs was six or seven per year in 1999 and 2000. The number of dot-com IPOs in Canada was very low—one in 1999 and five in 2000. IPO activity declined to the lowest point in a decade in 2001. Many Canadian VC firms have postponed IPOs for their technology-based holdings.

The Canadian Venture Exchange (CDNX) was created from the amalgamation of the Alberta and Vancouver Stock Exchanges in 1999 and in May 2001 was acquired by the Toronto Stock Exchange as a national junior exchange to provide access to small amounts of risk capital from angels and small investors. Technology, mining, and oil and gas securities are traded on the CDNX. In 2000 this exchange raised about $2 billion in capital. About a third of new listings on the TSE are graduates of the CDNX. The main problem in Canada with establishment of a national junior venture exchange is the cost of listing in up to thirteen separate jurisdictions. The cost of raising $1 million can therefore be as high as $100,000 (Volker 2001).

It seems possible that exits in the United States may become increasingly attractive to Canadian VC investors and entrepreneurs. Direct issuing costs on the TSE (fees and commissions) are lower than on the NASDAQ or NYSE. Indirect costs due to underpricing are also lower. It is complex and costly to go public simultaneously in both countries. In 1999 and 2000 only two Canadian companies listed exclusively on NASDAQ, and eight listed simultaneously on NASDAQ and the Toronto Stock Exchange (TSE). However the increasing involvement of U.S. venture capital in Canada will increase the availability of opportunities for successful IPOs in the United States for Canadian companies.

With the decline in opportunities to exit via an IPO, investors must face the problem of how to liquidate their investments. For holders of technology shares, acquisition looks like an attractive option. Most of the acquirers are foreign companies, raising the issue of the longer-term benefits to Canada if pathways to growing indigenous multinational firms are blocked. Increased involvement of pension funds in the market for Canadian technology equities would be good news for many.

CONCLUSIONS

During the 1990s the pool of venture capital under management in Canada more than quadrupled, from less than $3 billion to more than $12 billion, increasing again by about 50 percent in the boom year 2000. The Canadian venture capital industry underwent a process of deep maturation during the 1990s. The industry accumulated critical experience and competencies with respect to technology investing, syndication, internationalization of investment flows, specialty management within several kinds of investment firms, and extension of VC investment capability to a half-dozen Canadian city regions. The result is an institutionally heterogeneous industry that is currently managing close to $20 billion in venture investments.

In every country, the VC industry is very sensitive to fiscal and regulatory arrangements. In the mid 1980s, Canadian governments induced a significant infusion of venture capital investment with the introduction of legislation establishing LSVCCs and the tax incentives that make them attractive vehicles to retail investors. LSVCCs have economic and social development mandates that make them invest differently from other kinds of VC firms. To develop in Canada the kind of knowledgeable, proactive, "best-in-class" VC investment capability found in the United States, the Canadian tax system will have to offer analogous kinds of incentives for involvement in risky ventures that produce significant capital appreciation. The Canadian federal government has taken several steps since 1999 to make capital gains tax less of an inhibitor of venture investing. In general it appears that the policy system has taken notice of the importance of venture investing, but the modernization of aspects of the financial infrastructure that are embedded in Canadian intergovernmental relations does not lend itself to rapid solutions.

The involvement of Canadian pensions funds in venture investing remains a looming issue. Pension funds have significantly increased their contribution to venture capital in Canada during the 1990s, but the rate of pension participation in venture financing is still low compared to the United States. To accommodate the fiduciary needs and responsibilities of pension funds, U.S. VCs and pension fund managers developed best practices, third-party pools, private placement databases providing market information, and "a human resources component producing diverse investment specialists, intermediaries, market experts (known as gatekeepers) who act solely on behalf of fiduciary interests, and deal-making agents" (Falconer 2000). These are areas in which Canada can learn from the experience of the United States.

The Canadian venture capital industry has experienced a significant internationalization through syndication or strategic alliances with foreign, primarily American, VCs. Although Canada exports capital, most of the international flows are inbound. Very little is known about the dynamics or implications of these international venture capital flows on formation and growth of Canadian firms.

NOTES

1. The U.S. venture capital industry and Silicon Valley are the usual benchmarks against which innovation in Canada is compared, although the U.K. economy is more venture capital–intensive than the United States, and Massachusetts is a more venture capital–intensive region than California.

2. The Canadian Bankers Association defines small or medium business as ones with an authorized credit limit of less than $1 million.

3. The sample of respondents includes only firms that have attracted a first round of VC investment.

4. The seed stage is the riskiest, with an estimated risk-adjusted capital cost of 80 percent (Wetzel 1997), compared to the risks posed by investments at the start-up (60

percent), first stage (50 percent), second stage (40 percent), third stage (30 percent), and bridge stage (25 percent).

5. In a comparison of Canadian and U.S. venture capital investments, Cumming and MacIntosh (2000) find much higher average annual rates of return in the United States on investments using IPOs, acquisitions, and buybacks as exits. Canadian venture capital investments have a higher rate of return than their U.S. analogues when exiting via secondary sales.

REFERENCES

Amit, Raphael, James Brander, and Christoph Zott. 1998. "Why Do Venture Capital Firms Exist? Theory and Canadian Evidence." *Journal of Business Venturing* 13: 441–66.

Angus Reid Group. 2000. "Financing Services to Canadian Small and Medium-Sized Enterprises." Report prepared for the Business Development Bank of Canada.

Babbage, Maria. 2001. "Dispirited Venture Capitalists See Fewer Opportunities." *Toronto Business Journal*, 3 December.

Bachher, J. S. 2000. "Venture Capitalists' Investment Criteria in Technology-Based New Ventures." Ph.D. diss., University of Waterloo.

Baldwin, John R., and Joanne Johnson. 1996. "Business Strategies in More- and Less-Innovative Firms in Canada." *Research Policy* 25: 785–804.

Baldwin, John R., Tara Gray, Joanne Johnson, Jody Proctor, Mohammed Rafiquzzaman, and David Sabourin. 1997. "Failing Concerns: Business Bankruptcy in Canada." Ottawa: Statistics Canada, Catalogue No. 61-525.

Baygan, Günseli, and Michael Freudenberg. 2000. "The Internationalisation of Venture Capital Activity in OECD Countries: Implications for Measurement and Policy." Paris: Organisation for Economic Co-operation and Development, Directorate for Science, Technology and Industry, STI Working Paper 2000/7.

Bergeron, Michel Y., Lawrence Kryzanowski, Paul Beaulieu, and Yoser Gadhoum. 2000. *Financing-Related Issues and Difficulties for Canadian Biotechnology Companies.* Montreal: Chair in Management of Bio-industries, Ecole de Gestion, University du Québec à Montreal.

Best, Andrea, and Devashis Mitra. 1997. "The Venture Capital Industry in Canada." *Journal of Small Business Management* 35: 105–10.

Bruce, David. 2000. "Small Business Outlook 2001." Toronto: Canadian Federation of Independent Businesses, December.

Bruce, David. 2001. "Banking on Entrepreneurship: Results of CFIB Banking Survey." Toronto: Canadian Federation of Independent Businesses, March.

Business Development Bank of Canada. 2000. "Economic Impacts of Venture Capital: Eighth Annual Survey." Ottawa: Government of Canada.

Canadian Community Investment Plan (CCIP). 2001. *The Winning Formula: Facilitating Investment in Small Business Growth. Lessons from 22 Pilot Projects Under the Canadian Community Investment Plan.* Ottawa: Canadian Community Investment Plan, Industry Canada.

Canadian e-Business Opportunities Roundtable. 1999. "Submission to the Standing Committee on Finance." Ottawa: Canadian e-Business Opportunities Roundtable, November 9.

Canadian e-Business Opportunities Roundtable. 2000a. "Discussion with the Department of Finance." Ottawa: Canadian e-Business Opportunities Roundtable, January 7.

Canadian e-Business Opportunities Roundtable. 2000b. "Fast Forward 1.0." Toronto: Canadian e-Business Opportunities Roundtable/Boston Consulting Group.

Canadian e-Business Opportunities Roundtable. 2000c. "Submission to House of Commons Standing Committee on Finance." Ottawa: Capital Markets Team, Canadian e-Business Opportunities Roundtable/Boston Consulting Group.

Canadian Federation of Independent Business (CFIB). 2001. "Our Members' Opinions #47." Toronto: Canadian Federation of Independent Business, January.

Canadian Labour and Business Centre (CLBC). 1999. *Prudence, Patience, and Jobs: Pension Investment in a Changing Canadian Economy.* Ottawa: Canadian Labour and Business Centre.

Canadian Labour Market and Productivity Centre (CLMPC). 1995a. *Generating Growth: Improving Access to Capital by Small and Medium-Sized Enterprises.* Ottawa: Canadian Labour Market and Productivity Centre.

Canadian Labour Market and Productivity Centre (CLMPC). 1995b. *The Role and Performance of Labour-Sponsored Investment Funds in the Canadian Economy: An Institutional Profile.* Ottawa: Canadian Labour Market and Productivity Centre.

Canadian Labour Market and Productivity Centre (CLMPC). 1998. *Capital, Community, and Jobs: Local Solutions for Financing Investments in a New Economy.* Ottawa: Canadian Labour Market and Productivity Centre.

Canadian Venture Capital Association. *Enterprise.* Quarterly.

Chrétien, Prime Minister Jean. 2001. "Address in Reply to the Speech from the Throne." Ottawa, January 31.

Conference Board of Canada. 2001. *A Changing Demand for SME Debt Financing?* Ottawa: Conference Board of Canada, January.

Corkery, Karen, and Angie Brennand. 1999. "Seed Stage Investment Activity in Canada." Report prepared for the Advisory Council on Science and Technology, Ottawa.

Crane, P. L, and J. V. Poapst. 1971. "A Quantitative Study of the Sources of Venture Capital in Canada." In *Sources of Venture Capital: A Canadian Guide,* ed. P. McQuillan and H. Taylor, pp. 129–47. Ottawa: Department of Industry Trade and Commerce.

Cumming, Douglas J. 2001a. "The Convertible Preferred Equity Puzzle." Unpublished manuscript, March.

Cumming, Douglas J. 2001b. "The Determinants of Venture Capital Portfolio Size: Empirical Evidence." Unpublished manuscript, February.

Cumming, Douglas J., and Jeffrey G. MacIntosh. 2000. "Venture Capital Exits in Canada and the United States." Unpublished manuscript, November.

Cumming, Douglas J., and Jeffrey G. MacIntosh. 2002. "Venture Capital Investment Duration in Canada and the United States." *Journal of Multinational Financial Management* 11: 445–63.

Deloitte Touche. 2001. Canadian Technology Fast 50 website. http://www.deloitte.ca/en/Industries/TechComm/Fast50/

Doyle, Denzil. 1999. "Raising Venture Capital Aspects of Technological Change." *Canada–United States Law Journal* 5: 197–204.

Doyle, Denzil J. 2000. "Was That a Federal Push in the Right Direction or a Kick in the Pants?" *Silicon Valley North* 5 (11): 47.

Doyle, Denzil J. 2001. "Lack of Liquidity Hurts the Canadian High-Tech Industry." *Silicon Valley North* 6 (4): 39.

Falconer, Kirk. 2000. "Venturing Forth." *Benefits Canada,* November.

Fischer, Eileen, Rebecca Reuber, and Nancy M. Carter. 1999. "A Comparison of Multiple Perspectives on Rapid Growth Firms." Paper presented at the United States Association for Small Business and Entrepreneurship Conference, San Diego, January.

Gorman, Gary, and Wayne King. 1998. "Dynamics of Firm Growth in Atlantic Canada and Canada, 1989–1995." Paper presented at the Atlantic Schools of Business Conference, Acadia University, Wolfville, Nova Scotia.

Government of Canada. 2001. "Innovation Agenda for the Twenty-first Century." House of Commons, Parliament of Canada, Standing Committee on Industry, Science, and Technology, June. www.parl.gc.ca/infocomdoc/37/1/INST/studies/reports/indu04/06-toc-e.htm.

Grubel, Herbert. 2000. *Unlocking Canadian Capital: The Case for Capital Gains Tax Reform.* Vancouver: The Fraser Institute. http://www.fraserinstitute.ca/publications/books/capital_gains/

House of Commons. 2001. *An Innovation Agenda for Canada: The Fifth Report of the Standing Committee on Industry, Science, and Technology.* Ottawa: Government of Canada.

Jeng, Leslie A., and Philippe C. Wells. 2000. "The Determinants of Venture Capital Funding: Evidence across Countries." *Journal of Corporate Finance* 6: 241–89.

Jog, Vijay M. 1997. "Le contexte des Émissions Initiales au Canada." In *Le financement de la croissance au Canada,* ed. P. J. N. Halpern, pp. 399–449. Calgary: University of Calgary Press.

Johnstone, Harvey. 2000. "Financing High Tech Ventures in a Depleted Local Economy." Proceedings of the Thirtieth European Conference on Small Firms, Ghent.

Julien, Pierre André, and Richard Lachance. 2001. "Dynamic Regions and High-Growth SMEs: Uncertainty, Potential Information, and Weak Ties." *Human Systems Management* 20: 237–48.

Karaomerlioglu, D. C., and S. Jacobsson. 2000. "The Swedish Venture Capital Industry—An Infant, Adolescent, or Grown-up?" *Venture Capital* 2 (1): 61–88.

Kedrosky, Paul. 2001. "Deep Trouble for Venture Capitalists." *Financial Post,* April 21, p. D11.

Knight, Russell M. 1994. "A Longitudinal Study of Criteria Used by Venture Capitalists in Canada." *Journal of Small Business and Entrepreneurship* 11: 12–26.

Kortum, Sam, and Josh Lerner. 2000. "Assessing the Contribution of Venture Capital to Innovation." *RAND Journal of Economics* 31: 674–92.

Macdonald and Associates Limited. "Quarterly Overview of the Venture Capital Industry." Various quarters.

Macdonald and Associates Limited. 1998. "The Canadian Venture Capital Industry: Source of Capital and Implications for Industry Structure." Research paper prepared for the Task Force on the Future of the Canadian Financial Services Sector, September.

Macdonald, Mary. 1987. *Venture Capital in Canada: An Overview.* Ottawa: Investment Canada.

Macdonald, Mary. 1991. "Creating Threshold Technology Companies in Canada: The Role of Venture Capital." Report prepared for the Science Council of Canada.

Macdonald, Mary, and John Perry. 1985. *Pension Funds and Venture Capital: The Critical Links Between Savings, Investment, Technology, and Jobs.* Ottawa: Science Council of Canada.

MacIntosh, Jeffrey G. 1997. "Les sorties du marché du capital de risque au Canada et aux États-Unis." In *Le financement de la croissance au Canada*, ed. P. J. N. Halpern, pp. 309–98. Calgary: University of Calgary Press.

Mackay Task Force [Task Force on the Future of the Canadian Financial Services Sector]. 1998. Report, background papers, and research reports, Ottawa: Department of Finance, Government of Canada. http://finservtaskforce.fin.gc.ca/rpt/report.htm.

Martin, Paul. 2000. "Speech to the Toronto Board of Trade," 14 September.

Porter, Michael, and Roger Martin. 2000. "Canadian Competitiveness: Nine Years after the Crossroads." Paper presented at the CLSC Conference on the Canada-U.S. Manufacturing Productivity Gap, Ottawa, January.

PriceWaterhouseCoopers (PWC). 2000. *Survey of IPOs in Canada in 1999.* Toronto: PriceWaterhouseCoopers.

PriceWaterhouseCoopers (PWC). 2001. *Survey of IPOs in Canada in 2000.* Toronto: PriceWaterhouseCoopers.

Prowse, Stephen. 2000. "Angel Investors and the Market for Angel Investments." *Journal of Banking and Finance* 22: 785–92.

Quarter, Jack, Isla Carmichael, Jorge Sousa, and Susan Elgie. 2001. "Social Investment by Union-Based Pension Funds and Labour-Sponsored Investment Funds in Canada." *Industrial Relations* 56 (1): 92–115.

Riding, Alan. 1998. "Financing Entrepreneurial Firms: Legal and Regulatory Issues." Research paper prepared for the Task Force on the Future of the Canadian Financial Services Sector, September.

Royal Commission on the Economic Union and Development Prospects for Canada. 1985. *Report of the Royal Commission on the Economic Union and Development Prospects for Canada.* Ottawa: Government of Canada.

Sayegh, Jacques. 1992. "Venture Capital Redefined: New Directions and Opportunities for the '90s." *Canadian Banker* 99: 51–54.

Schreyer, Paul. 2000. "High Growth Firms and Employment." Directorate for Science, Technology, and Industry, Organization for Economic Cooperation and Development, Working Paper DSTI/DOC (2000) 3.

Secor. 1998. "Financing Knowledge-Based Small Business." Research paper prepared for the Task Force on the Future of the Canadian Financial Services Sector, September.

Sharwood, Gordon. 2001. "Tax-Free Rollover Receives Little Publicity." *Silicon Valley North* 24 (April).

Statistics Canada. 2000. "Small Business: A Statistical Overview." *The Daily,* 8 March.

Swift, Jamie. 1998. "Saving Our Jobs or Selling Our Souls? The Great Debate on Labour-Sponsored Investment Funds." *Our Times—Canada's Independent Labour Magazine.* http://www.ourtimes.ca/features/98save.html.

Vaillancourt, François. 1997. "Le Fonds de Capital de Risque des Travailleurs au Canada—aspects institutionnels, dépenses fiscals et création d'emploi." In *Le fi-*

nancement de la croissance au Canada, ed. P. J. N. Halpern, pp. 635–58. Calgary: University of Calgary Press.

Vardy, Jill. 2001. "Mentor Capitalists: Counsel and Cash: New Niche of Financiers Integral Parts of Startups." *Financial Post,* May 4, p. C9.

"The Venture Capital Fifty." 2001. *National Post Business,* April.

Volker, Michael. 2001. "The Way I See It." *Silicon Valley North,* May 29.

Wetzel, William E. 1997. "Venture Capital." In *The Portable MBA in Entrepreneurship,* ed. William D. Bygrave, pp. 184–209. New York: John Wiley and Sons.

9

Israel's Venture Capital Industry
Emergence, Operation, and Impact

Gil Avnimelech and Morris Teubal

PART A: OBJECTIVES AND BACKGROUND TO THE ISRAELI HIGH-TECH INDUSTRY TO POLICIES DIRECTED TO VENTURE CAPITAL

OBJECTIVES OF THE RESEARCH

This chapter focuses on Israel's venture capital (VC) industry, its emergence, and its operation during the 1990s, during which period the number of VC funds increased from 2 to over 100. The context for this chapter is the transformation of Israel's high-tech industry as a whole from the defense-dominated electronics industry of the 1970s and 1980s to the Silicon Valley model of the 1990s characterized by large numbers of SU (start-up) companies. During this period the largest share of high-tech was in the manufacturing industry; and information and communications technology's share in the business sector increased considerably, attaining one of the highest levels worldwide. Given the importance of venture capital,[1] an analysis of the waves of new SU companies should be done jointly with an analysis of the emergence and development of venture capital (and vice versa). This chapter cannot and does not undertake a full coevolutionary analysis; it does, however, make a serious attempt to understand the dynamics and the specificities of the wider high-tech context under which Israeli VC companies operate.

The approach adopted is an evolutionary and systemic approach rather than a focus on the operation of a mature venture capital industry, which has been more frequent in the literature (Gompers & Lerner 1999).[2] Our approach is evolutionary because we focus on the dynamics of venture capital, particularly an analysis of *emergence* and of *subsequent development* of the industry (and not only its *operation*); and because we will link these with core evolutionary concepts such as *variation, selection, and reproduction*. In fact, a lot of effort has been taken to set the context, which led to the central emergence events of the 1990s. This includes an understanding of the prior phase in the development of high-tech (the research and development, or R&D, penetration phase), and its links with innovation and technology policy. A major factor here was the operation of a background R&D support program since 1969–1970, which not only contributed to the "old" electronics industry but, indirectly, strongly stimulated VC industry emergence. This program was *strongly* complementary to the specific policies implemented during 1991–1995, which were more directly related to venture capital and to high-tech growth. Finally, our approach is also systemic because our analysis of VC takes place in the context of a new multicomponent "system of innovation" and "cluster" perspective of high-tech development. Thus VC development has influenced other system of innovation components as well as having been influenced by them.[3]

This analysis takes place at the meso (VC industry) level, where we focus on the evolution of the new industry in quantitative and qualitative terms and where we undertake a preliminary analysis of the *dynamics of emergence*. However, as mentioned, the approach taken leads us to strive to link variables at this level with the wider high-tech cluster *and* with the micro-VC company and fund level (which is the subject of follow-up research).

Specific Objectives

1. Analyze the emergence and development of Israel's venture capital industry during the 1990s, following an evolutionary and systems perspective and within the wider context of emergence of the new high-tech cluster of the 1990s.

   For the high-tech cluster as a whole and for venture capital we make a distinction between background conditions (e.g., the electronics industry of the 1980s, business sector R&D support, etc.); a preemergence phase (1990–1993); and an emergence phase (1993–1995)—the latter constituting Phase 1 of growth of the VC industry. Moreover, for venture capital we will also consider two postemergence phases: Phase 2, 1996–1998; and Phase 3, 1999–2000.

2. Analyze the role of policy in the above and arrive at policy implications.

   We will consider the role of business sector–oriented R&D policy (the backbone R&D Industrial Fund) both in creating Israel's high-tech industry (starting in 1969) and in complementing more specific policies directed toward venture capital; and we will provide a detailed analysis of targeted policies favoring VC in Israel and their impact, particularly Yozma—a government program and venture capital company implemented/operating between 1993–1997. The latter is widely regarded as having been the trigger of Israel's VC industry.

Structure of This Chapter

This chapter consists of two main parts: A and B. Part A provides the background to the VC industry as it emerged and operated during the 1990s. The background focuses on the evolution both of R&D and of high-tech industry/

business sectors; and it encompasses both "positive" as well as "normative" or policy aspects. High-tech and R&D till approximately 1990 preceded a clearly identifiable venture capital industry; and to some extent we might say that venture capital, as it emerged and developed during the 1990s, was an outgrowth of these developments. In contrast to this, High-tech and R&D in the 1990s are largely contemporaneous and coevolve with venture capital. They comprise the broader system, which both affects and is affected by VC. This sets the basis for closer looks at the dynamics of emergence and coevolution in Part B.

Part B outlines a conceptual model for the emergence and development of venture capital, including aspects of the above-mentioned coevolutionary processes. The emphases are twofold: first, an analysis of the *trigger* to the emergence of venture capital—the so-called Yozma program whose implementation began in 1993; second, an analysis of the *immediate preemergence* phase (1990–1993) and some analysis of the *emergence and postemergence phases* (1993–2000). The former "qualitative" analysis delves quite in detail into the particulars of the Yozma initiative and the Yozma policy process, its antecedents and reasons for success. The latter is based on data, some of it generated by the research team itself, as well as on qualitative analysis. We end up with a conceptual "Dynamic Coevolutionary Sequence" whose features represent the distinctive characteristics of the Israeli case. It summarizes what can be done at the *meso-level* of analysis.

THEORETICAL APPROACHES

Venture Capital in the Literature

Venture capitalists invest in new, unproven, entrepreneurial companies, particularly in high-tech areas, which are ignored by traditional financial institutions. These firms are characterized by a lot of asymmetric information problems, agency problems and conflicts of interests, significant intangible assets, and years of negative earnings, and they have uncertain prospects. As a result they are unlikely to receive bank loans or other debt financing from traditional investors. For many of these young firms, VC is the only potential source of financing. Gompers and Lerner 1999 and other researchers pointed out some of the mechanisms that VC companies use to reduce or to manage such problems. These include equity finance, convertible, or preferred securities; and staged and syndicated investing. The role of VC can be seen as taking an enterprise to a stage (e.g., an IPO or post-IPO stage) at which other forms of financial intermediation and corporate ownership and control are appropriate. VC structure and operation thus creates a way to overcome financial and organizational barriers that held back both innovation in large corporations and R&D project investment by traditional financial institutions.

More specifically venture capital performs two important roles: it overcomes market failure associated with equity issues of SU companies; and it provides other value-adding functions and activities to such companies. We briefly refer to each one of these.

Overcoming Market Failure in Equity Issues of Start-up Companies

Akerloff (1970) argues that asymmetric information can cause market failure in equity issues of young and risky firms. This will generally lead to IPO "underpricing," which VC can help overcome through a mechanism called "third party certification." Third party certification has value whenever securities are being issued in capital markets where insiders of the issuing firm and the outside investors have different information sets concerning the value of the offering firm. The presence of VC, as investors in a firm going public, reduces the underpricing of an issue, reduces the underwriter spread charged by the investment banker handling the issue, and increases the IPO valuation (Megginson and Weiss 1991).

For venture capitalists to effectively undertake such functions, as well as other value-adding functions, they have to undertake both *scanning* and *due diligence* activities. The first step is reading and evaluating a start-up company's business plan and meeting its managers. Due diligence is performed on a subset of companies scanned who are strong candidates for subsequent investment. It involves a detailed search of references; the solicitation of outside information from potential customers, suppliers and competitors about the quality of the technology and the entrepreneurial group; and often lasts for several months. During the due diligence process venture capitalists tend to make use of personal networking and business links. This helps them to get reliable information, which is very critical in this risky and uncertain business.

Value Added: Management Assistance and Networking

Some argue that venture capital plays a critical role in the innovation process, not only as a source of finance to innovation but through *other functions* that lie at the core of high-tech development (Saxenian 1998; Florida 1994). Venture capital provides a bridge between sources of finance, entrepreneurs, scientists, suppliers, and customers. According to Florida the U.S. venture capital industry played a critical rule in the innovation process in the United States and is one of the reasons why U.S. high-tech has become the world leader during the late 1980s and early 1990s.

The added value of VC companies might be an explanation for the observed lower underpricing and lower issuing costs experienced by VC-backed start-ups. In order to help start-up entrepreneurs—who generally have little management experience—to manage fast-growing companies, management assistance and training is required. Gorman and Sahlman (1989) found that lack of management skills is the most significant reason for start-up companies' failure. Venture capitalists typically try to add value to their portfolio companies through assistance to management in strategic decisions. Sapienza, Manigart, and Vermeir (1996) found that venture capitalists believe that their strategic involvement is their most important role in adding value to their portfolio companies. Moreover, they found that venture capitalists with experience in the portfolio companies' industry generated more added value than did venture capitalists without such prior experience. Also, venture capitalists with technology and entrepreneurial backgrounds generate more added value than do venture capitalists with financial backgrounds.

Venture capitalists also maintain close ties with investment bankers who can assist portfolio companies going public or going through an M&A (mergers and acquisitions) process. They also have ties with high-tech corporations that can open doors (e.g., of clients, for product testing) to their portfolio companies and assist in the scanning process. According to Florida (1994) venture capitalists are involved in four overlapping networks of agents related to the innovation process: financial institutions, entrepreneurs, professional business services, and the professional labor market.

According to Gompers (1995) and compared to start-ups not linked to VC, VC-backed start-ups on average go public younger; have less underpricing, cheaper underwriter costs, and higher valuation at the IPO; and perform better after the IPO. The superior performances of such companies is due to VC's good scanning, monitoring activities, reputational added value, networking added value, and management added value.

The Limited Partnership Venture Capital Company: Characteristics and Monitoring Mechanisms to Reduce Conflict of Interests

Venture capital in the Silicon Valley model of high-tech largely takes the form of limited partnerships (LP), although corporate venture capital companies and publicly traded companies coexist with this form of organization. This is also the case in Israel. In the LP form of organization, the VC company is a management company that manages one or more VC funds and that shares in their profits. The owners of the management company are termed general partners. Each VC fund has investors (called *limited* partners) and *portfolio companies*—that is, companies where venture capitalists have made investments in exchange for a share in their ownership. After raising the capital for a new VC fund, the fund is closed and the VC (management) company begins activities connected to investment. It starts by scanning, undertaking due diligence, investing, and undertaking an active role in management and decision making of portfolio companies. Since a VC fund operates typically for a period of seven years and since it has an obligation to reimburse investors in cash, a major activity of the VC is exiting, that is, selling the VC funds' ownership shares in its portfolio companies. In the United States and in Israel, the typical modes of exit are two: IPO (initial public offering) in the stock market or selling the companies through M&A deals.[4] The IPO exits are typically in NASDAQ (but increasingly in Europe), which is a *public* capital market where typically about 20 percent to 30 percent of ownership is eventually floated (after one issue or more). The selling exits include selling 100 percent (acquisition) or selling less than 100 percent (merger) of the company to another company, typically a large corporation whose technologies/products are complementary to those developed in the company concerned. The latter *private* capital market transaction is part of the M&A activity.[5]

Limited partnership contracts address obvious areas of conflict of interests between general partners and limited partners; and between the VC company and its portfolio companies. Both involve agency problems. Moreover, venture capitalists have means to reduce conflicts of interests between principals (limited partners, VC companies) and agents (general partners, portfolio companies). To deal with the latter group of conflicts, VC investments involve equity finance, the use of convertible securities, syndication and staging of investments, the use of the ratchet mechanisms, and many other mechanisms.

Systems of Innovation Perspective and Literature

The basic set of papers on the system of innovation or systems/evolutionary perspective can be found in the writings of Nelson, Lundvall, Edquist, and others.[6] In a recent paper, one of us has summarized this perspective by identifying the set of system components found in the literature and by distinguishing a set of "positive" from a set of "normative" general principles (Teubal 2002). This framework is directly applicable to high-tech clusters, which are regional high-tech sector systems of innovation (Saxenian 1998). The main objective of research following this perspective concerns not system "operation" but rather system dynamics, and more specifically the transformation of a system of innovation, for example, from a high-tech cluster without VC to one including VC.

There are five system components: the business sector; the supporting structure; links and interactions; institutions and markets; and culture and social structure. In such systems the business sector would include SU firms; non-SU firms involved in downstream production and marketing (as well as in R&D); VC companies; and an assortment of market agents involved in providing specialized services to high-tech. The supporting structure would involve universities, government laboratories, the segment of the VC industry that is either government owned or linked to government (Yozma funds in Israel), industry associations, policy institutions (like the Office of the Chief Scientist), and other nonmarket organizations of relevance for high-tech (e.g., the computer division of the Israeli army). The perspective emphasizes not only the importance of both market and nonmarket links but also, as applied to high-tech, the importance of international, cross-border links, for example, with global capital markets. Finally, under systems perspective, the role of institutions and culture is emphasized, for example, the importance of personal links and the culture of openness in Silicon Valley (Saxenian 1998). In what follows we briefly describe general principles, which are illustrated with examples pertinent to VC emergence in Israel. We then proceed to identify what research questions are asked by this perspective and link them with those asked in the specific VC literature.

"Positive" general principles include, among others, the importance of *learning* (such as interactive learning between venture capitalists and SU companies), of *new system components* (a distinct VC industry), of *cumulativeness*[7] *and VC-SU coevolution*, which could lead to a self-sustained process of high-tech growth; of *emergence of new demands*, for example, for the services provided by the new venture capitalists; of *fundamental uncertainty*; and of the *possibility of lock in*.

"Normative" general principles include *adaptive policy maker* (Metcalfe 1995), *policy as judgment*, and *an explicit strategy* rather than neoclassical optimizing policy makers in which priorities are obvious and policies can be determined with certainty. That is, the systems perspective recognizes the importance of identifying strategic priorities such as "creation of a VC industry" or "creation of a modern high-tech cluster," more generally speaking. Other "normative" general principles include, among others, *policy that is context specific*, for example, cluster-creating policies for one context need not be effective in another; *a portfolio of coordinated policies*, rather than simple support of R&D; and a *policy mix* involving both incentives and institutional changes as well as *horizontal and targeted programs*.

Both sets of principles will be applied in this chapter. We start by pointing out how an analysis of venture capital following this perspective would differ from the type of analysis (and the questions) usually followed (asked) in the specific VC literature surveyed above. To start with, the systems/evolutionary perspective would try to differentiate between high-tech clusters with venture capital (a "private" business enterprise support mechanism; see Cooke 2001) and those without venture capital. This will help explain the differential success of both at different phases in the process of globalization of the world economy, particularly of financial/capital markets. Moreover, the questions asked include the *emergence of venture capital* and, more generally, the *transition from VC-less systems of innovation to VC-based, SU-intensive systems*. One issue is whether *VC-SU coevolution* is necessary for successful emergence of a Silicon-type high-tech cluster. More generally, a discussion of VC dynamics and its impact cannot be conducted in isolation from the broader discussion of transition to the new system of innovation.[8]

A major aspect of the above is the role of venture capital (a) in the creation of SU companies; and (b) in their growth and evolution;[9] that is, the coevolution question could be considered a central aspect of the approach as applied to high-tech clusters. For several reasons, this goes beyond the measurement of differences between VC-backed and non-VC-backed companies, as is common in the specific VC literature (see Gompers 1995 and Lukomet 2000). Once we talk about coevolution, we cannot avoid dealing with the *substance* of VC added value and exits; with *learning* and other dynamic processes; and with *externalities and social impact*. Thus, measured impact may depend on learning and on other factors; and for this to be useful and indicative of future potential impact, it is important to know what has been learned and what constitutes relevant learning (see Part B, Section 3). Analyzing these issues requires delving into the substance of the relevant activities and into how they evolved through time, for example, how less sophisticated activities set the basis for more sophisticated and higher value activities; and the context under which successful learning has in fact taken place.

These are fundamental questions whose answers would shape how we measure; how we interpret the results we get; and what policy implications follow.[10] This would represent a first stage in the transition from an analysis of the operation of an existing (usually mature) VC sector to an analysis of emergence and postemergence evolution of such industries. A second reason for underpinning measurement with significant "premeasurement" research concerns identifying the nature of externalities and other aspects pertaining to the *social impact* (in contrast to the private performance) of VC companies, particularly the links between VC and high-tech growth more generally. It requires considering activities such as knowledge spillovers; collective learning; specific firm reputation and networking effects, which "spill over" or are made available to the emerging high-tech cluster as a whole; and novel types of backward and forward linkages (such as how more VC stimulates more SU and vice versa).

The systems/evolutionary perspective can consider such a rich set of interrelationships and dynamic, coevolutionary processes precisely because it provides a broad interpretative framework for the quantitative links established in the VC-specific literature. Thus the contribution of venture capital to high-tech growth will very much depend on three elements: (a) the stage of development of the VC industry and its capabilities; (b) the types of VC companies populating the industry (e.g., a limited partnership form versus other forms of VC organization; the distribution of experience and skills; etc.); and (c) other features of the broader system or high-tech cluster (e.g., universities—who may determine the pool of skills that may populate new SU companies, culture, or endogenous trends in entrepreneurship, to mention a few). These other features help explain the processes of evolution from a small VC sector to a large one, particularly through positive feedback effects, collective learning, and new industry entrants (VC-SU coevolution may lie at the heart of this). It may also show that in some contexts, early successes in VC and in SU might be followed by strong growth of the new industry; and that this will not be the case in other contexts.

We conclude that following a system or cluster perspective might, in some instances, enrich our interpretation of the results obtained from traditional VC analysis; while in other cases it may suggest a significantly different set of relationships for empirical testing.

R&D, HIGH-TECH, AND INNOVATION / TECHNOLOGY POLICY IN ISRAEL

In analyzing the background of the emergence of venture capital in the 1990s, we should (a) understand the evolution of high-tech; (b) analyze the dynamics of policy, particularly innovation and technology policy (ITP). Israeli high-tech has undergone at least two distinct periods since its emergence after the Six Days' War in 1967. The first corresponds to the process of introduction and diffusion of R&D throughout a prevailing R&D-less business sector overwhelmingly dominated by traditional and mid-tech industries; the second involves the transformation of high-tech into a Silicon Valley model with venture capital. Similarly we may distinguish two main periods in Israel's ITP. The first phase began in 1969–1970 with the establishment of the Office of the Chief Scientist (OCS) at the Ministry of Industry and Trade and ran until about 1990. The second phase began during the 1990s and ran until 2000–2001, when new sets of incentives programs were implemented.

The R&D Penetration Period (1970–1989)

High-Tech Industry and R&D

The Six Days' War and the subsequent French embargo generated new priorities for Israel with implications for R&D and high-tech industries. Self-sufficiency (or partial self-sufficiency) in the supply of sophisticated armament systems became one of the objectives of policy, with implications for the growth of military industries (some of them of a "high-tech" nature) and military R&D projects. Simultaneously, a government committee created to review policy recommended the stimulation of applied R&D and creation of a particular institution for implementing this objective in the various ministerial Offices of the Chief Scientist. Israel's R&D policy directed to the business sector resulted from the activity (and budget) of the most important of these bureaus— the one located in the Ministry of Industry and Trade. This office became the almost exclusive agency in charge of innovation and technology policy, especially that connected to R&D; and it was a significant factor in the development of a civilian R&D performance sector and to a civilian high-tech industry.[11]

During the first R&D Penetration period, which ran till about 1990, the basic R&D/innovation capabilities of Israel's business sector were generated. A civilian-oriented R&D-intensive, high-tech sector developed parallel, albeit with a lag, to the development of the military industries and defense-oriented high-tech. The share of this new high-tech sector in total product and exports of manufacturing increased from 6 percent to 24 percent and from 5 percent to 28 percent respectively between 1968 and 1983.[12] During the 1968–1987 period the pool of skills employed in manufacturing grew from 3,400 in 1968 to almost 20,000, and average industrial skill intensity increased from 1.3 percent to 5.8 percent. Civilian R&D that was performed in industry increased considerably in real terms—from $26 million (constant 1984–1985) dollars in 1969–1970 to $347 million, a twelvefold increase. Despite this enormous growth, military R&D overshadowed civilian R&D performed in the business sector. Military R&D during the early 1980s amounted to more than half of the total R&D, which, beyond military R&D, included both civilian R&D performed in the business sector and civilian R&D performed at universities and government laboratories. Its share in total national R&D was about 40 percent in the 1970s and rose to 65 percent in 1981.

The scope of R&D in the army enabled exploitation of economies of scale and the generation of research teams with strong networking among individual researchers. These effects could not have developed elsewhere, due to limited resources (U. Galil, March 28, 2001).[13] In addition, military R&D cooperation with the United States, Germany, and France presumably set the stage for the transfer of technologies from those countries to Israel. Moreover, the army became an efficient incubator of young researchers in many technological fields. During this period a deep process of restructuring of the military industries took place. Layoffs and spin-offs from the army and from army R&D seemed to have played an important contributory role in the emergence of the second *Silicon Valley (or Silicon Wadi) period* of Israel's high-tech development. Numerous entrepreneurs and engineers of this second period had worked previously in the military industries or performed military R&D. Moreover, the reduction in military expenditures also led to enhanced flows of engineers, technicians, and scientists to civilian rather than military R&D activities.[14]

The Backbone Industrial R&D Fund

The Israeli government's innovation and technology policy toward the business sector began in 1969 with the creation of the R&D Industrial Fund at the recently created OCS. This program was, and to some extent continues to be, the backbone of that country's R&D/innovation/technology strategy as far as the business sector is concerned.[15] It supports the R&D of individual companies whose objective is the creation of new or improved products (or processes) directed to the export market. This type of R&D could be termed "regular" or "classical" R&D to differentiate it from generic, cooperative R&D, which is a more infrastructural type of R&D. The latter's objective is to generate knowledge, capabilities, and components rather than directly marketable outputs. Its output would facilitate (or become inputs to) a subsequent "regular" R&D activity directed to new products or processes.

The 1984 R&D law further consolidated Israel's support of business sector R&D. Its objectives were to support knowledge-intensive industries, through expansion of the science and technology infrastructure and exploitation of existing human resources; and to create employment, including absorption of immigrant scientists and engineers.[16] The outcome was significant increases in R&D grants to industry.

The Industrial R&D Fund is an example of a *horizontal technology policy (HTP) program*, which is a program directed to the business sector as a whole and open in principle to all firms in that sector (rather than a *targeted program*, applicable to a specific industry or technology). These programs embody an important component of "neutrality in incentives." In Israel this expressed itself as a 50 percent subsidy to every R&D project submitted to the OCS, whatever the firm's industrial branch, whatever the product class toward which the proposed R&D was oriented, and whatever the technology underlying such a product class (see Teubal 1983, 1993). From $2.5 million in the late 1960s, the disbursements in the program reached almost $300 million in 1996–1997.[17]

Due to the central role played by the Industrial R&D Fund, Israel's explicit R&D strategy or innovation and technology policy (directed to the business sector) in the last thirty years can be termed *an HTP-led strategy*. That program was the first of the set of programs comprising Israel's program portfolio; and it was and still remains the dominant program in terms of government disbursements and probably (at least till the 1990s) in terms of impact.[18] Moreover, the dynamic processes unleashed by its successful implementation led to the other programs comprising Israel's innovation and technology policy of the last ten years.

A framework for understanding the impact of the Industrial R&D Fund is to adopt an evolutionary perspective to the implementation of the program. The objective of the program would then be *penetration and diffusion of regular R&D throughout the business sector*.[19] While a neoclassical perspective would focus on the need to provide incentives due to market failure (caused by knowledge spillovers by firms undertaking R&D), an evolutionary perspective would focus first and foremost on the absence of R&D and innovation capabilities as a major obstacle to diffuse R&D. Initially, when first implemented, such capabilities are nonexistent or exist only in small "islands" within the business sector. Therefore, according to this perspective, we should distinguish between two phases in program implementation—the first where such capabilities are absent (infant phase); the second when they have already achieved significant diffusion throughout the business sector (mature phase).

BIRD

In 1977, The Israel–United States Binational Industrial R&D foundation (BIRD-F) was established. The BIRD endowment was contributed equally by the governments of Israel and the United States in the amount of $60 million. The goal of the fund was to promote and support joint, nondefense, industrial R&D activities of companies from Israel and the United States. The idea was to enable young Israeli companies with pioneer technologies to calibrate with mature U.S. companies with strong appearance in global markets. Since its establishment, BIRD funds have supported more than 400 joint projects. BIRD had a significant effect on the Israeli global high-tech industry because of the opportunity for Israel to learn managerial skills from U.S. companies and to build Israel's high-tech reputation in the United States.

Learning in the HTP Infant Phase

The major objective during the infant phase is to promote learning about R&D and innovation. Much of this learning is collective learning, that is, R&D-performing firms mutually learning from each other; and a lot of this learning relates not directly to technology or R&D proper but to organizational and managerial factors. The top of figure 9.1 proposes a certain categorization of intrafirm learning processes, whereas the bottom indicates some specific aspects of collective learning during the period from 1969 to 1990 in Israel.[20]

Mature Phase Policy Restructuring

The evolutionary perspective to HTP states that after the infant phase of implementation of such a program (say five to ten years, depending on context), a number of developments will very likely take place: exhaustion of learning opportunities and associated externalities (in certain areas); new opportunities

INTRA Firm Learning about R&D/Innovation- Infant Phase of an HTP
1. Learning how to search for Market and Technological Information.
2. Learning to identify, screen, evaluate and choose new projects
3. Learning to generate new projects, including more complex ones
4. Learn to manage the innovation process (linking Design to Production & Marketing; Selection of Personnel; Budgeting; etc)

Collective Learning During the Implementation of the "Industrial R&D Fund"
Firms learned about the importance of marketing (thereby overcoming the previously held view that "my invention is so good that it will sell automatically")
Officials and experts of the OCS learned, partly through exchange of information within and informal 'policy network' a) to better asses the quality and potential of the projects submitted; b) how to help firms configure good projects
Firms acquired capabilities for identifying new projects, including "complex" projects which built upon prior 'simple' projects

Figure 9.1 INTRA Firm Learning about R&D/Innovation—Infant Phase of an HTP

for complex types of R&D projects (based on capabilities generated in simpler projects); and identification of possible areas of competitive advantage. The policy implications ideally would involve (a) likely reductions within the HTP program in average R&D subsidies together with greater selectivity; (b) the implementation beyond the HTP program of a number of additional programs, for example, targeted programs for specific areas/technologies or targeted/horizontal programs supporting generic, cooperative R&D projects. In Israel only a very limited adaptation did occur during the first phase, that is, until 1990.

Impact of ITP

The backbone regular R&D support program was widely regarded as having been a success in terms of stimulating R&D in the business sector, in stimulating exports resulting from R&D, and in contributing to the creation of a civilian high-tech sector or cluster during the 1980s (see Teubal 1993; Toren 1990; Justman and Zuscovitch 2000).

Silicon Valley Period (1990–2000)

The New High-Tech Cluster

The second period runs from 1990 till approximately 1998 and corresponds to the emergence and development of a distinct high-tech cluster largely modeled on Silicon Valley lines. This section will focus on this period because it is then that Israel's VC industry emerged and developed. The basic characteristics of this period (and some comparison with previous periods) are summarized in table 9.1.

Table 9.1
Israel's High-Tech Cluster of the 90s—Selected Structural Elements and Comparisons

	99/00	90	80
Number of SU:	~3000	~300	~150
Number of VC Companies:	~100	2	0
Funds Raised by VCs: M$	3400	~49	0
Capital Invested by VCs: M$	1270	~45	0
Accumulated No of IPOs (hi tech):	~130	9	1
Accumulated VC-backed IPOs:	~70	3	1
Share of Foreign Sources in Total SU funding:	67%	NA	NA
Share of IT Exports in Total Manufacturing Exports:	45.7%	~33%	~20%

Source: SU numbers come from three sources: CBS, OCS and IVA.

*Frequently the figures in the box are approximations due to gaps in the availability of data, the existence of various sources of information—including fragmentary information from non-official sources.

**Approximate figure for 1990–98.

We can observe that the high-tech cluster that emerged during the 1990s is very different from the military industries–dominated cluster of the 1980s. Its basic feature is that of being a SU-intensive high-tech cluster closely following the Silicon Valley model of high-tech in which both SU and VC increasingly play important roles (Teubal 1999). It is also much more integrated and linked with the United States and its high-tech clusters in Silicon Valley, Boston area, and elsewhere. Thus, the number of SU companies was estimated at 3,000 for 1999–2000, although other estimates show that this number was already reached in 1997 (Gelvan & Teubal 1997). The number of VC funds increased from one in 1991 to over a hundred toward the end of the decade (IVA 1997, 2000). In parallel to this, the economy continued the high-tech–biased structural change initiated in the 1970s but in an accelerated mode (Justman 2001). Within manufacturing (and also services), we observe a sharp increase in the weight of high-tech industry. Table 9.2 shows some basic data on IT high-tech manufacturing industries till 2000. There was a fourfold increase in sales, from over $3 billion to slightly over $12 billion. The share of these industries in manufacturing employment increased from 14 percent in 1980 to 19.5 percent in 1998—a higher share than all or most Organization for Economic Cooperation and Development (OECD) countries (Avnimelech et al. 1999).[21] The share of IT high-tech in total manufacturing exports has increased even more dramatically than the share of employment, reaching 45 percent in 1999. A similar picture emerges from recent data on Israel's information and communications technology (ICT) sector (OECD definition), where output increased 4 1/2-fold during the 1990s (CBS 2001). Moreover, the share of ICT growth in Israel's business sector was extremely high—74 percent in the year 2000 and 39 percent for the decade of the 1990s. Finally, a comparison between the share of ICT in Israel's business sector compared to the OECD's average (for 1997) shows that Israel's share (13.3 percent) was slightly less than double that of the OECD average (7.7 percent).

New Programs

Successful implementation of the core or backbone program, *through an evolutionary/dynamic process,* led to the emergence and implementation of a set of other programs in the early 1990s (see the program sequence in figure 9.2). Simultaneously with this, we see an expansion of the regular R&D support program till 1997. See data in table 9.3 and the summary of OCS activity for the year 1997.

Statistics

Table 9.3 summarizes OCS grants for all programs: support of regular R&D (what we termed the backbone support program, or Industrial R&D Fund), magnet, technology incubators, and other smaller programs that were implemented during the 1990s. The rate of growth of total grants declines considerably during the second half of the 1990s compared to the first half of the

Table 9.2
IT Hi-Tech Manufacturing Industry Sales, Exports and Employees

Year	Total Sales (000$)	Exports (000$)	Employees	Sale per Employee (000$)
1995	5,890	4,300	40,000	147
1996	6,500	4,880	42,000	155
1997	7,200	5,700	43,000	166
1998	8,030	6,550	44,700	180
1999	8,580	7,130	45,800	187
2000	12,500	11,000	53,800	232

Source: Israel Association of Electronic and Information Industries.

1) **Inbal** (1992) - a Government owned Insurance company, which gave partial (70%) guarantee to traded VC funds. Four VC companies were established under Inbal regulations.
2) **Yozma** (1993-97)—a 100 M$ Government owned Venture Capital company, which invested in 10 Funds which operated in Israel (8M$ per fund).
3) **Magnet Program** (1992-)—a 60/70 M $ a year Horizontal Program supporting cooperative, generic R&D involving two or more firms and at least one University. Widely regarded as a successful program
4) **Technological Incubators' Program** (1992--)—a year program supporting entrepreneurs during the Seed Phase of their project, for a period of three years. The incubators are privately owned and managed. Both they and the projects approved get financial support from the Government. The program complements the "Industrial R&D Fund" (projects could be submitted to either program). It contributed to the transformation of Israel's high tech cluster during the 90s, particularly in the early years.

Figure 9.2 New ITP programs—Silicon Valley period

Table 9.3
OCS R&D Grants (Nominal $ Million)

Year	Total Grants (Percent Change)	Regular R&D support	MAGNET	Technology Incubators	Miscellaneous	Royalties
1995	346 (9.4)	286	15	31	13	64
1996	348 (0.5)	276	36	30	5	91
1997	397 (14.1)	303	53	30	11	121
1998	400 (0.1)	307	61	30	2	133
1999	428 (7.0)	331	59	30	8	159
2000	440 (2.8)	334	67	32	8	154
2001	432 (-1.9)	330	64	32	6	176

Source: Office of the Chief Scientist.

decade, but the yearly absolute level of grants does not decline till 2001.[22] The figure for total grants includes royalties collected from the main backbone R&D support program (royalties are collected only on R&D programs leading to sales up to the real amount of the government subsidy, and at a rate of about 3 percent of sales). These royalties—shown in the last column of the table—

amounted to $64 million in 1995 (19 percent of total) and to $154 million in 2000 (35 percent of total), that is, their share of total disbursements has risen sharply during the second half of the 1990s. This means that total grants *net of royalties* declined by 9 percent between 1995 and 2001. Concerning structure, the first point is that the scope of regular (backbone) R&D support has not declined during the 1990s despite reductions in *net* government disbursements. The second point is that in 1995 the second and third programs in terms of disbursements were technological incubators and magnet respectively (with $31 million and $15.3 million respectively); and that a rank reversal of these two programs occurred in 1996. Since then, the second most important program in terms of scope of grants extended is the magnet program, with $66.6 million in disbursements in the year 2000 (15 percent of total). The scope of the technological incubators program remained more or less constant ($31.6 million in 2000), which means a significant reduction in its share of total OCS grants. Also, the number of projects in government-supported incubators declined between 1997 and 2000 (table 9.3). We also know that there was a decline of more than 20 percent in the number of firms requesting support between 1997 and 2000 and that there was a slight decline in the ratio of projects whose support was requested to projects that were approved.

PART B: BACKGROUND FACTORS AND TRIGGERS OF THE ISRAELI VC INDUSTRY AND STAGES IN ITS EVOLUTION

THE EMERGENCE OF VENTURE CAPITAL

Explanatory Factors and Conditions

Our understanding of the Israeli case is still patchy, but it is clear that there were a number of factors that explained emergence and development of the new form of IT high-tech involving large numbers of SU companies and venture capital (Gelvan and Teubal 1997 list some of these). The factors affecting the early phases of the industry are classified here into three groups: background structural conditions, preemergence conditions, and triggers. A fourth group of factors deals with conditions conducive to learning and cumulativeness. Figure 9.3 summarizes the various categories.

The preexisting backbone R&D support program affected both the supply and the demand for VC services: its R&D grants directly enhanced SU formation and "demand" (e.g., by engineers formerly working in the military, in MNE (multinational enterprises), or in large domestic companies; and by recent graduates). They also affected VC "supply" since R&D grants were complementary to VC investments, that is, start-ups could obtain such grants from the government while at the same time receive investments from VC companies (this represented indirect incentives to VC investments). The backbone

BACKGROUND STRUCTURAL CONDITIONS
Large Pool of qualified Scientists and Engineers, and Universities capable of adding to this flow   The prior existence of a Civilian Hi Tech industry with experience in R&D Projects/Innovation   Strong prior MNE presence in Israel (Motorola, IBM, DEC, Intel, etc)   Restructuring of the Military Industries
The prior existence of the Backbone, Horizontal program supporting R&D in the Business Sector   Special Institutions (Army, etc)
Liberalization of Capital Markets during the 80s, and of the economy more generally speaking   A successful price stabilization program;   The restructuring of Military Industries
Existence of a number of Communications Equipment companies (Tadiran, ECI, Fibronics,   PhaseCom etc) from which a number of important spinoffs of the 90s took place(e.g NiceCom   subsequently sold to 3-Com)

PRE-EMERGENCE CONDITIONS & TRIGGERS (late 80s-1993)
Globalization of Capital and Asset Markets-enhanced opportunities for SU technology companies   out of the US to float in NASDAQ (Israel was quick to make use of such opportunities)
Globalization of US Investment Banks; and their searching for opportunities in Israel;   Individuals(foreign and returning Israelis) coming to Israel to search for new investment   opportunities in High Tech   High Rate of Start Up Formation: 1988 – 1992
New Government Programs-both General and Targeted to VC: The Inbal program(1991),   Magnet(1992), Technology Incubators(1990) and Yozma(1993)

CONDITIONS ASSURING LEARNING AND CUMULATIVENESS(1993-96)
The Gulf War and initiation of the Peace Process-which contributed to reduce Israel's isolation,   making it more attractive for business and investments;   Continued Implementation of the R&D Support Scheme and of the Programs implemented in the   early 90s
Immigration from the former Soviet Union—a large number of engineers and medical doctors   settled in Israel and worked in High Tech
_ New Innovation opportunities world wide, particularly in Communications, due to the ongoing IT   Revolution and to the Liberalization of Telecommunications.   Cultural Shift favoring entrepreneurship

Figure 9.3 Emergence and development of Israel's VC industry and high-tech cluster of the 90s—explanatory factors

R&D support program thus contributed to the creation of a market for VC-related services in more than one way.

Restructuring of military industries in the mid 1980s had the effect that significant numbers of incumbent engineers and technicians began looking for alternatives in the civilian high-tech; and so did increasing proportions of new graduates. Table 9.4 provides some basic data on this matter.

Preemergence Conditions and Triggers (late 1980s to 1993)

Foremost here is the beginning of a new phase in the globalization process: foreign high-tech start-ups could for the first time systematically float in NASDAQ, provided the economy had adapted to the new opportunities. Part of Israel's adaptation involved new government programs that complemented the above-mentioned backbone R&D support program (which also continued to be

Table 9.4
Changes in Civilian and "Military" High Tech Employment: 1984–87
(transportation equipment and electronics sub-branches)

Employment	Military: Scientists & Engineers	Military: Total Employment	Civilian: Scientists & Engineers	Civilian: Total Employment
Absolute Change	- 370	- 5040	1560	7540
Relative Change	- 1.8 %	- 4.6 %	11.4 %	7.4 %

Various Sources

implemented). These programs included *targeted* programs supporting venture capital (Inbal and Yozma); and complementary programs raising the demand for VC services (e.g., Technology Incubators' Program). Simultaneously, foreigners and Israelis began searching for new investment opportunities in Israel; and three (pre-Yozma) VC companies began operating (Athena, Star, and Giza). The significant SU activity that appeared in the early 1990s provided *pointers toward the new model of high-tech* and a *potential for learning*. The actual trigger, as far as we know, was implementation of Yozma in 1993 and its operation throughout 1995–1996. This provided the critical mass for the onset of a cumulative, self-reinforcing process of growth of VC and SUs. Between $250 million and $300 million was raised during the three-year period, and significant amounts were invested.

Conditions Conducive to Learning and Cumulativeness (1993 to 1996)

Strong collective learning processes took place during these three years and beyond, triggered by Yozma, which contributed to attain the critical mass that made this process effective and self-sustaining. These processes concerned scanning, due diligence, investment, monitoring, and exiting of the portfolio companies of the new funds. This further stimulated entry of new VC companies and accelerated creation of second/third funds by existing Yozma VC companies. The feedback-cumulative process was also fueled by favorable changes in the *external environment*, in particular the rise of the NASDAQ index and deregulation of communications. Additional factors were the Oslo peace agreements, the Russian immigration, and domestic regulatory changes.[23]

VC Targeted Policies

There is wide consensus that one of the major factors triggering emergence of Israeli VC was Yozma. As mentioned, the implementation of this program cannot be considered as obvious and automatic. It might not have happened, but it did. As mentioned above, the factors responsible for Yozma included the vision, capabilities, and policy learning of Israeli policy makers at the time. We should not underestimate the importance of luck or randomness in the process. Let us recall some of the background conditions that were operating at the time and that *transformed Yozma into an effective trigger of Israel's new high-tech cluster:* the backbone R&D support program; the restructuring of the military industries and new innovation opportunities, particularly in the IT area. These factors, together with a *cultural shift* in which self-employment and enterprise were increasingly being considered prestigious in Israeli society, generated a spurt of SU activity during the early 1990s (it then transformed itself into a wave). More specifically, these factors ensured that at the beginning of the operation of Yozma (1993), there was a *clear excess demand for VC services.* The surfeit of SU included also some very high quality firms and entrepreneurs (Checkpoint, Memco, Galileo, and ESC among others) who made a significant direct and indirect contribution to emergence and subsequent cumulativeness. In addition, we should not underestimate the specifics of the design and implementation of Yozma.

The Policy Context

New national priorities emerged with the beginnings of the massive immigration from the former Soviet Union during the early 1990s. The government of Israel began searching for means to employ the thousands of engineers that came to this country. Simultaneously the military industries had laid off hundreds of engineers; and there were many attempts to create start-up companies, which largely failed.

One of the targets was enhancement of start-up formation and start-ups' survival. Till the 1990s, the percentage of successful young companies was extremely low, and the accepted view was that this resulted from weak management abilities. Experts in the field and officials in the Treasury (who had good B.A. training in economics) realized that despite massive government support for R&D there still was a clear "market failure"[24] that blocked the successful creation and development of start-up companies. The head of OCS, or Chief Scientist at the time, Ygal Erlich, pondered about how to make OCS support more effective. There was not then even one real success "similar to those we see today" (interview, January 1998). The basic problem was lack of capability to grow after the product development phase. Erlich arrived at what could be seen as a vision and strategic perspective for Israel's high-tech: that the missing link was marketing/management; and that the way to get it was to foster venture capital. At the time, there were only one to three venture capital companies but it was clear that the total capital available was inadequate for the task at hand.

Inbal

The Inbal program was implemented one year before the implementation of Yozma. Its central idea was to stimulate VC funds by guaranteeing the downside of their investments. The mechanism used was creation of a government insurance company ("Inbal") that provided a 70 percent guarantee to VC funds traded in the stock market (calculated as 70 percent of the value of their public issue). The program imposed certain restrictions on the investments of the protected funds. Four funds were established—Mofet, Marathon, Teuza, and Sdot Mop. They and the Inbal program as a whole were not a great success. Fund valuations in the stock market were like those of holding companies (i.e., low valuations). The funds encountered bureaucratic problems and had to go to great lengths in order to prepare regular period reports. All of them attempted to leave the program, which they eventually succeeded in doing. Today all the (former) Inbal funds are held by one holding company: Green Technology Holdings.

Policy makers and business executives alike learned from Inbal's weak impact: the difficulty in publicly traded VC of having investors contributing to the operation of the fund; the greater difficulty in exploiting reputation earned from early exits to increase the capital invested (in an LP form of organization it would be easy to rapidly raise a second fund); and absence of incentives relevant to the upside.

Yozma Program[25]

The Yozma program began operating in 1992. The explicit objective was to create a solid base for the industry, to learn the business from foreign partners, and to acquire a network of international contacts. It was based on a $100 million government-owned VC fund (with the same name) oriented to two functions: (a) investment in private VC funds ("Yozma Funds")—$80 million; and (b) direct investments in high-tech companies—$20 million. The basic idea was to promote the establishment of Israeli VC funds that invested in young Israeli high-tech start-ups with the support of government and with the involvement of foreign financial/investment institutions. Each fund would have to get the investment of one such foreign institution together with that of a well-established Israeli financial institution. When a fund fulfilled these conditions, the government would invest (through Yozma) around 40 percent (up to $8 million) of the funds raised. Each fund also had a call option on government shares, at cost (plus interest) and for a period of five years. This was the main incentive of Yozma beyond risk sharing with the government. It was not a simple supply incentive, as was common in other government VC support programs; rather, it was an incentive to the "upside." The program also ensured the realization of supply side learning through the compulsory participation of foreign financial institutions. Demand side support was provided not by Yozma itself but by the backbone R&D support and technological incubators programs (see above).

In total, ten private Yozma funds were created, but the Yozma program also included the $20 million directly invested by the government through the Yozma 1 Fund, which started operating in 1993. Also founded in 1993 were the five funds Gemini, Star, Concord, Pitango, and Walden; JVP was started in 1994; Medica and EuroFund were started in 1995; Genesis was started in 1996;

and Vertex was started in 1997. The total capital raised by Yozma funds was about $250 million ($100 million out of its government capital), and they invested in over 200 start-up companies.

Impact

The Yozma funds initiated a dynamic, cumulative process involving learning by doing and imitation, and learning from foreigners. It was a collective learning process that also contributed to exploitation of economies of scale and specialization. As mentioned, venture capital coevolved with start-ups; with high-tech more generally speaking; and with a whole range of specialized services supporting the new high-tech cluster.

An indication of the funds' success in triggering growth of the industry is their expansion, which took the form of follow-up funds. Each one of the Yozma funds (and some other funds, as well, that indirectly learned from the Yozma experience) was followed by one or more additional funds managed by an expanding but related core of managers. *The total sums managed by this group today is approximately $5 billion,* a large share of total funds managed today. Another measure of the success is the rapid entry of non-Yozma related funds, something triggered by the handsome profits obtained by Yozma funds.

STATISTICS AND DESCRIPTION OF THE ISRAELI VC INDUSTRY

Milestones and Capital Raised

In 1966, Discount Investment Corporation (DIC) and the Rockefeller venture fund invested in Elron Electronic Industries—the first Israeli venture capital–related investment. Later on, when Elbit and Elscint were spun off from Elron, DIC and Rockefeller realized an impressive return on their investment. In the late 1960s and 1970s, DIC, Elron, and Scitex had only few venture capital–related investments. In 1971, Fred Adler, an East Coast venture capitalist, invested in Elscint, which in 1972 become the first Israeli company traded on NASDAQ.

In 1985, following previous successes in venture investments in Israel, Fred Adler established with Dan Tolkowskey the first formal VC company—Atena (Elron was a limited partner in the fund, with 10 percent of equity). In the 1980s, only a few Israeli companies were VC-backed, including Fibronics, Optrotech, Biotechnology General, and Zoran.

In 1989, Meir Barel, an Israeli engineer working in a private equity fund in Germany (TVM), established Star Ventures, a VC company devoted to investments in Israeli and in Israeli-related and German start-ups. In the following three years, before it became a Yozma fund, Star founded three funds, raising $37 million.

Finally, in 1991/1992 and in 1993 the government launched the Inbal and Yozma programs (see above). During 1993 and thereafter, there was rapid growth of the Israeli VC industry, both in terms of capital raised and in terms of number of funds active in the industry (see table 9.5).

Total capital raised per year between 1991 and 1996 ranged from $58 million in 1991 to $397 million in 1996; and it grew from $727 million in 1997 to $3,288 million in the year 2000. In fact, during the second half of the 1990s, the Israeli VC industry became significant and had a huge influence on Israel's high-tech industry. It was then that the first foreign VC companies began to invest directly in Israeli start-ups. Later on, a few of them (e.g., Benchmark, Sequoia) established Israeli offices. We see that prior to the establishment of the Yozma funds there already was VC activity, although it was not significant amounts. The big jump occurred in 1993 when private venture capitalists raised $162 million compared to $27 million the year before (primarily Yozma funds). Note that during 1992 nonprivate venture capitalists played a dominant role in total capital raised—$133 million compared to $27 million in capital raised by private venture capitalists. This in part reflects the Inbal incentives on public VC raising of capital; but capital was also raised by the other two categories of financial institutions—private equity funds and investment companies.

These observations sustain our presumptions (also buttressed by qualitative evidence) that (a) there was already non-insignificant VC and VC-related activity prior to implementation of Yozma ($160 million raised in 1992)—a fact that may have been significant for Yozma's impact two to three years after; (b) Yozma's $200 million plus raised between 1993 and 1995 significantly contributed to create a critical mass that triggered a cumulative process of growth in the VC industry during the second half of the 1990s;[26] and (c) the dominant form of organization was, and is increasingly so, private VC companies (which means, in our case, limited partnerships).[27] A fourth conclusion is that the Inbal program did not *directly* generate, in its wake, a cumulative process of steady growth (although it did have important *indirect effects* through increased effectiveness of the Yozma program).

The Growth of SU and of VC-backed SU companies

Table 9.6 shows *gross addition* estimates of new start-up companies that began operating since 1991 (rows 2 and 3) and estimates of VC-backed SU (row

Table 9.5
Capital Raised by the Israeli VC Industry in the 90s

	1991	1992	1993	1994	1995	1996	1997	1998	1999	2000	Total
Private VCs	49	27	162	112	145	264	609	468	1575	3155	6566
Public VCs	0	54	42	0	0	0	27	8	44	35	210
Private Equity Funds	0	45	128	242	6	110	66	74	40	26	737
Investment Companies	9	34	40	20	5	23	25	125	93	72	446
Total Capital Raised	58	160	372	374	156	397	727	675	1752	3288	7959

*Source: IVA.

1). Row 3 figures are for new SU firms requesting OCS support. These are good estimates of new SU numbers before the onset of VC toward the mid-1990s (since there were no additional sources of finance till then).[28] Gross new SU prior to 1991/1992, that is, prior to implementation of Yozma, are estimated to range between 80 companies (row 2) and 143 companies (row 3). Significant increases took place during 1993 and 1994 (at least 100 and most probably around 380), and sharp increases were seen year by year after that (except in 1998). These increases reflect the impact of implementation of the Yozma program and the increased availability of VC. The *direct* impact of Yozma, as reflected in numbers of new VC-backed SU companies, is shown in the first row of the table (the indirect impact should also include the acceleration of SU formation itself starting in 1995—which led to a steady growth/cumulative process during the postemergence period after 1995). Thus, according to one measure of new SU, during 1991 and 1992 new VC-backed SU trailed behind new SU, whereas the reverse seemed to occur during 1993 and 1994—the first two years of implementation of Yozma. However, according to the alternative measure, the share of new VC-backed companies over new SUs increased from approximately 20 percent to approximately 50 percent between 1992 and 1993. (In general we see a sharp rise in the proportions of VC-backed SU companies whatever series we use.) The "swarming" of SU during the second half of the 1990s (except in 1996) meant a reversal of the reversal: new VC-backed companies increasingly trailed behind new start-ups.

Growth in Exits

IPOs

The first Israeli company with an IPO in NASDAQ was Elscint, a medical diagnostics company belonging to the Elron group, in 1972. This early beginning did not signal the beginning of a new era, however, as far as links with the U.S. capital market were concerned. Only small numbers of Israeli companies undertook IPOs in NASDAQ (or in other markets) till the late 1980s.

Today Israeli (or Israeli-related) companies traded in the United States (over 150 of them) are the third-largest group, behind only the United States and Canada. Moreover, the numbers of Israeli (or Israeli-related) companies that

Table 9.6
Gross Additions to SU Companies and to VC-backed SU Companies

	1991	1992	1993	1994	1995	1996	1997	1998	1999	2000	Total
VC backed SUs	10	20	80	90	80	200	219	252	338	513	1802
All SU	40	40	50	50	100	200	350	350	550	850	2605
First time OCS SU	34	109	165	218	146	200	170	165	138	126	1471

Source: IVA, OCS and Newspapers

are traded in the London-based AIM stock market are the second-largest after UK companies. Most of these companies are technology start-ups.

Table 9.7 shows total issues or offerings, both IPOs and subsequent company issues. Total offerings increased considerably during the 1990s compared to the previous decades, and during 1995 and beyond compared to 1991–1994 (all years except 1998 and, marginally, 1995).[29] IPOs jumped in 1993 and then again in 1996 with the first exits from Yozma. A related point is the increase in the share of VC-backed issues, from roughly 30 percent at or before 1997 to over 70 percent in 1999–2000. Moreover, most IPOs during the end of the decade must have been VC-backed. The picture that emerges is one of increasing maturity of Israel's high-tech industry (due to learning and other cluster effects such as the creation of the VC industry itself), a process that accompanied the increase in the NASDAQ index (which by itself would also induce an increase in IPOs).[30] We cannot avoid noting also that, prior to 1993, there was already a non-insignificant number of IPOs (twelve during 1991–1992 alone), and all except one were non-VC-backed issues. This in part reflects the fact that very good, high-quality SU began populating the scene in the early 1990s.

Mergers and Acquisitions

The picture about the emerging high-tech cluster would not be complete without a consideration of the phenomenon of M&A—one of the main mechanisms of exit for venture capital companies and for SU entrepreneurs and early investors. The phenomenon of M&A is not homogenous, since it comprises a variety of different types of transactions distinguished by, for example, degree of complexity and objectives of SU-acquiring companies (usually multinational corporations). Moreover, the "market" for M&A differs considerably from the "public" capital markets epitomized by NASDAQ. The term *private,* which could be attached to such (capital) markets, is supposed to indicate the

Table 9.7
Number of Offerings of Israeli Companies in NASDAQ*

YEAR	Total Offerings	Total IPOs	VC backed Offerings	Capital Raised (M$)
Before 90	10	9	3	
1991	3	3	0	
1992	9	9	1	225
1993	17	10	4	529
1994	10	9	2	336
1995	16	8	5	608
1996	31	22	13	1,037
1997	24	19	6	1,074
1998	13	12	5	907
1999	20	12	14	3,172
2000	27	20	20	2,842
Total 90's	158	126	69	10,730

*Most if not all VC-backed offerings are first offerings (IPOs).

fact that those who acquire SU are not the public at large but rather one specific company, usually a competitor or a company with a technology that is complementary to that of the SU itself. There is no clear marketplace where M&A transactions are negotiated and implemented. Markets are thin, and a lot of randomness exists about whether a particular transaction will take place. It follows that the conditions for an emerging cluster to enable M&A activity on *a continuous basis* differ from those required to provide access to public capital markets.

The Israeli case suggests that IPOs might have played a crucial role in creating the conditions for cluster emergence and that M&A entered in increasingly large numbers only later on, probably starting in 1994 (see partial data in tables 9.5 and 9.6, among other considerations). The connection could be described as follows: public capital market links early in the game generate conditions for the emergence (given a suitable government program like Yozma) of a distinctive VC industry during, in the case of Israel, 1994 and 1995. The new industry develops a capability for M&A, and in fact, many venture capitalists become oriented—during phase 1 of the industry—*toward* the M&A form of exiting rather than to the IPO strategy.[31] This will, in part, change once the strategy of many venture capitalists shifts toward the building of large companies (in which process IPOs become extremely important).With the onset of cluster maturity and with enhanced cluster reputation, MNEs start comingling, which creates a very strong wave of new M&A.

The sequence of events seems to be borne by the data. Tables 9.7 and 9.8 show that during 1996 and 1997 the number of *significant* VC-backed M&A (fourteen) was still 20 percent lower than IPO numbers for the period (total of nineteen); but that the former exceeded the latter by about the same percentage during the period from 1998 to 2000.

CONCLUSIONS AND MAJOR EMERGING ISSUES

This chapter analyzes *background conditions, policies,* and the processes leading to *emergence* of Israel's venture capital industry in the 1990s. The approach adopted is explicitly a systems/evolutionary perspective focusing on the broader high-tech cluster and on the links between VC and SU. We end up identifying and to some extent characterizing Israel's model of venture capital emergence and development and some aspects of the Silicon Valley model of high-tech that developed there in the 1990s.

Background Conditions and Horizontal R&D Incentives

Israel's venture capital industry and high-tech cluster of the 1990s is an outgrowth of high-tech as it developed during the 1970s and 1980s and that involved a large military-oriented component including a significant share of defense R&D in aggregate national R&D. Civilian high-tech industry grew in

Table 9.8
Selected VC-backed M&A Involving Israeli Companies, 1994–2000

	Number of significant VC backed Deals	Total Valuation of Deals (M$)	Average Value (M$)	Average 5 top	Biggest Deal (M$)
1994	2	62	31	16	53
1995	5	635	127	127	350
1996	10	950	95	119	200
1997	4	788	197	181	400
1998	14	2,604	186	305	412
1999	12	3,180	265	583	1,600
2000	21	10,500	574	1,874	4,800
Total 90's	68	18,719	275	1,982	4,800

Total Valuation of M&A Deals refers to the implicit value of 100% of the SU sold. Thus if the VC owns 20% of a company who is acquired for $100M, then the Valuation will be $100M. The Value of the deal, however, will be $20M.

parallel to the military-oriented component, although initially at a slower rate. Both components of high-tech reinforced each other till the mid-1980s (when severe resource constraints dampened further development of the military component, a fact that led to a successful shift of resources to civilian high-tech). During this period a large technological infrastructure was established, and a significant process of learning in connection with civilian R&D and in-novation took place. It was a period in which civilian-oriented R&D/innovation activities and R&D/innovation capabilities *penetrated* and *were diffused* throughout the business sector. Hundreds of companies, large and small, were performing R&D on a routine basis toward the end of the 1980s. They had learned how to search for good R&D projects, search for market information, link marketing and production to R&D, and shift from "simple" to "complex" R&D projects as well as learned how to manage the innovation process as a whole. All of this led to an R&D-performing segment of the business sector and also to a clearly identifiable civilian-oriented and electronics-oriented high-tech industry. This practical collective knowledge about R&D and innovation within the business sector was the basis upon which the future venture capital industry grew. A dominant share of VC company founders (and also an im-portant share of SU of the 1990s) were individuals who had prior experience with the electronics industry of the 1980s.

Targeted Cluster-Creating Policies

Despite the above successes and the increased numbers of SU created during the late 1980s and early 1990s, serious problems concerning SU survival and growth emerged. The rate of failure of SU companies did not increase during this period, and it gradually began to dawn on policy makers (particularly to the Chief Scientist at the time) that the twenty-year-old R&D support scheme, while necessary, was no longer a sufficient condition for further development of high-tech. The real problem was successful transition to the post-SU phase of new company growth; and the crux of the problem was identified as non-existence (with some exception) of a special financial institution developed in the United States during the preceding two decades—venture capital. Venture capital not only provided resources through the purchase of equity of SU companies, it also provided important value-adding functions and activities such as management, head-hunting, R&D and strategy focus, links with clients and strategic investors, and last but not least, a channel for linking both to public (i.e., stock market) and private (M&A deals, particularly with MNE) capital markets. Although capital markets were becoming global, not every country could exploit the new opportunities, and at that time the creation of a domestic venture capital industry was an essential precondition that Israel (in anticipation of other peripheral economies with a technology and skills orientation) readily generated.

Given the above-mentioned favorable background and new challenges, the mechanism for triggering a domestic venture capital industry was a *targeted VC support program entitled the Yozma program* in which a $100 million government VC company was set up early in 1993. Of these funds $80 million was invested in ten private funds of approximately $20 million each, and the remaining $20 million was invested directly by a government fund ("Yozma"). The program was a targeted program, that is, its incentives were directed to a particular sector—venture capital—rather than to the business sector as a whole. A condition for being part of the program was the involvement of a reputable foreign financial institution together with a reputable local financial institution. The incentive, beyond government's risk sharing with private investors, derived from the possibility of purchasing the government share approximately at cost. Yozma directly generated $250 million, which was invested in over 200 portfolio companies. The high and rapid returns obtained by these funds (the result of some very successful exits, both IPO and M&A) stimulated a Schumpeterian "swarming" process in which both follow-up funds to existing VC companies and completely new VC companies entered the market. These funds, the earnings of the first round of new companies, and the enhanced reputation of Israel's new high-tech cluster increased considerably the rate of SU creation and the numbers of successful exits. Thus a self-sustained growth process of a cumulative nature set in. This would correspond to the *reproduction phase* of evolutionary processes. It is important to point out that the policy process leading to Yozma began in the early 1990s; that several alternatives were probed, including another targeted government program (Inbal) with only very limited success (*variation*); and that a lot of search and even policy-relevant research took place before *selection* of the Yozma policy alternative.

Toward a Coevolutionary Dynamic Process

The data reported in this paper and other evidence shows an interesting dynamic sequence involving coevolution. It involves three phases and looks as follows:

- *Significant preemergence activity* (prior to 1993). We estimate that between 80 and 143 existing or new SU were founded in 1991–1992 only; preliminary successes with IPOs in NASDAQ totaled about twelve; there was some VC activity (Athena/Veritas, Star, Giza) and VC-related activity by other institutions and key individuals (Adi Shalev, Jay Morrison, etc.)—all of this generated conditions for the implementation of Yozma.

- *Policy-induced creation of critical mass.* Yozma generated a discontinuous jump in VC and VC- and SU-related activity during 1993–1996: large increases in VC capital raised and about 250 new VC-backed companies, compared to about 30 VC-backed SU during 1991–1992.

- *Cumulativeness and steady growth.* The above contributed to sharp increases in exits, particularly IPOs in NASDAQ: twenty-two in 1996 compared to between eight and ten during 1993–1995. These in turn generated a self-sustained process of steady growth characterized by a further increase in the number of start-ups and in VC-backed SU; by increases in the number of SU that grew beyond the SU phase; by further entry into the VC industry; and by sharp increases in public offerings and also in M&A deals and so on.[32]

- *Mergers and acquisitions.* They play some role during emergence but probably not (or much less so) in the preemergence period. On the other hand, they become an important mechanism of cumulativeness and steady growth *after* emergence of VC industry and once the high-tech cluster acquires an international reputation.

The above is the core of Israel's model of VC (and modern high-tech cluster) emergence. In the above process, special attention should be given to the pre-emergence period of 1991–1993. Star, one of the three VC companies operating then, *was already making profits* in the new activities characterizing the new model of *high-tech*. So were Giza and Mofet (an Inbal publicly quoted VC) and, to a lower extent, Athena/Veritas. There must have been significant numbers of *very good* SU companies around—created by returning Israelis, spun off from MNEs, founded by former employees of domestic electronics companies and from the defense and other industries. These represented *very rich pickings* for the small numbers of Schumpeterian investors and venture capitalists active during the period from 1991 to 1993.

This observation is consistent with a very rapid growth of VC and high-tech after Yozma. Yozma funds were extremely profitable—the success ratios were extremely high (work in progress) and all except two of the ten Yozma funds exercised their right to buy back the 40 percent government share—some of them after only one or two years of operation, when exits and realized profits were still scarce (this would not have happened in the absence of strong expectations of profitability: the purchase meant that the companies were renouncing their right of having the government share in any future losses). High private profitability must have led, through entry/imitation and expansion of existing companies, to the early onset of cumulativeness/takeoff in the VC industry as a whole.

The whole process took about six years: three years in which favorable "immediate pre-Yozma conditions" were created and three additional years for VC (and SU-intensive high-tech) cluster emergence. Yozma was implemented at the midpoint and triggered the process.

Further work will buttress these findings with microeconomic data. This will set the stage for cross-country comparative work on VC emergence and development.

NOTES

1. This has been amply confirmed by the literature (see below).

2. One notable exception is Florida's work, which, without being explicitly evolutionary, has dealt with aspects of the dynamics of VC industries in the United States. One of his main points is that the VC industry emerged by the workings of the market without explicit government supports (Florida and Kenney 1987; Florida 1994). This stands in contrast with the Israeli experience.

3. These are only the two *main* exiting mechanisms. Each one comprises a number of specific variants related to timing and purpose of exits, for example, selling of technology in early phases compared with mergers and acquisitions of companies' technologies and operations at a later stage.

4. Schwienbacher (2001) states that in the last five years in Europe the ratio of trade sales to IPO exceeds 2.5. The ratio in the United States varied between 1.1 and 1.7. Our partial figures for Israel show an M&A/IPO ratio *of less than 1*.

5. See Nelson and Winter 1982; Nelson 1993, 1995; Lundvall 1992; and Edquist 1996.

6. Krugman (1991), when referring to high-tech clusters, states that "small historical events start a cumulative process in which the presence of a large number of firms and workers acts as incentive for still more firms and workers to congregate at a particular location." This corresponds to the post variation/selection phase of evolutionary processes (*reproduction*) in which *imitation, learning, exploitation of scale economies,* and *system effects* (the latter could be the appearance of a new component of the supporting structure that considerably facilitates SU creation and development) increase the proportion of the selected variant in the total population. See also Teubal 2002.

7. This is one more instance of research on user-producer links and user-producer coevolution, which is quite common in the evolutionary/systems perspective. See Lundvall 1985 and Pyke et al. 1990.

8. This has been emphasized by Saxenian (1998) in her study of IT high-tech in the United States and by other researchers such as Cooke (2001) for biotech.

9. A systems/evolutionary perspective would indicate that such a dynamic viewpoint should also be considered in the analysis of the mechanisms used to reduce the effects

of asymmetric information, conflicts of interest, and agency problems—some of the major issues considered in the specific venture capital literature.

10. Creation of the Office of the Chief Scientist at the Ministry of Industry and Trade was probably the most momentous policy decision of the government of Israel, as far as innovation and technology policy is concerned. It became a specialized agency involved in promoting innovation by and for the business sector as a whole, with a focus from day 1 on *direct support of the business sector*. This became the central feature of the Israeli strategy for promoting innovation in the business sector.

11. See Teubal 1993 (p. 480). This is based on a three-way classification of industry: high-tech, other sophisticated (equivalent to mid-tech and including a metal working subgroup and a chemicals subgroup), and conventional (low-tech). The classification used then was based on skill intensity as measured by the share of scientists and engineers in total employment. Under this measure the average skill intensity of high-tech in 1984 was 16 percent compared to 6 percent and 2 percent for the other two categories respectively. The three industries comprising high-tech were electro-optics and fine machinery, aircraft and ships, and electronics and communications equipment. The first two are not the strongest product groups in the new high-tech cluster of the 1990s. Looking at the business sector as a whole (and not only at manufacturing), the most important groups are software and communications equipment (note that there was no separately identifiable software industry during the 1980s).

12. Lecture at the Hebrew University.

13. During the 1970s and 1980s the first foreign multinationals were also established in Israel, starting with Motorola in 1964 and followed by IBM, Intel, and Digital Equipment. These companies also became incubators of engineers and managers, the impact of which will be seen later on during the 1990s.

14. Till the early 1990s more than 90 percent of government disbursements to civilian R&D came out of this program.

15. It is well known that horizontal programs embody an element of selectivity by virtue of the particular activity being chosen, for example, regular R&D, generic-cooperative R&D, or technology transfer/adsorption. Thus Israel's Industrial R&D Fund, while formally neutral in the allocation of its incentives, and given its dominance over other programs for long periods of time, embodies strong selectivity of regular R&D relative to other possible technological activities. See, for example, Lall and Teubal 1998.

16. Another smaller program—BIRD—began operating toward the end of the 1970s. It was also successful and highly complementary to the main, backbone horizontal program.

17. Initial conditions in the ideal HTP (horizontal technology policy) model (see Teubal 1996, p. 7), which reflect the conditions prevailing in Israel in 1969, are (a) that R&D is practically nonexistent within the business sector; and (b) that its diffusion is a strategic priority of the country that is viewed as a necessary condition for growth of the business sector.

18. Learning, including experience-based learning triggered by increased R&D in the business sector, is the main factor leading to enhanced R&D/innovation capabilities.

19. The OECD average was 9.9 percent in 1996, and for the United States it was 11.8 percent.

20. Central Bureau of Statistics 2000.

21. A more systematic treatment of the cumulative process ensuing after 1993 would require microeconomic analysis of collective *learning, knowledge dissemination by Yozma*, and *links/other cluster effects*.

22. In fact both a market and an institutional/systemic failure.

23. Most of the material here was obtained from two interviews (January 1998 and May 2000) with Ygal Erlich, the CEO of Yozma and the architect (or one of the most important architects) of the program. Additional material was obtained from a lecture he gave at Pavia in February 2001 and from other sources.

24. Forty-six percent of total funds raised during 1994–1996 were from private VC (up from 35 percent during 1992–1994). About half are directly from Yozma funds; they may have indirectly influenced the others. Note, however, the importance of private equity funds in capital raised during 1993 and 1994. At least some of the Yozma funds emphasized early phase financing, in contrast to the policy of other venture capitalists. This would have a much larger effect on new SU companies compared to the effect of later phase financing. This mechanism also would have indirectly stimulated others to enter the industry.

25. Especially since 1996, when private VC funds represented 93 percent, with the ratio moving between 80 percent and 96 percent till the year 2000.

26. Also, SU after 1995–1996 did not always go for OCS grants since this could create difficulties in future M&A deals (an M&A would presumably involve an element of R&D implementation out of Israel and, correspondingly, a penalty on the company, according to OCS rules at the time).

27. No exception if we consider capital raised rather than numbers of offerings (see fourth column of table 9.3). Note that exits from Yozma first funds were supposed to take place during 1996–1998.

28. Both factors were certainly at work here. Note that the sharp increases in the NASDAQ index did not induce other high-tech clusters to float more companies, for example India, till 1999. Thus the fast response of Israeli firms to the growth of NASDAQ reflects *also* mounting capabilities and the effects of learning.

29. The "simple" types of M&A seem to be easier to learn during phase 1 of the VC industry (see next subsection) compared to "preparing a company for IPO." The latter requires paying attention to management, financial, and marketing capabilities because, to float, a company needs to sell a product (although it need not be profitable). In contrast, most mergers and acquisitions are based on the technology and technological excellence of SU and of its staff.

30. A previous study of the data security industry suggests that undertaking an IPO is a necessary but not sufficient condition for an SU to grow and become an indigenous company that takes on downstream production and marketing.

31. The 'simple' types of M&A seem to be easier to learn during phase 1 of the VC industry (see next subsection) compared to 'preparing a company for IPO'. The latter requires paying attention to management, financial and marketing capabilities since, for floating, a company needs a selling product (although it need not be profitable). In contrast, most M&A are based on the technology and technological excellence of SU and of its staff.

32. A previous study of the Data Security industry suggests that undertaking an IPO is a necessary but not sufficient condition for a SU to grow and become an indigenous company undertaking downstream production and marketing.

REFERENCES

Akerloff, G. 1970. "The Market for Lemons: Qualitative Uncertainty and the Market Mechanism." *Quarterly Journal of Economics* 84: 488–500.

Arrow, K. 1962. "Economic Welfare and the Allocation of Resources to Invention." In *The Rate and Direction of Inventive Activity*, ed. R. Nelson. Princeton, N.J.: Princeton University Press, National Bureau of Economic Research.

Avnimelech, G. 2001. "A Case Study of the Israeli Chip Design Sector." IFISE project, EU.

Avnimelech, G. 2002. "Exploring VC Added Value: A Study of the Israeli VC Industry." Master's thesis, Tel Aviv University.

Avnimelech, G., A. Gayego, and M. Teubal. 1999. "Globalization and Firm Dynamics in the Israeli Software Industry: A Case Study of Data Security." Typescript.

Avnimelech, G., A. Gayego, B. Toren, and M. Teubal. 1999. *Country Report: Israel.* TSER project "SME in Europe and Asia."

Avnimelech, G., and Y. Margalit. 1999. "R&D Policy in Israel." Bachelor of arts seminar paper, The Hebrew University.

CBS (Central Bureau of Statistics). 2000. "Development of Information and Communications Technologies in the Last Decade." Jerusalem: Central Bureau of Statistics, March.

Cooke, P. 2001. "New Economy Innovation Systems: Biotechnology in Europe and the USA." *Industry and Innovation* 3: 267–89.

Edquist, C., ed. 1996. *Systems of Innovation: Technologies, Institutions, and Organizations.* London: Pinter.

Florida, R. 1994. "VC and Industrial Competitiveness." Research report to the U.S. Economic Development Administration.

Florida, R. L., and M. Kenney. 1987. "Venture Capital-Financing Innovation and Technological Change in the USA." *Research Policy* 17: 119–37.

Gelvan, D., and M. Teubal. 1997. "Emergence and Development of a Venture Capital Industry in Israel: An Evolutionary and Policy Approach." Paper presented at a symposium in honor of Alexander Volta, Como, Italy.

Gompers, P. A. 1995. "Investment, Monitoring and the Staging of VC." *Journal of Finance* 38: 1461–89.

Gompers, P. A. 1996. "Grandstanding in the VC Industry." *Journal of Finance Economics* 42: 133–56.

Gompers, P. A., and J. Lerner. 1999. *The Venture Capital Cycle.* Cambridge, Mass.: MIT Press.

Gorman, M., and W. Sahlman. 1989. "What Do Venture Capitalists Do?" *Journal of Business Venturing* 4: 231–48.

IVA Yearbook. 1997. Tel Aviv: Giza Group.

IVA Yearbook. 1998. Tel Aviv: Giza Group.

IVA Yearbook. 1999. Tel Aviv: Giza Group.

IVA Yearbook. 2000. Tel Aviv: THCG Giza Israel.

IVA Yearbook. 2001. Tel Aviv: Israel Venture Capital.

Justman, M. 2001. "Structural Change and the Emergence of Israeli's High Tech Industry." In *The Israeli Economy 1985–98: From Government Intervention to Market Economy*. Volume in Honor of Michael Bruno. Jerusalem: Falk Institute for Economic Research.

Justman, M., and E. Zuscovitch. 2000. "The Economic Impact of Subsidized Industrial R&D in Israel." Paper presented at EUIP Conference, Eindhoven Technological University, Tillburg.

Krugman, P. 1991. *Geography and Trade*. Leuven, Belgium: Leuven University Press, and Cambridge, Mass.: The MIT Press.

Lall, S., and M. Teubal. 1998. "A Framework for Market Stimulating Industrial and Technology Policy." *World Development* 26: 1369–85.

Lerner, J. 2000. *Venture Capital and Private Equity—A Case Book*. New York: John Wiley and Sons.

Lukomet, R. 2000. "Venture Capital Funds and Their Contribution to the Development of Israel's High Tech Industries (in Hebrew)." Jerusalem: Falk Institute for Economic Research in Israel.

Lundvall, B. A. 1985. *User-Producer Interaction*. Aalborg: Aalborg University Press.

Lundvall, B. A., ed. 1992. *National Innovation Systems*. London: Pinter.

Megginson, W. L., and K. A. Weiss. 1991. "Venture Capitalist Certification in IPO's." *Journal of Finance*, pp. 879–903.

Metcalfe, S. 1995. "The Economic Foundations of Technology Policy: Equilibrium and Evolutionary Perspectives." In *Handbook of the Economics of Innovation and Technical Change*, ed. Paul Stoneman, ch. 11. Cambridge, Mass.: Basil Blackwell.

Nelson, R., ed. 1993. *National Systems of Innovation*. Oxford: Oxford University Press.

Nelson, R. 1995. "Recent Evolutionary Theorizing about Economic Change." *Journal of Economic Literature* 23: 48–90.

Nelson, R., and S. Winter. 1982. *An Evolutionary Theory of Economic Change*. Boston, Mass.: Harvard University Press.

Pyke, F., G. Becattini, and W. Sangenberger, eds. 1990. *Industrial Districts and Interform Cooperation in Italy*. Geneva: International Institute for Labour Studies.

Sahlman, W. A. 1990. "The Structure of Governance of Venture Capital Organizations." *Journal of Finance Economics* 27: 473–521.

Sapienza, H. J., S. Manigart, and W. Vermeir. 1996. "Venture Capitalist Governance and Value Added in Four Countries." *Journal of Business Venturing* 11: 439–69.

Saxenian, A. 1998. *Regional Development: Silicon Valley and Route 128*. Cambridge, Mass.: Harvard University Press.

Schwienbacher. 2001. "Innovation and Venture Capital Exits." Typescript, University of Namur.

Spiller, P., and M. Teubal. 1987. "Analysis of R&D Failure." In *Innovation Performance, Learning, and Government Policy*, ed. M. Teubal, ch. 2. Madison: University of Wisconsin Press. First published in *Research Policy* 6: 254–75.

Teubal, M. 1983. "Neutrality in Science Policy: The Promotion of Sophisticated Industrial Technology in Israel." *Minerva* 21: 172–79. Reprinted in *Innovation Performance, Learning, and Government Policy*, ed. M. Teubal, ch. 8. Madison: University of Wisconsin Press.

Teubal, M. 1986. *Innovation Performance, Learning, and Government Policy*. Madison: University of Wisconsin Press.

Teubal, M. 1993. "The Innovation System of Israel: Description, Performance, and Outstanding Issues." In *National Systems of Innovation*, ed. R. Nelson. Oxford: Oxford University Press.

Teubal, M. 1996. "A Catalytic and Evolutionary Perspective to Horizontal Technology Policy." *Research Policy* 25: 1161–88.

Teubal, M. 1999. "Towards an R&D Strategy for Israel." *The Economic Quarterly* (Hebrew), December.

Teubal, M. 2002. "What Is the Systems Perspective to Innovation and Technology Policy (ITP) and How Can We Apply It to Developing and Newly Industrialized Economies?" *Journal of Evolutionary Economics* 12: 233–57.

Teubal, M., N. Arnon, and M. Trachtenberg. 1987. "Performance in Innovation in the Israeli Electronics Industry: A Case Study of BioMedical Electronics Instrumentation." In *Innovation Performance, Learning, and Government Policy,* ed. M. Teubal, ch. 1. Madison: University of Wisconsin Press. First published in *Research Policy* 5: 354–79.

Teubal, M., and G. Avnimelech. 2001. "Which Peripheral Countries Benefit from Globalisation: Lessons from an Analysis of Company Growth, Acquisitions and Access to Complementary Assets in Israel's Data Security Industry." Typescript.

Teubal, M., and E. Boehm. 1998. "Creation of the Magnet Committee: A New Profile for Innovation and Technology Policy in Israel." Typescript.

Toren, B. 1990. "R&D in Israel." In *Industrial-Technological Policy for Israel,* ed. D. Brodet, M. Justman, and M. Teubal. Jerusalem: Jerusalem Institute for Israel Studies.

10

Fostering Innovation Financing in Developing Countries
The Case of Turkey

Dilek Çetindamar

INTRODUCTION

As has previously been emphasized in the introduction, one of the functions of a financial system is to support the start-up and growth of new technology-based firms. If the financial system is capable of performing this function, then the system will lead to opportunities for growth and development in the industrial sectors of the future. Industrialized countries (ICs) have for many years had the capability to develop mechanisms to support new industries and technologies (Carlsson 2002). In these ICs, this support is provided through a professional, dynamic system of innovation financing. One of the agents of this system is the venture capital industry (VCI), which has been defined quite clearly in both the introductory chapter and chapter 2, thus rendering unnecessary the need for its definition here. Suffice to say that the VCI consists of financial intermediary organizations that supply capital to firms in financial need, particularly those that are technology-based (Carlin and Mayer 1999; Smith and Smith 2000). This is not to deny the other roles of venture capital (VC) firms, such as setting strategy and enabling networking, which also need to be given the space they deserve. With this wide range of roles and the resultant direct support given to entrepreneurship and innovation, it can be seen that the VCI is one of the pillars supporting the so-called new economy (Senker and Vliet 1998). There are two questions that I want to address at this juncture. First, could this rejuvenating role of VC firms, so successful in ICs, be relevant for developing countries (DCs) too? Second, how can DCs construct an innovation financing system that is relevant to their economic and social context?

Before proceeding any further, I feel that it is necessary to define DCs, because, contrary to popular opinion, not all DCs are the same. There is a great disparity between different DCs, and they are categorized in many ways depending on the organization doing the categorization. For example, the United Nations has placed DCs into three groups in accordance with their level of income: low, middle, or high. While this categorization may be suitable for projects conducted by the United Nations, I prefer to use a technological classification. Because the focus of this paper is the VCI and its effect on the new economy, such a classification appears to be more appropriate.

Accordingly, DCs may be classified under the following four categories (Weiss 1990):

1. Countries with little or no technological infrastructure

2. Countries with some research capacity in agriculture but virtually none in other sectors

3. Countries with some agricultural and industrial research capacity

4. Countries with a significant amount of technological infrastructure

Regardless of the type of DC, financial problems have always been in existence from the dawn of their industrialization processes. These problems will linger for some time to come, as future wealth creation will depend on development driven by knowledge and technology (Grossman and Helpman 1991; Jalava and Pohjola 2002). Countries in category 4 will probably be sheltered from this to some extent, but DCs with the misfortune (in this regard) to fall into the other three categories will still suffer from the effects of this vicious circle.

Within this context, VC can play a role just as it does in ICs. However, our simple categorization of DCs shows us that the impact of VC on economic development may vary considerably depending on the country's level of technological development. In this regard, VC may contribute significantly to the industrialization of countries in groups 3 (such as Brazil and Turkey) and 4 (such as South Korea, Taiwan, and Singapore) due to two main reasons. First, these countries have a substantial base on which to construct a new economy. Their educated labor force and industrial experience can be sources leading to the transformation of the economy into an innovative and entrepreneurial structure (Najmabadi and Lall 1995). Second, these countries can produce competent and knowledgeable venture capitalists and entrepreneurs due to the available pool of professionals working in industry. With a proper incentive system, these professionals with production and sales experience might be attracted to work in VC firms or become entrepreneurs by setting up new firms.

It is my intention in this chapter to answer the questions posed in the first paragraph of the introduction. To accomplish this I will analyze the case of a type 3 developing country, Turkey. Exclusion of type 1 and 2 countries is due to the lack of industrial infrastructure in these countries. These countries cannot construct critical mass for the creation of researchers and entrepreneurs who can transform economy with innovations and generate enough profits to attract VC firms. There might be piecemeal VC investments, but the development of a VCI cannot be expected. I have chosen to focus on Turkey in part because I live and work here and, therefore, have access to the required information to make a proper and detailed analysis. In addition, this chapter focuses on an example of a country in which some research capacity and industrial experience exist. I will demonstrate in the subsequent discussion that the VCI may have more of a chance of contributing to economic and technological development in these types of countries. Turkey is a typical example of a country belonging to this category of DCs. It is heavily populated and has substantial research capability in agriculture and some in industrial sectors with a heavy industrial infrastructure. This industrial infrastructure can benefit a lot from a healthy innovation system generating innovations that can introduce high value-added products and production technologies to be used in existing industries (Grossman and Helpman 1991; Kim 1997). If it can be shown that the existence of the VCI can contribute to type 3 countries like Turkey, it is logical to expect that it will contribute to type 4 countries as well, since they have more research capabilities than the type 3 countries.

The organization of the chapter is as follows. After this short introduction, the role of VC in DCs will be discussed. In the third section I focus on the requirements of entrepreneurs, in other words, the demand side of the VC market. The specific example of Turkey will be used to identify important dimensions of the VC phenomena and its opportunities for DCs. The Turkish VC market is analyzed in the fourth section, where the actors in this market, the supply side, will be introduced. The financial conditions of Turkey and the developments in the VC market will be used to design a plausible innovation financing system for DCs in the fifth section. The last section will focus on general policy issues that might arise in DCs that are in the process of constructing a VC industry.

THE ROLE OF VENTURE CAPITAL IN DEVELOPING COUNTRIES

Evidence all around us shows that globalization is affecting every corner of the planet. It is no longer possible (as arguably it was in the past) for DCs to shut their eyes and their borders to what is going on in ICs. Therefore, DCs can not ignore the rise of the new economy in ICs nor can they expect the effects to pass them by without making any sort of impact (Grossman and Helpman 1991). The new economy produces visions of many different things to different people; however, my focus is on changes taking place in products, technologies, production processes, and industries. The world is experiencing the continual blurring of industrial boundaries and the introduction of new industries (Cooke 2001). The rapid growth of information and communication technologies, especially Internet technologies, has played and will continue to play a critical role in all these developments (OECD 2001; Jalava and Pohjola 2002).

Issues for Developing Countries

It is essential for DCs to take the necessary steps to invest in technological innovation as a means to increase productivity and competitiveness and to prevent potential threats (Grossman and Helpman 1991; Lall 1992; Weiss 1990). Unless DCs take these steps, even if only in a tentative manner to begin with, then these threats and problems will be realized. The major problems can be categorized under three headings, which are explained below using examples taken from the field of biotechnology.

First, DCs have country-specific problems that can never be solved by other countries' technologies (Lall 1992). For example, most of the biotechnology research in ICs (two-thirds of total research budgets in the United States) is oriented toward illnesses prevalent in their aging populations. In contrast to this research, the needs of DCs are dictated by statistics like the ones that show the rate of infant mortality being approximately 20 percent (Fransman, Junne, and Roobeek 1995). It appears obvious to me that DCs, if they are to develop, should conduct research in areas that are sine qua non for them, such as preventing child illnesses. With most of the research in ICs being specific to an IC's context, it is essential that DC scientists at work in ICs are able to develop their skills and bring these into the DC's context (Başağa and Çetindamar 2000).

Second, the increased strictness of the worldwide application of intellectual property rights laws has meant that DCs have encountered problems in making use of scientific findings in what could be referred to as the research black market (Senker and Vliet 1998). To make this even tighter, the World Trade Organization is at present introducing regulations that will limit the free diffusion of scientific developments. Researchers in ICs have also seen fit to increase patenting activities, thus obliging users to pay royalties. The major irony lies in the fact that while DCs have 80 percent of the total world gene resources, 99 percent of the license revenues based on technologies using DC-originated genes goes to ICs. The United States alone receives half these revenues (Forsman 2000). To right this obvious wrong, DCs need to develop the political power to influence the bargaining surrounding any regulation process and to protect their own rights. It is also essential for DCs to find a way to influence joint research activities conducted with DCs. As it stands at present, ICs are the ones in control of these joint ventures and subsequently the ones who gain the most. DCs must find a way to gain the knowledge and experience in biotechnology necessary to intervene and positively affect international biotechnology research and development (R&D) projects.

Third, there is a danger to the DCs of the substitution effect. ICs are known to have started producing some products in their laboratories, such as sugar substitutes. In the long run, it is very likely that many products traditionally imported from DCs could be produced in ICs. This will lead to severe trade reversal and significantly affect the DCs' trade balances. For a simple example of this issue, we only have to look at the laboratory production (in ICs) of high fructose corn syrup from maize, which threatens the livelihood of 50 million workers engaged in the sugar industry in DCs (Fransman, Junne, and Roobeek 1995). Even though the productivity of sugar producers in DCs is high, they may lack the ability to compete with the cheap, fabricated products of ICs. If this problem comes to fruition, it will inevitably lead to a reduction in the competitive advantage of DC producers.

Capturing the potential benefits of technological advancement and avoiding the threats that might arise from its absence depend on the nature of DCs' investments in science and technology (Başağa and Çetindamar 2000; OECD 1999; Weiss 1990). If we consider the complexity, high cost, and uncertainty of science, it is clear that it is almost impossible for countries to excel in all areas. Thus, DCs need to specialize in fields in which they can best utilize their resources, including skills, competencies, and capital (Najmabadi and Lall 1995).

At this juncture it is important to bear in mind that while ICs focus on high technologies that change the overall industrial structure accordingly, DCs cannot choose to specialize in high technologies alone. This is because they need to give priority to technologies that are going to be of immediate and direct use in their economy as it stands at the present time. In other words, DCs should allocate their limited resources to technologies that are appropriate for the existing industrial structure and can increase the value-added content of products and services produced in their countries (Kim 1997).

As already mentioned, the priority for investments in DCs should be given to directly applicable technologies. However, there are numerous advantages to allocating resources for R&D that has no immediate use for industrial purposes (Najmabadi and Lall 1995). First, this type of R&D increases the competence level of scientists and the level of scientific knowledge within the country. Second, some scientific findings can be exported abroad to countries that can then use these finding in their industries. This benefit can be exploited only if the host country has a strong intellectual property rights system (Senker and Vliet 1998). Otherwise, firms from ICs can exploit the scientific and technologic knowledge of DCs. To avoid this exploitation, it is necessary for firms, scientists, and entrepreneurs from DCs to be trained in legal and trade issues. Otherwise they will not be able to prevent any free riding or other opportunistic behavior that they might be faced with as they are exploited. Third, even if a brain drain occurs in the short term, there are long-term benefits that can offset it. This brain drain is caused by the departure of scientists who have inventions that cannot be commercialized within their own DC. The first benefit from brain drain is that success stories will motivate other scientists in the DC. The second benefit is that successful scientists can return to their countries or they can establish partnerships with local businesses and scientists, resulting in increased economic activities. India is a prime example of this benefit. Many successful Indian software producers left India to work in the United States and then used their expertise to become the main driving force in establishing the software business in India (Correa 1996). Many of these professionals either started companies in India or gave subcontracting work to existing companies. In either case, they were a force for economic growth. Let me add an important word of caution here: this long-term benefit is not something that can be relied upon as an automatic result of a brain drain. It is necessary for DCs to conduct policies that will serve to attract scientists and businesspeople living abroad to invest in their home country.

The Role of Innovation Financing in Industrial Renewal and Innovativeness

As I have been stressing throughout, the VCI has a crucial role to play in a DC's economic transformation process to the new economy, where the major developments are in the fields of science and technology (Aylward 1998; Sagari and Guidotti 1992; Rickne 2000). When we analyze the role of VC, we should do it in a broad context; as such, I have chosen to analyze VC under the following three headings: (a) VC as a financial input for industrialization, (b) VC as a financial and managerial tool for small and medium-sized enterprises (SMEs), and (c) VC as an innovation-financing source. The degree to which each of these exists in a country will be determined in conjunction with the functions of other financial organizations/actors in the system.

The VCI is in the position of being able to supply capital for industrialization in DCs. The vast majority of DCs import technologies from ICs and attempt to establish industries in their local markets (Humphrey 1995). In many DCs the heavy industries are under the control of state-owned enterprises, as was the case in many ICs until the late 1980s. These heavy industries require large investments, and this investment is of such a magnitude that state resources are required to ensure it is carried out. For many DCs of the time (e.g., Singapore, Japan, and South Korea), the second half of the twentieth century was a period of heavy industrialization (Lall 1992; Najmabadi and Lall 1995). This industrialization allowed these countries to jump from being DCs to becoming some of the most successful ICs. If we analyze these success stories, we see that these countries passed through a number of stages, ranging from imitation to innovation (Kim 1997). We must not forget that entrepreneurship and innovativeness have quite different meanings in DCs than in ICs. Entrepreneurs in ICs initiate unique products, services, and processes, whereas entrepreneurs in DCs might just imitate existing products, services, and processes in ICs that are considered to be "new" for their own local markets. However, such actions should not be taken to mean that entrepreneurs in DCs have no need of finance. Quite the opposite—these entrepreneurs need substantial amounts of capital even for this kind of imitative industrialization. The VCI can be one of the actors playing the role of supplying this finance (Smith and Smith 2000).

Another role of the VCI can be as a financial and managerial tool for SMEs, since financial resources are very limited in DCs. In general, start-up firms raise their capital from self-financing, family and friends, banks, government, stock markets, and large firms. However, many DCs do not have well-functioning bank and stock market systems that can support SMEs, as is the case in ICs (Sagari and Guidotti 1992). VC firms as private equity investors might bring a new alternative to entrepreneurs searching for capital for their business ideas. Equally important, the majority of DC firms are family-owned and not managed by professional managers. VC companies are in a position to help discipline these firms and aid them in a number of important managerial issues such as strategy, marketing, and networking (Sapienza, Manigart, and Vermeir 1996).

The VCI has many functions to perform in DC markets but its most important function is financing innovations. In order not to lose even more ground on ICs and in order to compete in the world markets, DCs need to understand the dynamics of the new economy, particularly entrepreneurship and innovativeness (OECD 1998, 2001). It is here that the main role of VC comes to the foreground, as an innovation-financing instrument that can contribute to the creation of the basis for the new industrialization wave (Carlsson 2002; Cooke 2001). This role is similar to the role of VC in ICs: a financial tool for new economy companies. In other words, VC increases the competitiveness of firms and/or countries in new technology fields (Kortum and Lerner 1998; Rickne 2000).

What I have discussed up to now looks very good on paper; however, DCs face many difficulties in creating and running a healthy VCI in their countries. Some of the important problems include low availability of financial resources; poor technological opportunities; small size and purchasing power of the domestic markets; lack of adequate skills; problems in entrepreneurial culture; difficulties with exit mechanisms; incomplete institutional and legal frameworks; economic instability; high inflation; and high interest rates (Sagari and Guidotti 1992; Aylward 1998). These difficulties, coupled with slow and inward-oriented economic growth, might hinder the development of the VCI in DCs. That is why it has been argued that VC operations in DCs could flourish only in areas of low technology, in craft work, and in the service sector (Sagari and Guidotti 1992). Suggested investment areas cover agribusiness; aquaculture; and horticulture such as food irradiation, manufacturing of tropical fruit juice concentrates, and marketing and distribution of fresh vegetables and flowers. Some countries such as Bulgaria are following this pattern, since VC investments in Bulgaria are in agriculture, food, and tourism (Mladenowa 2000).

However, restricting VC financing to low-technology industries will not lead to a restructuring of the economy. Instead it could prevent DCs from transforming their economies and developing technological capabilities (Lall 1992; Humphrey 1995). DC governments that follow such a policy would be making two mistakes in their long-run economic development. First, such a policy will limit them to low value-added products that cannot produce high economic wealth. Second, VC firms can profit in the short run but profits might not be sustainable in the long run since low technologies will not generate capabilities and innovative opportunities that are candidates for future investments.

A VCI should have a broader range of responsibilities, including fostering technology-based development. The example of Israel described in chapter 9 shows that the VCI can drive rapid industrialization based on high-technology products and services. This rapid industrialization can then lead to DCs becoming ICs, which we must assume to be their long-term goal.

ENTREPRENEURS IN TURKEY

This section focuses on the demand side issues in the VC market. To analyze demand, I will begin with the entrepreneurial culture in Turkey and then try to paint a picture showing the degree of financial problems that entrepreneurial firms find themselves in at the present time.

Entrepreneurial and innovative countries such as the United States have societies that encompass entrepreneurs and that support their innovative endeavors (OECD 1998; Hisrich and Peters 1998). This cultural environment motivates scientists and researchers to take risks and establish firms in order to commercialize their findings. Education plays a special role in creating and sustaining this culture, since entrepreneurs are also educated with regard to the managerial capabilities and skills that they will require should they ever run their own company. Entrepreneurs are also encouraged to be risk takers, which facilitates the establishment of companies with alternative technologies (Swedberg 2000). With the laws of competition being akin to the law of the jungle, only the fittest survive and the weak perish. Even though failure may be considered a negative, in fact, entrepreneurial culture benefits a lot from it. By examining the reasons behind failure, firms and scientists develop a diverse knowledge set that can be utilized in the subsequent product and technology creation processes. In short, failed companies and entrepreneurs are not indefinitely penalized as failures but are conceptualized to be part of the ordinary process of innovation.

Comparative studies of the entrepreneurial cultures in the European Union (EU) and the United States indicate that the United States outperforms EU countries in many respects (Senker and Vliet 1998; OECD 1998). The main reason behind this is the institutional infrastructure, such as simple and efficient regulation systems for taxation and employment.

Because the main factor behind success appears to be the institutional infrastructure, it is pertinent to examine Turkey in this regard. Like many DCs, Turkey has an institutional structure that is a bureaucratic minefield. This excessive bureaucracy creates many problems that hinder entrepreneurial motivation. On a societal level, entrepreneurial culture might be considered a new development. Turkey has been a latecomer to industrialization, with the private sector only starting to take shape around the 1950s. Most production is done by state-owned corporations and the large family-run conglomerates. Most of the SMEs are run by families, not by professional managers. University graduates' career plans involve working in large companies, since starting up a firm is considered a big risk. Therefore, no tradition of entrepreneurialism exists.

Besides bureaucracy, another problem is the lack of collaboration among universities, research organizations, and firms. In ICs, close collaborations and networks facilitate easy and fast transfer of technology to companies (Senker and Vliet 1998). This, in turn, leads to rapid commercialization. When researchers do not show interest in the problems of corporations and, similarly, corporations do not trust researchers' capability in solving their problems, technology transfer will not function (Maeda 2001). The entrepreneurial climate is hindered by mistrust, miscommunication, and negative attitudes toward each other. This is exactly what is being experienced in the Turkish case. The innovation survey conducted by the State Institute of Statistics (SIS) collected data from more than two thousand firms in 1998. The results show that only 4 percent of innovative firms consider universities as a source of knowledge and technology, while only 2.7 percent of them see government research agencies as a source (SIS 1998). These figures show a worrying amount of mistrust among organizations.

On top of the lack of a supportive entrepreneurial culture, entrepreneurial firms, particularly SMEs, have significant financial problems, like their counterparts in ICs (Van Auken 1999). The financial resources available to entrepreneurs are highly limited in Turkey. SMEs receive only 3 percent to 4 percent of the total bank credits given to private sector firms. The government recognized this figure as being exceptionally low and so decided to create new financial resources for SMEs in 1991 by establishing the Credit Guarantee Fund Corporation. However, it had a limited role since it gave guarantees only to a state-owned bank, Halk Bank (Başlar 2000). In recent years, some trade banks such as Pamukbank have been offering credits to entrepreneurs. But still, these funds have not been enough to satisfy the demand. Furthermore, the banking crisis in 2001 caused additional difficulties for SMEs. In 2001, twelve banks went bankrupt due to a combination of mismanagement and corruption. Entrepreneurs could get financial input from the stock market rather than from banks, but the Turkish stock market is not a feasible source for SMEs, because they cannot satisfy the conditions for being traded in this market. Government sources, in the form of grants and soft loans, are not sufficient either.

The limited availability of resources is a particular problem when it comes to funds available (or not, as the case may be) to innovative firms. A number of studies clearly show that technology-based firms face significant financial difficulties. For example, a study of 820 SMEs shows that these firms cannot perform innovative activities because of financial problems (Taymaz 2001). Almost 90 percent of firms complain about the high costs of R&D, and 82 percent of them indicate limited financial resources as the core problem of SMEs. In addition to financial problems, SMEs mentioned several other reasons that prevented them from conducting innovative activities: economic risk (80 percent), limited skilled labor (54 percent), organizational problems (53 percent), lack of knowledge about technology (50 percent), and regulative problems (47 percent).

Interestingly enough, similar problems also exist for large firms that attempt technological development. A study of 426 large firms indicates that finance is the main reason behind their lack of innovation (Taymaz 2001). According to the study, their major two problems were the same as the ones faced by SMEs: high costs and limited financial resources. The remaining problems look familiar too: economic risk (86 percent), regulative problems (56 percent), and organizational problems (52 percent).

Because of this capital gap, the government has started two special programs for financing SMEs based on technology: grants given by TIDEB (Technology Observation Directorate) and soft loans distributed by TTGV (Turkish Technology Development Association). Table 10.1 shows the distribution of financial support provided by these organizations. Both the number of companies receiving grants and loans and the amount received substantially increased during the period from 1991 to 1997. Still, when the Turkish government's support to private sector R&D is compared with many ICs' data, it is significantly lower. For example, in 1996, the share of government resources utilized in private sector R&D expenses was 1.9 percent in Turkey, 9.7 percent in the United Kingdom, and 15.2 percent in the United States (OECD 1999).

The results of the analysis that I have just described are based on general statistical data that does not focus on a specific technology field. However, I will now examine data based on two firms working in biotechnology and information/communication technologies. This examination will allow us to understand specific problems of technologies that are accepted as constituting the basis of the new economy. The results of the two surveys are summarized next.

The information and communication technologies sector consists of firms involved in telecommunication, computers, office equipment, software, computer services, electronic components, and communication instrument production. These firms together constitute a large industrial sector in Turkey with a turnover of $11.3 billion in 1999 (*Etkileşim* 2000). However, these firms do not conduct R&D activities. According to 1997 data, in spite of the healthy turnover, these firms spent only $1.5 million on R&D.

Thirty-three firms involved in information and communication technologies were included in the survey, and the majority of them are located in Istanbul (Çetindamar 2000). The results of the study can be summarized as follows:

- In the start-up process, firms used individual and family savings. Two firms received financial support from corporate partners, two firms managed to receive credit by giving away half the ownership of the firm, one firm received a loan from TTGV, and one firm, two years after its foundation, received credit from a bank.
- The summary of the technology performances of the firms is as follows: only four firms are owners of patents, two firms have patent applications in process, and one firm owns a copyright. More than half the firms (60 percent) have structured R&D departments. Most of them (57 percent) have technology creation activities and production.
- The firms in the survey list the problems of their sector as follows: lack of finance (61 percent of firms), skilled labor (51 percent), infrastructure problems (45 percent),

Table 10.1
The Number of Firms Receiving Loans and Grants from TIDEB and TTGV,
and the Total Amount Received, 1991–97

	1992	1993	1994	1995	1996	1997
Number of firms TYDEB		2	7	61	157	224
Amount TYDEB*		30	4,915	12,943	24,167	36,934
Number of firms TTGV	7	20	26	31	56	71
Amount TTGV*	341	3,434	6,077	5,483	11,101	25,035

* Thousand US dollars, purchasing power parity.
Source: Taymaz, 2001.

lack of R&D (42 percent), insufficient incentive structure (40 percent), and unfair competition (36 percent).

• The firms in the survey expect the government to take action in the following areas: setting a stable government policy for the industry (56 percent of firms), increasing incentives (51 percent), investing in infrastructure (48 percent), increasing the financial opportunities (42 percent), reducing bureaucracy (40 percent), and developing standards (33 percent).

Similar results can be observed in the innovation survey conducted by SIS. Almost all the firms surveyed by SIS used internal resources to establish their firms. The main problem preventing their innovative activities was finance.

Another conclusion gleaned from the above-mentioned studies is that Turkey does not yet have a technology-creating industry in the information and communications area. Firms operating in the industry generally import their technologies and then sell the products to local customers. Both the low R&D budgets and the lack of patents indicate that firms do not have the capability or the desire to develop original technology. If we look at the development life-cycle of a firm in a DC, we can see that, in general, DC firms start with imports but then move into basic assembly operations. At a later stage they develop production capabilities for imitative products, and in the most advanced stages they start producing original products and technologies (Lall 1992; Kim 1997). Considering this process, it would not be wrong to say that Turkish information and communication technology firms are in the early stages of the development cycle. On a positive note, though, there are a few signs that Turkey is progressing to a new stage. Firms in the innovation survey have indicated that they want to invest in technology creation and reduce their dependence on imported technologies. Thus, in the coming decade, the financial needs of these firms can be expected to rise and with it greater demand for a systemized VCI.

Biotechnology firms that have been recently established in Turkey have a total market size of $950 million in 1999 for biotech products. Twenty-nine firms were sampled for the survey of biotechnology firms (Başağa and Çetindamar 2000). Because biotechnology is a generic technology, firms in the survey come from a number of different sectors: pharmaceuticals and diagnostics, food industry, environment, and industrial enzymes. The survey yielded three significant results:

- One of the twenty-nine sample firms was the recipient of VC, and eleven firms received R&D support from government resources. One of the firms is located in a technopark.
- Twenty-four firms (82 percent) have independent R&D departments. R&D expenses show a negative correlation with the size of the company. For example, the largest firm spends only 5 percent of its sales volume on R&D (in absolute terms, $1.5 million), while a small diagnostic firm spends almost 60 percent of its sales volume on R&D (in absolute terms, $450 thousand).
- Firms taking part in the survey suggested that the following actions needed to be taken in order to improve the biotechnology based industries' performance: R&D spending both in firms and research organizations needs to be increased (72 percent of firms); financial support should be given to firms doing R&D (44 percent of firms); and there should be a structure supporting a coherent strategy and providing incentives for the establishment of biotechnology firms (27 percent of firms).

This study shows that biotechnology firms are conducting R&D activities even though biotechnology is one of the most complicated high technologies in existence worldwide. As these technology-producing firms encountered more and more financial problems, they applied for all financial sources available, including VC and government organizations. It appears they were successful in getting financial support.

Data summarized in this section highlights the acute financial needs of Turkish entrepreneurs, particularly SMEs and technology-producing firms. Turkey needs to find ways to create a diverse financial system in order to produce opportunities for entrepreneurs that will aid them in their attempts to develop technologies and commercialize their products in local and global markets.

THE INFRASTRUCTURE OF THE TURKISH INNOVATION FINANCING SYSTEM AND SUGGESTIONS FOR DEVELOPING COUNTRIES

The harsh reality of the situation in Turkey is that it cannot claim to be in possession of a VC market yet. So few VC firms are in existence in the market that to even declare that the (practically nonexistent) VCI was at a very early stage of start-up would be a hoax.

The present state of affairs does not present a very pretty picture; however, the maturity dimensions of the VCI (Karaomerlioglu and Jacobsson 2000) are as follows:

- Size: Turkey has only two venture capital firms, and the total VC fund size is approximately $150 million (*Globus* 2000).
- Diversity: Turkey does not have a set of diverse VC actors.

- Competence: It is fair to say that the competence level of venture capitalists is very low. There are a number of reasons for this. First, none of the VC firms exited from their investments, thus completing the investment process and gaining the learning experience that would come along with this step. Second, there are only a few portfolio firms, showing limited learning capability. Third, banks finance VC firms and venture capitalists come from a financial background; thus, they are unable to contribute to the nonfinancial value-adding activities required by investee firms.

Because Turkey and many DCs are at the very early stages of launching their VC industries, they should learn from the experiences of ICs. As I proposed in chapter 1, DCs should approach the establishment of a VCI as the creation of a system that will transform the structure of their economy into an entrepreneurial and innovative one. In this chapter, the focus will be on the VC organization as an important actor in the innovation-financing system. However, I will examine VC within a wider system, taking in all the actors and institutions. This examination will identify the role of different actors and institutions in the development of the VCI.

Following the suggested model in chapter 1, I will analyze the infrastructure of the VC industry in Turkey with regard to four dimensions: sources of finance, institutional infrastructure, exit mechanisms, and entrepreneur and innovator originators. This analysis will assess the existing infrastructure and identify gaps in the system. In each of the following sections, I will start by discussing the experience of Turkey, and then, through a combination of this empirical data and available literature, I will draw some general conclusions for DCs with respect to the particular components of the innovation-financing system.

Sources of Finance

When we talk about sources of finance in the VCI we are generally referring to two discrete groups of organizations: those, such as VC firms, that directly invest in innovative firms; and indirect investors who use VC firms as a vehicle for their investments, for example, pension funds. In this section I am mainly interested in looking at the group of direct investors. Included in this group are the many previously mentioned actors in the VCI as well as financial organizations who invest directly in entrepreneurial firms (such as technoparks and incubators, investment banks, governments, and the stock market).

Although the main focus of this chapter is the VCI, I have chosen here to extend the analysis to include all of the organizations involved in innovation financing. I have done this for three main reasons. First, VC firms are not the only providers of financial support for innovation (Christensen 1997). There are other organizations that also provide this mode of support and that function in a complementary role to the venture capitalists by serving at different growth stages. Second, I strongly believe that DCs are not in the position to put all their eggs in one basket when it comes to financial support for innovation. By this I mean that they cannot afford to rely just on the VCI and nobody else. Thus, it is essential for policy makers to be able to create the conditions whereby the financial organizations are able to function effectively together as part of a greater whole. Third, VC firms do not exist in a vacuum, and they may depend a great deal on the other financial mechanisms that are in existence in the country. For example, in Germany, banks are highly active in the private equity market, and therefore, VC firms often find themselves working together with banks in assessing and selecting their investments (Carlin and Mayer 1999; Jeng and Wells 2000). Another example shows that the high involvement of Swedish corporations as investors to high-technology firms has slowed down the development of the VCI in Sweden (Lindholm-Dahlstrand and Çetindamar 2000). As a result of situations like this, the financial organizations in existence in a country have a direct impact on the skills and roles that the VC firms are able to develop.

I have utilized the following sources to identify the important actors involved in the innovation-financing system in Turkey:

- Secondary sources from various business journals and daily newspapers (*Globus* 2000; *Milliyet* 2001; *Sabah* 2000; *Radikal* 2001)
- Conference presentations (Erdal 2000; Kanbak 2001)
- The list supplied by the European Venture Capital Association (EVCA)
- The Information and Communications Technology Exhibition conference (September 7, 2000) in Istanbul and interviews with the workshop participants of the Forum on Raising VC Funding for Entrepreneurs (September 7, 2001)
- An MBA project on a corporate VC model for Turkey (Dumanlı et al. 2001)

The actors involved in the theater of the Turkish innovation-financing system can be put into eight groups, as shown in Table 10.2. The interviews conducted with the workshop participants were able to support the belief that the organizations listed in the table are the major financiers.

Actors in the Turkish Venture Capital Market

Business angels: There is no accurate data available showing the extent to which business angels invest in innovation companies in Turkey. It is, however, common knowledge that wealthy businesspeople do invest in other companies at the behest of the entrepreneurs. The entrepreneur informally approaches the businessperson, and if the businessperson recognizes that there is potential profit in the venture, then he or she may choose to invest.

VC firms: At the present time there are only two officially registered VC firms in Turkey. They are Vakıf and ış VC partnerships established by Vakıf Bank and İş Bank, respectively.

Vakıf VC was established in 1996 with an available fund of TL 500 billion ($6 million). This money was provided by the government-owned Vakıf Bank. It has been the recipient of more than five hundred project applications since

Table 10.2
The Actors in the Turkish Innovation Financing System

Financial resource	Firm names
Actors in the VC market:	
Venture capital	Vakıf VC partnership, İş VC partnership
Corporate VC	Girişim, Borusan, Esas, İlab, IBM, Koç, Teknoloji conglomerates
Private equity partnerships	Sparx Asset Management, Safron, AIG Blue Voyage Fund, Alliance capital, Taurus Capital Partners, Turkish Venture Capital Partners, Silkroad ventures, Commercial Capital Partners, EMEA Technology Investment, Softbank, Nomura, Merill Lynch
Intermediary financial org.	ATA yatırım**, Strategic Business Development and Valuation, Dundas Ünlü & Company, PDF, Corporate Financial Services, KapitalNet, OTS Investment and Financial Consultancy
Other financial org.:	
Investment banks	Garanti Investment, Yapı Kredi Investment, Demir Investment**, K Investment Securities**, TEB Private Equity, Nurol bank**, Citibank Venture Capital, Deutsche Bank, Türkiye Sınai Kalkınma Bank – EIB
Technoparks and Incubators	IncubaTR, İxir/ Okyanux*, Superonline, Ericsson CREA World, Tofaş, Siemens, GOSB- SU-Wertheimer, technoparks
Government org.	Small and Medium Enterprises Development Organization (KOSGEB), Technology Monitoring and Evaluation Board (TIDEB), Technology Development Foundation Of Turkey (TTGV)
Stock market	İstanbul Stock Market

Org.—Organizations.
*It went bankrupt.
**Turkish members of the European Private Equity and VC Firms Association.
Source: A number of sources indicated in the text.

its launch in 1996 and has made investments in three of these. All three of the firms that Vakıf VC invested in are small start-up firms that are technology based. Two of these portfolio firms are located in a technopark within a university, while the other one operates out of a free trade zone.

İş VC was established toward the end of 2000, but has not made any investments up to the present date. This lack of movement can be attributed in part to the volatility of the Turkish economy caused by the recession that began in February 2001 and by the devaluation of the currency by 100 percent in one year.

This recession and devaluation has cooled a lot of the interest that was beginning to build in the VCI. Many of the large family-owned conglomerates were beginning to show interest in establishing VC firms prior to the recession, but now bankers and investors are very cautious and the VCI will have to be patient for the time being.

Foreign-owned firms have also not seen fit to enter the market up to now, although on occasion they use local intermediary financial organizations to make some investments.

Corporate VC: Corporate VC is a relatively new phenomenon for Turkey. Of the companies that carry out VC activities, few, if any, have an actual VC department. The VC investments that take place are done in an ad hoc manner on a very informal level. As a result, it is impossible to know how many firms are conducting VC operations as well as the funds available.

Recently, though, we have been able to observe some changes taking place in the corporate structure. Large conglomerates and some computer companies are starting up VC units. Some computer companies (such as ılab, IBM, Koç, and Teknoloji Conglomerates) have private equity partnerships with start-up companies in the field of information technology. For example, Koç Bilgi invested in a spin-off company (called Geveze) operating in the incubator of Boğaziçi University. As would be expected, although computer companies may invest in technology-based firms, the conglomerates show no particular tendency toward technology and will invest in whatever they see as likely to bring them the best returns. An example is Girişim Conglomerate, which invested in a textile-retailing company.

Foreign private equity partnerships: As mentioned previously, there is not a great deal of foreign involvement in the Turkish VCI. However, there are two groups of private equity firms at present operating in Turkey: firms that have local partners, and firms that have no local office or partner but invest through the local intermediary financial organizations. Two examples of the former are Turkish Venture Capital Partners and Silk Road. Some examples of the latter are Europe-Middle East-Africa (EMEA), Zouk Ventures, and Softbank. EMEA's fund originates from Egypt and has investments in two Turkish firms (Probil and Gordon). Zouk Ventures is a British private equity firm, and Softbank is a Japanese one.

The first foreign private equity investor in Turkey was a Japanese firm called Sparx Wealth Management. During the period from 1995 to 1999 they invested in six firms: Ünal Tarım, Arat Tekstil, GDS Holding, Tekstilbank, Rant Leasing, and Eka Elektronik. Their investments totaled $40 million, and they concentrated on low-technology firms. Another foreign firm, Safron, entered the Turkish market in 1999 by investing in two nontechnical firms (Banker Trust and Jumbo). Interestingly, another international private equity firm, AIG Blue Voyage Fund, invested in a local football club (Galatasaray) in 2000.

Merrill Lynch is another international firm at present investing in Turkey. It invested in a technology-based firm (Termo Teknik) in 1997 and cashed in its investment in 1999. In 2000, it invested in a retail chain company (BIM; Başlar 2000; *Globus* 2000).

Intermediary financial organizations: The role of intermediary financial organizations is to act as brokers or go-betweens among entrepreneurs and financial organizations. They either concentrate on finding capital for entrepreneurs or help them find suitable investors. These intermediaries are not VC firms as such, but they perform some of the tasks of VC firms and they further complement the VC market in a number of ways.

First, they search for a suitable investor for each entrepreneur, depending on the type of project and the entrepreneur. Second, these intermediaries act as local representatives of foreign investors and help them work with local firms, while at the same time convincing them to invest in Turkey. Third, they help entrepreneurs in a number of ways: training entrepreneurs in the art of writing business plans; preparing entrepreneurs for interviews; helping entrepreneurs calculate their financial needs and value their firms; and giving detailed information regarding the legal aspects of contracts and, when the need arises, drawing up the terms of contracts for entrepreneurs in their agreements with investors.

Some of the intermediary financial firms are consultancies. These firms employ experts in corporate financing. The most active consultancy firms are companies like Strategic Business Development and Valuation, Dundas Ünlü Project Management–Financial Consultancy, OTS Investment and Financial Consultancy, and Corporate Financial Services. In this market, we also find some foreign consultancy firms in operation.

Investment bankers can also be considered intermediaries but in this chapter the term *intermediary* refers to firms offering corporate financing services (such as public offering, mergers and acquisitions, privatization, financial consultancy, portfolio management, international transactions, and private equity).

Other Financial Organizations with Funds Available for Innovative Firms

Investment banks: Turkey has more than seventy banks, of which twenty-two are foreign owned and thirteen are investment banks. Considering that the population of Turkey is 65 million and that the gross national product is $200 billion, the number of banks indicates a high concentration. The five big banks constitute almost half of the total assets (47 percent) in banking.

Banks, particularly investment banks, give credit to entrepreneurs to finance their debts. Some banks (such as Garanti, Yapı Kredi, and Türkiye Ekonomi banks) have special corporate financing sections that specialize in transactions of this sort. Some other banks have opened independent branches that operate solely as corporate financial service providers. These organizations supply either debt financing or private equity financing. Two examples of this are Demir Yatırım (belonging to Demir bank) and K Investment Securities (belonging to Bank Kapital). These two firms and Nurol Bank are also members of the EVCA.

There are very few foreign investment banks operating in Turkey, and of these, only two are particularly important in the field of private equity investments. The two banks that I am referring to are Citibank and Deutsche Bank. Both of these banks have VC departments. In addition, there are also some funds that have been made available from international organizations. The World Bank established the IFC (International Finance Corporation) in order to give loans to DC firms. The IFC has been in operation in Turkey since 1963 and has invested in 143 projects with the grand sum of $5.2 billion during the period from 1963 to 1997. In 2001, IFC invested $37 million in four Turkish firms (Şişe Cam, Arçelik, Günkol, and Ipek Kağıt; IFC 2001). In recent years,

OPIC (The Overseas Private Investment Corporation) financed by the U.S. government has given financial support to firms of U.S. origin investing in DCs. It is expected that in the future OPIC will allocate some funds for investments in Turkey that will be coordinated in collaboration with a local investment bank.

Because of a lack of data, investment banks' financial contributions to entrepreneurs are not known. The only data available comes from Türkiye Sınai Kalkınma Bank, which received $12 million from the European Investment Bank (EIB) in 2000 to be used as a VC fund for Turkish entrepreneurs (Başlar 2000).

Technoparks and incubators: Incubators support entrepreneurs at the very early stages of their projects, even before they establish firms. By making use of incubators, entrepreneurs have access to cheap office space and equipment along with legal and managerial support from the incubator's administration. These incubators are established either by private firms or by government institutions. Here, the focus will be on the private incubators, while government-supported incubators will be discussed in the next section.

The main differences in the types of incubators stem from differences in their goals and the services they provide to entrepreneurs. A number of incubators establish VC funds, as in the case of ıxir's VC fund, called Okyanux. The general practice, though, is for incubators not to invest in entrepreneurs' ideas but to concentrate on helping the entrepreneur raise funds from the myriad of financial organizations.

Many IT firms have established incubators that have been active since 1998. These incubators support entrepreneurs from the stage of idea generation to the stage of production. Successful projects are either purchased by the owner of the incubator or are established as independent firms in which the owner of the incubator sometimes holds minority shares. The better-known incubators in Turkey specialize in the Internet and in software projects such as IncubaTR, Superonline, and Ericsson Crea World.

In recent times there have been a number of new incubator projects. One of these, Siemens Business Accelerator, has been established by the German multinational Siemens. It began its operations in November 2001, and its stated aim is to supply office space, infrastructure, consultancy, and financial help. On top of this, it also intends to link entrepreneurial firms with local and international companies. Similarly, a local car manufacturer (Tofaş) is working on a new incubator idea that has been called a "tech-ubator." The main focus of this, as we might expect, will be the automotive industry. Entrepreneurs who are developing original technology in the field of automotive production will be supported in this new incubator (Nahum 2001). Another example is the consortium Gebze Industrial District–Sabancı University–Wertheimer Foundation (Israel), which aims to operationalize an incubator based on the Tekfen model in Israel (Kanbak 2001).

At the present time there are three technoparks in Turkey. The Scientific and Technical Research Council of Turkey–Marmara Research Center

(TÜBITAK-MAM) began operating in 1991; however, due to a variety of problems it was not able to experience the expected growth and level of success. In 2000, the status of this technopark changed and it also became a free trade zone. Time will tell whether or not this change brings the advantages that its previous status could not. The other two technoparks are located on the grounds of state universities: one in Middle East Technical University (was opened in 2001) and the other in Yıldız Technical University (expected to open in 2004).

Government resources: There are three main government organizations that are supporting entrepreneurs in Turkey. These are KOSGEB (the Small and Medium-Sized Enterprise Development Directorate), TIDEB (Technology Monitoring and Evaluation Board), and TTGV (Technology Development Foundation of Turkey).

KOSGEB was established in 1990 with the intention of helping SMEs increase their competitiveness by developing their productivity and absorption capacities (KOSGEB 2001). Due to the generality of its mission, KOSGEB has no specific focus on technology-based firms. However, KOSGEB has recently begun to establish incubators at universities, referred to as technology centers. Since 1996, seven technology centers have opened in universities (Ankara, Boğaziçi, Istanbul Technical, Yıldız Technical, Middle East Technical, and Karadeniz Technical Universities, and Gebze High Technology Institute). These centers supply innovative entrepreneurs with office space and finance for both the seed stage and the start-up stage. In the five-year-period of the centers' existence, two hundred firms have been able to take advantage of the facilities they offer.

The Scientific and Technical Research Council of Turkey established TIDEB in 1995 with a mission to support the R&D activities of Turkish firms (TIDEB 2001). Its main role is in supplying research grants to firms conducting R&D. The amount given is up to a maximum of 60 percent of a firm's total R&D expenses and is given for a period of three years. During the period from 1995 to 1999, TIDEB gave $489 million in support. The organization has strict criteria for firms wishing to receive this support, and it is only given to those firms that are developing new products or production technologies, increasing product quality and standards, or applying technologies to decrease costs.

TTGV was established in 1991 as a result of cooperation between the World Bank, the Turkish government, and the private sector (TTGV 2001). TTGV's main operation is in providing soft loans to companies conducting R&D. It prefers to specialize in projects that will be ready for commercialization within two years. The maximum it is able to provide to each firm is either $2 million or 50 percent of the R&D costs for a maximum of four years. In the period between 1991 and 1999, TTGV supported 363 projects at a financial cost of $68.8 million. Besides this soft loan provision, TTGV also has two specialized loan programs. The first one deals with loans to companies that are located in technoparks. The amount of the loan varies but is a maximum of 20 percent of the total project costs and is available for a period of two years. The second program applies to companies that provide technology services such as test laboratories. Again, TTGV is prepared to cover 20 percent of the total costs, but because of the large amounts involved in these kinds of companies, the organization has set an upper limit of $1 million on the loan. Another option available for these service firms, assuming certain criteria are met, is for TTGV to become a partner for them. Other than loans, TTGV also has grants available for SMEs that are intended to encourage SMEs to purchase technology-based services such as those involved in the patenting process.

The stock market: The Turkish Stock Market was established in 1985 as the Istanbul Stock Market (ISM). Due to the general economic instability that has beset Turkey in the past seventeen years, the stock market has not yet been able to reach the position of being a financial resource for SMEs. The most recent figures for 2000 indicate that there were around three hundred firms with a total transaction volume of $375 billion. Compare these figures to the United States, where the New York Stock Exchange (NYSE) had 2,862 firms listed in 2000 and its transaction volume was $0.9 trillion (NYSE 2002).

In addition to the small size of its national stock market, Turkey has no stock market for technology-based start-up firms like the United States has with NASDAQ and Germany has with its Neuer Markt. The largest stock market in the world is in the United States, with more than 4,700 firms listed and a $1.4 trillion transaction volume in 2000 (NASDAQ 2002). In the late 1990s, many European countries established their own national markets similar to NASDAQ but many of them could not grow. The best example of this problem is the experience of Easdaq, which was established in 1996 to serve technology-based firms from all European countries. In 1998, this market had only thirty-nine listings with a market capitalization of $270 million (*Economist* 1998). Even though European countries have well-functioning stock markets, they still experience problems running specialized markets for technology firms. Considering this fact, it is normal to expect that it will be even more difficult for DCs to set up these special markets in an environment in which ordinary stock markets do not function efficiently, as in the case of Turkey.

Suggestions for Possible Financial Resources

In DCs there is a limit to the number of financial organizations that are able and willing to contribute funds to VC. ICs, on the other hand, have a multiplicity of organizations that contribute to VC, including banks, pension funds, insurance firms, and government programs. This luxury is not one that is proffered to DCs, as has been demonstrated by the example of Turkey.

The VC funds available in Turkey are limited to the capital received from banks, large firms, and foreign private equity firms. The two private Turkish VC firms (Vakıf and İş Risk firms) are in the enviable position of being able to receive funds from their owners' banks. Large firms (i.e., those not specializing in VC) either conduct casual/ad hoc investments in the corporate venturing field or set up incubators and look for potential firms that they may wish to acquire and make part of their conglomerates. If we examine the strategy of foreign private equity firms with relation to Turkey, we can see they do not have a fixed budget set aside for the Turkish market but instead conduct their investments through local intermediary financial firms in a rather ad hoc manner.

In DCs there appears to be a general condition whereby venture capitalists over-rely on banks for their funds (Sagari and Guidotti 1992). As I discussed earlier, having only one source of funds puts the industry in a potentially very unhealthy situation. We only have to look at the example of Japan, an IC, to see the problems that such a dependence can cause (Finlayson 1999). As a result of relying on banks as their main source, Japanese VC companies became too bureaucratic and risk-averse. Banks influence the management teams that VC firms select, and banks enforce some of their own assessment and selection criteria. This control, in turn, limits the activities of VC companies that become suppliers of financial services, with little or no managerial support being given to portfolio firms. However, an issue of perhaps greater importance is how the crisis in the banking sector negatively affected the VC industry, causing a slow-down. The lesson for DCs to learn here is that similar problems are likely to happen to them if they have too great a reliance on the banking sector and have no diversity to create a balance and help them deal with any crisis that may occur.

As in ICs, there is in DCs the potential for the use of pension funds as a resource for VC. The drawback for Turkey is that the law forbids this. In addition, the state of the private pension fund industry is not as developed as in ICs, and as a result, almost all pension funds are managed by the government, which does not create a particularly ripe climate for a change in the law in the foreseeable future. There is the potential for insurance companies to be a source of funds because there is no law preventing this practice. However, for reasons known only to them, none of the government-owned or private-owned insurance companies have yet shown an interest in supporting VC firms. This is probably due to the fact that the insurance industry has only recently become liberalized and as such is still in a conservative mode of operation. This conservative mode dictates that the industry is risk-averse and not likely to invest in what is seen as the high-risk VCI. Another potential source is government funds; however, these funds are likewise not forthcoming. Most of the government financial programs available at the present time are either debt financing or grants.

In the short term, Turkey and other DCs need to attract foreign VC funds to invest in their countries. This inflow from foreign VCs will serve two useful functions. First, it will bring in much-needed capital, a scarce resource in all DCs, and second, these investors will bring a level of competence and professionalism that is largely unavailable in DCs at this juncture. The issue of competence and professionalism is crucial for a successful VCI and will be discussed in greater depth in the institutional section that follows.

When we compare DCs to ICs, we see a marked difference not only between the investors in VC funds but also between the actors directly operating in the VC market. In ICs, the VCI is generally at a stage of maturity such that there is a diversity of VC firms already, and this diversity will continue to grow. In DCs, however, diversity might be problematic from the demand point of view. Some financial organizations might not be established because of insufficient market demand. For example, stock markets require a critical mass of firms to be listed in order to have significant transactions that can attract investors and offer different services for their customers. If industrial firms in a country are limited, they do not constitute a sound base for the efficient functioning of financial organizations, preventing different actors from coming to the fore.

Institutional Infrastructure

The history of government-initiated financial organizations in Turkey is very modern and not particularly extensive. It dates back only as far as 1986, when the Development and Support Fund and Technology Support Agency were both established (Başlar 2000). In spite of the government's intention to model the goals of the agency on the U.S.-established Small Business Investment Corporations, this step was never realized due to political instability at the time. The next action taken by the government was to pass the law entitled "Risk Sermaye Ortaklığı" (the VC Partnership Law) in 1993. As a result of this law, two VC firms were able to establish themselves as private equity firms. This section of this chapter will give a summary of the existing institutional infrastructure in Turkey and continue with suggestions for DCs regarding their infrastructure.

Turkish Institutional Infrastructure for the Venture Capital Industry

Certain institutional features are essential for the three key actors in the VCI: venture capitalists, fund providers, and entrepreneurs. In order to have a healthy and well-functioning VCI, there needs to be a carefully designed and operationalized incentive structure.

The incentive structure for VC management is related to laws regulating the establishment and management of VC firms. The first law dates back to 1993. A section of the stock market law legislated in 1993 allows for the establishment of VC firms but only if they are listed in the stock market by the end of their first year with a minimum of 10 percent of their funds. According to the law, it is imperative that this figure reach 49 percent within three years (Tuncel 1995). These firms can be established as partnerships as long as the partnership will last a minimum of ten years. This law was originally seen as taking advantage of an article of the tax law that gives tax rebates to firms operating in the stock market. By removing taxes from VC investments, it is expected that investors in VC will be the beneficiaries of certain advantages that they would not have access to if they chose to invest through other channels. This tax advantage is a great incentive for fund providers. Although the tax issue is interpreted as a definite positive development, venture capitalists have two complaints about the law. First, VC private equity firms are forced to offer 49 percent of their funds on the stock market within three years of their establishment. Because VC firms generally exist on a small scale, they find this a hard target to achieve. Furthermore, they consider being listed on the stock market as a high risk for small VC funds. Second, VC firms listed on the stock market face greater restrictions in their wage structure than do other forms of VC firms that are not listed in stock markets. Venture capitalists want to become partners to funds they are managing but they are not allowed to. Related to this issue is the use of stock options in VC firms. By giving stocks to employees, venture capitalists aim to increase motivation and productivity. However, stock options are forbidden in Turkey.

Another set of incentives has been directed toward entrepreneurs, related particularly to the commercialization and firm establishment processes. In order to support entrepreneurship, regulations for opening and closing firms need to be easy and simple. However, in Turkey the opposite is the case. According to a study carried out by the Turkish Employee Unions Federation, Turkey is listed as the thirteenth most bureaucratic country in the world (*Milliyet* 2001). Some data will enable us to understand this issue more clearly:

• In Turkey, an entrepreneur spends around 20 percent of his or her time on bureaucratic issues; this rate is 8 percent in the EU.
• The setting up of a firm takes, on average, 2.5 months.
• An entrepreneur needs 172 signatures from various government agencies in order to receive approval to invest.
• The total cost of the setting-up procedure is around 4 percent of total capital.
• The time needed to get permission to construct a plant can take up to two years.

Other important regulations that affect entrepreneurship are related to R&D, taxation, technology trade (import and export), and intellectual property rights. These regulations might not seem to directly affect VC. However, if the VCI is going to foster entrepreneurial firms based on technology and innovation, the appropriate regulations in these fields will be an incentive not only for inventors but also for attracting VC investments. Entrepreneurs and venture capitalists will not enter into any long-term and uncertain technology investments unless they know that they have a more than reasonable chance of receiving appropriate rewards for their investments and that there are potentially high profits from it. This is particularly the case with patents. If the guarantee given by patents is forthcoming, then entrepreneurs and venture capitalists will find the courage to make risky investments and continue their R&D activities. The Turkish Patent Institute was initially established in 1879 but it was not revised until 1995 (Taymaz 2001). The final revision was done in 2000 in order to comply with the EU patent laws.

There was nothing resembling an incentive system in Turkey until the 1990s. There have been two recent movements in a positive direction with the legislation of the Technology Developments Act (April 2000) and Technology Districts Act (June 2001). The former is oriented toward the technological advancement of SMEs. It incorporates a wide variety of support schemes including financial support as well as training and consultancy. The latter is focused on the establishment of technoparks and technology districts. This act allows the private sector to set up technoparks with the built-in advantage that investment and tax rebates are given to all activities conducted in these areas. As a simple example of this, firms located in these technoparks do not pay taxes for the first five years of their existence. This act also includes incentive schemes that encourage university professors to work in the technoparks.

Besides these two acts, the government passed a law in 1987 to regulate capital gains and corporate taxes. Accordingly, corporations performing R&D can delay payment of up to 20 percent of their capital gains and corporate taxes for three years without any interest charged from the time of payment. Moreover, R&D organizations are left out of the taxation system.

Suggestions for the Institutional Infrastructure

The specific policy suggestions for the institutional changes in DCs that have been suggested are as follows (Sagari and Guidotti 1992; Jeng and Wells 2000; Mason and Harrison 1999; Gompers and Lerner 1998; Gompers et al. 1998):

1. Incentives to investors—rebates, tax credits, deductions from taxes, or taxable income of amounts invested in eligible VC institutions. In addition, the existence of a favorable regime allowing the use of capital losses incurred to offset capital gains or ordinary income (e.g., as in France, Belgium, United Kingdom, Ireland). This type of statutory framework guides the portfolio choices of institutional investors, which affects their role as suppliers of funds. In particular, incentives should be directed toward pension funds so that this rich source could be invested in VC funds. Another incentive scheme should be developed for business angels. Because wealthy individuals have large pools of capital, attracting them to invest in VC funds could be highly rewarding for DCs that have limited capital sources.

2. Incentives to the VC institution, including tax relief on income received from portfolio companies (e.g., as in South Korea, Netherlands, Brazil) or exemption from corporate tax for a predetermined period (e.g., as in Singapore). The regulations regarding the formation of VC firms should be directed toward encouraging a limited partnership structure because this form of company has been shown to be the best structure from the incentive point of view, namely, incentives for venture capitalists and employees of VC firms. As a further step, it is of the utmost importance that stock options for employees are allowed.

With regard to the competence of venture capitalists, Turkey, like other DCs, should be aware of the problems arising from their poor manufacturing structure. These problems have the effect of limiting the industry and the technology-specific competence. Because the profile of competence is strongly path-dependent and because the learning of new competencies is constrained by the earlier specialization profiles, DCs with a limited number of industries and technologies will face significant problems in the field of competence.

As a result of this competence issue, DCs should focus on competence and find ways to resolve problems preventing the accumulation of competence in the industry. One way of doing this could be to attract foreign investors and multilateral agencies such as the World Bank and to enter into collaboration with them to ensure the provision of technical assistance, the transference of managerial skills, and the training of local personnel for their VCI. Singapore has shown that this is possible because it has managed to establish links with competent venture capitalists in Silicon Valley in the United States (Sagari and Guidotti 1992). Another route could be to apply the method used by venture capitalists in the United States: either employ experienced senior managers from medium-sized and larger corporations, or work with successful entrepreneurs. A third possibility to increase competence could be to give incentives to managers in the business world to start VC firms.

3. Specific laws that legislate clear definitions of VC and new technology-based firms and their procedures. Some examples of laws in place in ICs are the rules governing the establishment of VC subsidiaries by banks and insurance companies. Similarly, the rights of minority shareholders, incorporation regulations, treatment of bankruptcies, and legal liability of corporate directors should be in place (as in France, Australia, Canada, Germany, Korea, Mexico, the Netherlands, and Portugal). The amount of bureaucracy in the process of the establishment of firms should be reduced.

There are a number of indirect incentives that might lead to a flourishing of VC firms, and one of these is regarding intellectual property rights. In general, it can be observed that DCs have weak regulative structures that need to be changed. Unless a system is in place that ensures the protection of intellectual property rights regarding inventions and innovations, entrepreneurs will not be prepared to invest large amounts of money. Incentives that encourage R&D and technoparks will not only protect intellectual property rights but will also help to encourage entrepreneurs to part with their money. As they invest, we will see a transformation of scientific and technological developments into commercial use.

The existence of financial resources per se is not enough, though, for an entrepreneurial economy to flourish. Financial resources can contribute to an economy only if there are technological opportunities that can utilize this capital as an economic input. As shown in the case of the United States, capital is necessary but not a sufficient condition for technological development. That is why governments need to provide a number of incentives that will support technological and industrial developments. For example, similar to the support given by the Indian government that helped create a software industry, DCs can develop policies based on the technological strengths of their countries and entrepreneurial development (Correa 1996).

These incentives, however, will not be enough on their own, and DCs need to find answers to the question of how to stop the brain drain of researchers and entrepreneurs. Within these answers there is a place for regulations and incentives. The situation in most DCs today is that the vast majority of researchers have almost no incentives to transfer their ideas to companies, and they do not want to start their own firms. In such a situation, it is only natural that some of them are attracted to go abroad where they can be rewarded for their innovations. One possible solution to prevent this brain drain could be to give patenting rights to university researchers for their inventions, similar to the stipulations established in the Bay-Dohle law that was legislated in 1981 in the United States. This law is considered to be the turning point for universities, because researchers were rewarded for their innovations (Bygrave and Timmons 1992; Kortum and Lerner 1998). In addition to such an arrangement, researchers need to be allowed to work in the private sector for a short period of time as a means to increase the technology transfer as well as improve the relationship between universities and firms.

DCs that are able to develop an entrepreneurial culture will stimulate entrepreneurs who will then demand and use VC funds. The starting point for all of this needs to be a change of attitude in society. A simple first step would be for universities to provide courses in entrepreneurship. Many entrepreneurs have the courage to start up firms without having the necessary managerial and production knowledge. That is why management training should also be considered for entrepreneurs who already have companies. In Turkey, KOSGEB established The Entrepreneurship Institute in 1998. This institute organizes lectures and seminars—both for entrepreneurs who want to start firms and for managers of SMEs—related to managerial problems they are facing in their daily operations. In the long run, it is essential for there to be a diffusion of the institute's functions throughout all the regions of the country. In addition to long-term training, there is also a need for regular seminars and conferences.

As a final issue regarding entrepreneurs, governments may consider supporting the intermediary organizations, particularly service-providing companies such as law offices and engineering design firms. Most of the entrepreneurial firms are small, and they cannot employ high-paid specialists such as lawyers in their companies. Therefore, they prefer to outsource some activities that are not core to their business but are necessary for the functioning of firms both at the start-up process (such as issuing patents and completing legal procedures) and at the development stage (such as keeping records of licensing and having accountant services). In general, there is not a great proliferation of these types of professional service firms in DCs. This in turn hinders the rapid growth of technology-based entrepreneurial firms, because they need to solve all their problems themselves with limited internal resources that will take more time than would buying from specialized firms. If we look at the example of Turkey, we see that this market is only served by some government organizations, such as KOSGEB and TTGV, and a few private consultancy firms. The government might take a role in establishing some incentive system specifically tailored toward the establishment and functioning of these types of service firms.

Exit Mechanisms

Exit Mechanisms in Turkey

The Turkish stock market is called Istanbul Stock Market. It was established in Istanbul in 1985, and its new firms market started in 1995. In addition to the already existing manufacturing and services indexes, the technology index came into operation in 2000 (IMKB 2001). There has been effort exerted to start a technology market similar to NASDAQ but the fruits of the labor have still not been observed. Istanbul Stock Market is small because of recurring economic crises in the country, resulting in instability in stock trades. Because of these problems, the stock market is not only a weak financial resource for firms but also a less desirable exit mechanism. Due to the lack of a market in which technology-based firms are traded, VC firms cannot exit from their investments through IPOs.

The remaining exit possibilities for VC firms are sales to local firms and public offering in the European or U.S. stock markets. An observation of the "exits" that have taken place so far in Turkey do not show any listings in foreign markets. Corporate VC has been seen to conclude with the acquisition of the investee firms by the parent companies. Foreign private equity investors have used trade sales for their exit.

Suggestions for Exit Mechanisms

Because VC firms generally prefer the stock market for their exit, DCs should take steps, if possible, to establish and successfully run a stock market purely for the technology-based firms (akin to NASDAQ). Otherwise, DCs may use solutions such as listing their firms on the European and U.S. markets. Israel is the best example of this solution; it has the distinction of being the home country of the second most traded foreign firms in the U.S. stock market, after Canada (see chapter 9). There are a number of alternative suggestions for smoothing the creation of these exit possibilities for VC firms. First, entrepreneurs can be trained in the workings of foreign markets. Second, regulations should be legislated in such a way that entrepreneurs will not be penalized for going abroad for a stock market listing. The government can supply incentives for intermediary organizations that will help entrepreneurial firms become listed in foreign markets.

The development and successful functioning of stock markets in DCs can be considered a long process, and they may never be developed to the level that exists in ICs. Thus, DCs should focus on other sources of exit mechanisms and make them function as efficiently as possible. Some of these mechanisms are: the acquisition of portfolio firms by a third party, the secondary sale of VC shares to a third party, the sale of VC shares to the entrepreneur, and the abandonment of the investment. Regulations governing the acquisitions and shares of firms should be simple and tax relief should be given to VC firms for these types of transactions.

Entrepreneur and Innovation Generators

Turkey, like many DCs, suffers from a lack of innovative capabilities and the nonexistence of an entrepreneurial culture. As much as Turkey needs a supply of capital, it also needs ideas and people who will take ideas and turn them into successful commercial products and services (Christensen 1997; OECD 1998; Swedberg 2000). If this need is addressed, a healthy environment for the development of the VC industry can be constructed. This section will briefly introduce the scientific and technological capabilities available in Turkey and highlight what organizations may be able to serve as the potential generators of entrepreneurs and innovators.

The Turkish Innovation System

The stronger the national innovation system in a country is, the more opportunities exist for innovativeness and entrepreneurs. The innovativeness of a country can be measured either by inputs such as R&D expenditures or by outputs such as patents and the export of high technology-based products (Eurostat 2001).

ICs invest substantially in their innovation systems. One way in which this can be shown is by the measurement of R&D expenses related to gross national product. This rate in 1998 was 1.86 percent in EU countries, 2.58 percent in the United States, 3.03 percent in Japan, and 3.77 percent in Sweden, the highest R&D spender (OECD 1999). The Turkish figure is a miserly 0.5 percent. Firms in ICs conduct R&D, whereas the government is the main source for R&D in DCs. This is also the case in Turkey, where universities and government constitute 74 percent of R&D (OECD 1999).

The Turkish SIS conducts R&D surveys each year among manufacturing firms. The number of firms in this survey increased from 126 in 1991 to 223 in 1997, and the R&D expenses of these companies increased from $169 million to $296 million in the same time period (Taymaz 2001). The number of companies in the R&D survey is low, representing only 2 percent to 3 percent of all manufacturing companies. However, it is the only available data, because like many DCs, Turkey has an inadequate and immature data collation system. The results of this survey show that R&D firms mainly use their internal resources (90 percent of all expenses) for R&D activities and that these activities are basically development activities (70 percent of all activities). Based on this industry analysis, the main R&D performer is the machinery production industry, whose R&D spending constitutes almost 70 percent of all R&D expenditures. The second most prolific R&D performer is the chemical industry, representing 12 percent of all R&D. Traditional industries such as food and textile are poor R&D performers. These two industries have only 3.5 percent and 3.3 percent of all R&D, respectively.

Because Turkey does not allocate large resources to R&D, scientific production is not especially fruitful. If scientific output is measured by the number of articles published and number of patents issued, we see a low rate of performance. With respect to the articles published in 1995, Turkey had only 3 publications per 100,000 people, whereas this figure was 56 for the EU, 77 for the United States, and 42 for Japan. Similarly, the Turkish patent applications to the European Patent Office in 1995 were equivalent to 0.05 patents per 1 million people, whereas it was 9.9 for South Korea, 72.4 for the United States, 92.1 for Japan, and 72.4 for the EU (Taymaz 2001; OECD 1999).

Turkey exhibits poor performance not only in creating technology but also in transferring and using technologies created abroad. The results of the manufacturing survey conducted by SIS show that only 5 percent of 7,241 firms participating in the survey made use of transferred technology in 1997. The R&D survey conducted by SIS shows that 28 percent of the 223 firms made use of R&D transfer technology. The results of these two surveys clearly indicate that firms conducting R&D also utilize foreign resources. However, the low percentage rates are not particularly promising for a country whose stated aim is to reach the economic level of ICs.

Another performance criteria for the innovation system could be the value-added economics coming from technology-based industries. The export figures shown in table 10.3 indicate that Turkish exports are based on low technology. South Korea has approximately two-thirds of the population of Turkey, but its export, based on high technology, is almost ten times higher than the Turkish figure.

The overall performance of Turkey with respect to innovation does not show a particularly bright picture. This picture does not become any brighter when we examine information and communication technologies, both important pil-

Table 10.3
The Distribution of Manufacturing Industry's Exports Based on the Type of Technology, Selected OECD countries, 1996

Countries	High Technology	Middle – High Technology	Middle – Low Technology	Low Technology
US	26,8	45,9	11,2	15,4
Germany	11,3	57,9	15,7	13,7
Japan	23,6	58,6	14,7	2,9
South Korea	23,7	34,6	21,9	19,8
OECD Average	17,4	45,8	17,5	18,7
Turkey (*)	2,5	17,9	21,1	58,2

(*)Calculated from State Institute of Statistics data.
Source: OECD, 1999.

lars of the new economy. Turkey has increased investments in the information infrastructure but has still not been capable of attaining the EU level. In 1999, industries based on information and communication technologies as a percentage of gross national product was 2.6 percent in Turkey, whereas it was 5.9 percent in the EU and 7.8 percent in the United States. During the period between 1992 and 1997, there was yearly growth of 0.1 percent in Turkey, whereas the corresponding figures in the EU and the United States were 1.8 percent and 1.2 percent, respectively (OECD 1999).

Suggestions for Entrepreneur and Innovator Generators

The development of the VCI goes hand-in-hand with a well-functioning national innovation system that will generate entrepreneurs and innovators. This can be clearly observed in the United States, where VC is concentrated in high-technology regions such as Silicon Valley and Route 728 rather than in financial centers such as Chicago and New York (Florida and Smith 1990). It is clear that DCs need to find ways of creating entrepreneurs and innovators. The most likely establishment capable of rising to this task is academia.

As the Turkish example shows, universities are the main conductors of R&D, so it is natural to expect their graduates to be potentially skillful entrepreneurs and researchers who will become recipients of VC funds (Maeda 2001). DCs need to continue investing in the scientific infrastructure and even increase their investments if they want to close the technological gap that exists between them and ICs (Najmabadi and Lall 1995).

As important as having strong research organizations and universities may be, it is even more essential for DCs to follow the correct policies regarding the setting up of the institutional infrastructure, as discussed in the institutional infrastructure section. For example, DCs need to develop an entrepreneurial culture that will motivate researchers to become entrepreneurs. Related to this, the cultural attitude among researchers and businesspeople needs to change in order to establish communication between them. This is not just a problem in DCs; even many European countries complain about this gap that prevents the transfer of their scientific findings into economic use (Senker and Vliet 1998). Many suggestions have been put forward to combat this problem. For example, a suggestion has been made to set up technology transfer mechanisms such as technoparks and incubators in universities or with the collaboration of universities. Germany is a proponent of this model, and so are some of the astonishingly successful DC examples, such as Israel and Ireland, which can both now be referred to as ICs (Maeda 2001; Murphy 2000).

POLICY DISCUSSION

This chapter has analyzed the VCI in Turkey within the context of DCs by focusing on the VC's role as an innovation-financing tool in DCs. This analysis makes it possible to identify some alternative courses of action that may lead the way to the development of entrepreneurship and innovativeness in DCs. This section will put forward some suggestions for actors influential in the VCI (Çetindamar 1999).

The Distribution of Responsibilities

Government

The role of the government can be summarized under six headings:

- Establishing the infrastructure for VC firms
- Supplying financial support
- Supporting VC firms during periods of crisis
- Developing policies that will increase demand for VC
- Increasing entrepreneurship
- Developing national technology strategies

Establishing the infrastructure for VC firms: The government is the crucial element in establishing and developing a VC industry, since it is responsible for creating the institutional infrastructure within which VC firms will operate. As discussed in the institutional infrastructure section, DC governments should legislate a set of laws that will regulate the functions of VC firms, VC funds, fund investors, portfolio firms, exit mechanisms, and entrepreneurial firms.

Supplying financial support: Another crucial role of the government in establishing the VCI is providing direct financial contributions to VC funds. The governments of many ICs supply capital either as investors in VC firms or by forming state-owned VC firms. One surprising fact about the United States is that in spite of the fact that it has the most mature and developed VCI, the U.S. government still has Small Business Investment Corporations that supply VC funds to entrepreneurial firms in their start-up stages.

Although the governments of DCs should consider investing in VC funds, they should be careful to prevent corruption and misuse of these funds. Turkey, like many DCs, is a victim of political corruption. For this reason it is necessary for some precautionary measures to be put in place. For example, financial support to the VCI can be conducted through investments in successful private sector VC firms rather than by setting up state-owned VC firms. This practice is widely applied in Sweden and China. Around eighty Chinese VC firms have received a total of $360 million from the government and have invested these funds in local, technology-based firms (Folta 1999).

The government can also supply financial support to the VCI through indirect means such as loans and debt financing given to entrepreneurial firms. After providing support to these entrepreneurial firms in the seed stage, the government functions as an intermediary investor that complements the VCI.

Supporting VC firms during periods of crisis: The establishment of a VCI requires a long period of time, since it necessitates a learning process for developing competencies and skills in solving nonfinancial problems of portfolio firms. For example, the Swedish VCI has gone through a thirty-year learning process, as described in chapter 6. During this period, there may be critical times when government intervention and direct financial support could be the determining factor in the industry's survival. This type of government support has been observed in ICs such as Sweden and the United States.

Regarding the supplying of financial support to the VC industry in times of financial crisis, the fear of failure and loss of tax revenue might create doubt in the minds of politicians. Considering that around one-third of investments in VC ends up in bankruptcy, this may well be a valid fear. That is why government policies should try to assuage this fear by being transparent to the public and by explaining the rationale behind their support of the industry. By stimulating entrepreneurial culture, the government can reduce the burden of failure, since even failure may be advantageous through the opportunity for learning created. In addition to increasing managerial and technical knowledge, there are also the beneficial effects of the experience gained by both venture capitalists and entrepreneurs. If we look at the United States, we can see that many Small Business Investment Corporations established in the 1960s failed. However, if we dig further, we see that the unsuccessful venture capitalists of that period were the successful founders of VC firms in the 1970s (Bygrave and Timmons 1992; SBA 1999). This and similar examples should be directly explained to the electorate as a means to win their support for this policy.

Developing policies that will increase demand for VC: Besides supply side precautions (such as installing infrastructure and financial support), government policies can foster the VCI by also supporting the demand side. This could be done in a number of ways. For example, the majority (79 percent) of governmental financial support for entrepreneurs in the United States is done through direct technology purchases (OECD 1999). When we look at other countries in the world, we see that this rate is 76 percent in the United Kingdom and 46 percent in Japan. When the government is an important customer for technology products, it gives incentives for entrepreneurs and researchers to become innovative. By creating demand for local producers to meet, the government initiates and provides opportunities to local entrepreneurs. The Ministry of Defense in Turkey has started this kind of technology acquisition policy in recent years. It is crucial for all DCs to adopt similar policies.

Increasing entrepreneurship: DCs should learn from the experience of ICs in developing an entrepreneurial culture. It is essential for DCs to legislate for the protection of intellectual property rights, the opening and managing of incubators, the provision of help for firms with access to diversified innovation financing resources, the granting of permission to university researchers to start up companies, and the training of entrepreneurs. In Turkey, the recently enacted Technology Districts Act could be an important factor in creating an entrepreneurial environment.

Developing national technology strategies: Because VC is not by itself enough for the entrepreneurial and innovative economy, governments need to construct a comprehensive national innovation system (Lundvall 1992). Policies regarding technology, education, industry, and entrepreneurship should be integrated to ensure that they are able to complement one another and benefit from synergy. DCs in general lack such a comprehensive perspective and are not particularly visionary in their outlook. Turkey has not yet started to plan its future with regard to technology. With the exception of a few incentives, such as R&D loans, Turkey still lacks a systematic innovation system (Göker 1998). R&D loans and grants have existed in small amounts so far, but their impact on companies receiving the funds has been extremely positive in terms of company sales and growth (Taymaz 2001). Thus, Turkey should first plan its future and then increase its R&D incentives to reach EU levels.

Firms

Producer firms: The majority of firms in DCs are small scale and oriented toward low value-added products. Therefore, the product innovativeness of these companies is limited. As latecomers to the family of ICs, firms in DCs use technology in production that is generally licensed from foreign countries, and these firms are highly dependent on this foreign technology for such aspects as maintenance. As a result, few companies can develop innovative capability and use it to gain competitive advantage (Humphrey 1995). Any crisis has the potential to have a devastating effect on firms because of their low profit margins. This situation can change if firms gain competitiveness through innovativeness and enter new economic areas, particularly niche markets. In a nutshell, firms need to change their mentality regarding a number of issues.

First, firms need to start investing in R&D. Even though the internal financial resources of firms are limited, new resources such as government loans and the EU's international research programs have become available in recent years. South Korea, Japan, Singapore, and Ireland are successful examples of countries that have utilized international research consortiums for their technological development (Najmabadi and Lall 1995). Firms should actively search for these new opportunities in order to benefit from them. In the 1990s, Turkish firms started to realize the importance of international collaborations. A signal of this new development is the increase in the number of Turkish projects in the EUREKA program. EUREKA is a European program that has been set up to fund R&D projects for firms from various European countries. Turkey became a member of this program in 1985, but the number of Turkish projects has increased significantly since 1995. The total number of projects involved with EUREKA reached twenty-nine in 2001.

Second, firms should increase their relationships with universities and research organizations. By developing strong ties with scientific organizations, firms can tap into resources such as skilled researchers, scientific knowledge, and inventions that can then be transferred into economic value. Many successful IC firms have not only in-house research capabilities but also competencies gained from the external resources of their networks (Lundvall 1992).

If firms can increase their relationships with universities, they can influence the direction of the scientific world toward their needs.

Third, large corporations in DCs should change their attitude toward state-of-the-art technologies. Many companies in Turkey are highly bureaucratic and conservative. Their management needs to find ways of integrating entrepreneurship into their managerial system. Because corporations have large financial resources, a positive decision to support innovation can positively affect the flow of funds into VC funds.

Actors of the innovation-financing system: The main task of financial organizations is to come together to create a VCI. This task incorporates a number of steps. First, these organizations need to attract VC funds from abroad. They need to become members of international associations not only to improve capital flow but also to reap the benefits from the resources of these networks. For example, the Turkish members of EVCA could increase collaboration with European VC firms and bring EVCA services, such as training, to the local firms. This step will increase the competence level of venture capitalists and further increase trust and networking relationships among local and foreign firms. Second, financial organizations in DCs should cooperate in their investments as successful VC firms in ICs have. Third, DC firms should come together and form associations or various types of networks in order to collaborate on a number of issues: lobbying for changes in regulations, training venture capitalists, providing legal and support services, and informing each other about entrepreneurs and/or technological opportunities.

In DCs, networks need to be extended to include business angels. Reaching out to business angels and informing entrepreneurs about these individuals can lead to an activation of these resources. Business angels can form their own independent network too. As discussed in chapter 3, the networks of business angels can increase the effectiveness of the overall VC market, so the actors of the innovation-financing system should try to include all these independent individuals in their work and networking. It is essential for DCs to incorporate business angels into the VCI as a means to overcome the problem of limited capital.

The final point is that financial organizations should contribute to the entrepreneurial culture. This step will reap long-term benefits for firms operating in the VC market. The most important benefit is that firms will create a favorable environment for entrepreneurs, who will then become customers for VC funds. Increasing public awareness of entrepreneurship can also help change the perception of failures. Unless there is endorsement of failure, financial firms will find it difficult to raise funds for VC investments. Many institutional investors hesitate in giving funds to risk organizations. Moreover, investors might tend to control firms that they invest in, as has often been observed in the Turkish case. By educating investors about entrepreneurship and the way VC functions, the actors in the VC market will be able to make the environment they work in more comfortable and conducive to success.

Intermediary organizations: The majority of firms in DCs are family-owned SMEs with limited resources. Intermediary organizations such as trade and industry chambers could bring their members together and set up collaborations to work on technological developments that cannot be undertaken by any one of the members individually. Another role that intermediary organizations can function in is as the bridge between research organizations and firms. Industrial associations can set up centers that will educate their members, provide consultancy in the field of technology, and help in the technology transfer stages.

Universities and Research Institutes

Another policy that DCs must implement regards increasing the technological opportunities in their countries. If there is no demand and no technological base, the supply of VC cannot contribute to their economic growth at all. A study in the United States has clearly shown that VC is a necessary but not, on its own, sufficient condition to stimulate high technology economic development (Florida and Smith 1990). In addition to VC, there must be a strong scientific base that can create opportunities for VC firms to capture and transform into economic profits. Technological capabilities are needed not only to attract VCI investments but also to transfer technologies and ensure the efficient utilization within the local economy (Weiss 1990). Therefore, the study suggests, policy makers should build a strong technological infrastructure and integrated industrial base. To do so, several policies can be recommended. First, policy makers should stimulate early-stage VC to encourage start-ups. Second, DCs should aim to be innovative in finding technology niches, such as engineering services, where they can become competitive with ICs. The success of India in the software industry could be an inspiring example for other countries (Correa 1996). Third, DCs should support an educational infrastructure that will produce well-qualified scientists and entrepreneurs. Fourth, governments should support pure and applied science that fosters entrepreneurship.

Government policies are just one side of the coin with respect to universities and other research organizations, since these organizations themselves have significant responsibilities in the field of increasing innovativeness and entrepreneurship. These responsibilities are as follows:

- Conducting advanced scientific research and increasing scientific knowledge
- Supplying high-quality education
- Improving relationships with firms
- Prioritizing industrial and societal needs when considering the allocation of research budgets and researchers
- Producing graduates with a level of practical knowledge that is easily adaptable to an industrial setting
- Increasing awareness about innovativeness and entrepreneurship
- Ensuring that training for managers, venture capitalists, and financial experts is up-to-date and state-of-the-art

Concluding Remarks

DCs face a dilemma: to choose between development based on traditional industries with low value-added products or development based on a new industrial structure with high technology products. Plumping for the second choice will transform their economy with a series of radical structural changes. Innovativeness and entrepreneurship will be the basis of the new construction. For this process to start, DCs should begin with an in-depth analysis of their existing technological infrastructure so that they can identify and solve whatever problems prevent the national innovation system from functioning in an efficient manner. All this data can then be fed into a planning process that will create immediate strategy and actions for the development of a scientific base, innovativeness, entrepreneurial culture, and innovation financing. In the process of restructuring for economic development, Turkey, like other DCs, will need to construct a well-functioning dynamic system of innovation financing with VC as one of the prime elements.

In order to make VC function, DCs need to consider all the dimensions of the innovation financing system within the context of their own country. They need to have entrepreneurs, investors, innovators, and venture capitalists. Even though this chapter places an emphasis on the role of VC, it should not be exaggerated and all efforts should not be expended only on the development of VC markets. ICs are able to focus most of their efforts on VC because they have a number of alternative well-functioning financial mechanisms such as stock markets and investment banks. However, DCs have to consider their own economic structure and build a healthy functioning financial system with a range of financial organizations rather than just relying on VC. Depending on the country-specific conditions, DCs should develop a balanced and varied mix of financial instruments, including: VC, business angels, private equity partnerships, technoparks and incubators, intermediary financial organizations, corporate VC, investment banks, government resources, and the stock market. Business angels, technoparks, and incubators will have special value for DCs, since they can be immediately mobilized and they are competent in nonfinancial services as well. This will buy time until a competent VCI is created, and it will speed the creation of a critical mass that can attract formal VC firms.

DCs have to follow long-term strategies and plans with consistent policies (Najmabadi and Lall 1995). However, this necessitates economic and political stability where inflation and interest rates are low, there is confidence in the market, and there is public support and trust for policies. When all these have been achieved, the macroeconomic environment will motivate entrepreneurs and innovations will become profitable. Such an environment can also attract funds from both local and foreign resources that will flow to VC funds that can then be used to revitalize existing industries and establish new ones.

Funds are an important ingredient of an entrepreneurial society but as long as there are no technological opportunities, they will not be used efficiently. DCs should ensure efficient use by investing in scientific and technologic developments. In this process, governments, firms, and universities have their own roles and responsibilities. They need to be active and cooperative to ensure the efficient functioning of the overall system. Rather than relying on one financial mechanism such as VC, diverse mechanisms such as government funds and business angels have to be in a position to complement each other and serve different functions in the growth of entrepreneurial and innovative firms.

Structural transformation is not an easy task for Turkey or for many other DCs. However, in the technological age, DCs have to face up to the challenge and make a decision for the future. If DCs miss the boat, the gap between ICs and DCs will widen further. It is important to remember that innovation financing is one element of the overall transformation and even this task is not easily achievable in the short term. However, if there is a delay in starting, the goal of having a well-functioning VCI will be postponed further. Turkey and other DCs should start to work on a feasible innovation financing system that will fit into their overall industrial and technological structure. If they succeed, they will see a boost to the welfare of their countries; if they fail, however, their economic problems will become more and more serious.

REFERENCES

Aylward, A. 1998. *Trends in Venture Capital Finance in Developing Countries.* World Bank, Washington, DC: IFC. Discussion Paper No. 36.

Başağa, H., and Çetindamar, D. 2000. *Uluslararası Rekabet Stratejileri: Biyoteknoloji Raporu [International Competitiveness Strategies: Biotechnology Report].* Istanbul: TÜSIAD.

Başlar, A. 2000. "Türkiye'de Risk Sermayesi [Venture Capital in Turkey]." *Ekovitrin,* October.

Bygrave, W. D., and J. A. Timmons. 1992. *Venture Capital at the Crossroads.* Boston, Mass.: Harvard Business School.

Carlin, W., and C. Mayer. 1999. "Finance, Investment, and Growth." CEPR Discussion Paper No. 2223.

Carlsson, B. 2002. *New Technological Systems in the Bio Industries: An International Study.* Eindhoven: Kluwer.

Çetindamar-K., D. 1999. "The Role of Venture Capital for Innovation in Developing Countries." *Sixteenth International Association of Science Parks Conference.* August 31–September 4, Istanbul, Turkey.

Çetindamar, D. 2000. "Türkiye'de Bilişim Sektörü [Turkish Information and Communication Technology]." *TUBISAD-Sabancı University Venture Capital Conference.* September 7, Istanbul.

Christensen, J. L. 1997. *Financing Innovation.* TSER Project Report: Innovation Systems and Europe 3.2.3. Denmark: Aalborg University.

Cooke, P. 2001. "New Economy Innovation Systems: Biotechnology in Europe and the USA." *Industry and Innovation* 3: 267–89.

Correa, C. M. 1996. "Strategies for Software Exports from Developing Countries." *World Development* 24 (1): 171–82.

278 The Growth of Venture Capital

Dumanlı, Z. Ö., A. E. Kazancı, Ö. Öğüç, T. Şarlıgil, T. Tatar, and B. Tüzemen. 2001. *Venture Capital in Turkey.* Project Report, Sabancı University Graduate School of Management.

The Economist. 1998. "Europe's Great Experiment." June 13.

Edquist, C. 1997. *Systems of Innovation.* London: Pinter.

Erdal, C. 2000. "Vakıf Risk [Vakıf Risk Capital Firm]." *TUBISAD-Sabancı University Venture Capital Conference.* September 7, Istanbul.

Etkileşim. 2000. "Bilişim Pazarının Geliri 11 Milyar Dolar [The Industry Based on Information and Communication Technologies earns 11 Billion Dollars]." *Etkileşim,* May, pp. 22–23.

Eurostat. 2001. *Science and Technology in Europe: A Statistical Panorama of the EU Knowledge-based Economy.* No. 33/2001.

Fenn, W., N. Liang, and S. Prowse. 1995. *The Economics of the Private Equity Market.* Washington, D.C.: Federal Reserve Bank.

Finlayson, G. E. 1999. "Japan: The Changing Venture Capital Market." *International Financial Law Review,* Supplement: Private Equity and Venture Capital, pp. 14–19.

Florida, R., and J. D. F. Smith. 1990. "Venture Capital, Innovation, and Economic Development." *Economic Development Quarterly* 4 (4): 345–61.

Folta, P. H. 1999. "The Rise of Venture Capital in China." *The China Business Review* 26 (6): 6–15.

Forsman, Z. K. 2000. "Biotechnology: A Legal Challenge for Turkey." *Biotechnology: Opportunities and Challenges Workshop,* October 6–7, Ýstanbul.

Fransman, M., G. Junne, and A. Roobeek. 1995. *The Biotechnology Revolution?* Oxford: Blackwell.

Globus. 2000. "A'dan Z'ye Risk Sermayesi: Fon Bulmanın Yeni Yolu [Venture Capital from A to Z: Ways of Raising Funds]." *Globus,* August, pp. 105–13.

Gompers, P. A., and J. Lerner. 1998. *The Determinants of Corporate Venture Capital Success: Organizational Structure, Incentives, and Complementaries.* National Bureau of Economic Research Working Paper No. 6725, Massachusetts.

Gompers, P. A., J. Lerner, M. M. Blair, and T. Hellmann. 1998. "What Drives Venture Capital Fundraising?" *Brookings Papers on Economic Activity,* pp. 149–204.

Göker, A. 1998. *Niçin Bilim ve Teknoloji Politikası [Why Science and Technology Policy].* Ankara: TÜBITAK, 1998.

Grossman, G. M., and E. Helpman. 1991. *Innovation and Growth in the Global Economy.* Cambridge: MIT Press.

Hisrich, R. D., and M. P. Peters. 1998. *Enterpreneurship.* New York: McGraw-Hill.

Humphrey, J. 1995. "Industrial Organization and Manufacturing Competitiveness in Developing Countries." *World Development* 23 (1): 149–63.

IFC (International Finance Corporation). 2001. www.ifc.org.

IMKB (Istanbul Menkul Kıymetler Borsası [Istanbul Stock Market]). 2001. www.imkb.gov.tr.

Jalava, J., and M. Pohjola. 2002. "Economic Growth in the New Economy: Evidence from Advanced Economies." *Information Economics and Policy* 14 (2): 189–211.

Jeng, L. A., and P. C. Wells. 2000. "The Determinants of Venture Capital Funding: Evidence across Countries." *Journal of Corporate Finance* 6 (3): 241–89.

Kanbak, Y. 2001. "Gebze Organize Sanayi Bölgesi–Sabancı Üniversitesi–Wertheimer Inkübator Girişimi [Incubator of Gebze Industrial District–Sabancı University–

Wertheimer]." *Matchmaking Event for Entrepreneurs in Information Industry,* September 7, Ýstanbul.

Karaomerlioglu, D. C., and S. Jacobsson. 2000. "The Swedish Venture Capital Industry—an Infant, Adolescent, or Grown-up?" *Venture Capital* 2 (1): 61–88.

Kim, L. 1997. *Imitation to Innovation: The Dynamics of Korea's Technological Learning.* Boston, Mass.: Harvard Business School.

Kortum, S., and J. Lerner. 1998. "Does Venture Capital Spur Innovation?" Working paper, Harvard Business School, Boston, Mass.

KOSGEB [Small and Medium-Sized Enterprise Development Directorate]. 2001. www.kosgeb.gov.tr.

Lall, S. 1992. "Technological Capability and Industrialization." *World Development* 20 (2): 165–86.

Lindholm-Dahlstrand, Å., and D. Çetindamar. 2000. "The Dynamics of Innovation Financing in Sweden." *Venture Capital* 2 (3): 203–21.

Lundvall, B. 1992. *National Systems of Innovation: Towards a Theory of Innovation and Interactive Learning.* London: Pinter.

Maeda, N. 2001. "Missing Link of National Entrepreneurial Business Model-Issues of High-tech Start-up in Japan in Comparison with US and German Model." *PICMET Conference,* July 29–August 2, Portland, Oregon.

Mason, C. M., and R. T. Harrison. 1999. "Venture Capital: Rationale, Aims, and Scope [editorial]." *Venture Capital* 1 (1): 1–46.

Milliyet. 2001. "Bürokraside Avrupa Lideriyiz [Turkey is bureaucracy leader in Europe]." *Milliyet,* October 28.

Mladenowa, I. 2000. *Venture Capital Financing ("A Comparative Study of US, European and Bulgarian Experience").* Sofia: Economic Policy Institute.

Murphy, M. 2000. "Ireland: Venturing Far and Near." *European Venture Capital Journal* 75: 46–50.

Nahum, J. 2001. "Tofaş—Techubator." *Matchmaking Event for Entrepreneurs in Information Industry,* September 7, Istanbul.

Najmabadi, F., and S. Lall. 1995. *Developing Industrial Technology: Lessons for Policy and Practice.* Washington, D.C.: World Bank.

NASDAQ. 2002. http://www.nasdaq.com.

NYSE (New York Stock Exchange). 2002. http://www.nyse.com.

OECD (Office for Economic Cooperation and Development). 1998. *Fostering Entrepreneurship: The OECD Jobs Strategy.* Paris: OECD.

OECD. 1999. *OECD Science, Technology, and Industry Scoreboard 1999.* Paris: OECD.

OECD. 2001. *Science, Technology, and Industry Outlook: Drivers of Growth—Information Technology, Innovation, and Entrepreneurship.* Paris: OECD.

Radikal. 2001. "Dış; Yatırımı Unut [Losing Foreign Investment]." *Radikal,* November 9.

Rickne, A. 2000. *New Technology-Based Firms and Industrial Dynamics.* Ph.D. diss., Industrial Dynamics Department, Chalmers University of Technology, Gothenborg, Sweden.

Sabah. 2000. "Para Bilişime Akacak [Money Will Flow to Information and Communication Technologies]." *Sabah,* September 6.

Sagari, S. B., and G. Guidotti. 1992. *Financial Markets, Institutions, and Instruments: Venture Capital—The Lessons from the Developed World for the Developing Markets.* Oxford: Blackwell Publishers.

Sapienza, H. J., S. Manigart, and W. Vermeir. 1996. "Venture Capitalist Governance and Value Added in Four Countries." *Journal of Business Venturing* 11: 439–69.

SBA (Small Business Administration). 1999. http://www.sba.gov/SBIR/otacc.html.

Senker, J., and R. V. Vliet. 1998. *Biotechnology and Competitive Advantage.* Cheltenham, UK: Edward Elgar.

SIS (State Institute of Statistics). 1998. *Inovasyon Anketi [Innovation survey].* Ankara: SIS.

Smith, R. L., and J. K. Smith. 2000. *Entrepreneurial Finance.* New York: John Wiley.

Swedberg, R. 2000. *Entrepreneurship.* Oxford: Oxford University Press.

Taymaz, E. 2001. *Ulusal Yenilik Sistemi: Türkiye Imalat Sanayiinde Teknolojik Değişim ve Yenilik Süreçleri [National Innovation System: Technological change and Innovation in the Turkish Manufacturing Industry].* Ankara: TÜBITAK / TTGV/DIE.

TIDEB [Technology Observation Directorate]. 2001. http://www.tideb.tubitak.gov.tr.

Tuncel, K. 1995. *Risk Sermayesi Finansman Modeli [Venture capital financial model].* Ankara: SPK.

TTGV [Turkish Technology Development Association]. 2001. www.ttgv.gov.tr.

Van Auken, H. E. 1999. "Obstacles to Business Launch." *Journal of Developmental Entrepreneurship* 4 (2): 175–87.

Weiss, C. 1990. "Scientific and Technological Constraints to Economic Growth and Equity." In *Science and Technology: Lessons for Development Policy,* ed. R. E. Evenson and G. Rains. Boulder, Colo.: Westview.

Part III
Industry Experiences

11

The Role of Venture Capital Financing for Young Bioscience Firms

Annika Rickne

INTRODUCTION

The last two decades have seen an expanding venture capital industry in both Europe and the United States, contributing to the success of corporations such as Intel, Netscape, and Amazon. Indeed, there are many young technology-based or science-based firms that have benefited greatly from the actions of venture capital companies. With the aim of enhancing growth of such firms, it is pertinent, therefore, to understand in depth the function that venture capital companies play for firm formation and firm development as well as for firm performance (Bygrave and Timmons 1992). The microeconomic behavior of venture capital companies (henceforth VCC) has accordingly been analyzed in a number of studies focusing on such areas as selection and investment processes (e.g., Fried and Hisrich 1994) and investment activities and relations between VCCs and firms (e.g., Sapienza 1992; Fried and Hisrich 1995). This chapter gives a detailed analysis of the exact *resource and knowledge exchange* that takes place between a venture capital company investor and a young firm, with the aim of understanding the precise workings of the venture capital industry.

Indeed, it is well known that young technology-based or science-based firms rely heavily on other actors for innovation and firm development. Technology and product development, managerial analysis, and other activities often take place at the interface between the firm and its partners, be they other companies, research organizations, financiers, or policy organizations. Resources and knowledge are sourced into the firm from an array of partners—developed with these partners—with needs shifting over time (Churchill and Lewis 1983), and resulting in learning, innovation, and firm growth.

In this context, a venture capital company is one type of actor that may potentially be of great importance to science-based firms, providing, for example, financial assets; support in recruitment; managerial and marketing guidance; and advice for product development and contacts. Indeed, even in its very definition of venture capitalist investors, the European Venture Capital Association (EVCA) includes requirements of equity financing and active management support (EVCA 1997). Such intense support by a VCC often adds significant value to the firm (Fredriksen 1997), and some studies argue that the outcome of active VCC involvement may even be higher firm performance, compared with non-venture-backed firms, in terms of both growth rates and employment creation (EVCA 1997).

Even though the role of VCCs for resource and knowledge mobilization is well recognized both in studies taking a resource-based view of firm development and in studies with an innovation system approach, there are gaps in the understanding of the exact nature of such exchange and influence. Therefore, this chapter sets out to examine in detail what role VCCs play in the formation and development of young science-based firms, with particular attention to resource and knowledge exchange. While the focus of this chapter is on *how young firms experience* the influence of VCCs, the study also takes into account how venture capital companies themselves view their role. Thus, the first issue to be investigated is to what extent and in what way venture capital companies were involved in the very *formation process* of the entrepreneurial firms. This analysis has revealed three mechanisms of influence, each of which will be discussed: financing the venture, providing the initial technology base, and enhancing the clustering of innovations. The second issue concerns how venture capital companies influence the *development path* of the firms. Again, particular attention is given to the function of the venture capital companies in providing the new firms with resources and knowledge. A number of mechanisms are discussed: financing and risk sharing, managerial expertise and guidance, creation and diffusion of technology, legitimization, and networking.

After discussion of the VCCs' role in firm formation and development, some attention is devoted to analyzing whether spatial proximity between financier and firm is of any importance. This issue is especially relevant to policy advice on how, and where, to create a competent capital market.

This analysis is based on evidence from seventy-three entrepreneurial bioscience firms with a core competence in the area of biocompatible materials. An internationally comparative approach is taken, and the firms are located in Sweden, Ohio, and Massachusetts, respectively. This approach offers a sample of regions with capital markets at varying levels of maturity.

The chapter is structured as follows. After a brief note on methodology, I discuss the role of venture capital companies in the firm formation process. Mechanisms of influence on the firms' development paths is discussed in the fourth section. The fifth section concerns the issue of whether spatial proximity to venture capital companies is of importance to young science-based firms. And the final section discusses the main conclusions. The analysis will have two types of results, one in which conclusions are drawn for management on how to view partnerships with venture capital companies, and one in which a set of policy recommendations is given for each of the three regions on how to enhance the functionality of the capital market for entrepreneurial firms.

THE RESEARCH DESIGN

This chapter analyzes a population of seventy-three young science-based firms that develop biocompatible materials and related products. In biomedical devices, designed for use in close physical contact with the human body, the choice of material is crucial. Clearly, the development of new materials is not only a key element for the growth of a set of biomedical industries, it is in fact one of the drivers of this growth. This study thus does not concern firms within only one specific industry but rather firms dealing with a set of technologies that relate to and transform a number of industries.

As the term implies, *young science-based firms* are companies that are in some sense *young* and have a strong *scientific and technological focus:* in other words, they are (relatively) new firms having scientific technological competence as a dominant variable that affects their competitive advantage. Some of these firms will work with new technologies, being a part of the entrepreneurial activity that follows a technological discontinuity. These firms are active in shaping new industries and new innovation systems. Others have found a niche in a much more mature industry but may still be part of a reconfiguring process. In this chapter, the young firms in focus have been established to exploit opportunities within a specific technology: biomaterials. The *newness* means that the company is a *new entity*, where the meaning of *new* differs among different industries and innovation systems. Here the concept of young is operationalized in two ways: (1) biomaterials firms established within the period from 1975 to 1998 qualify as young in this study, because this period marks the start of the establishment of firms with the specific aim of exploiting inventions related to biomaterials; (2) all new entities are included, that is, even when the new firm is formed by an older company's efforts to enter the technological field.

To find the young firms, it proved useful to apply several methods simultaneously, given the inherent uncertainties in each method, and a triangulated approach was used. Biomaterials technologies can be incorporated into many products, and the first step was to identify these existing or potential products. Firms developing such products were found through searching a number of directories. Next, to verify that the firms had a competence profile involving biomaterials technologies, a patent method was used in addition to the reading of corporate documentation. Finally, more firms were added to the population by asking each firm to point to additional actors, each of which were scrutinized with regard to technology and product profile.

This chapter examines the role of venture capital for young science-based firms by analyzing in what ways and to what extent the biomaterials firms have acquired resources and knowledge from such partners. In this analysis, the role of venture capital companies is set in relation to the role of other types of actors. Therefore, for each firm, its entire set of relations with all types of actors (VCCs, companies, customers, universities, other organizations, and so forth) was mapped over time. For each relationship, the type and extent of flow of resources and knowledge (technology, finance, market-related resources, management and extended networks) were assessed.[1]

In this type of exploratory study, it is crucial to triangulate the data sources so as to obtain strong findings. Therefore, five different sources of information, both quantitative and qualitative data, about the young firms and their patterns of networking and resource flows were used: (1) extensive written company information,[2] (2) databases on collaborations,[3] (3) interviews with the firms,[4] (4) interviews with several of the inventors of the firms' initial technology,[5] (5) interviews with some of the firms' partners (financiers, companies, etc.) in order to give insight into the young firm's development from an outside perspective.

Although the focus in this chapter is on *how young firms experience* the influence of VCCs, the study also analyzes how venture capital companies themselves view their role in firm development. Therefore, eleven VCCs were interviewed. The VC firms were located within the three selected regions,[6] and all named bioscience as one of their focus areas for investment.

For all types of interviews, semistructured guides with closed-ended as well as open-ended questions were used. The length of the interviews varied from 1.5 to 7 hours, and they went in depth into the evolution of the biomaterials company or the activities of the venture capital firms.

VENTURE CAPITAL COMPANIES AND FIRM FORMATION

The issue in focus in this section is to what extent and in what way venture capital companies were involved in the very formation process of the new firms. The analysis has revealed three mechanisms of influence, each of which will be discussed here: (a) financing the venture, (b) providing the initial technology base, and (c) enhancing clustering of innovations.

Financing the Start of the New Venture

The primary function of the capital market is, naturally, to provide financing, in this way enabling the operations of the firms and sharing their risks. Indeed, a key to success for young science-based firms is to raise capital quickly and in sufficient amount in relation to the choice of low-hurdle or high-potential projects. A number of studies have pointed out the problems experienced by young or small firms in raising money for start-up or development, taking this fact as a partial explanation of inhibited growth (Landström and Winborg 1995; Binks and Ennew 1996).

A definition of a capital market must include all the actors that may provide the firm with financial assets for its establishment and development as well as the structure of that market and the institutions guiding it. In this broad sense, not only is it the traditional actors of capital markets, such as banks, that may be of importance in providing capital, but it is also customers, acquirers, governmental bodies, bridging organizations, venture capital companies, and business angels. For example, the first publicly held American venture capital company was formed in 1946, and its successes, along with tax incentives, spurred further investments in technology by banks and insurance companies as well as private risk takers (Saxenian 1994). Governmental or military agencies may also function as capital providers; military contracts provided the foundation for many U.S. start-ups from the 1950s onward.

The focus of this chapter, however, is on venture capital companies. The competence of VCCs enables them to address the problems of information asymmetry, adverse selection, and risk assessment (Chan 1983). In this study on biomaterials firms, VCCs provided one-third of the new firms with initial financing (see table 11.1). There are substantial differences with regard to this

Table 11.1
Financial Sources for the Start of the New Venture (Percentage of firms receiving financing from each type of source)[a]

	Firms in Sweden	Firms in Ohio	Firms in Massachusetts	**All firms [b]**
Venture capital company	13	42	43	**33**
Research foundations	63	33	4	**29**
Founder	31	75	4	**27**
Other organization [c]	25	58	4	**24**
Biomedical company [d]	25	17	22	**22**
Parent firm or new owner	38	8	17	**22**
Public offering	0	8	4	**4**
Development with customer	6	0	4	**4**

[a]As the analysis is of the total population of biomaterials firms, located in the three regions, the actual differences are significant in themselves.

[b]Note that the sum of each column exceeds 100% as each firm connects to several sources.

[c]Other organizations include technology-transfer units, bridging organizations, consulting firms, military units, R&D organizations.

[d]Biomedical company other than parent or owner

$N_{TOT} = 51$, $N_S = 15$, $N_O = 12$, $N_M = 24$

source, depending on where the firms are located. Over 40 percent of the U.S. firms report initial VCC financing, while the corresponding figure for Swedish firms is only 13 percent.

Start-up financing from venture capital companies should be compared with other types of sources. Next, a comparison with research grants, founder investment, corporate funding, financing by other organizations, and public funding is provided. Note that traditional financial sources, such as bank loans, are not included.

Due to the science-based character of the field, research grants (from government-supported policy units, for instance) were vital for 29 percent of the firm formations (see table 11.1). Again, this figure differs widely between regions, with as many as 63 percent of the Swedish firms having research grants at start-up compared with only one-third of the Ohio firms and only one firm in the Massachusetts sample.[7]

Confirming previous studies on the importance of private investments by the entrepreneurs (see, e.g., Berger and Udell 1998), the founding team provided part of the start-up capital in 27 percent of the cases. Whereas most firms in Ohio rely partly on private savings (75 percent), only 31 percent of the Swedish start-ups do, and this financial source is of minor importance in Massachusetts. It is likely that access to other sources (e.g., VCCs) makes the savings of founders less central.

Organizations such as the military, bridging organizations,[8] R&D organizations, or consulting firms provide initial capital to 24 percent of the firms. These types of sources are by far most influential in Ohio (58 percent), but are also important in Sweden (25 percent). Other biomedical companies than the parent firms are of equal significance in the regions, providing one-fifth of the firms with money for start-up. A firm may also rely on a parent company for financing (22 percent), and the parent firm is often at least a partial owner. The importance of a parent company or owner is particularly pronounced in Sweden, where it provides initial financing to 38 percent of the firms. Finally, neither public offering nor development with customers are common routes of financing at start-up.

This comparison reveals that VCC financing is the single principal source for start-up capital. Even though there seems to be some substitutability between different types of financial sources, and there are substantial regional differences, the role of VCC is clearly imperative for firm formation to come about.

Providing the Initial Technology Base

Many new science-based firms are formed as a response to a specific technological opportunity, be it the possibility of exploring a scientific breakthrough or a new or improved technology to bring to market. Thus, the science and technology that are to form the initial knowledge base of the firm have often been developed by other organizations prior to firm establishment. Indeed, almost all the companies in the population initially sourced their science and technology platform from the developments in an existing organization, either in the form of human capital, intellectual property, or artifacts. Cutting-edge activities in universities and other research institutes, but also in companies, are therefore crucial to firm formation.

Venture capital companies are involved in these early explorative efforts in at least four ways. First, due to the science-based character of biomaterials, universities, medical schools, and hospitals have played a crucial role in the formation of the biomaterials field, and the initial technology emanates from such research groups in 71 percent of the firms. Several venture capital companies invest in such basic science projects at universities, obtaining rights to commercialize scientific results. For example, Senmed Ventures in Ohio invested in Professor Ronald Fournier's work on an artificial liver as well as in other research projects. Indeed, a majority of the venture capitalists interviewed state an interest in investing in new and original technology that may be developed for a range of applications. Such technology may open up opportunities for VCCs to establish several firms from one base of scientific research. Not only does this yield benefits with regard to possibilities of focusing the VCCs' scientific knowledge base, but greater economic returns may also develop. In this way the venture capitalists engage in the very selection of how to direct scientific research into product development. On the commercialization side, venture capital companies often urge each particular young firm to focus on a well-defined application, deselecting other options. Thereby, the VCCs take part in the technology selection process for the firms as well. Given that long-term financing is provided, a focused application strategy is often beneficial for the young firm, concentrating resources and increasing market opportunities. Another effect of such focus is that unused technological opportunities lie open for exploitation by other actors, providing possibilities for additional firm establishments.

Second, venture capital companies are also involved in early explorative efforts through the support of experimental activities in other companies. In one-third of the firms, the initial technological opportunity originates from scientific and technological activities in another company. For example, a significant part of the technology platform of Alkermes Inc. in Massachusetts was acquired from the young VCC-backed firm Enzytech Inc. (Massachusetts).[9] The history of biomaterials-related firms reveals that venture capital companies have often supported such development.

Third, it is clear from the previous discussion that the establishment of new ventures within the field of biomaterials depends on access to previous technological development. VCCs specialize in matching technological opportunities with market opportunities, functioning as a bridge between research and commercialization. For example, the now very successful company Genzyme Inc. was formed by a venture capital group that brought in initial technology on the isolation of enzymes from Professor Henry Blair at Tufts New England Enzyme Center. In the initial phase, before the company had even been officially formed, the founding team also took on board a research-oriented consulting firm formed by a number of professors, BioInformation Associates, to help develop the company's technological plan. The collaboration with Bio-Information Associates lasted for ten years, guiding the company from being a five-employee company to one with 3,500 employees and substantial sales and profit.

Fourth, interestingly enough, for a small part of the American ventures (10 percent of the U.S. firms), the initial technology on which they based their business idea had in fact been developed by the venture capital company that financed the start-up. Thus, the venture capital firm actually held competence enough to be active in technological development. This is presumably due to long experience from similar start-ups and the technological learning that resulted. However, it is important to acknowledge that these cases are exceptions: many VCCs in the United States and Sweden have executives with degrees in management and financing but not a strong scientific or technological background.

After this discussion of the various ways VCCs take part in early explorative technology development efforts, one additional interesting observation can be made. There are indications from the data that the scientific and organizational origins of the biomaterials firms influence not only their initial technological profile but their further choices of applications as well. The analysis of firm formation within biomaterials has shown that before firm establishment, a range of activities takes place and a range of actors is involved. Technology is developed in an experimental fashion, often in cooperation among several R&D organizations and companies. The outcome of science and technology developments is by no means given in advance but unfolds over time, and this unfolding depends on exactly which actors are involved and what information and knowledge they share (see also Shane 1997) and which problems come into focus. In this way, the technological focus of the new firm is a product of whatever activities and actors have been parts of the pre-firm process. The active search for technology by venture capital companies may thus partially establish the direction of future technological choices.

In summary, VCCs help provide the young firms with their initial technology base by engaging in early explorative efforts to develop new science and technology in research organizations as well as in companies. Not infrequently, the VCC guides the technology and application selection process and thereby spurs firm formation through its active search for technology matched by competence in evaluation, technology development, and management. In addition, VCCs may function as bridges between academia and industry, paving the way for new research to be inserted into new or existing industrial applications. In some cases, the VCC executives may even have competence to engage in technological development themselves.

Enhancing the Clustering of Innovations

Innovations and firm formation tend to cluster, both in that scientific and technological breakthroughs often lead to several related innovations and firms that are brought forward, and in that some research centers (within universities or firms) tend to spin out more than one company. One example is the research group of Professors Robert Langer at Massachusetts Institute of Technology and Joseph Vacanti at Harvard Medical School, who started searching in 1983 for ways to grow liver tissue and also worked on a number of other applications (skin, cartilage, bone, urethras, heart valves, tendons, intestines, blood vessels, and breast tissue). The idea was to take isolated cells, let them multiply outside the body, and then place them in a polymer scaffold. Patents were filed in 1987, and the company Neomorphics was established with U.S.$4 million in venture capital financing and was sold at an early stage to Advanced Tissue Science (California), with which the Langer group has retained contact on a consultant basis. To get the most out of the technology, the technology-transfer unit at MIT split up the licenses by applications, and MIT retained the rights to use the technology for specific tissue. Through the initiative of The Parker Medical Group, this technology led to the formation of Reprogenesis Inc., which works on wound treatment and kidney failure among other things. The company Focal was also established on the basis of technology developed in this research group.

Why is it that interrelated clusters of inventions are found in some regions but not in others? The interviews suggest four types of explanations. First, the educational system must ensure continuous development of human capital in a particular field. For example, in Sweden, osseointegration and related technologies have been built on the successful diffusion of competence through the education of Ph.D. students. Second, the existence of tight networks that allow for competence spillovers seems to be influential in creating clusters of inventions. Third, there must be inventive researchers (individuals or teams) who see the commercial potential of their basic research and are able to take the technology from the lab into a company setting. Such competence may be built through a committed university/corporate policy to encourage entrepreneurial efforts, for example, or by role models. Fourth, financial providers with know-how in the specific field are needed. When virtuous circles are created and the four processes are reinforced, innovations and firm formation cluster.

Venture capital companies play a role in this type of clustering process. They do so, first, by encouraging serial entrepreneurship through maintaining close links with research groups, urging technological opportunities to be commercialized; and second, by gaining enough scientific and technological competence to see potential synergies in grouping technological opportunities and to understand how to split the commercialization of a technological platform into several linked applications.

VENTURE CAPITAL COMPANIES AND FIRM DEVELOPMENT

In order both to induce firm growth and to gain access to information on firm development, thereby reducing risks of moral hazard, venture capitalists are often deeply involved in firm activities, even if not on a daily basis (Binks, Ennew, and Reed 1992; Black and Gilson 1998). Levels of VCC involvement are bound to differ—ranging from a laissez-faire approach and monitoring to intense management—depending on a firm's characteristics and development phase, for example, as well as on the preference and competence of the VCC and whether it is a lead or following investor (Dixon 1991; Steier and Greenwood 1995). However, a substantial number of VCCs, especially lead investors, do invest their time heavily into the investee firms (Sahlman 1990; Sapienza and Gupta 1994; Elango et al. 1995; Reid 1996). This section examines the *mechanisms* by which venture capital companies impact the development of young science-based firms. Particular attention is given to their role in resource and knowledge mobilization. A number of mechanisms are discussed: financing and risk sharing, managerial expertise and guidance, creation and diffusion of technology, legitimization, and networking.

Financing and Risk Sharing

Using the broad definition of a capital market, the empirical evidence shows that all the young firms use several different sources of financing during their lifetime, each firm using two to six sources. The most prevalent source of financing was other biomedical companies (used by 67 percent of the firms; see table 11.2). The Massachusetts firms, especially, rely on corporate collaborations when it comes to capital supply, with as many as 78 percent of the young firms having connections to other companies that provide not only technological or market-oriented resources but monetary supply as well. This figure should be compared with 67 percent for the Ohio-based firms and 50 percent for the Swedish firms. In such agreements, the incumbents cooperate with biomaterials firms and pay for most, if not all, R&D costs, or they acquire technology or distribution licenses and bring the products into their own organizations. Either way, development of the specific application is not infrequently completed in cooperation with the partner who will handle distribution. Thus, while corporate partnerships may be regarded as a part of technology and product development and of the marketing process, they may also be categorized as a financial source, in fact, the most common financial source.

Venture capital companies are the second most common source of capital, providing financing to 59 percent of the firms (see table 11.2). It is worth noting

Table 11.2
Financial Sources for Firm Development (Percentage of firms receiving financing from each type of source)[a]

	Firms in Sweden	Firms in Ohio	Firms in Massachusetts	All firms [b]
Biomedical company [c]	50	67	78	**67**
Venture capital company	25	50	87	**59**
Public offering	19	33	48	**35**
Research foundations	25	42	17	**25**
Parent firm or new owner	25	8	13	**16**
Other organization [d]	13	33	4	**14**
Founder	6	8	0	**4**

[a]As the analysis is of the total population of biomaterials firms, located in the three regions, the actual differences are significant in themselves.
[b]Note that the sum of each column exceeds 100% as each firm connects to several sources.
[c]Biomedical company other than parent or owner
[d]Other organizations include technology-transfer units, bridging organizations, consulting firms, military units, R&D organizations.
$N_{TOT} = 51, N_S = 15, N_O = 12, N_M = 24$

that as many as 87 percent of the Massachusetts-based firms acquire VCC financing, while the corresponding figure is 50 percent in Ohio and only 25 percent in Sweden.

Another financial source for firm development is public offerings (35 percent), a route most often taken by firms in Massachusetts (48 percent) and Ohio (33 percent) and more seldom in Sweden (19 percent). Engaging in long-term science-based product development, one-fourth of the firms retain their link to research foundations, especially so in Ohio (42 percent), as compared with Sweden (25 percent) and Massachusetts (17 percent). Parent companies or new owners provide financing to 16 percent of the firms. Their importance is particularly pronounced in Sweden, where they not only provide initial financing but are also long-term financiers to one- fourth of the firms, as compared to 13 percent in Massachusetts and to only one firm in Ohio. Finally, other organizations such as the military, bridging organizations, R&D organizations, or consulting firms provide capital to 14 percent of the companies studied, while founder investment is of minimal importance (4 percent).

Thus, regarding the structure of the capital markets for young biomaterials companies, it is clear that the firms acquire financing from *many different types of sources.* It is also clear that the type of sources *differs between the locations* as well as *over time.* Some observations may be pointed out from this comparison.

First, a capital market needs to be defined very broadly and to include not only such traditional actors as banks and financial organizations but also actors such as related companies, early customers, and bridging organizations. A diversified, competent, and patient capital market able to provide financing in all stages of firm development is crucial. For example, most firms source a considerable part of their financing from other companies, either from other biomedical companies or from their parents. This is interesting because many studies on financing patterns of young firms use the traditional definition of a capital market, which includes only financial organizations. This chapter argues that, at least in the case of science-based industries, in order to fully understand the role of financing for firm establishment and development it is more revealing to include all forms of organizations providing financing to the firm.[10]

Second, the fact that venture capital companies in a global market choose to invest in a particular firm may be seen as an indication of high firm potential with regard to technology and product development as well as with regard to market outcome. Likewise, corporate partnerships may signal success in product development. Thus, the higher figures of VCC investments and corporate partnerships involving financing and public offerings in the Massachusetts-based firms could be an indication of higher potential or performance on the firm level. Such signals of high potential or high performance may be sent to other investors and partners, creating virtuous circles. Indeed, venture capital backing does signal firm value, and partly because of this their IPOs are often priced higher (Megginson and Weiss 1991; Brav and Gompers 1997). On the other hand, the access to financing in Massachusetts may be an indication of a more well functioning capital market in Massachusetts, meaning not only that money is available, but that the exact capital sources needed by the firms are available at the right cost, that control is appropriately divided, and that the needed competencies are being brought into the firm (Storey 1994).

Third, it is clear that VCC financing is extremely essential to the development of these young science-based firms. Indeed, it is the second most prevalent form of financial input analyzed in the study. The venture capital company functioning as the lead investor also has a key role in helping the firm create a stable group of investors and obtain additional financing (Sahlman and Gorman 1989; Fredriksen 1997).

Fourth, one trait that cannot be stressed enough in the type of long-term development processes analyzed here is *patient financing,* meaning that not only are the amount and timing key, but so is long-term commitment from financiers. What financial assets do is absorb risk and buy learning time. For example, cautiousness on the part of regulatory bodies forces the companies to have enough financial backing to be able to wait for approval. Therefore, if the firm is expecting to be able to engage in development projects that do not give a return on investment for quite some time, it is essential for that firm to have relatively large capital resources. The firm Alkermes Inc. (Massachusetts) is one example; this company received more than U.S.$90 million in funding from VCCs and corporate deals before any product was on the market. Today, it is clearly seen that this has contributed to Alkermes' success. There are also counterexamples of firms in which the financiers misjudged the time frame of the investment and therefore backed out, leaving the young firm in a predicament.

Finally, the majority of the firms analyzed do not seem to choose the route of sticking mainly to internal financial sources, which thereby risks slowed growth, in order to retain full control over business operations (Myers 1984; Bhide 1992; Winborg and Landström 1997). Rather, the entrepreneurs are directed toward growth strategies involving financial alternatives that distribute ownership and control to actors other than the founding team.

Managerial Expertise and Guidance

Even though the science-based firms analyzed in this study are knowledge intensive, this does not imply that they do not face the traditional disadvantages of small firms, for example, lack of managerial competence. Consequently, the financier needs to have a competence that goes beyond the selection of firms, the evaluation of investment objects, and risk assessment (Eliasson 1996, 1997). Financiers also have to be able to provide a set of managerial resources to the young firm. A capital market that provides such resources can be described as a competent capital market.

The majority of the biomaterials firms financed by venture capital state that executives in the VCC take an active part in strategic management; in Sweden 81 percent, in Ohio 72 percent, and in Massachusetts 100 percent of the firms say so. Interviews reveal that through their economic and management expertise VCCs may guide the firm's strategic and operational choices through a number of means. One way is for the VCCs to be highly active in recruiting new management. Sometimes even one of the investors at the VCC will step in as a temporary manager engaging in day-to-day operations. A second mode is for VCCs to get involved in the board of directors, both by joining in themselves and by appointing new external members to the board. Third, managerial involvement also concerns how to organize the firm activities and structure routines, adding a layer of bureaucracy, for better or worse, to the entrepreneurial firm. It is important to note that VCC financiers may also function as *incubators*, providing not only facilities and equipment but also administrative support. This has been the case for several regionally financed firms in Massachusetts, and some in Ohio, but not in Sweden. The VCCs are, thus, highly influential in setting the firms' strategic and operational path.

To understand the relative importance of VCCs in firm management, these figures need to be related to how many firms actually are financed by VCCs as well as to the importance of other sources of management. First, it is clear that more than half the population (53 percent) relies in part on VCC management. Its importance varies between the three regions, however, with 25 percent of the biomaterials firms in Sweden getting management support, compared to 42 percent in Ohio and 78 percent in Massachusetts. Second, almost half the firms (47 percent) stated that managerial guidance from other biomedical companies was of great consequence. This is especially true in Sweden and Massachusetts (44 percent versus 57 percent, respectively), while the Ohio-based firms benefit less from firm cooperation in this respect (33 percent). The conclusion is that with regard to the entire population, VCC and corporate management are equally important, but there are substantial group differences. At this point there can be only speculation as to whether the differences between the three groups of firms are due to variations in supply in the three regions or due to variations in firm characteristics and potential for growth.

The VCCs often see their connections to a range of experienced managers, along with their other ways of aiding strategic management, as one of their more central types of inputs to the investee firm. On the part of the young firms, the managerial support is welcomed by some and seen as an opportunity not only for growth but also for a scientifically oriented founding team to stay focused on its core competencies. However, the issue of VCC-induced management shifts is by no means a simple one. For instance, in the cases where the analyzed biomaterials firms have split into two separate companies at an early stage, it is not infrequently because the initial founding team either was unhappy with how this firm was developing or wanted to focus on another application. Indeed, it is true in two-thirds of the cases in the study that the founder sold or left the earlier firm and started a new company, bringing technological assets along.[11] Therefore, unless the VCC possesses the necessary range of competencies in scientific opportunities, product development, and market preferences, the founding team of a science-based firm may feel that the managerial guidance provided by the VCC is of less value. Indeed, this was the case in several of the firms interviewed. Given the inherent uncertainty about technological and market outcome, it is not always clear to what extent the VCC guidance was more correct in assessing the most prosperous path of development in those cases where it conflicted with the view of the founders. The empirical material indicates that when a VCC invests in a science-based firm, it may be critical that the founding team stay within or in close contact with the firm management for an extended period of time.

While the competence base of many VC investors has traditionally been in the areas of finance and management, an increasing number of VCCs have, as was shown earlier, accentuated scientific, technological, and industrial competence. Advice based on this type of specialized competence is highly valued by the firms, as the strategic guidance may be more tuned to the company's specific needs (Fredriksen 1997). In particular, this specialized competence may be primary when the technology or industry is immature and in early phases of firm development (Bonaldo 2001).

Creation and Diffusion of Technology

Innovation processes of new firms include choice of technological approach, development of one or several platform technologies, the whole process of product and process development and testing, and marketing and distribution. The firm often reaches outside its own organizational borders in these innovative activities to acquire technology or to cooperate. Indeed, many firms source technological opportunities from, for example, research organizations (universities, hospitals, and so forth), partner companies, customers, or other organizations. As will be seen, venture capital companies also have a function in the process of creation and diffusion of technology.

The biomaterials firms thus have a number of sources of technology-related resources. First, in all three locations, cooperation with research organizations turns out to be an essential source of technological ideas (to 71 percent of the firms) and technological intellectual property or artifacts (69 percent), for outsourcing of clinical trials (84 percent), and for the supply of material and equipment (25 percent). Second, the development of a product such as an implant or a drug delivery system requires profound interaction with the users,[12] and 61 percent of the firms consider that discussions with customers provide specific technological ideas that are useful for technology and product development. Third, it is evident as well that other companies influence technological development through ideas (55 percent); technological IP or artifacts (69 percent); the provision of material, parts, complementary products, or equipment (57 percent); and to some extent, clinical trials (10 percent). Fourth, other organizations or groups of individuals that may matter to the innovation process are scientific boards, military organizations, and bridging organizations.

Finally, it may be surprising in this context that venture capital companies may help the young firm in its invention processes, either by taking an active part in technology creation or by diffusing technology from other actors in their networks. Interestingly enough, in the United States, venture capital companies have provided technological ideas (17 percent and 13 percent in Ohio and Massachusetts, respectively) and IP or artifacts (8 percent and 9 percent in Ohio and Massachusetts, respectively; see table 11.3). VCC partners have been also helpful to the U.S. firms with respect to the provision of material, components, or equipment. No venture capitalists have provided Swedish firms with these types of functions.

The data just presented allows for a number of conclusions. It was clear that a variety of sources for technology supply are available and used by the young firms. Because a company often does not know in advance what it will need, it is essential to open up a rather wide range of "technological channels," in other words, networks to possible state-of-the-art partners. Venture capitalists may, in fact, be one of these types of partners. Also, although the degree of "scientification" of technological change varies among different technological fields, the process of this change is undergoing a significant shift from engineering-based to science-based (Grupp 1994). Therefore, capabilities in basic and applied

Table 11.3
Technologically Related Resources Provided by Venture Capital Companies

	Technological ideas	Technological intellectual property and/or artifacts	Material, component or equipment
Firms in Sweden	0	0	0
Firms in Ohio	17	8	17
Firms in Massachusetts	13	9	9
All firms	**10**	**6**	**8**

[a]As the analysis is of the total population of biomaterials firms, located in the three regions, the actual differences
 are significant in themselves.
$N_{TOT} = 51, N_S = 15, N_O = 12, N_M = 24$

science are of increasing importance to firms. This suggests that the role of
universities (technical and natural science) may be taking on a more central
function in the innovation process. In addition, it suggests that the venture
capitalists need to master scientific and technological skills in order to select
ventures for investment, to guide and manage the firms, and to provide technological advice and development. Indeed, although some studies have indicated that in order to reduce risk VCCs need a diversification strategy when it
comes to technological fields and industries in which to invest (Norton and
Tenenbaum 1995), the present study indicates that a specialization strategy
would increase the possibilities of guiding the portfolio firm to success (see
also Ruhnka and Young 1992). Thus, specialization of investment span would
decrease risk for the VCC. As demonstrated, some VCCs have already attained
a level of technological knowledge that allows them to *contribute to the technology creation process* in the science-based firms.

   Another mechanism by which VCCs take part in technology and product
development is by facilitating diffusion of scientific and technological opportunities, created within research organizations or other firms, into young companies. Traditionally, the diffusion from universities and hospitals can be
facilitated by university-based or other types of technology-transfer units. For
example, the technology licensing office at MIT has been highly influential in
bringing technological solutions to the market. Likewise, bridging organizations like the Edison Biotechnology Center in Cleveland, Ohio, have taken on
a similar role. However, in spite of the efforts by technology-transfer units and
bridging organizations, many of the biomaterials firms interviewed, especially
in Sweden and Ohio, state that they have lacked support in the start-up process.
Indeed, the university aid may be restricted due to limited resources as well as
lack of experience in skills like networking, negotiating, and contract writing.
It is in this context that VCCs are vital through *facilitating* the science and
technology diffusion. This issue has already been discussed in relation to firm
formation (see section 3), and it is as true for further firm development. Some
of the venture capital companies have had enough competence to seek out

interesting scientific and technological opportunities, both at universities and in other firms, and feed them into the young firm.

Legitimization

For a certain technological path to develop, it needs to be legitimized (Lundgren 1994). Acceptance takes time, and many companies have encountered a great deal of skepticism when they have tried to do something technologically new. The case of osseointegration is an example of a new technology that was hindered by lack of legitimization. Indeed, first academia, then regulatory authorities, and later customers showed skepticism toward the new technology, and only through strategic action—in this case persistent education of customers—was legitimization achieved with time. Technology and product development are evaluated in an iterative process between the firm, corporate partners, the financial organizations (such as VCCs), regulatory agencies, and eventually, the public market. The legitimization of technology is a social and political process in the sense that it is not necessarily the technology with the best fit to a certain application problem that is chosen. By investing in a young firm that is working with a certain technology, the venture capital companies may function as a warrant for the high potential of the technology.

Moreover, the young firm itself needs to be legitimized in order to obtain financing, collaborations, and regulatory approval. Working with a technology that is seen as legitimate may in itself be positive for building valuable relations and may facilitate the financing process. A venture capital company is also part of this process of firm legitimization as well. First, it may help to legitimize a firm in relation to other financiers. Second, in the effort to obtain corporate collaborations the VCC can have a legitimizing effect. Such corporate agreements in turn give legitimacy in the capital market as well as in the technology and product market (see also Mønsted 1998). Indeed, to provide a new venture with second- or third-round financing, the financial market often needs the assurance of an established company investing in the new firm through a distribution license or R&D cooperation. Thus, by partnering with a firm, a related company provides legitimacy for the technology and market potential. Third, the companies within the biomaterials field struggle with a lengthy period of technology and product development in tandem with a period of clinical trials before regulatory approval is granted. An understanding of regulations is therefore crucial, as is the actual contact with regulatory authorities.

As proven in the case of biomaterials, venture capital companies can provide credibility in contacts with regulatory agencies. Interestingly, regulations may be either an inducing or an obstructing factor in the *technology* legitimization process. For example, with Swedish regulatory approval of dental implants based on osseointegration came the legitimization of the technology in academia as well as among users. However, in the U.S. market, the situation was the reverse, with regulatory caution causing a halt in the process of legitimization and thereby in diffusion. In a situation like this, the potential influence of the VCC may be even more pronounced.

Networking

Another major mechanism of influence by a VCC is building and enhancing the firm's *networks*. The empirical data shows that VCCs have provided two-thirds (66 percent) of the interviewed biomaterials companies with extended networks. Interestingly, in Sweden all VC-backed firms are provided with extended networks, while this is not the case for the American firms, where the figures are 59 percent versus 62 percent for firms in Ohio and Massachusetts, respectively.

These figures may be compared with the influence of biomedical companies and university researchers in augmenting a firm's network. Slightly less than half of the biomaterials firms (47 percent) state that other biomedical companies have been influential in this respect. Even though parent firms and owners are of great consequence to young firms, it is not only, and perhaps not primarily, these companies that help with management and networks. Instead, the firms link up with other biomedical companies in collaborative agreements, and are managed by and gain access to a larger network in the process. University researchers, too, share their networks with the new ventures. Indeed, more than half the population indicates that they have gained access to new contacts to add to their network through cooperation with university researchers. This finding is especially true for firms in Sweden and Massachusetts.

The considerable importance of VCCs in network building has three explanations. First, it seems as though the origin of the firms matters a great deal, not only for the technological profile (as discussed in section 3) but for network formation as well. The networks that are formed in early pre-firm activities seem to retain their influence in the young firm. Indeed, it is not always the problem in focus that directs what partner the firm should seek to cooperate with. Rather, the exact choice of network formation is highly path-dependent, because it is a function of the previous relationships of the company as well as key individuals. In interviews, it was stressed again and again that relationships are established between individuals, not between organizations. With personal relationships being this imperative, the early networks of the key individuals in firms have proved to be influential for a firm's network embeddedness. Such relations direct the path of development early on, but they may also continue to influence the firm's later development. It may be said that the firm follows a "relational pathway" strategy of networking. Through each relationship, a firm is enclosed in a "new" network: that of its partner. The possibility of utilizing this new network is often essential and is a major benefit of the relationship. In this way, one relationship leads to another, building a web of relations. As the network expands, more actors are included, and each of these actors may provide the young firm with resources and facilitate the development process. Given that VCCs are highly significant in the firms' early phases, they are also essential for network creation.

A second explanation for the considerable importance of VCCs in network building rests with the fact that corporate deals not infrequently come about with the active participation of a venture capital firm. The financier may function as a node in the network. The VCC network can also prove valuable in identifying potential firm acquisitions or even acquirers (see, e.g., Bygrave and Timmons 1992). For example, the venture capital financier of Polymedica Inc. not only provided capital and management but also pointed the way to the firm Matrix Medica, which was subsequently acquired.

A third way in which VCCs influence network building is that they not only provide insight into customer needs, as discussed earlier, but also connect the firm with customers through their wide networks.

THE SPATIAL DIMENSION

This section is concerned with whether spatial proximity of venture capital companies is of importance to young science-based firms. From the previous analysis it is obvious that connection to a competent VCC financier may be highly beneficial for a young science-based firm. However, nothing has been said so far about the *location* of the financiers themselves. Therefore, this section looks at where the financiers are located and whether their location matters.

For a further analysis of where the financiers are located, they have been classified into location in close proximity, as opposed to location within the same "common market" (EU versus United States) or a more distant location, outside the "common market." Accordingly, table 11.4 gives the percentage of biomaterials firms interviewed that have financiers located (a) within the region (i.e., Sweden, Ohio, or Massachusetts, respectively), (b) within EU (for Swedish firms) versus within the United States (for firms in Ohio or Massachusetts) or (c) outside EU versus United States. The pattern that emerged for location of VCC financiers is that 41 percent of the biomaterials firms have received regional VCC money, 20 percent from a VCC within the EU versus U.S. market, and only 8 percent from a VCC located outside the EU versus U.S. market (see table 11.4).[13] All in all, the data shows that for this group of firms it is much more common to acquire financing from regional VCC partners. Interestingly, this patterns holds regardless of the type of financier, that is, whether the financier is a parent or owner, another biomedical company, a venture capital company, another organization, or a customer. It is also true with regard to both financial means for start-up (first year of activities) and financial means for further firm development. The only exception is development financing from a biomedical company. Thus, almost regardless of phase of financing or

Table 11.4

Location of the Firms' Financiers Providing Startup Financing Versus Development Financing (Percentage of biomaterials firms receiving financing from partners at each type of location)[a]

Type of financier	Phase	Location Regional	Within EU / US [b]	Outside EU / US [c]
Parent or Owner	Startup	22	0	0
	Development	12	4	0
Biomedical company [d]	Startup	18	4	0
	Development	37	39	22
Venture Capital Company	Startup	33	2	2
	Development	41	20	8
Other organizations [e]	Startup	22	2	0
	Development	12	6	0
Customer	Startup	4	2	0
	Development	4	6	4

[a]As the analysis is of the total population of biomaterials firms, located in the three regions, the actual differences are significant in themselves.

[b]In EU for Swedish firms versus in US for firms in Ohio or Massachusetts.

[c]Outside EU for Swedish firms versus outside US for firms in Ohio or Massachusetts.

[d]Biomedical company other than parent or owner.

[e]Other organizations include technology-transfer units, bridging organizations, consulting firms, military units, R&D organizations.

$N_{TOT} = 51, N_S = 15, N_O = 12, N_M = 24$

type of financier, the young science-based firms in this study more often *choose a regional partner.*

There are, however, some variations in these patterns of regional financing between the three groups of firms. Table 11.5 displays the location of VCC financiers for biomaterials firms in Sweden, Ohio, and Massachusetts, respectively. It is clear that the firms in Ohio and Massachusetts often source financing from VCCs located within their own region, but they also source money from VCCs located in other U.S. states. Swedish firms do not have this sourcing pattern within the EU. Instead, Swedish firms almost exclusively source money from Swedish VCCs.

The regional patterns of financing displayed in table 11.4 leave the question of why it is that geographically proximate agreements are so common. It can be concluded that connections to VCCs in close proximity have historically been of considerable importance for this population of firms—but why is it so?

One answer is that there is clearly a strong *path dependence* in connections. Firms have a certain degree of inertia toward stepping onto a new path of relationships and often build on earlier networks (David 1985, 1988, 1993).

Table 11.5
Location of the Firms' VCC Financiers (Percentage of biomaterials firms receiving financing from partners at each type of location)[a]

	At startup	For growth
Percentage of Swedish firms financed by VCC located		
within Sweden	13	25
within EU	0	0
outside EU	0	6
Percentage of Ohio firms financed by VCC located		
within Ohio	42	17
within US	8	42
outside US	0	8
Percentage of Massachusetts firms financed by VCC located		
within Massachusetts	43	65
within US	9	30
outside US	9	9
Percentage of all firms financed by VCC located		
within its own region	33	41
within EU versus US [b]	2	20
outside EU versus US [c]	2	8

[a]As the analysis is of the total population of biomaterials firms, located in the three regions, the actual differences are significant in themselves.
[b]In EU for Swedish firms versus in US for firms in Ohio or Massachusetts.
[c]Outside EU for Swedish firms versus outside US for firms in Ohio or Massachusetts.
$N_{TOT} = 51$, $N_S = 15$, $N_O = 12$, $N_M = 24$

Because most of the companies analyzed spring from a regional context (see section 3), the regional connections are strong. Thus, the regional dimension is retained and reinforced in the firms' patterns of financing.

Another, partly different, answer is that regional connections are *preferred* by the biomaterials firms. As stated in interviews, such preference can, for example, be due to ease of communication, cultural similarities, and so forth. The VCCs too may *prefer* investments in close proximity. Indeed, interviews with venture capital companies indicate that this is the case. Venture capital managers often feel that in order to be able to properly guide and manage a young firm, it should not be located more than a one- to two-hour drive away.

A third explanation lies in confinement of *search space*. Such geographical restrictions can either be imposed by the young firm or by the venture capitalist. First, the biomaterials firm may have *perceived* the financial market as geographically delimited. For example, the Swedish firms that were analyzed seem not to have viewed the European VC market as their home market for capital but instead felt restricted to the Swedish VCC market. This indicates a spatially confined search space on the part of the young Swedish firms. It is worth noting that the variations between Swedish and American biomaterials firms, as displayed in table 11.5, indicate that the American firms *perceive* the VC market as national rather than delimited by state. Naturally, the U.S. venture capital market benefits from having the same language, culture, and much of the same regulatory system. Thus, even though there are indeed large differences between the setup of VC markets in different states within the United States, the American science-based firms that were analyzed search for capital in a larger geographical arena than do their Swedish counterparts. Second, the VCCs too may have a confined search space, resulting in geographically skewed financing patterns. Capital is attracted to regions that contain plenty of technological and commercial opportunities and many start-up firms. Indeed, this is where VCCs prefer to locate. Accordingly, a venture capital company located in such a region perhaps does not feel the need to search outside the region for investments. This results in financial connections of high spatially proximity.

Notably, as visible in tables 11.4 and 11.5, not all financial connections are within close spatial proximity. On the contrary, many of the American biomaterials companies receive monetary means for growth from VCCs in U.S. states other than their own. This is true for 42 percent of the Ohio firms and 30 percent of the firms in Massachusetts. This may be because VCCs that are located outside high-opportunity regions like Massachusetts direct some of their investments to these regions.[14] The Swedish firms, however, do not attract capital from such an enlarged region, that is, the EU. Even so, the overall picture is that patterns of financial connections are spatially skewed. The concluding section will outline some policy implications of this finding.

CONCLUDING DISCUSSION

This final section discusses the main conclusions. After a brief summary, two topics will be touched upon: (a) how management of young science-based firms should view partnerships with venture capital companies, and (b) how to enhance the functionality of the capital market for entrepreneurial firms.

Summarizing the Findings

The analysis in this chapter has revealed that venture capital companies play a vital role for both firm formation and firm development and growth. Three issues have been examined: (a) the role of VCCs in firm establishment, (b) their influence on the firms' development paths, and (c) the possible relevance of spatial proximity.

In exploring to what extent and in what way venture capital companies were involved in the very formation process of the new firms, this chapter discussed start-up financing, the provision of the initial technology base, and the clustering of innovations. It was clear that financing from VCCs is a very substantial source of start-up capital. In addition to spurring firm formation through financial means, the support for science and technology exploration in research organizations and companies forms the basis for the young firms' technological base. More directly, some VCCs even actively develop parts of a young firm's technological foundation. Venture capital companies also enhance the clustering of inventions and firms by encouraging serial entrepreneurship and by grouping technological opportunities and linking applications.

In the analysis of if and how VCCs influence the firms' development paths, a number of mechanisms were discussed: financing and risk sharing, managerial expertise and guidance, creation and diffusion of technology, legitimization, and networking. With regard to financing, it is clear that the firms acquire money from many different types of sources, pointing to the need to define the capital market broadly. Venture capital companies were found to be the second most prevalent form of financial input. The biomaterials firms did not shy away from external financing from fear of losing management control but inclined toward VCC financing. Venture capital companies are especially vital because of their ability to act as patient financiers, to absorb risk, and to buy learning time for the young firms. The VCCs may also, through their investment decision, take part in creating virtuous circles, spurring further financing, corporate partnerships, and higher pricing of IPOs.

Most of the firms backed by venture capital have been provided with managerial expertise and guidance through a newly recruited management team, active participation in the board of directors, and advice on organizing of routines and processes. The interviews made it clear that VCC-induced management shifts may be highly valued and indeed a route to success, but only if the VCC contained the necessary scientific, technological, and market competencies. It is often important to keep the linkages to the initial founding team as the bearer of visions for technology as well as market development.

Perhaps surprisingly, VCCs take part in the biomaterials firms' processes of technology and product development. Indeed, a few American VCCs have provided technological ideas as well as intellectual property and material, components, or equipment to their investee firms. Venture capital companies may also facilitate science and technology diffusion from research organizations and other firms. It is becoming increasingly critical for venture capitalists to have such scientific and technological skills if they are to form a competent capital market. This study suggests that one fruitful route to acquiring and maintaining such competencies is for the VCCs to adopt specialization strategies in the selection of technological areas in which to invest.

In the intricate process of legitimizing technology, product development, and new firms, the actions of a VCC partner may be crucial. The VCC, by its investment decision, may be seen as a warrant of the high potential of the technology. In addition, a VCC partnership gives credibility to the young firm in the face of other financiers, potential corporate partners, and regulatory authorities.

A majority of the biomaterials firms state that the VCC is influential in building and enhancing the firm's network. This is due to the fact that VCC activity in the firms' early phases sketch the future networks that will be formed, but it is due as well to their influence in spurring corporate deals and connecting the firm with customers.

With regard to the spatial dimension, the analysis revealed that the patterns of VCC financing are spatially skewed in favor of geographically close connections. This is especially true in Sweden, whereas several of the American biomaterials companies have been financed by VCCs in U.S. states other than their own. However, regardless of where the young firms are located, connections with more remote VCCs—that is, outside the EU or the United States—are scarce. A number of reasons for the importance of geographical proximity were highlighted: a strong path dependence on how connections are selected and formed, the preference of the biomaterials firms or the VCC respectively, or a confined search space.

Conclusions for Management

This analysis leads to some conclusions in this section on how management could view partnerships with venture capital companies. As venture capital companies seem to play such a vital role for both firm formation and firm development and growth, it is naturally important that management have a clear understanding of such influences so that it will be able to make appropriate choices.

One of the first issues for a managerial team is what financial sources to choose. While this study confirms earlier findings that venture capital companies are often a common and crucial source for start-up capital, it is not self-evident that the founding team should turn to a VCC in the process of firm formation. Instead, the potential benefits often need to be weighed against the possible risk of losing control of both the path of firm development and revenues. Less demanding financial sources may mean that the founding team can retain control over business operations but may also involve the risk of slowing down growth. Even though this chapter has not discussed whether the VCC-backed firms perform differently from the firms without VCC backing, evidence indicates that important knowledge and other resources may be introduced into the young firm from its VCC partners. However, this knowledge transfer is not always available; it is to a large degree a function of the experience and competence of the particular VCC team. Thus, because there is a broad variety of potential financial sources in the start-up phase, the firm needs to evaluate these sources and assess the degree to which a particular VCC may provide not only start-up financing but also assistance in the formation of the initial technology base. For later financial choices, the firm should assess the VCC's ability to provide managerial guidance, technological expertise, and competence as well as networks to customers, partners, and financiers. This is not an easy assessment, of course, but because the choice of financial partner may prove crucial, its importance is high.

With regard to scientific and technological guidance by the VCC partner, this analysis has highlighted a number of important mechanisms. As was pointed out earlier, with the increased scientification of technological change, venture capital companies may be expected to focus their attention on selected fields in order to master necessary scientific and technological competence. In situations of uncertainty regarding technology and applications, such specialized competence may be of particular value. A firm that has teamed up with a technologically competent financier may think of the VCC partner as an important link in the process of building the firm's technological competence base. The main contribution of VCCs is often found in networking activities, where they may feed scientific and technological opportunities, created within research organizations or other firms, into the company, or they may link the firm to customers crucial for product development. In special instances, the VCCs themselves may even contribute to the technology and product creation.

It is important for management to recognize that a not unusual trap for a VCC seems to be to disconnect too early in the firm's development from the scientific origin of the firm.[15] For example, a VCC may impose a very different path of technology or product development than the one indicated by the founding team or by scientific advisories. Although the new path has sometimes been a correct choice, it may also be an effect of too weak a scientific and technological competence base on the part of the VCC. This study indicates that by keeping close links to the scientific origin (be it through the founding team, the university from which technology is licensed, or by other channels), the scientific and commercial aspects of innovation may be balanced.

The VCC's role as a node in the network cannot be stressed enough. A range of resources such as management, connections to customers, corporate deals, identification of partners, and further financing are mobilized through VCC partners. In such networking processes, the key is legitimization, both of the technology and of the firm. In this, the VCC partner plays a crucial role, for example, in arranging further financing from other venture capitalists or business angels, in obtaining corporate collaborations, and in setting up other forms of partnerships. It is imperative that a firm assess the magnitude and character of the VCC network before entering into a relationship with a venture capital company.

Managers must also pay attention to the issue of search space. This study demonstrated that financial sources in close proximity are selected more often than distant ones. Even though there are often sound reasons for these patterns—a virtuous path dependence or sheer preference—there is also the risk of being locked in by a confined search space. This has been the case, for example, in a number of instances in the study, where lack of regional VCC financing (either in terms of volume, type of investment area, or investment phase) has stopped promising innovations or slowed firm growth. In these cases, an enlarged geographical search space may have been the solution.

In conclusion, this chapter has pointed out a set of mechanisms by which a venture capital company may influence the development path of a young science-based firm. In order to be able to select the most appropriate VCC partner and to benefit fully from the relationship, it is crucial that the management team is well aware of these mechanisms. The mechanisms should not be seen as givens, but they are formed in the intertwining connection between the firm and the VCC.

Policy Recommendations

The aim of this final section is to briefly point out how to enhance the VC market for young science-based firms. This analysis has displayed two types of problems regarding financing of biomaterials firms. One problem is that there is relatively less diversity in the capital markets in Sweden and Ohio in terms of types of actors (companies, venture capital firms, business angels, and so forth) who provide financing to biomaterials firms. Another problem is that, especially in the Swedish capital market, there is a lack of actors who have the competence not only to evaluate the potential of the technological opportunity and the founding team but also to provide the firm with scarce competencies, guidance, and understanding. For the Swedish biomaterials firms especially, the venture capital industry has displayed a low functionality.

Access to a competent VC industry can be created by at least two different, and complementary, routes. The first, and perhaps swiftest, would be to link young science-based firms to regions where the competent capital may be found. The biomaterials firms should be encouraged to form close links with VCCs in other locations. The spatially delimited networks need to be broadened; firms should go more often to where the money is. Regional policy could in this context facilitate connectivity to the international capital market. It is acknowledged that in this case study, because of cultural barriers, it may be easier for entrepreneurs in Ohio to gain access to financiers located in more vibrant regions within the United States than it would be for Swedish firms to do the equivalent. This situation may change with a more integrated European market.

The second route is to strengthen the regional/national venture capital industries. This point is central, because the financial search process has been found to be often somewhat spatially delimited on the part of the young firm and because venture capitalists prefer proximity to their objects of investment. Such a structural change may bring with it more than money; additional resources and functions may follow. For example, venture capital companies may support firm development by incubation; by providing management, market knowledge, and networks; and by diffusion of technologies and products. With time, the learning process may even involve support in technology creation.

The creation of a regional VC industry can be accomplished by attracting extra-regional actors to locate in the region. Money goes where the opportunities are, but only if the region is reasonably attractive in other dimensions as well (university and company partners, entrepreneurship culture, and so forth). Venture capital companies may hesitate to locate in a region with less visible entrepreneurs and fewer incumbents. Each potential investment object competes with good projects in other regions, and in this choice the determining factor may very well be the characteristics of the regional milieu. A regional venture capital industry can also be created by encouraging new actors to establish and by encouraging current financial organizations to redirect their activities.

In Sweden, policy measures have been taken during the last few years to enhance the function of the capital market, for instance through changes in laws for taxation. The exit possibilities have increased with the development of the stock market. In addition, strong technological development in Sweden, especially in the area of information and communication technology, has attracted foreign VCCs as well as spurred the establishment of new actors. These processes are now jointly bearing fruit with a growing number of venture capital companies, business angels, and corporate venturing initiatives. Already, the stock of venture capital actors, nationally based as well as foreign, has been increased considerably in Sweden, and a recent study identifies as many as ninety-six actors (Karaomerlioglu and Jacobsson 2000). However, the industry has not yet matured, and it remains to be seen how many of these actors will provide only risk capital, and how many will also provide competence.

NOTES

1. Note that with regard to questions on the firms' financing processes, the capital market was not predefined; rather, the questions probed at how and by which sources each step of the technology, product, and market development was financed.

2. Annual reports, press releases, product information, shareholders' reports, IPO documentation, patents and publications, licensing agreements, and so on.

3. A *directory* provided by Recombinant Capital Inc., containing all American biotechnology firms' formal alliances, gave us the possibility to verify and sometimes complement the data on networking for biotech-related firms in this population.

4. In small companies, one face-to-face interview with the present manager, supplemented with secondary company information and sometimes additional telephone conversation, was judged sufficient, while further interviews (with present or former company officials) were needed in the larger companies. For companies not active today, we interviewed the founder as well as the previous manager.

5. Regardless if they were part of the firm or were from a research organization or another company. These researchers have often been very involved in the firm development, be it as the inceptor and holder of the vision, as a scientific advisor, or as a chief scientist or manager within the firm.

6. Note, though, that the geographical location of the entire set of VCCs that have financed each young firm may be more dispersed (see section 5).

7. This is particularly interesting because although Massachusetts is the U.S. state that is receiving by far the most health-related federal R&D funding (COSEPUP 1998), in the field of biomaterials, start-up grants are more prevalent in Sweden and Ohio.

8. Bridging organizations refer to organizations created to link actors to each other, for example, that link university research to industry, or entrepreneurs to larger firms. These organizations can be created by policy measures (e.g., Edison Biotechnology Center in Ohio) or as private initiatives (e.g., Massachusetts Technology Collaboration).

9. Note that the science, technology, and product development process is by no means linear.

10. Indeed, in hindsight this study would have benefited from including also, for example, bank loans and sales.

11. This multiplying process of new firms can be seen as a feature of strength, given that we view experimentation and increased diversity as advantageous for regional and national development. Note, though, that for this population we know little so far about the positive or negative effects at the firm level. That is, it remains to be seen whether splitting into two companies is good for firm performance.

12. That is, surgeons and other physicians as well as patients.

13. As was stated earlier, 59 percent of the biomaterials firms have received development financing from a venture capital company (see section 4). Each firm may have acquired finance from several different VCCs located in different places.

14. To overcome the managerial difficulties of guiding a firm in spite of a geographical distance, either the young firm with time moves closer to the lead investor or the VCC locates a manager within proximity of the young firm.

15. This should not be confused with the often necessary need to more tightly focus the firm's mission and operations. Managerial guidance by a VCC has often proved crucial in this respect.

REFERENCES

Berger, A. N., and G. F. Udell. 1998. "The Economics of Small Business Finance: The Roles of Private Equity and Debt Markets in the Financial Growth Cycle." *The Journal of Banking and Finance* 22: 613–73.

Bhide, D. 1992. "Bootstrap Financing: The Art of Start-Up." *Harvard Business Review,* November–December, pp. 109–17.

Binks, M. R., and C. T. Ennew. 1996. "Growing Firms and the Credit Constraint." *Small Business Economics* 8: 17–25.

Binks, M. R., C. T. Ennew, and G. V. Reed. 1992. "Information Asymmetries and the Provision of Finance to Small Firms." *International Small Business Journal* 11 (1): 35–47.

Black, S. B., and R. J. Gilson. 1998. "Venture Capital and the Structure of Capital Markets: Banks versus Stock Markets." *Journal of Financial Economics* 47 (3): 243–77.

Bonaldo, M. 2001. *A Cross Sectional Study of Investment Activity in the Italian Venture Capital Industry.* Gothenburg: Department of Industrial Dynamics, Chalmers University of Technology.

Brav, A., and P. Gompers. 1997. "Myth or Reality? Long-run Underperfomance of Initial Public Offering: Evidence from Venture Capital and Non-Venture Capital Backed IPOs." *Journal of Finance* 52: 1791–1821.

Bygrave, W., and J. Timmons. 1992. *Venture Capital at the Crossroads.* Boston: Harvard Business School Press.

Chan, Y. 1983. "On the Positive Role of Financial Intermediation in Allocations of Venture Capital in a Market with Imperfect Information." *Journal of Finance* 38: 1543–61.

Churchill, L., and W. Lewis. 1983. "The Five Stages of Small Busienss Growth." *Harvard Business Review,* May–June.

COSEPUP. 1998. "Materials Science and Engineering Benchmarking Report." Committee on Science, Engineering, and Public Policy. www2.nas.edu/cosepup.

David, P. A. 1985. "Clio and the Economics of QWERTY." *American Economic Review* 75: 332–37.

David, P. A. 1988. *Path Dependence: Putting the Past into the Future of Economics.* Institute for Mathematical Studies in the Social Sciences Technical Report 553, Stanford University.

David, P. A. 1993. "Path Dependence and Predictability in Dynamic Systems with Local Network Externalities: A Paradigm for Historical Economics." In *Technology and the Wealth of Nations: The Dynamics of Constructed Advantage,* ed. D. Foray and C. Freeman. London: Pinter.

Dixon, R. 1991. "Venture Capitalists and the Appraisal of Investments." *Omega International Journal of Management Science* 19 (5): 333–44.

Elango, B., V. Fried, R. Hisrich, and A. Polonchek. 1995. "How Venture Capital Firms Differ." *Journal of Business Venturing* 10: 157–79.

Eliasson, G. 1996. "Spillovers, Integrated Production, and the Theory of the Firm." *Journal of Evolutionary Economics* 6: 125–40.

Eliasson, G. 1997. *Competence Blocs and Industrial Policy in the Knowledge-Based Economy.* Stockholm: Department of Industrial Economics and Management, The Royal Institute of Technology.

EVCA (European Venture Capital Association). 1997. *A Survey of Venture Capital and Private Equity in Europe.* EVCA Yearbook.

Fredriksen, O. 1997. *Venture Capital Firms' Relationship and Cooperation with Entrepreneurial Companies.* Department of Management Economics, Linkoping University.

Fried, V. H., and R. D. Hisrich. 1994. "Toward a Model of Venture Capital Investment Decision Making." *Financial Management* 23 (3): 28–37.

Fried, V. H., and R. D. Hisrich. 1995. "The Venture Capitalist: A Relationship Investor." *California Management Review* 37 (2): 101–13.

Grupp, H. 1994. "The Dynamics of Science-Based Innovations Reconsidered: Cognitive Models and Statistical Findings." In *Economics of Technology,* ed. O. Granstrand, pp. 223–52. Amsterdam: North-Holland.

Karaomerlioglu, D. C., and S. Jacobsson. 2000. "The Swedish Venture Capital Industry—an Infant, Adolescent, or Grown-up?" *Venture Capital* 2 (1): 61–88.

Landström, H., and J. Winborg. 1995. "Small Business Managers' Attitude Towards and Use of Financial Sources." Frontiers of Entrepreneurship Research, Babson College.

Lundgren, A. 1994. *Technological Innovation and Network Evolution.* London, Routledge.

Megginson, W. C., and K. A. Weiss. 1991. "Venture Capital Certification in Initial Public Offerings." *Journal of Finance* 46 (July): 879–903.

Mønsted, M. 1998. "Networking for Legitimacy—Overcoming Uncertainties in Small High Tech Firms." Tenth Nordic Conference on Small Business Reserach, Växjö University, Sweden.

Myers, S. C. 1984. "The Capital Structure Puzzle." *Journal of Finance* 39 (3): 575–92.

Norton, E., and E. Tenenbaum. 1995. "The Effects of Venture Capitalists' Characteristics on the Structure of the Venture Capital Deal." *Journal of Small Business Management*, October, pp. 32–41.

Reid, G. 1996. "Financial Structure and Growing Small Firm: Theoretical Underpinning and Current Evidence." *Small Business Economics* 8: 1–7.

Ruhnka, J., and J. Young. 1992. "Some Hypotheses about Risk in VC Investing." *Journal of Business Venturing* 6: 115–33.

Sahlman, W. 1990. "The Structure and Governance of VC Organizations." *Journal of Financial Economics* 27: 473–521.

Sahlman, W., and P. Gorman. 1989. "What Do Venture Capitalists Do?" *Journal of Business Venturing* 4: 231–48.

Sapienza, H. 1992. "When Do Venture Capitalists Add Value?" *Journal of Business Venturing* 7: 9–27.

Sapienza, H., and H. Gupta. 1994. "Impact of Agency Risks and Task Uncertainty on Venture Capitalist–CEO Interactions." *Academy of Management Journal* 37 (6): 1618–32.

Saxenian, A. 1994. *Regional Advantage Culture and Competition in Silicon Valley and Route 128.* Cambridge, Mass.: Harvard University Press.

Shane, S. 1997. *Luck, Knowledge, and the Discovery of Entrepreneurial Opportunities.* Cambridge: Massachusetts Institute of Technology.

Steier, L., and R. Greenwood. 1995. "Venture Capitalist Relationship in the Deal Structuring and Post Investment Stages of New Firm Creation." *Journal of Management Studies* 32 (3): 337–57.

Storey, D. 1994. *Understanding the Small Business Sector.* New York: Routledge.

Winborg, J., and H. Landström. 1997. *Financial Bootstrapping in Small Business: A Resource-Based View on Small Business Finance.* Frontiers of Entrepreneurship Research, Babson College.

12

Conclusion

Dilek Çetindamar

The aim of this final chapter is to bring together the important lessons that can be derived from the experiences of the various countries discussed in this book. The focus here is the identification of some important implications for policy with regard to the formation and development of the venture capital industry (VCI). The wide spectrum of examples that have been presented offers a prime position from which to glean some comparative results.

THE EVOLUTION OF THE VENTURE CAPITAL INDUSTRY

The evolution of the VCI displays a cyclical character. Positive macroeconomic conditions such as rapid economic growth provide a fertile ground for the venture capital (VC) business, and in a similar vein, negative conditions lead to desertification and a subsequent slowdown in the activities of the VCI. This cycle can be clearly seen in the rapid diffusion and growth of the VCI in many European countries during an economic upswing.

An understanding of the life-cycle of the VCI is highly valuable for policy makers, since the importance of factors affecting the industry might change depending on whatever stage of development a country is in. Moreover, the discussion of maturity raises issues related to the functions of the VCI. In other words, the characteristics of a mature industry is what countries aim to achieve because the VCI is expected to function most efficiently and effectively in its mature stage. As shown in chapter 6, the stage of the VCI in a country is determined by three main measures: size, diversity, and competence.

The measurement of *size* can be the total cumulative funds raised for the private equity investments, or the total funds invested in portfolio firms, or the total number of firms operating in the VCI. When size is adjusted in relation to gross domestic product, it can be easily used to make comparisons between countries. This is, in fact, how national VC associations collect data and make comparisons. However, there are two complications in determining the exact size of the VCI: business angel funds and foreign funds. The total funds raised by business angels are difficult to determine unless business angels start to institutionalize their activities and expose themselves. The networking trend among business angels, as shown in chapter 3, might solve this problem. With respect to the foreign funds, it is clear that the heightened globalization of VC activities complicates the calculation of VC funds in a country, as was shown in the examples of Denmark and Canada.

The size of the industry is important in the sense that it directly shows the resources available to entrepreneurs. Instinctively, we might consider that the larger the size of the VCI, the more mature it is. In fact, this is correct to a large extent. As has been shown in a number of countries, such as Denmark and Israel, the VCI could not develop before a critical mass had been accumulated. The threshold may change from country to country depending on its gross national product, but once this size is reached, industry associations can be built and the industry becomes institutionalized in the eyes of the public and the government.

The *diversity* of the VC industry is related to the existence of a wide variety of actors operating as VC firms. If there is a wide variety of VC firms able to be differentiated from each other with respect to their investment in a specific industry or technology or geography or stage of investee firm, then these VC firms can offer different services and satisfy different needs of entrepreneurial firms. For example, some VC firms are establishing internal business incubators in which they supply not only finance and managerial advice but also facilities, equipment, and administrative support (see chapters 7 and 11). This kind of rich portfolio of services can be supplied only with a diverse set of VC firms. That is why their absence becomes a source of complaint, as in the case of biomaterial firms in Sweden mentioned in chapter 11. The diversity concern is another reason why business angels and buyout specialists should be seen as important actors in the VCI. As chapters 3 and 4 demonstrate, these actors have a unique role in adding value to finance-seeking entrepreneurial firms.

As shown in the study of the Swedish VCI evolution in chapter 6, a VCI might grow in size and diversity but not attain a *competent* position in which it develops knowledge and skills that can solve nonfinancial problems of portfolio firms. Venture capitalists develop experience either in their previous career or during their work in VC firms. Thanks to this broad range of experience, they are able to reduce the risks associated with technology-based firms in a way that other financial experts are not able to. In other words, competent venture capitalists can evaluate the commercial potentials of early-stage projects and ideas much better than financial experts can (Eliasson 1997). The value of competence increases during the investment process, because the competence of venture capitalists helps to solve managerial, marketing, and networking problems of investee firm.

The experiences in many countries, such as Denmark, Israel, Sweden, and the United States, highlight that the competence of the industry does not develop easily. In the case of the United States, even though the first VC firm was established in 1946, we might argue that the industry did not become mature until the 1980s, a period of four decades. Hence, maturity refers to a substantial size, diversity of actors, and high competence of VC firms. Considering that the definition of VC and the role of VC in an entrepreneurial and innovative economy emphasize the value-added contribution of venture capitalists, the competence issue is the central characteristic expected from a well-functioning industry.

The greater the number of investments and the greater the variety of investee firms, the more competent venture capitalists become due to increased opportunities for learning available in the process. Until the industry reaches maturity, which requires a long learning period, the industry experiences many fluctuations and shake-ups, and many VC firms might fail due to a lack of competence. Similar to a natural selection process, only the fittest survive, and successes and failures build up skills and knowledge needed to run VC activities.

THE VENTURE CAPITAL INDUSTRY AS THE CORE OF THE INNOVATION-FINANCING SYSTEM

The popularity of the VCI is based on the observation that it plays a direct and significant role in the process of innovation and technology-based development in modern economies, as discussed in chapter 2. Studies have clearly shown that VC is one of the main driving forces behind development in many high-technology industries, including information technology and biotechnology (Sharp 1995; Swann and Prevezer 1996; Carlsson 2002). This makes VC firms, business angels, and buyout specialists critical players in any national innovation system.

VC firms provide two functions to entrepreneurial and innovative firms: finance and managerial services. As illustrated previously, innovative firms in many countries (such as Canada, Denmark, Israel, Sweden, and Turkey) are experiencing financial difficulties. The existence of VC closes the capital gap for firms seeking finance for start-up and as working capital in the early stages of their ventures. With respect to the second function of VC firms, we see a set of services that venture capitalists can supply under the umbrella of management. The main managerial services can be listed as:

- Risk sharing
- Managerial guidance in investee firm's search for technology as well as markets
- Speeding up the diffusion of technology and commercialization
- Legitimization of start-up and technology-based firms
- Networking among innovators, investors, universities, suppliers, and customer firms.

All of these value-added contributions of VC make this financial intermediary organization one of the main infrastructure elements of the new economy. This central position can be accredited to the support VC provides to the innovative and entrepreneurial economy by allowing various innovations to get off the ground and by selecting successful ones for further development.

As observed throughout this book, organizations and institutional infrastructure in a country have substantial impact on the establishment and development of the VCI. Following is a summary of the determinants of the VCI under the four categories suggested in chapter 1: sources of finance, institutional infrastructure, exit mechanisms, and entrepreneur and innovation generators.

Sources of Finance

The structure of the VCI depends on the availability of funds in a country or the flow of foreign funds into the country. Funds determine the size of the industry as well as the characteristics of the VC firms. Fund providers are either wealthy individuals or organizations such as pension funds, banks, insurance companies, and large corporations. In the majority of countries that have experienced strong growth in the VCI, we see that pension funds were the main source of funds for VC firms. For example, pension funds constitute at least one-third of the funds in the United States, the United Kingdom, Ireland, Japan, and Denmark. In Canada, labor unions have created a new type of capital source for VC firms that is unique in the world. Having diverse sources of funds reduces any potential fragility of VC firms, since any crisis in one of the sources can be balanced with increased contributions of others. At the very least, the effects of a shock can be reduced if not balanced completely. Besides risk, relying on limited sources can restrict the behavior of VC firms, as has been shown in a number of studies. For example, VC firms receiving funds from banks might tend to be more conservative because bank-originated concerns might be influential in the decision processes.

Institutional Infrastructure

Regulations, rules, customs, and culture in a country can influence both the demand and supply side of the VC market. If the institutional infrastructure has been correctly established, as discussed in chapters 6 and 10, motivation will take place in the three main actors of VC (fund providers, venture capitalists, and entrepreneurs). In effect, this means that investors will volunteer to put their capital into VC funds, highly competent professionals will be attracted to become venture capitalists, and entrepreneurs will create demand for the services provided by VC firms. Institutional arrangements regarding investors and venture capitalists lay the ground for the effective functioning of the supply side, while institutional arrangements for entrepreneurs regulate the demand side.

The tools involved in creating the essential institutional infrastructure consist of a number of incentive mechanisms. Incentives to investors might take the form of reductions in capital gains tax, tax credits, or deductions from taxes or taxable income of amounts invested in eligible VC institutions. In addition to these incentives, some governments may allow the use of capital losses incurred to offset capital gains or ordinary income (e.g., France, Belgium, United Kingdom, Ireland). Control over who can invest in VC funds might be an important issue, since laws related to investors such as pension funds or foreign funds might limit or expand the flow of funds into VC (e.g., Israel). Incentives to the VC management could include tax relief on income received from investee companies (e.g., Korea, Netherlands, Brazil) or exemption from corporate tax for a predetermined period (e.g., Singapore). Allowing stock options to be given to venture capitalists or employees in VC firms can attract competent professionals into the industry. One incentive for entrepreneurs could be laws defining new technology-based firms and their procedures. For example, the rights of minority shareholders, incorporation regulations, labor market rigidity, accounting standards, treatment of bankruptcies, and legal liability of corporate directors should be in place (e.g., France, Australia, Canada, Germany, Korea, Mexico, the Netherlands, and Portugal). Regulations affecting innovation, such as patent laws and intellectual property rights, also affect the decisions of entrepreneurs and venture capitalists. In addition to all these formal rules, culture and customs in a society affect the VCI. For example, a culture that embraces entrepreneurship will have more chances of attracting entrepreneurs that will demand VC funds. As chapter 5 mentions, the slow growth of the VCI in Germany is attributed to both a cultural and an institutional aversion to risk taking in that country.

Even though there are positive developments in establishing VCIs in many developing countries, the volume of VC is still at very low levels compared to industrialized countries. This situation could be attributed to weaknesses in the incentive structures and the poor technological opportunities available in these developing nations.

Exit Mechanisms

As shown in chapter 5, the development of the VCI is highly sensitive to the use of IPOs as exit mechanisms. This influential role of stock markets initiated the establishment of specialized stock exchange markets, such as Neue Markt and AIM, in a number of countries in Europe. Even though stock markets play a strong role as an exit route for VC firms in situations in which those firms have maximum control on the exit process and expectation of high profit, there are a few exceptions, such as the Danish example. Other examples are in Canada and Turkey. Canadian VC firms use a number of alternative exit routes, including share-for-share mergers with the U.S. companies. VC investments in Turkey conclude with trade sales and acquisitions. These appear to be reasonable exit routes in countries that have a weak stock market or no stock market at all. Israel is an interesting example in the area of exit mechanisms. Besides trade sales, Israeli VC firms utilize foreign stock markets as an efficient way of exiting VC investments.

Entrepreneur and Innovation Generators

Although the size of VC is an important measurement for the development of the VCI, on its own it is not enough, since this factor does not take into consideration the demand issue. Clearly, if there is not enough demand, funds will not be used or they will be used inefficiently. Because VC firms are profit-seeking service firms, they are always on the lookout for ideas and people. Therefore, if local demand is not satisfactory, VC funds might emigrate to locations where there is more demand. This point has been well illustrated by the case of the transfer of funds raised in Chicago and New York to California and Massachusetts. This example shows a shift of funds within a country; however, considering that VC funds have started to globalize, policy makers need to pay attention to demand issues in order to keep funds in the local economy. The most successful examples in terms of demand creation are Israel and Ireland; both countries have a high percentage of scientists and researchers thanks to long-term government programs.

Industrialized countries have strong national innovation systems in which science is conducted by a broad range of actors. In the majority of European countries and also in the United States, universities and research organizations are on the front line shoulder-to-shoulder with defense industries and private businesses. However, some countries, such as Japan, rely on private business for technological development. Thus, the organizations that can produce entrepreneurs and innovators are expected to be mainly large corporations rather than universities. In developing countries, as shown in the case of Turkey, public organizations and universities conduct the majority of research and development activities. Hence, universities and research organizations are the most likely candidates for the production of entrepreneurs and inventors.

Once organizations succeed in supplying entrepreneurs and inventors, the next step is to establish mechanisms that will connect them to the commercial world. Studies about the commercialization gap between Europe and the United States in the biotechnology field indicates the European failure to transfer technology from universities (Carlsson 2002; Martin and Thomas 1998). In such an instance, venture capitalists can play a unique role, not just as a financial supporter but also as a network enabler. This is clearly observed in chapter 11, which described VC firms that helped young science-based biomaterial firms to form networks both in their formation and development processes.

POLICY SUGGESTIONS

The performance of the industry is influenced by its size, diversity, and competence. All these characteristics of the industry can be influenced by institutional infrastructure that shapes financial resources, exit mechanisms, and entrepreneur and innovation generators. Policy makers need to structure these institutions in such a way as to lay strong foundations for the establishment and development of the VCI. Additionally, there are two important policy considerations related to the institutional infrastructure that deserve to be discussed briefly: the role of government and the interactions of institutions within the financial system.

The Role of Government

The government as an institution-building unit has a critical role in the process of establishing and developing a VCI. The contributions of government can take four forms:

- Establishing institutional infrastructure
- Supplying capital for VC funds
- Financing early-stage investments
- Fostering demand for VC

First, the government supplies the appropriate institutional infrastructure that enables the establishment and functioning of organizations. For example, the government may establish a stock market or provide tax incentives encouraging the establishment of entrepreneurial firms. In fact, all aspects of the incentive structure mentioned earlier are directly created by government initiatives. Regulations may function as attractive incentives for fund providers, venture capitalists, and entrepreneurs. An example of this is when the Employee Retirement Income Security Act in the United States allowed pension funds to be invested in VC funds in 1978. As a result of this act, the share of pension funds in total VC funds increased significantly, from 15 percent to 50 percent in eight years (Bygrave and Timmons 1992). The government can encourage networks of foreign and local corporations to coinvest in high technology start-up firms, as has been the successfully applied policy in Israel. This helped not only to attract funds into Israel but also to increase the competence of Israeli VC firms.

Second, the government can supply capital to VC funds either by directly establishing VC funds (e.g., Israel and Portugal) or by indirectly supporting VC funds of independent firms (e.g., the Netherlands and Norway). Although the degree of involvement varies, industrialized countries, by and large, have started their VCI through some form of financial support. In addition to the financial support of governments in the establishment period of the VCI, they might help VC firms in times of crisis, as seen in Sweden, Denmark, and the Netherlands. With the support of government funds, the cyclical behavior of the VCI can be smoothed out. Thus, governments need to commit themselves and have patience enough to wait until the industry reaches its maturity. Governments must realize that this process takes a long time due to the amount of learning required for the industry to become competent. When the government finishes its stabilization role, it can reduce its support programs for VC, but this does not mean a reduction of the size of the VCI, as demonstrated by the experiences in the Netherlands and in Israel.

Third, the government plays a complementary role for the VCI by supplying the early-stage financing. The governments of many advanced countries are engaged directly or indirectly in supplying capital to new technology-based firms such as the European Seed Capital Fund Pilot Scheme (Murray 1998). In the seed phase, the uncertainties are so great that VC firms may not be prepared to invest enough to sustain a sufficiently high degree of experimentation in the economy.

Finally, the development of the VCI can be explained not only by supply side factors but also by demand for funds. Governments support education and scientific research through a number of special incentive schemes such as grants and awards or loan guarantee schemes for small firms. By creating skilled researchers, entrepreneurs, and finance experts, governments indirectly contribute to the development of the VCI, since educated people are more likely to become entrepreneurs and venture capitalists.

The Financial System

VC is just one of the financial organizations available to help entrepreneurs; others include banks, the government, stock markets, large companies, and business associates such as suppliers or buyers (Christensen 1997; Gompers and Lerner 1998). The development of VC needs to be considered within the broader context of the whole financial system. Policy makers should take care not to ignore the suggestion that a healthy and sustainable economic growth necessitates a diversified financial system (Fenn, Liang, and Prowse 1995; Carlsson and Jacobsson 1997).

Consideration of the financial system as a whole is necessitated by the fact that an entrepreneurial firm goes through a number of stages in its life-cycle, from start-up to maturity. During each stage, varying financial needs of entrepreneurial firms can be satiated by different financial organizations, as demonstrated in figure 12.1. These organizations both collaborate and compete with each other, but either way, not only entrepreneurs but also investors benefit. They cooperate since they can complement each other through the formation of networks so they can coinvest, inform each other about potential investments, and provide each other with consulting and other services. This cooperation is particularly useful for venture capitalists who need to accumulate

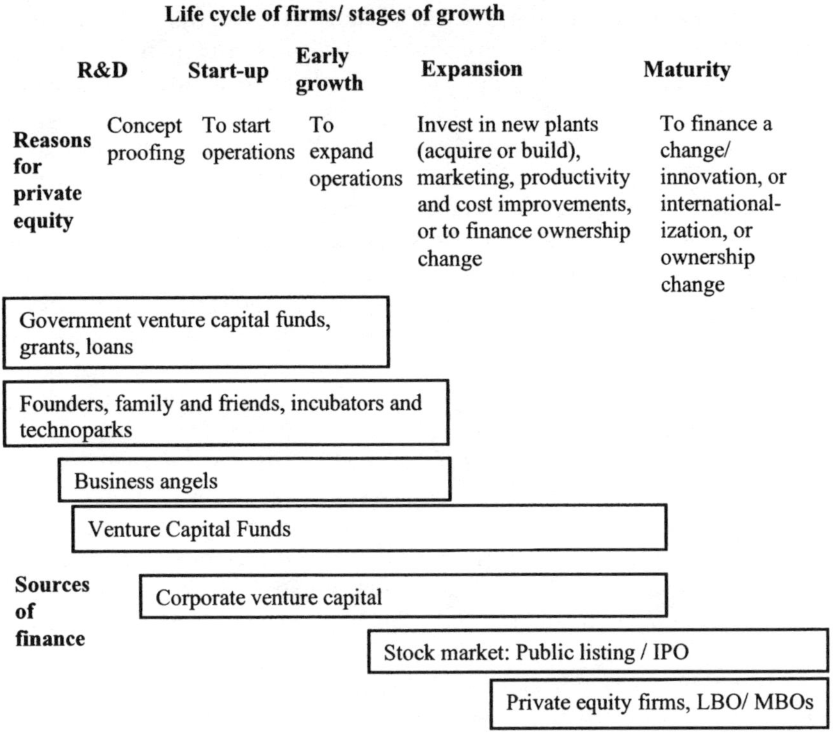

Life cycle of firms/ stages of growth

	R&D	Start-up	Early growth	Expansion	Maturity
Reasons for private equity	Concept proofing	To start operations	To expand operations	Invest in new plants (acquire or build), marketing, productivity and cost improvements, or to finance ownership change	To finance a change/ innovation, or international- ization, or ownership change

Government venture capital funds, grants, loans

Founders, family and friends, incubators and technoparks

Business angels

Venture Capital Funds

Sources of finance   Corporate venture capital

Stock market: Public listing / IPO

Private equity firms, LBO/ MBOs

Figure 12.1 Life cycle of firms

and use a wide variety of knowledge to understand and help innovative firms. Also, they might cooperate to enable each other to invest in a particular en- trepreneurial firm at different periods of this firm's life-cycle. They compete, but even this competition is in their favor, because they will excel in what they are doing and subsequently increase their competence. Either way, the com- petition or cooperation of financial organizations is to the benefit of entrepre- neurial firms, because the VC firms will develop a wide range of services that will be available to the entrepreneurs.

It is impossible to identify any "best" financial mechanism, since these al- ternative financial sources have advantages and disadvantages (Lindholm- Dahlstrand and Çetindamar 2000). For example, the government has a special role in seed financing by supporting entrepreneurs independent of technology and industry focus. This attitude can create equal opportunities to a plethora of entrepreneurs and innovators by providing finance at the most risky stage of their operation. Hence, government funds are considered to be the mecha- nism bridging the capital gap between the research and start-up stages of en- trepreneurial firms. Once firms receive government support and pass the seed stage with legitimacy, it becomes easier to attract resources from other sources. However, the disadvantage of government financing comes from the fact that any contribution it makes is limited to capital alone; its industrial and managerial expertise is nonexistent.

The same issues also have to be discussed for VC firms. As previously mentioned, they supply many benefits to entrepreneurial firms, including: increasing commercialization, supporting the fast growth of firms, developing networks with customers and suppliers, giving legitimacy, reducing risk, and supplying managerial and strategic skills. There may, however, be some disadvantages at the macro level. Venture capitalists tend to invest only in (1) firms with high returns, (2) high-growth technologies and industries, and (3) successful technology regions. Because of this tendency, venture capitalists neglect many potentially successful firms, technologies, and regions. Zider's study (1998) showed that VC firms in the United States invest in firms with expected returns of 25 percent to 35 percent per year, concentrate on information technology firms, and localize in technology clusters such as Silicon Valley.

Therefore, it is essential for a healthy financial system to consist of all these complementary financial organizations. This ensures that, in line with the priorities of each country, the advantages of each organization are maximized and the disadvantages are minimized. The availability of financial organizations to which entrepreneurial firms can apply, depending on their stage of development as shown in figure 12.1, varies in accordance with each country's economic, political, and social structures. For example, because banks are able to have private equity partnerships in Germany and Japan, they are thus the main capital source for entrepreneurial firms (Jeng and Wells 2000) in spite of the fact that the VCI is at a mature stage in both these countries. This example shows the need for all countries to form an innovation-financing system in accordance with the peculiarities of their own institutions.

To make the financial system work efficiently, it is essential to create networks that can facilitate cooperation among financial organizations. This is particularly useful for any information flow regarding VC firms, deals, investment opportunities, revenues, and the performances of VC firms. The availability of information is necessary to create a transparent and reliable environment not only for investors but also for venture capitalists. The government or associations of financial organizations might initiate or support networks of business angels, VC firms, and entrepreneurs. Networks can (1) increase trust and awareness about VC firms and business angels, (2) speed up the diffusion of competencies, and (3) create a lobbying instrument for financial organizations.

The suggestion to create a mixed structure of financial instruments for financing innovation is particularly important for developing countries. Size, diversity, and competence can be used to measure the performance and evolution of VC firms. If there is no critical mass of VC funds, it will not be possible to establish a VCI. Moreover, regarding the competence issue, developing countries should be aware of the problems arising from their poor manufacturing structure that will limit industry-specific and technology-specific competence. Because the profile of competence is strongly path-dependent and the learning of new competencies is constrained by earlier specialization profiles, developing countries with a limited number of industries and technologies will face significant competence problems. These potential problems do not mean that developing countries should avoid establishing a VCI but rather that governments should be aware of these problems and take measures to try to solve them.

FURTHER STUDY

In a rapidly changing environment, the new economy demands entrepreneurs and innovations that will rejuvenate old industries and create new ones. This demand highlights the role of VC as a scaffold that finances innovations. Thus, we will continue to see the diffusion of VC across countries.

This book concentrated on the innovation-financing feature of VC firms and presented the experiences of many countries in the establishment and development of the VCI at the macro level. The analysis of the country-specific cases shows the variety of institutional factors. However, there are a number of interesting research issues not dealt with in this book that deserve further study. For example, the problems faced by developing countries in establishing their VCI need to be analyzed further through empirical studies. Similarly, the increased transnational developments of VC activities necessitate an in-depth analysis of the impact of international funds on the local VC. Although this book touched on how leveraged buyouts add value to companies, there is a lack of empirical studies that can quantify their economic impact relative to other VC firms' impact. The relationship between country conditions and the dominance of business angels, VC firms, and buyout specialists could be another interesting path to follow. For example, the limited availability of financial organizations in developing countries highlights the need for increased activity by business angels in these economies. Another possible route of research could be to analyze how institutional infrastructure might impact VC firms, dependent of course on the type of VC firm. As has been shown, labor market rigidity and the IPO effects do not affect VC firms investing in the early development stages. This contrasts quite markedly with those investing in the later stages. This kind of comparison needs to be conducted for all the factors that have an impact on a VCI. An alternative research question to pursue is an analysis of VC firms in different countries on a micro level. Such an analysis could increase the understanding of the day-to-day working of VC firms. In particular, the analysis would help measure the competence of VC firms and reveal what skills and knowledge sets are at a developed stage in different countries.

REFERENCES

Aylward, A. 1998. *Trends in Venture Capital Finance in Developing Countries*. World Bank, Washington, D.C.: IFC (International Finance Corporation) Discussion Paper No. 36.

Branscomb, L. M., and J. H. Keller. 1998. *Investing in Innovation*. Cambridge, Mass.: MIT Press,.

Branuerjelm, P., D. Çetindamar, and D. Johansson. 2002. "The Support Structure of the Biomedical Cluster: Research, Intermediary, and Financial Organizations." In *New Technological Systems in the Bio Industries: An International Study*, ed. Bo Carlsson. Eindhoven: Kluwer.

Bygrave, W. D., and J. A. Timmons. 1992. *Venture Capital at the Crossroads*. Boston, Mass.: Harvard Business School.

Carlsson, B. 2002. *New Technological Systems in the Bio Industries: An International Study*. Eindhoven: Kluwer.

Carlsson, B., and S. Jacobsson. 1997. "Diversity Creation and Technological Systems: A Technology Policy Perspective." In *Systems of Innovation: Technologies, Institutions, and Organizations*, ed. C. Edquist. London: Pinter.

Christensen, J. L. 1997. *Financing Innovation*. TSER Project Report: Innovation Systems and Europe 3.2.3. Denmark: Aalborg University.

Cooke, P. 2001. "New Economy Innovation Systems: Biotechnology in Europe and the USA." *Industry and Innovation* 3: 267–89.

The Economist. 1997. "IPO Venture Capitalism." January 25.

The Economist. 1998. "Europe's Great Experiment." June 13.

Eliasson, G. 1997. *The Venture Capitalist as a Competent Outsider*. KTH/IEO/R-97/6-SE. Stockholm: The Royal Institute of Technology.

Fenn, W., N. Liang, and S. Prowse. 1995. *The Economics of the Private Equity Market*. Washington, D.C.: Federal Reserve Bank.

Finlayson, G. E. 1999. "Japan: The Changing Venture Capital Market." *International Financial Law Review*. Supplement: Private Equity and Venture Capital, pp. 14–19.

Florida, R., and J. D. F. Smith. 1990. "Venture Capital, Innovation, and Economic Development." *Economic Development Quarterly* 4 (4): 345–61.

Gifford, D. 1997. "Venture Capital: The Visible Hand at Work." *Harvard Business Review* 75 (4): 12–14.

Gompers, P. A., and J. Lerner. 1998. *The Determinants of Corporate Venture Capital Success: Organizational Structure, Incentives, and Complementaries*. National Bureau of Economic Research Working Paper No. 6725 Cambridge, Massachusetts.

Jeng, L. A., and P. C. Wells. 2000. "The Determinants of Venture Capital Funding: Evidence across Countries." *Journal of Corporate Finance* 6 (3): 241–89.

Lindholm-Dahlstrand, Å., and D. Çetindamar. 2000. "The Dynamics of Innovation Financing in Sweden." *Venture Capital* 2 (3): 203–21.

Maeda, N. 2001. "Missing Link of National Entrepreneurial Business Model-Issues of High-Tech Start-up in Japan, in Comparison with US and German Model." PICMET Conference, July 29–August 2, Portland, Oregon, USA.

Martin, P., and S. Thomas. 1998. "The Commercialization Gap in Gene Therapy: Lessons for European Competitiveness." In *Biotechnology and Competitive Advantage*, ed. J. Senker and R. V. Vliet. Cheltenham, U.K.: Edward Elgar.

Mason, C. M., and R. T. Harrison. 1999. "Venture Capital: Rationale, Aims, and Scope [editorial]." *Venture Capital* 1 (1): 1–46.

Moore, B. 1994. "Financial Constraints to the Growth and Development of Small High-Technology Firms." In *Finance and the Small Firm*, ed. A. Hughes and D. Storey. London: Routledge.

Murray, G. A. 1998. "Policy Response to Regional Disparities in the Supply of Risk Capital to New Technology-Based Firms in the European Union: The European Seed Capital Fund Scheme." *Regional Studies* 32 (5): 405–19.

Murray, G. C. 1996. "Evolution and Change: An Analysis of the First Decade of the UK Venture Capital Industry." *Journal of Business Finance and Accounting* 22 (8): 1077–1107.

OECD. 2001. *Science, Technology, and Industry Outlook: Drivers of Growth—Information Technology, Innovation, and Entrepreneurship.* Paris: OECD.

Sagari, S. B., and G. Guidotti. 1992. *Financial Markets, Institutions, and Instruments: Venture Capital—The Lessons from the Developed World for the Developing Markets.* Oxford: Blackwell Publishers.

Sapienza, H. J., S. Manigart, and W. Vermeir. 1996. "Venture Capitalist Governance and Value Added in Four Countries." *Journal of Business Venturing* 11: 439–69.

Sharp, M. 1995. "The Role of Private Companies and the State in the Promotion of Biotechnology: Options for Government." In *The Biotechnology Revolution*, ed. M. Fransman, G. Junne, and A. Roobeek. London: Blackwell.

Swann, P., and M. Prevezer. 1996. "A Comparison of the Dynamics of Industrial Clustering and Biotechnology." *Research Policy* 25 (7): 1139–58.

Zider, B. 1998. "How Venture Capital Works." *Harvard Business Review*, November-December, pp. 121–39.

Index

About the Contributors

GIL AVNIMELECH holds a master's degree (with honor) in financial economics; has worked as an analyst performing equity research on technology companies; and has participated in numerous projects on venture capital and high-tech. He has researched and published in the areas of firm strategy, mergers and acquisitions, IPOs, venture capital, and R&D policy. He is currently involved with Morris Teubal and others in writing a book on Israeli high-tech.

DILEK ÇETINDAMAR has been Associate Professor of Technology Management at Sabancı University in Turkey since 1999. She graduated from the Industrial Engineering Department at Boğaziçi University and received her Ph.D. in management from Istanbul Technical University. She has worked at the following universities: Boğaziçi University, Case Western Reserve University (USA), Portland State University (USA), and Chalmers University of Technology (Sweden). She participated in many international projects (including United Nations and European Union projects) and published many articles and two books. She received the Turkish Young Industrialists Association's award for her study published as *Venture Capital, Entrepreneurship, and the Future of Turkey*. Her main interest and research topics are technology management, development economics, entrepreneurship, and industrial economics.

JESPER LINDGAARD CHRISTENSEN has, since 1989, been a member of the IKE research group of Aalborg University. As Associate Professor in the Department of Business Studies, he is teaching both business administration and economics. His research includes various aspects of innovation theory and practice. He has a broad knowledge of innovation and innovation policy and has specialized in financial aspects of innovation. He is currently investigating Danish business angels, the Danish venture capital market, development in financial systems, and interfirm collaboration. Previously, he was the daily coordinator of a three-year research project on the Danish Innovation System in Comparative Perspective ("DISKO"). In addition, he conducted some of the

analyses for DISKO, including an analysis of the collaboration between industrial firms and technological institutes and an analysis of the role of business
angels in Denmark.

CHARLES H. DAVIS is Professor in the Faculty of Business at the University
of New Brunswick in Saint John where he teaches courses in innovation management and e-business. He received his Ph.D. in science and technology policy
from the Université de Montréal. His current research projects focus on enterprise integration, IT-enabled services, and customer relationship
management.

STAFFAN JACOBSSON received his Ph.D. in economics at the University of
Sussex, England, in 1986 and is currently Professor of Science and Technology
Policy at the Department of Industrial Dynamics, Chalmers University of Technology, Gothenburg, Sweden. His current interest lies mainly in issues related
to the diffusion of renewable energy technology and transformation of the
energy system to a more sustainable one.

LESLIE ANN JENG is currently Senior Vice President of Research for the Private
Equity Research Group (PERG). Leslie graduated from the University of Penn-
sylvania in 1991 with a dual degree in mathematics and finance. She earned
her Ph.D. in business economics from Harvard University in 1998. In 1998,
she joined the faculty in the Finance and Economics Department at Boston
University School of Management. In 2000, she joined PERG. Her research
has focused primarily on private equity and insider-trading performance eval-
uation. Her most recent papers include "The Determinants of Venture Capital
Funding: An Empirical Analysis" (coauthored with Philippe Wells, *Journal of
Corporate Finance* 2000) and "Estimating the Returns to Insider Trading: A
Performance-Evaluation Perspective" (coauthored with Andrew Metrick and
Richard Zeckhauser, forthcoming in *The Review of Economics and Statistics*).
Her previous work experience includes investment banking at Goldman Sachs
and consulting at Cornerstone Research.

ARMAN KÖSEDAĞ received his master of science and Ph.D. degrees in finance
from Louisiana State University. During his graduate study at LSU, he was
employed as a research and teaching assistant by the Department of Finance.
After earning his Ph.D. degree in the spring of 1997, he worked as a Visiting
Assistant Professor for the Department of Finance at Oklahoma State University until May 1999. In 1999, he joined the Graduate School of Management
at Sabanci University, where he currently teaches financial management, corporate finance, and financial risk management classes in the MBA and EMBA
programs. He has published in *Journal of Business Finance and Accounting,*

International Review of Financial Analysis, and *Review of Financial Economics.* His current research interest focuses on leveraged buyouts (including reverse LBOs and reLBOs) and dividend policy. He is a member of Financial Management Association International.

JULIAN LANGE is Associate Professor of Entrepreneurship and the Benson Distinguished Entrepreneurship Fellow at Babson College. He was CEO of Software Arts, the company that created VisiCalc—the first electronic spreadsheet, he served as an Assistant Professor of Business Administration (Finance) at Harvard Business School, and he continues to serve on boards and as a consultant to private sector firms and public agencies. Dr. Lange is founder and president of Chatham Associates, a management consulting firm that assists businesses in building competitive advantage. His research is concerned with venture capital and angel investing, the financing of high-growth entrepreneurial ventures, the impact of the Internet on entrepreneurial companies, and the use of distance learning and multimedia in entrepreneurship training and education. Dr. Lange is a Phi Beta Kappa, magna cum laude graduate of Princeton University and also holds M.B.A., A.M., and Ph.D. degrees from Harvard University.

BENOÎT LELEUX (M.Sc., M.Ed., MBA, Ph.D. INSEAD) is the Stephan Schmidheiny Professor of Entrepreneurship and Finance at IMD (Lausanne, Switzerland). He was previously Visiting Professor of Entrepreneurship at INSEAD and Director of the 3i VentureLab and Associate Professor and Zubillaga Chair in Finance and Entrepreneurship at Babson College, Wellesley, Massachusetts (USA). Dr. Leleux is a world-reputed specialist in the field of venture capital and corporate venturing. He is also a director and/or advisor to numerous start-up companies and venture capital funds in Europe and the United States. His research papers have appeared in journals such as the *Strategic Management Journal,* the *Journal of Business Venturing,* and *Venture Capital.* He is the author of *A European Casebook on Entrepreneurship and New Ventures* (Prentice Hall, 1996) with D. Molian.

ANNIKA RICKNE is an Assistant Professor at the Department of Industrial Dynamics, Chalmers University of Technology in Sweden. She also functions as a Program Manager at Chalmers Advanced Management Programs and as a Program Leader for the Doctoral School at the School of Technology Management and Economics. The main focus of her research is economic growth initiated by new scientific or technological knowledge that creates opportunities that reshape existing knowledge fields and industries or gives rise to the evolution of new ones. Leading themes have been, for example, to understand the development process of new technology-based firms in the context of their innovation networks, the relationship between universities and industry, and issues of firm growth. Her empirical work focuses on knowledge-intensive sectors, especially bioscience-related fields.

BERNARD SURLEMONT (INSEAD MBA and Ph.D.) is Professor of Entrepreneurship at HEC Lausanne University (Switzerland). His research interests focus on technology start-ups and university spin-offs. He has published several articles in these fields in key journals. He is on the board of several investment funds and spin-off companies. Professor Surlemont provides expertise to the EU commission for business angels support and coaching systems for high-growth start-ups.

MORRIS TEUBAL is Professor of Economics at the Hebrew University of Jerusalem and is actively involved there in the creation of a new Center for High Tech, Biotechnology, and Globalization Studies. His areas of interest are (a) systems of innovation—both positive and normative aspects, particularly the systems perspective to innovation and technology policy (ITP); (b) growth policies of successful high-tech companies—both in information technology and in biotech areas; and (c) high-tech clusters—their emergence, evolution, and reconfiguration, including studies of venture capital. He has published in both orthodox and evolutionary-related journals and, together with Gil Avnimelech and other colleagues, is presently preparing a book on Israel's high-tech cluster of the 1990s.

PHILIPPE C. WELLS currently works as a Vice President at Bain Capital. He graduated from Yale University in 1991 with a B.A. in economics. He then spent two years at the Boston Consulting Group. He obtained his Ph.D. in economics from Harvard University in 1998. He has been at Bain Capital since 1998.